Deep Learning, Reinforcement Learning, and the Rise of Intelligent Systems

M. Irfan Uddin
Kohat University of Science and Technology, Pakistan

Wali Khan Mashwani
Kohat University of Science and Technology, Pakistan

A volume in the Advances in Computational Intelligence and Robotics (ACIR) Book Series

IGI Global
PUBLISHER of TIMELY KNOWLEDGE

Published in the United States of America by
IGI Global
Engineering Science Reference (an imprint of IGI Global)
701 E. Chocolate Avenue
Hershey PA, USA 17033
Tel: 717-533-8845
Fax: 717-533-8661
E-mail: cust@igi-global.com
Web site: http://www.igi-global.com

Library of Congress Cataloging-in-Publication Data

Names: Uddin, M. Irfan, 1982- editor. | Mashwani, Wali Khan, 1972- editor.
Title: Deep learning, reinforcement learning, and the rise of intelligent systems / edited by: M. Irfan Uddin, Wali Khan Mashwani.
Description: Hershey PA : Engineering Science Reference, [2024] | Includes bibliographical references. | Summary: "By providing a comprehensive exploration of deep learning, reinforcement learning, and intelligent systems, the book can contribute to expanding the collective knowledge base of the research community. It covers fundamental principles, advanced techniques, and real-world applications, offering researchers a deeper understanding of the subject matter"-- Provided by publisher.
Identifiers: LCCN 2023051804 (print) | LCCN 2023051805 (ebook) | ISBN 9798369317389 (hardcover) | ISBN 9798369317396 (ebook)
Subjects: LCSH: Deep learning (Machine learning)--Industrial applications.
Classification: LCC Q325.73 .D47 2024 (print) | LCC Q325.73 (ebook) | DDC 006.3/1--dc23/eng/20231213
LC record available at https://lccn.loc.gov/2023051804
LC ebook record available at https://lccn.loc.gov/2023051805

This book is published in the IGI Global book series Advances in Computational Intelligence and Robotics (ACIR) (ISSN: 2327-0411; eISSN: 2327-042X)

British Cataloguing in Publication Data
A Cataloguing in Publication record for this book is available from the British Library.
All work contributed to this book is new, previously-unpublished material.
The views expressed in this book are those of the authors, but not necessarily of the publisher.
For electronic access to this publication, please contact: eresources@igi-global.com.

Advances in Computational Intelligence and Robotics (ACIR) Book Series

ISSN:2327-0411
EISSN:2327-042X

Editor-in-Chief: Ivan Giannoccaro, University of Salento, Italy

MISSION

While intelligence is traditionally a term applied to humans and human cognition, technology has progressed in such a way to allow for the development of intelligent systems able to simulate many human traits. With this new era of simulated and artificial intelligence, much research is needed in order to continue to advance the field and also to evaluate the ethical and societal concerns of the existence of artificial life and machine learning.

The **Advances in Computational Intelligence and Robotics (ACIR) Book Series** encourages scholarly discourse on all topics pertaining to evolutionary computing, artificial life, computational intelligence, machine learning, and robotics. ACIR presents the latest research being conducted on diverse topics in intelligence technologies with the goal of advancing knowledge and applications in this rapidly evolving field.

COVERAGE

- Cyborgs
- Pattern Recognition
- Computational Intelligence
- Intelligent Control
- Heuristics
- Brain Simulation
- Fuzzy Systems
- Natural Language Processing
- Automated Reasoning
- Robotics

IGI Global is currently accepting manuscripts for publication within this series. To submit a proposal for a volume in this series, please contact our Acquisition Editors at Acquisitions@igi-global.com or visit: http://www.igi-global.com/publish/.

The Advances in Computational Intelligence and Robotics (ACIR) Book Series (ISSN 2327-0411) is published by IGI Global, 701 E. Chocolate Avenue, Hershey, PA 17033-1240, USA, www.igi-global.com. This series is composed of titles available for purchase individually; each title is edited to be contextually exclusive from any other title within the series. For pricing and ordering information please visit http://www.igi-global.com/book-series/advances-computational-intelligence-robotics/73674. Postmaster: Send all address changes to above address.

Titles in this Series

For a list of additional titles in this series, please visit:
http://www.igi-global.com/book-series/advances-computational-intelligence-robotics/73674

Empowering Low-Resource Languages With NLP Solutions
Partha Pakray (National Institute of Technology, Silchar, India) Pankaj Dadure (University of Petroleum and Energy Studies, India) and Sivaji Bandyopadhyay (Jadavpur University, India)
Engineering Science Reference • © 2024 • 330pp • H/C (ISBN: 9798369307281) • US $300.00

AIoT and Smart Sensing Technologies for Smart Devices
Fadi Al-Turjman (AI and Robotics Institute, Near East University, Nicosia, Turkey & Faculty of Engineering, University of Kyrenia, Kyrenia, Turkey)
Engineering Science Reference • © 2024 • 250pp • H/C (ISBN: 9798369307861) • US $300.00

Industrial Applications of Big Data, AI, and Blockchain
Mahmoud El Samad (Lebanese International University, Lebanon) Ghalia Nassreddine (Rafik Hariri University, Lebanon) Hani El-Chaarani (Beirut Arab University, Lebanon) and Sam El Nemar (AZM University, Lebanon)
Engineering Science Reference • © 2024 • 348pp • H/C (ISBN: 9798369310465) • US $275.00

Principles and Applications of Adaptive Artificial Intelligence
Zhihan Lv (Uppsala University, Sweden)
Engineering Science Reference • © 2024 • 316pp • H/C (ISBN: 9798369302309) • US $325.00

AI Tools and Applications for Women's Safety
Sivaram Ponnusamy (Sandip University, Nashik, India) Vibha Bora (G.H. Raisoni College of Engineering, Nagpur, India) Prema M. Daigavane (G.H. Raisoni College of Engineering, Nagpur, India) and Sampada S. Wazalwar (G.H. Raisoni College of Engineering, Nagpur, India)
Engineering Science Reference • © 2024 • 362pp • H/C (ISBN: 9798369314357) • US $300.00

For an entire list of titles in this series, please visit:
http://www.igi-global.com/book-series/advances-computational-intelligence-robotics/73674

IGI Global
PUBLISHER of TIMELY KNOWLEDGE

701 East Chocolate Avenue, Hershey, PA 17033, USA
Tel: 717-533-8845 x100 • Fax: 717-533-8661
E-Mail: cust@igi-global.com • www.igi-global.com

To my wonderful sons Aaban Uddin and Imad Uddin:

May your intelligence be as limitless as deep learning, and your laughter as rewarding as a perfectly trained model!

Irfan Uddin

Table of Contents

Detailed Table of Contents

Reinforcement learning (RL) is a dynamic and evolving subfield of machine learning that focuses on training intelligent agents to learn and adapt through interactions with their environment. This introductory article provides an overview of the fundamental concepts and principles of RL, elucidating its core components, such as the agent, environment, actions, and rewards. This study aims to give readers an in-depth introduction to RL and show examples of its different uses in various domains. RL can allow agents to learn through interaction with an environment, which has led to its enormous interest. The core ideas of RL and its essential elements will be covered in this study, after which it will go into applications in industries including robotics, gaming, finance, healthcare, and more. The fundamental ideas of RL will become clearer to readers, and they will recognize how transformative it can be when used to address challenging decision-making issues. These applications demonstrate the versatility and significance of RL in shaping the future of technology and automation.

Computer vision has benefited from deep learning, making it possible to create complex systems. Computer vision has seen radical changes using deep learning techniques, specifically transfer learning for computer vision. It enables computers to understand and interpret visual data, such as images and videos, with great precision. Transfer learning in particular, is a deep learning technique that has transformed several areas of computer vision, including face recognition, semantic segmentation,

the use of transformers and their manifold versions. The chapter also highlights the current limitations and potential future developments in the field.

Deep reinforcement learning has shown remarkable results across various tasks. However, recent studies highlight the susceptibility of DRL to targeted adversarial disruptions. Furthermore, discrepancies between simulated settings and real-world applications often make it challenging to transfer these DRL policies, particularly in situations where safety is essential. Several solutions have been proposed to address these issues to enhance DRL's robustness. This chapter delves into the significance of adversarial attack and defense strategies in machine learning, emphasizing the unique challenges in adversarial DRL settings. It also presents an overview of recent advancements, DRL foundations, adversarial Markov decision process models, and comparisons among different attacks and defenses. The chapter further evaluates the effectiveness of various attacks and the efficacy of multiple defense mechanisms using simulation data, specifically focusing on policy success rates and average rewards. Potential limitations and prospects for future research are also explored.

Human action recognition is a fundamental research problem in computer vision. The accuracy of human action recognition has important applications. In this book chapter, the authors use a YOLOv7-based model for human action recognition. To evaluate the performance of the model, the action recognition results of YOLOv7 were compared with those using CNN+LSTM, YOLOv5, and YOLOv4. Furthermore, a small human action dataset suitable for YOLO model training is designed. This data set is composed of images extracted from KTH, Weizmann, MSR data sets. In this book chapter, the authors make use of this data set to verify the experimental results. The final experimental results show that using the YOLOv7 model for human action recognition is very convenient and effective, compared with the previous YOLO model.

Facial emotion recognition (FER) is the task of identifying human emotions from facial expressions. The purpose of this book chapter is to improve accuracy of facial emotion recognition using integrated learning of lightweight networks without increasing the complexity or depth of the network. Compared to single lightweight models, it made a significant improvement. For a solution, the authors proposed an ensemble of mini-Xception models, where each expert is trained for a specific emotion and lets confidence score for the vote. Therefore, the expert model will transform the original multiclass task into binary tasks. The authors target the model to differentiate between a specific emotion and all others, facilitating the learning process. The principal innovation lies in our confidence-based voting mechanism, in which the experts "vote" based on their confidence scores rather than binary decisions.

This book chapter presents a real-time system for detecting the stability of a player's billiard shot, based on the YOLOv8 neural network. The system comprises a real-time object detection model and a real-time slope monitoring system. The model focuses on detecting four classes: The cue ball, hand, cue stick tip, and the bridge hand (hand support point). The project involved iterative model training on a custom dataset, eventually achieving a YOLOv8 model with 95% accuracy. The stability of a player's shot is detected by simulating slope change of cue stick during aiming, using the cue stick tip and bridge hand. Overall, the project highlights the immense potential of YOLOv8 in sports applications.

In this book chapter, the authors propose a low-cost distance estimation approach to develop more accurate predictions from a 3D perspective for vehicle detection and ranging by using inexpensive monocular cameras. This distance estimation model integrates YOLOv7 model with an attention module (CBAM) and transformer, as well as extend the prediction vector as the fundamental architecture to improved high-level semantic understanding and enhanced feature extraction ability. This integration significantly improved detection and ranging performance, offering a more suitable and cost-effective solution for distance estimation.

In this book chapter, the authors propose a method for player pose recognition in billiards matches by combining keypoint extraction and an optimized transformer. Given that those human pose analysis methods usually require high labour costs, the authors explore deep learning methods to achieve real-time, high-precision pose recognition. Firstly, they utilize human key point detection technology to extract the key points of players from real-time videos and generate key points. Then, the key point data is input into the transformer model for pose analysis and recognition. In addition, the authors design a human skeletal alignment method for comparison with standard poses. The experimental results show that the method performs well in recognizing players' poses in billiards matches and provides real-time and timely feedback on players' pose information. This research project provides a new and efficient tool for training billiard players and opens up new possibilities for applying deep learning in sports analytics. In addition, one of these contributions is the creation of a dataset for pose recognition.

Global cyber dangers related to phishing emails have increased dramatically, particularly after the COVID-19 epidemic broke out. Many companies have suffered significant financial losses as a result of this kind of assault. Even though many models have been developed to distinguish between phishing efforts and genuine emails, attackers always come up with new ways to trick their targets into falling for their scams. Many companies have suffered significant financial losses as a result of this kind of assault. Although phishing detection algorithms are being developed, their accuracy and speed in recognizing phishing emails are not up to par right now. Furthermore, the number of phished emails has alarmingly increased lately.

To lessen the negative effects of such bogus communications, there is an urgent need for more effective and high-performing phishing detection algorithms. Inside the framework of this study, a thorough examination of an email message's email header and content is carried out. A novel phishing detection model is built using the features of sentences that are extracted. The new dimension of sentence-level analysis is introduced by this model, which makes use of k-nearest neighbor (KNN). Kaggle's well-known datasets were used both to train and evaluate the model. Important performance indicators, including the F1-measure, precision, recall, and accuracy of 0.97, are used to assess the efficacy of this approach.

Preface

Artificial intelligence (AI) is an ever-evolving field and through different innovations and discoveries in the field, there is a need to further research its subtopics such as deep Learning, Reinforcement Learning, and Intelligent Systems. To see the current advancements in the field, this book on the topic *Deep Learning, Reinforcement Learning and the Rise of Intelligent Systems* is a collection of comprehensive research techniques and their applications in different domains.

In the book, the authors have explored advanced topics such as Reinforcement Learning, Transfer Learning, Generative AI, Adversarial Deep Reinforcement Learning, Computer Vision, AI Systems Interpretability, and their applications in different domains. Researchers from different research institutions have written well-crafted chapters and have demonstrated the latest techniques, theories, and implementations in the domain of intelligent systems.

AI has continuously reshaped our lives through different advancements in industries, and societies. Therefore, we must understand these technologies in AI. In the book, we have not only explored the theoretical foundations of AI but also have shown real-world examples in different domains. The theoretical knowledge and practical examples in the book make it an invaluable resource in academia for researchers, and students who are interested to understand the knowledge and applications of intelligent systems.

The audience of the book is very diverse. It can be used by researchers to understand and see how the knowledge can be applied in their research work. It can be used by instructors in teaching a course on AI, intelligent systems, or deep learning. It can be used by professionals who are interested in applying AI techniques at a commercial level. It can be used by students to further extend their knowledge and understanding of the field.

In the book, there are a total of twelve different chapters and each chapter has its importance and application. A summary of the chapters is given below.

Chapter 1, "An Introduction to Reinforcement Learning and Its Application in Various Domains," authored by Samina Amin, sets the stage by providing a comprehensive introduction to reinforcement learning. It explores its applications across various domains, laying a solid foundation for the subsequent chapters.

Chapter 2, "Transfer Learning for Computer Vision: From Theory to Implementation by Qadeem Khan," takes us through transfer learning, particularly focusing on its applications in computer vision. This chapter serves as a bridge between theoretical concepts and their practical implementation.

Chapter 3, "The Importance of Interpretability in AI Systems and its Implications for Deep Learning: Ensuring Transparency in Intelligent Systems," authored by Muhammad Adnan, tackles a critical aspect of AI i.e., interpretability. In an era where AI decisions impact our lives, understanding and ensuring transparency in intelligent systems is very important.

Chapter 4, "Generative AI From Theory to Model: Unleashing the Creative Power of Artificial Intelligence" by Asim Wadood, explores the domain of generative AI, providing insights into the creative potential of artificial intelligence. This chapter covers the theoretical foundations and practical applications of generative models.

Chapter 5, "Robust Adversarial Deep Reinforcement Learning," authored by Di Wang, gives details into the robustness of deep reinforcement learning using adversarial techniques. The insights provided contribute to enhancing the resilience of intelligent systems.

Chapters 6 to 10, "Computer Vision Applications from Auckland University of Technology, New Zealand," authored by Chenwei Liang, Wei Qi Yan, GuanQun Xu, Boning Yang, and Xiaoxu Liu, present a series of chapters focusing on practical applications of computer vision. These range from human action recognition and emotion recognition to real-time billiard shot stability detection and vehicle detection, showcasing the diversity of intelligent systems.

Chapter 11, "Analysis Model at Sentence Level for Phishing Detection," authored by Sonali Mishra, explores the application of deep learning in phishing detection at the sentence level, emphasizing the wide-reaching applications of intelligent systems in cybersecurity.

In summary, the book *Deep Learning, Reinforcement Learning, and the Rise of Intelligent Systems* contains topics ranging from theories, techniques, and applications. The authors from different locations have contributed to this book demonstrating the international collaboration to shape this advanced field of AI. The book is a comprehensive resource for all those who are interested in understanding the theory, techniques, and applications of intelligent systems and can use this book as a guide if they are working on their application. We enjoyed working on this book and we are happy to receive chapters from authors on the different aspects of AI. We hope that the book will serve as a light that can illuminate the path towards AI shaping the lives of humans and empowering them in different diverse domains.

M. Irfan Uddin
Kohat University of Science and Technology, Pakistan

Wali Khan Mashwani
Kohat University of Science and Technology, Pakistan

Chapter 1
An Introduction to Reinforcement Learning and Its Application in Various Domains

Samina Amin
https://orcid.org/0000-0003-4811-6806
Institute of Computing, Kohat University of Science and Technology, Pakistan

ABSTRACT

Reinforcement learning (RL) is a dynamic and evolving subfield of machine learning that focuses on training intelligent agents to learn and adapt through interactions with their environment. This introductory article provides an overview of the fundamental concepts and principles of RL, elucidating its core components, such as the agent, environment, actions, and rewards. This study aims to give readers an in-depth introduction to RL and show examples of its different uses in various domains. RL can allow agents to learn through interaction with an environment, which has led to its enormous interest. The core ideas of RL and its essential elements will be covered in this study, after which it will go into applications in industries including robotics, gaming, finance, healthcare, and more. The fundamental ideas of RL will become clearer to readers, and they will recognize how transformative it can be when used to address challenging decision-making issues. These applications demonstrate the versatility and significance of RL in shaping the future of technology and automation.

DOI: 10.4018/979-8-3693-1738-9.ch001

INTRODUCTION/PRELIMINARIES

RL is a specialized field within machine learning that is primarily oriented towards solving control problems. It amalgamates the benefits of dynamic programming with a trial-and-error approach. In RL, an agent-based control paradigm is adopted, wherein the agent learns by interacting with the controlled environment. RL draws inspiration from the natural learning process that occurs through interactions with the environment, mirroring how biological systems learn (Amin et al. 2023) (Sutton and Barto 2018). Like other forms of learning, it revolves around establishing connections between states and actions to optimize specific rewards. Nevertheless, the primary challenge in this type of learning lies in the fact that, unlike conventional machine learning approaches, the learner must autonomously discover the optimal actions for specific situations. Consequently, a learning agent needs to comprehend the environment, select actions that maximize rewards, and adapt its behavior accordingly, even in the face of environmental uncertainties. RL systems are well-suited for unsupervised, real-time implementation, as they construct their understanding of the environment through exploration. Figure 1 illustrates a general RL framework. The formalization of RL is achieved through the utilization of a Markov decision process (MDP), which serves as a discrete-time stochastic control process (Amin et al. 2023). MDP offers a structured mathematical foundation for modeling the decision-making process within this framework.

Figure 1. Representation of RL structure

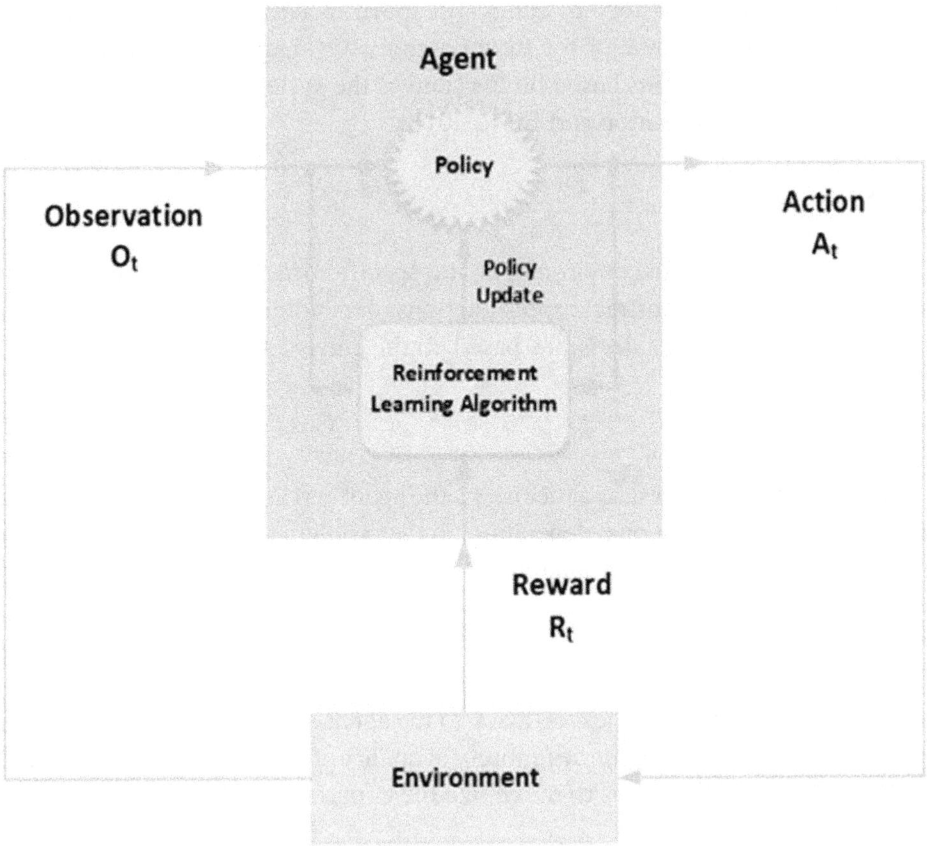

- Agent

The learner or decision-maker interacts with the environment. The agent observes the current state, selects actions, and receives feedback from the environment.

- Environment

The environment's behavior can be described by the state it assumes at a given time, denoted as S(t), which is characterized by a set of attributes or values. Each state is associated with a reward or immediate cost, represented as R(t), that is generated upon entering that state. At each time step, the agent has a choice of taking one of several possible actions, denoted as A(t), which influence the subsequent state of the system, S(t + 1), and consequently the rewards or costs experienced, with probabilities governing these transitions. The agent's decision-making process, considering the current state, is shaped by its past experiences. In this manner, an RL system utilizes its history of actions in specific states and the corresponding rewards to update its strategy for future actions. Over time, the agent evolves a policy for selecting actions based on the state of the system during its interactions with the environment (Sutton and Barto 2018).

- State

A representation of the environment at a specific time. States can be as simple as raw sensory data or abstract representations, depending on the problem. In RL, the agent typically makes decisions based on the current state.

- Action

The set of possible choices or decisions the agent can make at each state. Actions can be discrete or continuous, depending on the problem. The agent selects actions to transition from one state to another.

- Reward

A scalar value that provides feedback to the agent after each action. The reward signal quantifies the immediate desirability or quality of an action taken in a particular state. The agent's objective is to maximize the cumulative reward over time.

- Policy (π)

A strategy or mapping that the agent uses to determine which action to take in each state. The policy defines the agent's behaviour. It can be deterministic (direct mapping from state to action) or stochastic (probabilistic mapping).

- Value Function

A function that estimates the expected cumulative reward, or "value," associated with being in a particular state. It helps the agent assess the desirability of different states.

Exploration and Exploitation

Balancing the trade-off between exploring unknown states and exploiting the knowledge gained from already visited states is a fundamental challenge in RL.

Different strategies, such as epsilon greedy or UCB (Upper Confidence Bound), are used to address this issue.

Markov Decision Process (MDP)

An MDP is a mathematical framework used to model RL problems. It consists of a finite set of states, a finite set of actions, a transition function that defines the probability of moving from one state to another after taking an action, and a reward function.

In addition, an MDP is a tuple with the elements s, a, r, pi, where S is the discrete finite state space, A = {a_1, a_2, a_3, ...} is the discrete finite action space, and [0, 1] is the discount factor. The notation r: s a x R is the agent's reward function, and p: s x a is the transition function. The discount factor [0, 1] significantly depicts the concept that rewards are reduced by a factor < 1 at each time step. It can be supposed that the transition probabilities p (s_1|s, a) are static for all t = 0, 1, 2,... and $Xs_{02}S$ p(s_1|s, a) = 1 for every s, s_0 2 S as well as every action a_2 (Amin et al. 2023).

APPLICATIONS OF REINFORCEMENT LEARNING

RL algorithms, such as Q-learning, Deep Q-Networks (DQN), Policy Gradient methods, and Actor-Critic methods, are designed to optimize the agent's policy to maximize the expected cumulative reward. RL has applications in various domains, including robotics, game playing, autonomous vehicles, recommendation systems, healthcare, and education, among others as follows.

Robotics and Autonomous Systems

RL has a significant impact on robotics and autonomous systems, enabling machines to learn and adapt to their environments, make decisions, and perform tasks autonomously (Ibarz et al. 2021). RL is used to train robots to perform tasks like walking, grasping objects, and navigating environments. It enables robots to adapt to unforeseen changes in their surroundings (Singh, Kumar, and Singh 2022), (Kober, Bagnell, and Peters 2013).

RL is used to control the movements and actions of robots. By training RL agents in simulations or real-world environments, robots can learn how to navigate, manipulate objects, and interact with their surroundings. RL enables robots to perform tasks like picking and placing objects, assembly, and more (Singh, Kumar, and Singh 2022), (Gu et al. 2017).

RL in robotics and autonomous systems has the potential to enhance the adaptability and intelligence of these machines, enabling them to perform tasks more efficiently, make autonomous decisions, and operate in dynamic and unpredictable environments.

Gaming

Gaming has become an indispensable part of the lives of many people today, including you, me, and a substantial portion of the population. By employing RL algorithms to optimize games, we can anticipate enhanced performance in our preferred genres, such as adventure, action, or mystery.

To illustrate this, we can consider the case of AlphaGo (Sewak 2019), (Silver et al. 2018), a computer program that achieved a remarkable feat in October 2015 by defeating the most skilled human Go player and subsequently becoming the top-ranked Go player itself. The key to AlphaGo's victory was RL, which allowed it to continually improve its skills by facing and adapting to unexpected gaming challenges. Similar to AlphaGo, numerous other games are available, where we can enhance the gaming experience by implementing predictive models that teach how to excel even in intricate scenarios through RL-enabled strategies (Lample and Chaplot 2017).

RL in gaming is a promising area that has the potential to create more immersive and dynamic gaming experiences while also streamlining game development and testing processes.

Image Processing

Image Processing serves as a pivotal technique for enhancing the quality and utility of images by extracting valuable information. This process involves several key steps, including:

- Acquisition of the image through devices such as scanners.
- Analysis and manipulation of the image.
- Utilizing the resultant image, post-analysis, for various purposes such as representation and description.

In this context, the field of machine learning offers a powerful approach, particularly through the utilization of deep neural networks, which are grounded in RL frameworks (Dhiman et al. 2023), (Furuta, Inoue, and Yamasaki 2019), (Bernstein and Burnaev 2018). Deep neural networks can significantly streamline and augment this evolving image-processing technique. They enable improvements in image quality or concealment of specific image information, which can later be employed for various computer vision tasks.

J. Valente et al., (Valente et al. 2023) carried out an extensive review of developments in AI design and the optimization strategies put out to address image processing issues. Despite the encouraging outcomes, this field of study continues to encounter numerous obstacles. They addressed the primary and more recent advancements, uses, and innovations about image processing applications, and we suggest future research paths in this rapidly evolving and ever-changing topic.

RL in image processing is a promising area that can lead to more efficient and adaptive image analysis and manipulation, benefiting applications in computer vision, healthcare, robotics, and many other domains.

Self-Driving Cars

Deep RL for autonomous driving has been proposed in several studies. There are several factors to consider with self-driving automobiles, like different locations' speed limits, drivable zones, and preventing crashes (Cao et al. 2021).

Trajectory optimization, motion planning, dynamic pathing, controller optimization, and scenario-based learning policies for highways are a few autonomous driving activities where RL may be used. For instance, automatic parking policies can be learned to accomplish parking. Q-learning can be used to change lanes, and learning an overtaking policy while avoiding collisions and continuing at a steady pace can be used to execute overtaking (Katrakazas et al. 2015), (Mir et al. 2022), (Song et al. 2023). The purpose of the autonomous racing vehicle AWS DeepRacer is to test RL on a real track. It controls the throttle and direction using an RL model, and it visualizes the runway using cameras.

RL in self-driving cars is a critical component that enables these vehicles to operate safely, make decisions in complex traffic scenarios, and adapt to a wide range of driving conditions. It plays a key role in making autonomous driving a reality.

Healthcare

Machine learning and artificial intelligence play a significant role in the healthcare sector, and RL is no different. It finds application in automated medical diagnoses, optimizing resource allocation, aiding drug discovery and development, and enhancing health management (Datta et al. 2021), (Coronato et al. 2020).

A key application of RL lies in the realm of dynamic treatment regimens (DTRs). In the development of a DTR, a practitioner or system considers a collection of clinical observations and patient assessments. Leveraging historical patient outcomes and medical records, the learning system can subsequently provide recommendations for treatment approaches, medication dosages, and appointment scheduling at each phase of the patient's healthcare journey. This proves highly advantageous for making time-sensitive decisions regarding the most effective treatment for a patient at any given moment, all while minimizing the need for extensive consultations and resource expenditure from multiple stakeholders[1]. RL can be used to personalize treatment plans for patients based on their health data. RL algorithms can learn from historical patient outcomes and continually adapt treatment recommendations to achieve better outcomes (M. Liu, Shen, and Pan 2022).

To enhance healthcare decision-making, in Ref. (Dai et al. 2020) the development of human body simulators using deep neural networks for healthcare research was proposed. Initially, Y. Dai et al., (Dai et al. 2020) established a deep neural network-based model for the human body system. Their analysis unfolds, and they recognized that DNN-based models can replicate real-world scenarios, including those health states that may be otherwise unattainable. Subsequently, the authors integrated deep RL (DRL) with conceptual embedding techniques to investigate effective healthcare strategies for these simulated human bodies. They introduced a virtual human body simulator, which can receive interventions and represent its concealed states through high-dimensional images. Additionally, they presented a DRL-based treatment module capable of diagnosing latent health states based on image observations and selecting interventions to nurture the simulated body toward a desired state. Healthcare is an ever-evolving process that necessitates continuous monitoring of an individual's health status and timely intervention, as depicted in Figure 2. Historically, individuals would typically visit a hospital or doctor when they felt unwell, where various medical devices would be employed to collect patient data, diagnose their health conditions, and prescribe treatments. However, a more effective healthcare approach involves proactive intervention before individuals experience discomfort. In the present day, the widespread integration of embedded systems and wearable devices enables continuous monitoring of human health parameters, regardless of location or time.

Figure 2. Health status and timely intervention using RL
Figure source: Dai et al. 2020

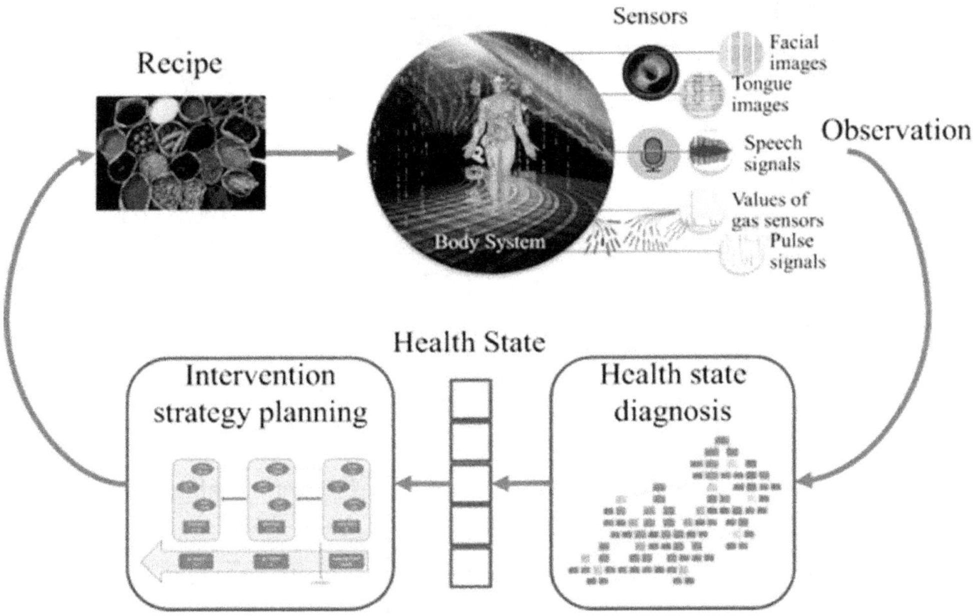

A. Coronato et al., (Coronato et al. 2020) aimed to present a comprehensive overview of how RL is utilized in the healthcare field, with a focus on its potential to facilitate the creation of personalized treatments in alignment with the broader concept of precision medicine. By harnessing pervasive sensors, diverse 5G networks, and intelligent processing and control systems, intelligent health systems can continuously observe individuals' daily lives and deliver smart healthcare services to both residents and travelers, all without imposing any restrictions on their activities. Intelligent health can encompass a range of applications, such as remote monitoring, pandemic control, at-home care, and even remote surgical procedures (refer to Figure 1 for an illustration).

Figure 3. Intelligent health system components adapted from Coronato et al. 2020

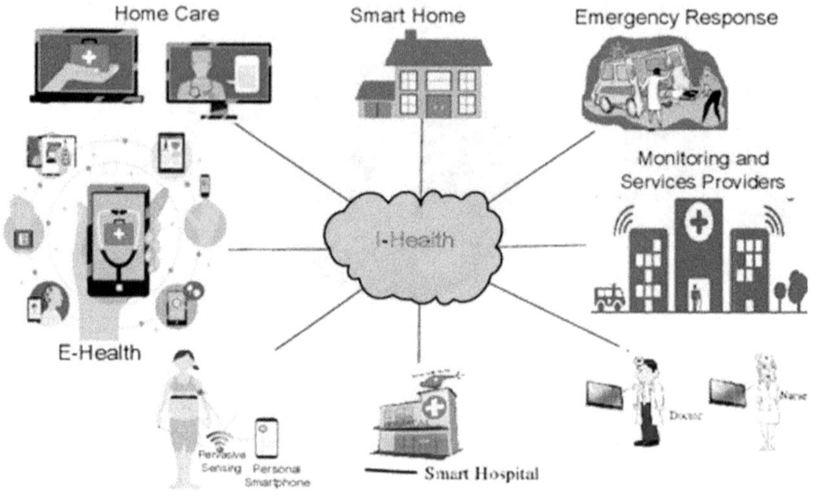

Figure 4 illustrates a classification system for RL in the context of intelligent health systems, covering various methodologies, use cases, obstacles, and areas of ongoing research. The illustration serves as a flowchart diagram, explaining the various components and uses of RL in the context of intelligent healthcare systems. The three primary sections of the flowchart are Open Research Directions, RL Fundamentals and Applications, and intelligent health Systems. The architecture, advantages, and difficulties of intelligent healthcare systems are outlined in Figure 4 on intelligent health systems. The history, techniques, and applications of RL in intelligent healthcare systems are explained in RL fundamentals and applications. Future directions for RL research and its applications to intelligent healthcare systems are also highlighted (Coronato et al. 2020).

Figure 4. A classification system for RL in the context of I-Health systems, covering various methodologies, use cases, obstacles, and areas of ongoing research (Coronato et al. 2020)

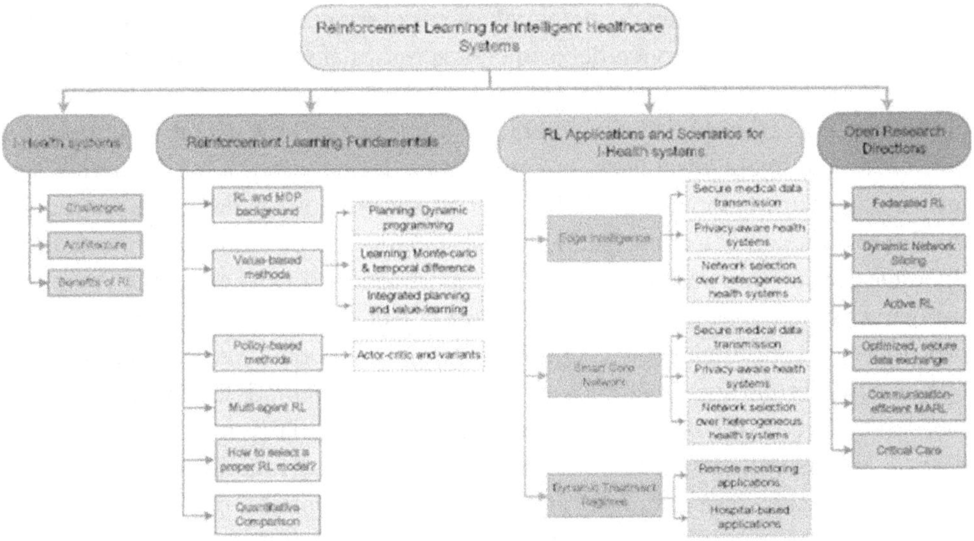

To implement RL in healthcare, it is important to follow ethical and regulatory guidelines, ensure patient privacy, and validate the models with rigorous testing. Some challenges and considerations include the interpretability of RL models, data quality, and the need for collaboration between machine learning experts and healthcare professionals.

In summary, RL has the potential to enhance healthcare by optimizing treatment decisions, personalizing medicine, improving resource allocation, and contributing to more efficient and effective healthcare processes. As technology and healthcare data continue to evolve, RL will likely play an increasingly important role in the healthcare industry.

Natural Language Processing

RL in natural language processing (NLP) finds application in various areas, such as machine translation, question answering, text summarization, and predictive text generation. By analyzing typical language patterns, RL-based models can mimic and predict everyday speech patterns, encompassing not only syntax (word and sentence structure) but also diction (word choice) and the language employed.

In 2016, scientists from Microsoft Research, Ohio State University, and Stanford University employed this learning to create conversation, much like chatbots do. They employed policy gradient approaches to reward crucial traits including coherence, informativity, and simplicity of answering questions while simulating discussions between two virtual agents[2]. This study was distinctive in that it considered both the immediate question and the potential effects of a solution on subsequent events. These days, customer service departments across many large corporations apply this NLP method to RL.

Newer neural models for generating dialogues show great potential for conversational agent responses, but they often lack foresight by predicting one utterance at a time without considering their impact on future interactions. Predicting the future direction of a conversation is essential for creating coherent and engaging dialogues, prompting traditional NLP dialogue models to incorporate RL. This paper introduces an approach that combines these objectives, leveraging DRL to model prospective rewards in chatbot dialogues. The proposed model simulates conversations between two virtual agents, employing policy gradient methods to reward sequences that exhibit three valuable conversational attributes: informativeness, coherence, and ease of response, all of which are linked to forward-looking functions (Li et al. 2016).

E. Choi et al., (Choi et al. 2017) introduced a framework for question-answering designed to efficiently handle longer documents while either maintaining or enhancing the performance of cutting-edge models. Many successful reading comprehension methods rely on recurrent neural networks (RNNs) but executing them over extensive documents proves to be unmanageably slow due to challenges in parallelization across sequences. Drawing inspiration from how people typically approach document reading by first skimming the content, identifying pertinent sections, and then engaging in a more careful reading to derive answers, their approach combines a rapid, coarse-grained model for selecting relevant sentences with a more resource-intensive RNN for generating answers from these selected sentences. To achieve this, authors treated the sentence selection process as a latent variable, and it is jointly trained based on the answer through RL. They provided an RL-based method for answering questions in the context of lengthy texts. They began their process by picking a few passages from the document that were pertinent to the subject at hand. After that, a slow RNN is used to generate responses for the chosen sentences. Figure 0 shows a Hierarchical question answering involves a two-step process: initially, the model chooses pertinent sentences to form a document summary (d^) in response to the query (x), and subsequently, it generates an answer (y) using both the summary (d^) and the query x.

Figure 5. Hierarchical question answering involves a two-step process
Figure source: Choi et al. 2017

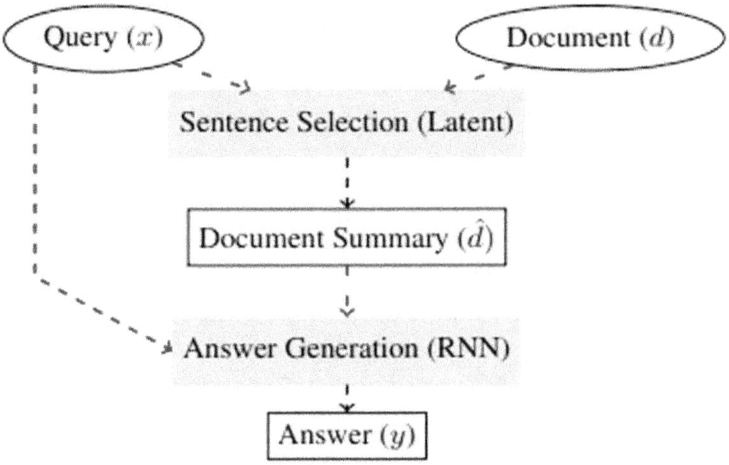

In article (Paulus, Xiong, and Socher 2017), abstractive text summarization is achieved by a combination of supervised and RL. Their objective is to use attentive, RNN-based encoder-decoder models in larger documents to tackle the summarization challenge. In this research, the authors present a neural network with a novel intra-attention that continually generates different outputs while attending to the input. They combine RL with conventional supervised word prediction in their training techniques. Figure 6 depicts the computation of the intra-attention context vector, along with the encoder's temporal attention, and how they are utilized in the decoder.

Figure 6. A representation of the combined encoder and decoder attention functions. The two context vectors, denoted as "C," are computed by attending to both the encoder's hidden states and the decoder's hidden states. With these two contexts and the current decoder hidden state, labeled as "H," a new word is generated and incorporated into the output sequence.
Figure source: Paulus, Xiong, and Socher 2017

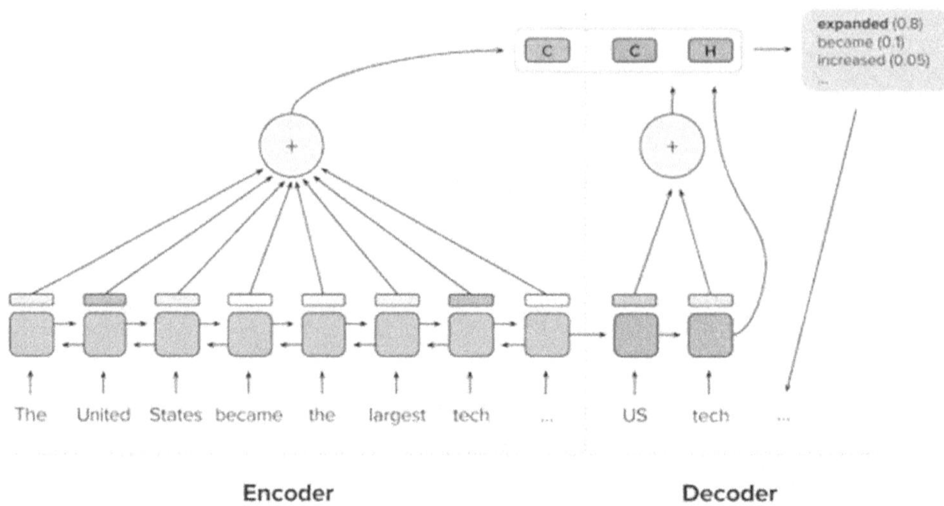

A. Grissom et al.,(Grissom II et al. 2014) presented an approach based on RL for simultaneous machine translation, which involves generating a translation while continuously receiving input words. This method is particularly valuable when translating between languages with significantly different word orders, such as from verb-final languages like German to verb-medial languages like English. In traditional machine translation, the translator typically needs to wait for the entire source material to appear before initiating the translation process. The authors overcome this limitation by proactively predicting the final verb. Through RL, they acquired the ability to determine when to trust predictions regarding unseen portions of the sentence in the future. Additionally, they introduced an evaluation metric to gauge both the speed and quality of the translation. In Figure 7, as each German word is received, the system progresses to a new state, comprising the source input, the translation in progress in the target language, and predictions regarding unseen words. Subsequently, the translation system must decide based on the information available in the current state. This decision leads to the reception and translation of additional source words, advancing the system to the next state. In the given example, during the initial stages where the source-language words are few, the translator refrains from producing any output due to insufficient information at that particular state. However, upon reaching State 3, the system exhibits a high level of confidence in predicting the verb "gefahren." Supported by the observed German input, the system is now self-assured enough to take action on this prediction, enabling the production of an English translation

Figure 7. In the process of simultaneous translation from the source language (German) to the target language (English), the agent decides to delay its translation process until after step 3. At this stage, the agent has gained enough confidence to predict the final verb in the sentence, which occurs in step 4. With this additional information, the agent can initiate the translation into English, influencing subsequent translation steps (5). As the remaining part of the sentence unfolds, the system can proceed to translate the rest of the sentence.
Figure source: Grissom II et al. 2014

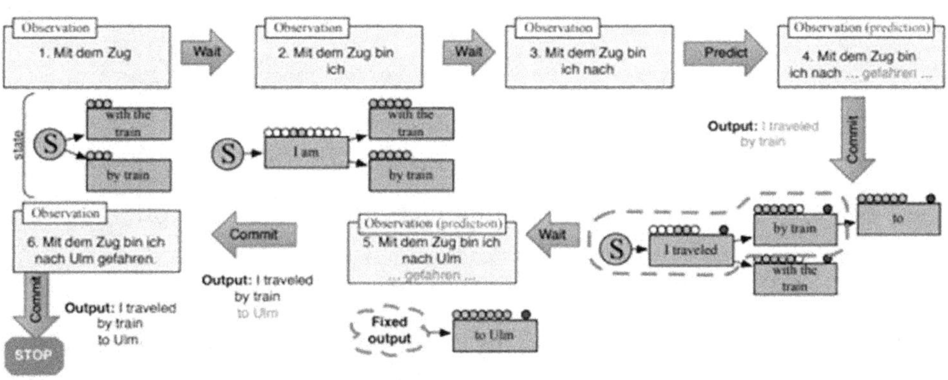

J. Li et al., (Li et al. 2016) demonstrated the integration of these objectives by employing DRL to model future rewards in chatbot dialogues. Their model simulates dialogues between two virtual agents, utilizing policy gradient methods to incentivize sequences that exhibit three valuable conversational qualities: informativity, coherence, and ease of response (associated with forward-looking functionality). They assessed the model's performance in terms of diversity, dialogue length, and human judgments, revealing that the proposed algorithm generates more interactive responses and facilitates more sustained and engaging conversations in dialogue simulations. This research represents an initial stride toward developing a neural conversational model that focuses on the long-term success of dialogues. They conducted simulations of dialogues involving two virtual agents who engage in a turn-based conversation as depicted in Figure 8. The simulation process unfolds as follows: Initially, a message from the training dataset is provided to the first agent. This agent encodes the input message into a vector representation and begins the decoding process to create a response. Using the immediate output from the first agent in conjunction with the existing dialogue history, the second agent updates its state. It accomplishes this by encoding the entire dialogue history into a representation and then utilizing a decoder RNN to generate responses. These responses are subsequently relayed back to the first agent, and this iterative process continues

Figure 8. Dialogue simulation between the two agents
Figure source: Li et al. 2016

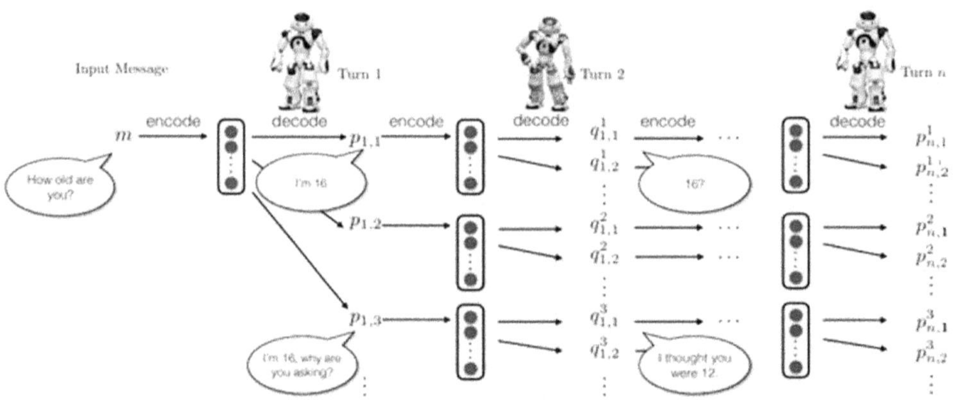

RL in NLP holds the potential to create more context-aware, responsive, and adaptive language models and applications, making it a valuable approach for improving human-computer interactions, content generation, and language understanding.

Recommender Systems

RSs have found widespread application in various real-life scenarios, aiding us in discovering valuable information. Specifically, RSs based on RL have gained significant attention in recent years due to their interactive nature and autonomous learning capabilities. Empirical evidence suggests that RL-based recommendation methods often outperform supervised learning methods. However, there are multiple challenges associated with implementing RL in RSs (Y Lin et al. 2023), (Chen et al. 2023).

In the past, the recommendation challenge was typically viewed as a classification or prediction task. However, there is now a growing consensus that framing it as a sequential decision problem more accurately captures the dynamics of user-system interaction. As a result, it can be conceptualized as a MDP and addressed using RL techniques. Unlike conventional recommendation approaches such as collaborative filtering and content-based filtering, RL excels in managing the continuous, evolving user-system interplay and factoring in long-term user engagement (Afsar, Crump, and Far 2022).

X. Xin et al.,(Xin et al. 2020) introduced a novel methodology, self-supervised RL, tailored for tasks involving sequential recommendations. Their method extends conventional recommendation models by incorporating two distinct output layers: one for self-supervised learning and the other for RL. The RL component serves as a regularizing factor, guiding the supervised layer to prioritize specific rewards, such as suggesting items likely to result in purchases rather than mere clicks. Meanwhile, the self-supervised layer, utilizing a cross-entropy loss, furnishes robust gradient signals to facilitate parameter updates. Building upon this framework, they introduced two distinct models: self-supervised Q-learning and self-supervised actor-critic. These innovative frameworks are seamlessly integrated with four leading-edge recommendation models.

While RL is a natural fit for maximizing long-term rewards, applying RL to enhance long-term user engagement remains challenging. User behaviors are highly diverse, encompassing both immediate feedback (e.g., clicks) and delayed feedback (e.g., dwell time, revisits). Additionally, achieving effective off-policy learning, particularly when combining bootstrapping and function approximation, remains an evolving area. To tackle these challenges, (Zou et al. 2019) introduced an RL framework called FeedRec, designed to optimize long-term user engagement. FeedRec consists of two key components: A Q-Network, implemented using a hierarchical LSTM, is responsible for modeling intricate user behaviors. An S-Network, which emulates the environment, supports the Q-Network and mitigates convergence instability in policy learning. Extensive experiments conducted on synthetic data and a real-world large-scale dataset demonstrate that FeedRec effectively enhances long-term user engagement and surpasses existing state-of-the-art methods.

L. Huang et al., (Huang et al. 2021) presented an innovative interactive RS that leverages DRL. In their approach, they treat the recommendation process as an MDP, which models the interactions between the RS (the agent) and the user (the environment) using an RNN. Furthermore, they employed RL to fine-tune the model, aiming to enhance long-term recommendation accuracy to the maximum extent. I. Munemasa et al., (Munemasa et al. 2018) proposed an RS based on DRL. In DRL, a multilayer neural network is used to update the value function

In recent times, distance learning has gained significant diversity and popularity. Many universities are actively expanding their offerings of online courses, including MOOCs, SPOCs, SMOCs, SSOCs, and more, providing learners with a plethora of options. However, the process of selecting the right course from this multitude of choices can be quite intricate. M. Agrebi et al., (Agrebi, Sendi, and Abed 2019) introduced a personalized RS that utilizes DRL to suggest the most suitable course for individual learners based on their unique profiles, requirements, and competencies. To assess the effectiveness of the system, they conducted testing on a group of actual students, and the results from their study strongly support the robustness of RS.

Jian-Wei Tzeng et al., (Tzeng et al. 2023) designed the actor–critic framework of RL to recommend personalized exercises in MOOC. In the context of online learning, learners typically seek courses that align with their preferences and cater to their future growth requirements. Consequently, there is a significant demand for the creation of efficient personalized course recommendation systems designed to assist learners in selecting appropriate courses. M. Agrebi et al., (Yuanguo Lin et al. 2022) introduced an innovative course recommendation model called hierarchical RL with a dynamic recurrent mechanism. This model incorporates a profile constructor with autonomous learning capabilities, aimed at delivering personalized course recommendations.

RL in RS can lead to more effective, personalized, and adaptive recommendations, ultimately enhancing the user experience and achieving business objectives in various domains. Figure 9 illustrates (a) deep learning-based RS and (b) DRL-based RS), by finding that deep learning-based RS typically update their recommendation policy only during the training phase. This often necessitates re-training, which can be computationally inefficient when users' interests undergo significant changes. In contrast, DRL-based RS continuously updates its recommendation policy as new rewards are obtained over time (Chen et al. 2023).

(a) DL-based recommender system
(b) DRL-based recommender system

Figure 9. Contrasting (a) deep learning-based RS and (b) DRL-based RS), by finding that deep learning-based RS typically update their recommendation policy only during the training phase. This often necessitates re-training, which can be computationally inefficient when users' interests undergo significant changes. In contrast, DRL-based RS continuously updates its recommendation policy as new rewards are obtained over time.
Figure source: Chen et al. 2023

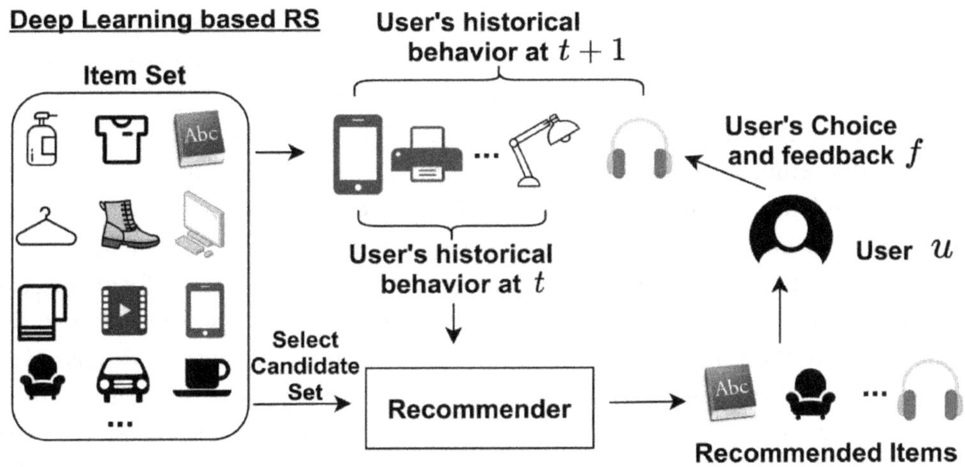

(a) Deep learning based recommender systems

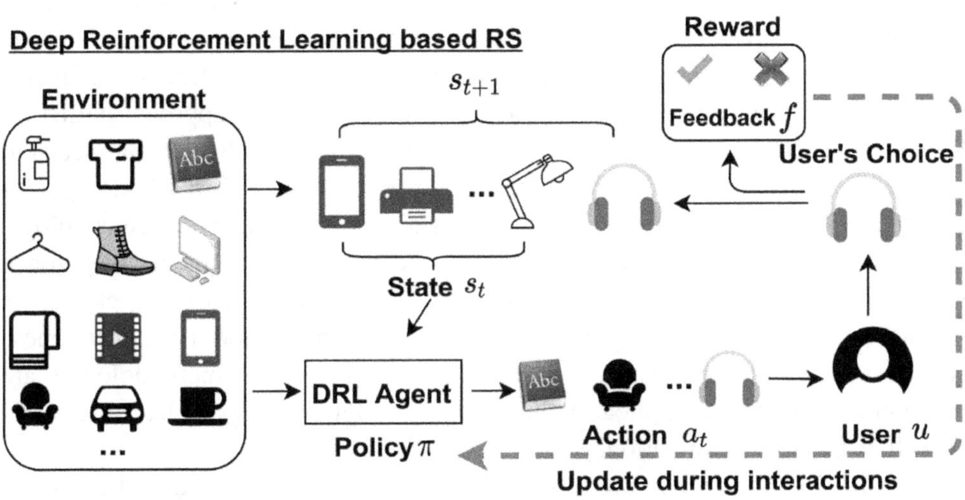

(b) Deep reinforcement learning-based recommender systems

Education

Incorporating RL into the realm of education can instigate a substantial transformation in students' learning methods and teachers' assessment of student advancement. The application of RL in education facilitates tailored and flexible learning, permitting adjustments to the challenge level in response to a student's performance. Consequently, this has the potential to enhance students' motivation and active participation significantly (Fahad Mon et al. 2023). RL can create personalized learning paths for students. It adapts the difficulty of tasks and the pace of learning to individual needs (Bassen et al. 2020), (S. Liu et al. 2018).

S. Liu et al. (S. Liu et al. 2018) proposed the development of a cyber-physical system that employs multiple sensors, including cameras and a quiz creator, to monitor students' learning progress. They leveraged RL techniques to offer tailored learning guidance within a smart classroom setting. To elaborate, their smart learning recommendation system collects data on students' heartbeats, quiz performance, eye blinks, and facial expressions, enabling the determination of their learning states. Subsequently, they employed RL to suggest appropriate learning activities based on these individual learning states. The process of interactive learning recommendations in a sensor-equipped smart classroom can be conceptualized as an MDP. Preliminary simulation results highlight the effectiveness of this intelligent learning RS. This research lays the groundwork for future intelligent learning environments designed to enhance personalized education. D. Shawky et al., (Shawky and Badawi 2019) introduced an approach that flexibly adapts to the most influential factors in the learning process, accommodating variations among individual learners and diverse learning contexts, be it individual or collaborative learning. This approach harnesses RL to construct an intelligent learning environment. It not only offers a means to recommend suitable learning resources but also establishes a methodology for continually assessing students' evolving states and their acceptance of the technology. R. Hare et al., (Hare and Tang 2023) presented a hierarchical multi-agent RL approach with experience sharing, aimed at enhancing the intelligence of non-player characters within Metaverse learning environments to enable personalization. The effectiveness and advantages of this proposed framework and associated methodologies are illustrated through their application in Gridlock, a Metaverse-based learning game, as well as extensive simulations.

Overall, RL in education aims to create a more individualized and engaging learning experience, with a focus on helping students achieve their full potential while providing educators with valuable tools for informed decision-making.

IMPLICATION AND FUTURE WORK SUGGESTIONS

RL holds significant implications for automation, personalization, and improved AI systems across a wide array of domains. By automating complex decision-making processes, RL can drive cost savings, efficiency, and resource optimization. In healthcare, education, recommendation systems, and content delivery, RL enables highly personalized experiences, enhancing user satisfaction and engagement. Moreover, RL contributes to the development of more sophisticated and adaptable AI systems capable of handling real-world uncertainties and adapting to changing conditions. It also has the potential to expedite scientific discoveries in fields such as chemistry, biology, and physics and to promote sustainability and safety in energy management, transportation, and robotics.

As RL continues to expand its reach, future work should concentrate on improving sample efficiency, transfer learning, exploration strategies, robustness, human-AI collaboration, ethical and regulatory frameworks, generalization, interpretable AI, offline RL, multi-agent RL, and the real-world deployment of RL solutions to address new challenges and harness its full potential while ensuring responsible and ethical use.

CONCLUSION

To conclude, this book chapter attempts to provide a basic library, for scholars and researchers interested in understanding RL and its numerous applications across various domains. It gives scholars and researchers the information and inspiration to study and contributes to the fascinating field of RL by offering both theoretical concepts and practical insights.

REFERENCES

Afsar, M., Crump, T., & Far, B. (2022). Reinforcement Learning Based Recommender Systems: A Survey. *ACM Computing Surveys*, *55*(7), 1–38. doi:10.1145/3543846

Agrebi, M., Sendi, M., & Abed, M. 2019. "Deep Reinforcement Learning for Personalized Recommendation of Distance Learning." In *World Conference on Information Systems and Technologies*, 597–606. Springer. 10.1007/978-3-030-16184-2_57

Amin, S., Irfan Uddin, M., Alarood, A. A., Mashwani, W. K., Alzahrani, A., & Alzahrani, A. O. (2023). Smart E-Learning Framework For Personalized Adaptive Learning and Sequential Path Recommendations Using Reinforcement Learning. *IEEE Access : Practical Innovations, Open Solutions, 11*, 89769–89790. doi:10.1109/ACCESS.2023.3305584

Bassen, J., Balaji, B., Schaarschmidt, M., Thille, C., Painter, J., Zimmaro, D., Games, A., & Fast, E. (2020). Reinforcement Learning for the Adaptive Scheduling of Educational Activities. In *Proceedings of the 2020 CHI Conference on Human Factors in Computing Systems*, (pp. 1–12). ACM. 10.1145/3313831.3376518

Bernstein, A. V., & Evgeny, V. (2018). Reinforcement Learning in Computer Vision. In *Tenth International Conference on Machine Vision (ICMV 2017).*

Cao, Z., Xu, S., Peng, H., Yang, D., & Zidek, R. (2021). Confidence-Aware Reinforcement Learning for Self-Driving Cars. *IEEE Transactions on Intelligent Transportation Systems*, *23*(7), 7419–7430. doi:10.1109/TITS.2021.3069497

Chen, X., Yao, L., McAuley, J., Zhou, G., & Wang, X. (2023). Deep Reinforcement Learning in Recommender Systems: A Survey and New Perspectives. *Knowledge-Based Systems*, *264*, 110335. doi:10.1016/j.knosys.2023.110335

Choi, E., Hewlett, D., Uszkoreit, J., Polosukhin, I., Lacoste, A., & Berant, J. (2017). Coarse-to-Fine Question Answering for Long Documents. In *Proceedings of the 55th Annual Meeting of the Association for Computational Linguistics (*Volume 1*: Long Papers)*, (pp. 209–20). IEEE. 10.18653/v1/P17-1020

Coronato, A., Naeem, M., De Pietro, G., & Paragliola, G. (2020). Reinforcement Learning for Intelligent Healthcare Applications: A Survey. *Artificial Intelligence in Medicine*, *109*(September), 101964. doi:10.1016/j.artmed.2020.101964 PMID:34756216

Dai, Y., Wang, G., Muhammad, K., & Liu, S. (2020). A Closed-Loop Healthcare Processing Approach Based on Deep Reinforcement Learning. *Multimedia Tools and Applications*, no. 2017.

Datta, S., & Li, Y. (2021). Reinforcement Learning in Surgery. *Surgery, 170*(1), 329–32. https://doi.org/10.1016/j.surg.2020.11.040

Dhiman, G., Kumar, A. V., Nirmalan, R., Sujitha, S., Srihari, K., Yuvaraj, N., Arulprakash, P., & Raja, R. A. (2023). Multi-Modal Active Learning with Deep Reinforcement Learning for Target Feature Extraction in Multi-Media Image Processing Applications. *Multimedia Tools and Applications*, *82*(4), 5343–5367. doi:10.1007/s11042-022-12178-7

Furuta, R., Inoue, N., & Yamasaki, T. (2019). Pixelrl: Fully Convolutional Network with Reinforcement Learning for Image Processing. *IEEE Transactions on Multimedia*, *22*(7), 1704–1719. doi:10.1109/TMM.2019.2960636

Grissom, I. I. (2014). Don't until the Final Verb Wait: Reinforcement Learning for Simultaneous Machine Translation. In *Proceedings of the 2014 Conference on Empirical Methods in Natural Language Processing (EMNLP)*, (pp. 1342–52). ACL. 10.3115/v1/D14-1140

Gu, S., Holly, E., Lillicrap, T., & Levine, S. (2017). Deep Reinforcement Learning for Robotic Manipulation with Asynchronous Off-Policy Updates. In *2017 IEEE International Conference on Robotics and Automation (ICRA)*, (pp. 3389–96). IEEE. 10.1109/ICRA.2017.7989385

Hare, R., & Tang, Y. (2023). Hierarchical Deep Reinforcement Learning With Experience Sharing for Metaverse in Education. *IEEE Transactions on Systems, Man, and Cybernetics. Systems*, *53*(4), 2047–2055. doi:10.1109/TSMC.2022.3227919

Huang, L., Fu, M., Li, F., Qu, H., Liu, Y., & Chen, W. (2021). A Deep Reinforcement Learning Based Long-Term Recommender System. *Knowledge-Based Systems*, *213*(1), 106706. doi:10.1016/j.knosys.2020.106706

Ibarz, J., Tan, J., Finn, C., Kalakrishnan, M., Pastor, P., & Levine, S. (2021). How to Train Your Robot with Deep Reinforcement Learning: Lessons We Have Learned. *The International Journal of Robotics Research*, *40*(4–5), 698–721. doi:10.1177/0278364920987859

Katrakazas, C., Quddus, M., Chen, W.-H., & Deka, L. (2015). Real-Time Motion Planning Methods for Autonomous on-Road Driving: State-of-the-Art and Future Research Directions. *Transportation Research Part C, Emerging Technologies*, *60*, 416–442. https://doi.org/10.1016/j.trc.2015.09.011. doi:10.1016/j.trc.2015.09.011

Kober, J., Bagnell, J. A., & Peters, J. (2013). Reinforcement Learning in Robotics: A Survey. *The International Journal of Robotics Research*, *32*(11), 1238–1274. doi:10.1177/0278364913495721

Lample, G., & Chaplot, D. S. (2017). Playing FPS Games with Deep Reinforcement Learning. In *Proceedings of the AAAI Conference on Artificial Intelligence*. AAAI. 10.1609/aaai.v31i1.10827

Li, J., Monroe, W., Ritter, A., Galley, M., Gao, J., & Jurafsky, D. (2016). Deep Reinforcement Learning for Dialogue Generation. *ArXiv Preprint ArXiv:1606.01541*. doi:10.18653/v1/D16-1127

Lin, Y., Lin, F., Zeng, W., Xiahou, J., Li, L., Wu, P., Liu, Y., & Miao, C. (2022). Hierarchical Reinforcement Learning with Dynamic Recurrent Mechanism for Course Recommendation. *Knowledge-Based Systems, 244*, 108546. doi:10.1016/j.knosys.2022.108546

Lin, Y., Liu, Y., Lin, F., Zou, L., Wu, P., Zeng, W., Chen, H., & Miao, C. (2023). A Survey on Reinforcement Learning for Recommender Systems. *IEEE Transactions on Neural Networks and Learning Systems*, 1–21. doi:10.1109/TNNLS.2023.3280161 PMID:37279123

Liu, M., Shen, X., & Pan, W. (2022). Deep Reinforcement Learning for Personalized Treatment Recommendation. *Statistics in Medicine*, *1*(23), 1–23. doi:10.1002/sim.9491 PMID:35716038

Liu, S., Chen, Y., Huang, H., Xiao, L., & Hei, X. (2018). Towards Smart Educational Recommendations with Reinforcement Learning in Classroom. In *2018 IEEE International Conference on Teaching, Assessment, and Learning for Engineering (TALE)*, (pp. 1079–84). IEEE. 10.1109/TALE.2018.8615217

Mir, I., Gul, F., Mir, S., Mansoor A Khan, N. S., Abualigah, L., Abuhaija, B., & Amir, H. (2022, September 06). A Survey of Trajectory Planning Techniques for Autonomous Systems. *Electronics (Basel)*, *11*(18), 2801. doi:10.3390/electronics11182801

Mon, F., Bisni, A. W., Hayajneh, M., Slim, A., & Abu Ali, N. (2023). Reinforcement Learning in Education: A Literature Review. [MDPI.]. *Informatics (MDPI)*, *10*(3), 74. doi:10.3390/informatics10030074

Munemasa, I., Tomomatsu, Y., Hayashi, K., & Takagi, T. (2018). Deep Reinforcement Learning for Recommender Systems. In *2018 International Conference on Information and Communications Technology (ICOIACT)*, (pp. 226–33). IEEE. 10.1109/ICOIACT.2018.8350761

Paulus, R., Xiong, C., & Socher, R. (2017). A Deep Reinforced Model for Abstractive Summarization. *ArXiv Preprint ArXiv:1705.04304.*

Sewak, M. (2019). In M. Sewak (Ed.), *Deep Q Network (DQN), Double DQN, and Dueling DQN BT - Deep Reinforcement Learning: Frontiers of Artificial Intelligence* (pp. 95–108). Springer Singapore. doi:10.1007/978-981-13-8285-7_8

Shawky, D., & Badawi, A. (2019). In A. E. Hassanien (Ed.), *Towards a Personalized Learning Experience Using Reinforcement Learning BT - Machine Learning Paradigms: Theory and Application* (pp. 169–187). Springer International Publishing. doi:10.1007/978-3-030-02357-7_8

Silver, D., Hubert, T., Schrittwieser, J., Antonoglou, I., Lai, M., Guez, A., Lanctot, M., Sifre, L., Kumaran, D., Graepel, T., Lillicrap, T., Simonyan, K., & Hassabis, D. (2018). A General Reinforcement Learning Algorithm That Masters Chess, Shogi, and Go through Self-Play. *Science*, *362*(6419), 1140–1144. doi:10.1126/science.aar6404 PMID:30523106

Singh, B., Kumar, R., & Singh, V. P. (2022). Reinforcement Learning in Robotic Applications: A Comprehensive Survey. *Artificial Intelligence Review*, *55*(2), 1–46. doi:10.1007/s10462-021-09997-9

Song, X., Gao, H., Ding, T., Gu, Y., Liu, J., & Tian, K. (2023). A Review of the Motion Planning and Control Methods for Automated Vehicles. *Sensors (Basel)*, *23*(13), 6140. doi:10.3390/s23136140 PMID:37447989

Sutton, R. (2018). *Reinforcement Learning : An Introduction*. The MIT Press.

Tzeng, J.-W., Huang, N.-F., Chuang, A.-C., Huang, T.-W., & Chang, H.-Y. (2023). Massive Open Online Course Recommendation System Based on a Reinforcement Learning Algorithm. *Neural Computing & Applications*. Advance online publication. doi:10.1007/s00521-023-08686-8

Valente, J., António, J., Mora, C., & Jardim, S. (2023). Developments in Image Processing Using Deep Learning and Reinforcement Learning. *Journal of Imaging*, *9*(10), 207. doi:10.3390/jimaging9100207 PMID:37888314

Xin, X., Karatzoglou, A., & Arapakis, I., & Joemon, M. (2020). Self-Supervised Reinforcement Learning for Recommender Systems. In *Proceedings of the 43rd International ACM SIGIR Conference on Research and Development in Information Retrieval*. ACM.

Zou, L., Xia, L., Ding, Z., Song, J., Liu, W., & Yin, D. (2019). Reinforcement Learning to Optimize Long-Term User Engagement in Recommender Systems. In *Proceedings of the 25th ACM SIGKDD International Conference on Knowledge Discovery & Data Mining*. ACM. 10.1145/3292500.3330668

ENDNOTES

1. https://onlinedegrees.scu.edu/media/blog/9-examples-of-reinforcement-learning
2. https://neptune.ai/blog/reinforcement-learning-applications

Chapter 2
Transfer Learning for Computer Vision:
From Theory to Implementation

Qadeem Khan
Kohat University of Science and Technology, Pakistan

ABSTRACT

Computer vision has benefited from deep learning, making it possible to create complex systems. Computer vision has seen radical changes using deep learning techniques, specifically transfer learning for computer vision. It enables computers to understand and interpret visual data, such as images and videos, with great precision. Transfer learning in particular, is a deep learning technique that has transformed several areas of computer vision, including face recognition, semantic segmentation, object detection, and image categorization. This powerful technology is essential in applications such as autonomous vehicles, healthcare, surveillance, and more, since it has improved our capacity to identify, locate, and classify objects in images as well as comprehend complex visual scenes. In computer vision, transfer learning is a method that allows us to use previously taught models to tackle new problems. Benefits include shortened training times and efficient feature extraction. This chapter provides a brief help for implementation of transfer learning for computer vision.

INTRODUCTION

Computer vision (Jose Sigut, 2020) is a multidisciplinary area of artificial intelligence (AI) and computer science that deals on enabling computers to interpret and understand visual information from the world, much like the human visual system.

DOI: 10.4018/979-8-3693-1738-9.ch002

It is originated from the development of algorithms, techniques, and technologies that allow computer systems to extract, process, analyze, and make sense of visual data, such as text, images and videos which has some specified meaning. Computer vision is an evolving field with constant advancements in algorithms, hardware, and applications. As technology it continues to progress, computer vision is likely to have an increasingly profound impact on various industries and everyday life.

As computer vision continues to evolve, it finds applications in an ever-expanding range of domains, including healthcare, transportation, entertainment, and more. The integration of computer vision with other AI technologies is expected to lead to even more advanced and versatile visual perception systems in the future.

With the development of deep learning (Mohmannad Reza Iman et.al, 2022) algorithms, the field of computer vision—which analyzes and comprehends visual information—has seen a dramatic progress. Deep learning, a branch of artificial intelligence that draws inspiration from the composition and operations of the human brain, has shown to be revolutionary across a range of fields. When used in computer vision, it gives devices the ability to see, process, and understand images and videos with the improved precision and efficiency.

This synergy of computer vision and deep learning has catalyzed groundbreaking advancements, enabling applications ranging from autonomous vehicles and medical imaging to industrial automation and entertainment. Deep learning methods, particularly convolution neural networks (CNNs) and recurrent neural networks (RNNs) (Dimitrios Kollias, Stefanos Zafeiriou, 2021), have demonstrated an exceptional ability to automatically extract meaningful features from raw visual data (Atif Khan, M. Irfan Uddin et al, Scientific Programming 2020), facilitating tasks such as object recognition, image classification (), and even image generation.

In this chapter, we focus on the evolution of computer vision technology with a focus on transfer learning (), exploring the fundamental concepts, recent developments, and real-world applications that underscore the transformative potential of this synergy. Through an examination of key algorithms and methodologies, we aim to elucidate the promising prospects and challenges in the ever-evolving realm of computer vision, emphasizing the role of transfer learning as a catalyst for the next frontier in visual intelligence.

WHAT IS COMPUTER VISION?

Computer vision (Jesús Martínez, 2021) sometimes also called machine vision is a technology of computer science which is used to extract the properties from a given an image or more, extract properties of the 3D world. With a few modifications of human eyesight, computer vision functions quite similarly to human vision. The benefit to human sight is that it has lifetimes of context to learn how to distinguish things, measure their distance from one another, detect motion, and determine whether an image is faulty.

Instead of using retinas, optic nerves, and a visual brain, computer vision uses cameras, data, and algorithms to teach robots to accomplish similar tasks in a fraction of the time. A system trained to inspect goods or monitor a manufacturing asset can fast outperform a person in terms of analysis—it can examine thousands of products or processes in a minute and detect subtle flaws or problems.

How Computer Vision Works in Terms of Image Processing and Machine Vision?

Huge amount of data () is required for computer vision. It repeatedly analyzes data in order to identify differences and, eventually, identify pictures. For instance, a computer must be given a tone of x-rays photos and associated objects in order to be trained to identify cancer tissues. Only then will the computer be able to distinguish between x-rays, particularly ones that are defect-free.

Figure 1. Low level computer vision

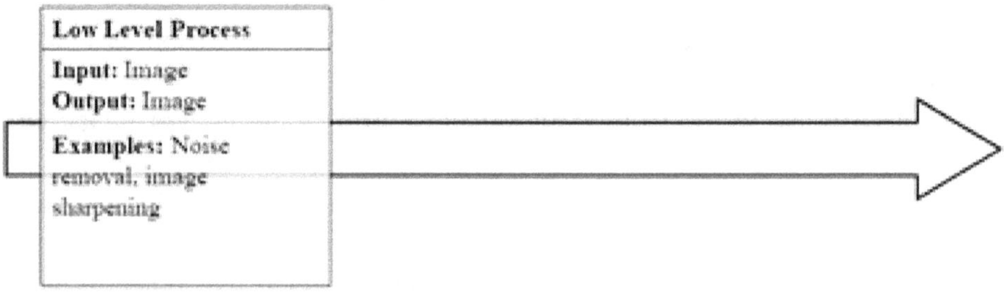

we can classify the computer vision into three different levels. These levels specify the complexity levels of computer vision. Figure 1 defines the basic and low level processing of computer vision in which the input is an image and the output is also an image. Here the system cannot get the images or record a video from the surrounding using a camera. Figure 2 demonstrates the example of photo restoration (Xibei Liu,et al,2023) technique.

Figure 2. Example of low level of computer vision

The second level is more advanced than the first level in which the system the system takes an image and also creates an image as in output but performs much complex tasks like object recognition and segmentation in the image. This is shown in the figure 3 as shown bellow.

Figure 3. Mid revel computer vision

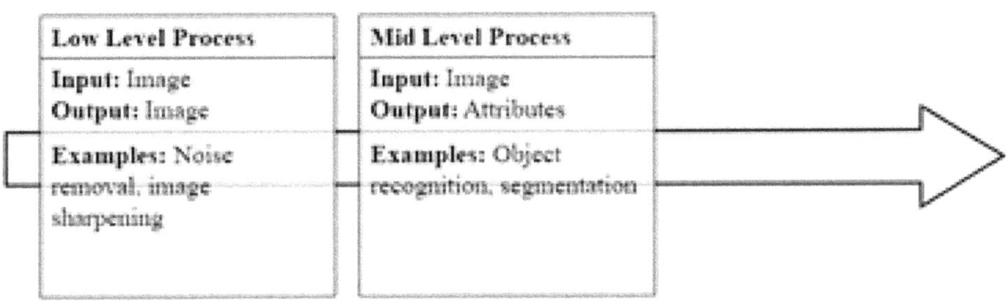

The image segmentation is a common example of mid level processing of computer vision and is a fundamental task in computer vision that involves dividing an image into multiple segments or regions with the goal of simplifying or changing the representation of an image into something more meaningful and easier to analyze. The primary objective of image segmentation is to group together pixels that belong to the same object or share similar visual characteristics, while separating them from pixels that belong to other objects or backgrounds. It is a so much important step in various computer vision applications, including object recognition in image or in video, object tracking, scene understanding, and medical image analysis. The examples of image segmentation or color segmentation is shown in the following figure 4 here.

Figure 4. Example of image segmentation

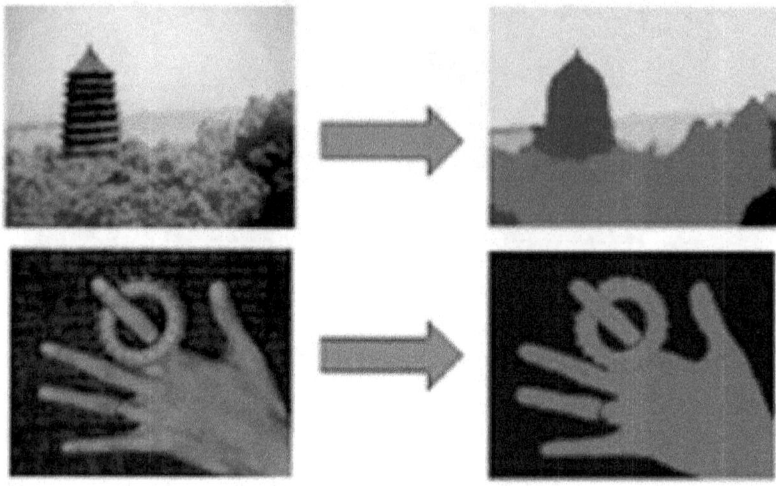

The final level of computer vision is the high level of computer vision and is shown in the figure 5.

Figure 5. High level computer vision

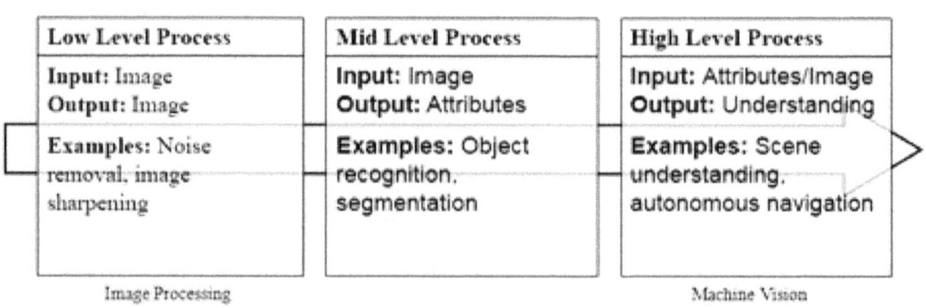

In this level the computer vision system takes the attributes or image as a input and creates the understanding of the environment. The example of this level of computer vision is the scene understanding and the autonomous navigation systems. Scene understanding is a significant area within computer vision and artificial intelligence that aims to enable machines, such as computers and robots, to comprehend and interpret the content of a visual scene or environment. It goes beyond basic image analysis and object recognition and seeks to provide a higher-level understanding of the relationships between objects, their interactions, and the context in which they exist. Scene understanding involves recognizing objects, their attributes, and the overall scene structure. Here are some key aspects of scene understanding. Autonomous navigation systems are a critical component of various autonomous and robotic applications (Laurel D. Riek,, 2013), enabling machines to navigate and move in their environment without human intervention. These systems rely on a combination of sensors, algorithms, and decision-making processes to safely and effectively navigate through spaces. Here are key aspects of autonomous navigation systems. This is shown in the figure 6.

Figure 6. Example of high level computer vision

COMPUTER VISION APPLICATIONS

Computer vision has a wide range of applications across various industries and domains. It involves the use of algorithms, machine learning (Muhammad Adnan et al 2022), and image processing to enable machines to understand and interpret visual data such as images and videos. Here are some key computer vision applications:

- IBM has utilized the computer vision to develop My Moments in the year of 2018 for Masters golf tournament. IBM Watson displayed Masters footage and identify the videos and audio of the wonderful golf events. It enabled computer vision to provide the important events about the Master golf to the viewers.
- Google Cloud Vision is a cloud-based machine learning service provided by Google that offers a wide range of computer vision capabilities for developers and businesses. It enables users to analyze and extract valuable information from images and videos.
- Computer vision is a fundamental technology used in self-driving cars to enable them to perceive and navigate their environment autonomously. It allows these vehicles to understand and react to the visual information captured by cameras, Lidar, radar, and other sensors.

TRANSFER LEARNING

Transfer learning (Ling Shao, 2013) is an important machine learning methodology where involves adapting or fine-tuning a model that has been trained on one job to a second related task. . It makes it easier to apply the first task's knowledge to enhance performance (Rashid Naseem et al, 2020) on the second task. This technique is especially useful when we have limited amount of data for the accomplishment of the second task, as it helps us to reuse the knowledge already gained for the first task.

Given the enormous computational and time resources needed to develop neural network models on computer vision and natural language processing tasks, as well as the significant skill gains they offer on related problems, using pre-trained models as the starting point is a popular deep learning approach.

Let us explain the transfer learning from a simple daily life example. If a player knows about the ice skating and the player want to learn about the ice hockey then this will be easier to transfer the learning of ice skating and transfer some skills into the ice-hockey. This will save the time and resources of learning a new sport. The transfer learning of artificial intelligence does the same process by gaining the skills from the previous task and transfer them into a new task. This is shown here in the figure 8.7 bellow.

Figure 7. Example of transfer learning
(Swedish Championship, 2015)

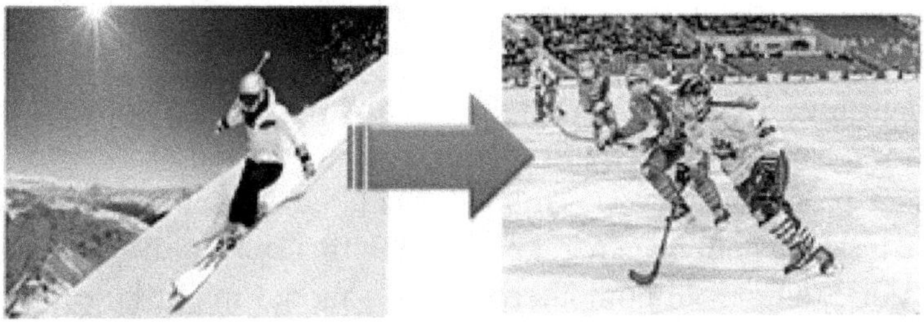

Transfer learning has various advantages which makes it unique over other deep learning technologies. These are very essential to make the computer system more versatile. The advantages include:

- **Reduced Training Time**: Training a model from scratch on a target task can be time-consuming and resource-intensive. Transfer learning can significantly reduce the training time, as much of the feature extraction and pattern recognition have already been learned during pre-training.
- **Improved Performance**: Transfer learning often leads to better performance on the target task compared to training from scratch, especially when there is limited data available for the target task. The size of a new dataset extracted from the previous data set should be relatively small so that the performance could be optimized.
- **Generalization**: Transfer learning models can leverage the general knowledge acquired during pre-training, which can lead to better generalization on the target task. This make the transfer learning more beneficial for all sort of tasks to be accomplished.

Transfer learning is worldwide used in various domains and areas of computer technology, including computer vision, natural language processing, and speech recognition. Pre-trained models like BERT for NLP and ResNet for image classification have shown the effectiveness of this technique. Researchers and practitioners often fine-tune these pre-trained models on specific tasks, achieving state-of-the-art results in various applications.

HOW TRANSFER LEARNING WORKS?

Transfer learning works in three pre-defined phases as explained here.

1. **Pre-training**: A deep neural network model (typically a convolutional neural network for computer vision tasks or a recurrent neural network for natural language processing tasks) is trained on a large dataset for a source task. This source task is usually a general problem with a substantial amount of labeled data. For example, in computer vision, a model might be pre-trained on a massive dataset of images with labels for various categories.
2. **Feature Extraction:** After pre-training, the learned model is used as a feature extractor. The weights of the earlier layers of the model (usually the convolution layers) are frozen, and the output of these layers is treated as a set of features that represent the input data. These features capture hierarchical, abstract representations of the data's underlying patterns.
3. **Fine-tuning:** The pre-trained model, along with the extracted features, is further trained on the target task with a smaller dataset. The weights of the later layers (often fully connected layers) are fine-tuned for the specific task, while the weights of the earlier layers remain fixed. Sometimes, task-specific layers are added on top of the pre-trained layers for task-specific learning.

Layered architectures used in deep learning systems are capable of learning distinct characteristics at various layers. Higher-level features are compiled in the first layers and become finer-grained features as we move deeper into the network. To obtain the final output, these layers are ultimately connected to the final layer, which in the case of supervised learning is often a completely connected layer. This allows popular pre-trained networks (such Google Inception Model, Microsoft ResNet Model, and Oxford VGG Model) to be used as fixed feature extractors for various tasks without requiring their final layer. The layered architecture of the machine learning transfer learning is shown here in the figure 8.8

The filters that are learnt in these levels of convnet can be utilized by other convents if some of the layers learn the same kind of feature. In convents, this is referred to as transfer learning, and it is quite effective.

Figure 8. Transfer learning mechanism

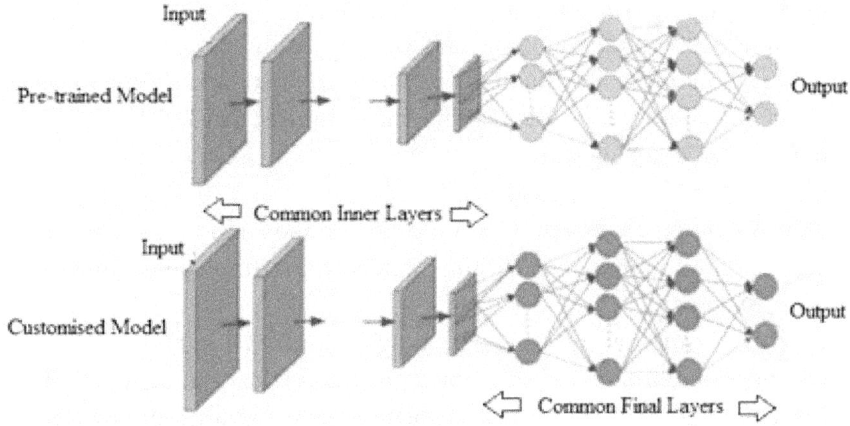

TRANSFER LEARNING IN COMPUTER VISION

Transfer learning is widely used in various computer vision applications, such as image classification, object detection, image segmentation, and facial recognition. For example, you can adapt a pre-trained model, which has learned to recognize a broad range of objects, to identify specific objects in your images.

The goal of computer vision is to empower robots to perceive, understand, and evaluate visual information from their surroundings. Creating intelligent machines that are capable of tasks like object identification, recognition, tracking, and segmentation, which often require human-level visual perception is the aim of computer vision. Multiple methods and strategies are used in computer vision, allowing models to be trained on massive volumes of visual data, including pictures and movies. Deep learning and neural network advancements have played a major role in the several recent successes in computer vision.

Here are some of the renown examples of computer vision applications using transfer learning.

1. GPT Image Production: The realistic visuals from textual descriptions have recently been produced using OpenAI's GPT-3 and above language model. The neural network is trained on descriptions in plain language, allowing the model to produce precise and detailed visuals images are created and capture in the described scene.
2. Object Detection: The object detection models obtain the high accuracy on a different datasets, such as COCO, Pascal VOC, and ImageNet. These

architectures are based on deep learning architectures e.g. Faster R-CNN YOLOv5, and RetinaNet to improve accuracy and speed.

3. Autonomous Vehicles Control: Computer vision is used for autonomous vehicles to mobilize itself and understand the surrounding. The most modern system for autonomous car driving including the NVIDIA's DRIVE AGX implemented deep learning algorithms to enabled a car to detect the path and road and also different obstacles.
4. Medical Computer Vision: Computer vision is used to enhance the medical treatment and diagnosing the lung cancer, brain tumor detection, and other cancer diagnosing.
5. Robotics: Computer vision is so much essential for robotics in order to understand and interact with environment and also to understand the human interaction with the robot. For this purpose, deep learning algorithms are used to implement the reasoning abilities in the robotics world.

TRANSFER LEARNING PRE-TRAINED MODELS OF KERAS

There are wide verity of models used for transfer learning in computer. Strong pre-trained models from the ImageNet (Stanford University,2020) contests are available through Keras. You can use these models without weights or with pre-trained weights. Preparing the models such that the trained model would be expected is a practice. For example, the pre-trained model can anticipate that the pixel will be within a specific value or that the picture would be scaled within a certain range. Ensuring that the input data are in the format that the model expects is necessary to optimize its performance. Several Keras pre-trained models (Google Keras, 2023) include:

- XCeption
- VGG16
- VGG19
- ResNet50
- ResNet101
- InceptionV3
- MobileNet
- DenseNet etc.

PYTHON IMPLEMENTTAION OF TRANSFER LEARNING FOR COMPUTER VISION

Here in this section, the VGGNet 16 is used for object detector using python In this important section, we'll categorize a whole new image using the VGGNet model. There is an important dataset of flowers images available at www.robots.ox.ac.uk/~vgg/data/flowers/102/. The image taken from this dataset will be fed into the VGGNet model to identify its name as a label. This is a lovely image of flower as shown in the following figure 9.

Figure 9. Flower image for classification

Step One: Loading Flower.jpeg

In this step, the above image is loaded into *input_image* variable using *load_image* function from the memory of computer system.

```
from keras.applications.vgg16 import VGG16, preprocess_input,
decode_predictions
from keras import Input
from keras.preprocessing.image import load_img, img_to_array

#load the image
input_image = load_img('flower.jpeg', target_size=(224, 224))
```

Step Two: Converting Flower.jpeg to Array

In this step, the above image loaded *input_image* variable is converted into arrays as the machine learning models can work on the numbers or numeric datatypes.

```
input_image = img_to_array(input_image)
```

Step 3: Preprocessing the 3-Dimensions Array to 4-Dimenstions Array

In this step, the array (3, 224, 224)is converted into 4-dimensions as the VGGnet model need 4-dimensional array of (1, 3, 224, 224). This is because the possibility of many samples or batches of photos being fed into the model at simultaneously, an additional one dimension has been included. Additionally, the picture has to be ready for the model. For this task, the preprocess_input function is employed to convert the dimensionality of the array. Now let's preprocess the image and give it a new form for the model.

```
input_image = my_image.reshape((1,input_image.shape[0], input_
image.shape[1], input_image.shape[2]))
input_image = preprocess_input(input_image)
```

Step 4: Calling the VGGNet Model for Predication

In this step, the VGG16 model is loaded into model parameter and then *predict* function is called to make the predication and the results are stored in the variable as shown in the bellow code.

```
model = VGG16()
prediction = model.predict(input_image)
```

Step 5: Results

In this step, the probability is converted into actual label by using the *decode_predictions* function. The item with the highest probability is return as all items are stored with the probabilities of the descending order. This is implemented in the following code.

```
prediction = decode_predictions(prediction)
item = prediction[0][0]
print(f"{item[1]} with a probability of {int(item[2]*100)}%")
```

CONCLUSION

In this chapter, the computer vision is deeply covered in terms of transfer learning. The computer vision is one of the important aspect of image processing and artificial intelligence. We are using the computer vision technology in may form in our daily life activities like identification, detection of an object, sensing a change of an event in the scene or in a video etc. there three different levels of image processing and computer vision. The transfer learning is used as an important technique for classification or detection in the image or videos. There are many algorithms of transfer learning for computer vision. These algorithms are also called models which are pre-implemented techniques. VGGNet is one of the important model which we have implemented on the flower image. The VGGNet model has successfully detected the image of flower with the probability of more than 50%.

REFERENCES

Adnan, M., Alarood, A. A. S., Uddin, M. I., & ur Rehman, I. (2022). Utilizing grid search cross-validation with adaptive boosting for augmenting performance of machine learning models. *PeerJ. Computer Science*, *8*, e803. doi:10.7717/peerj-cs.803 PMID:35494796

Atif Khan, M. & Uddin, I. (2020). *Summarizing Online Movie Reviews: A Machine Learning Approach to Big Data Analytics*. Scientific Programming.

Aziz, F., Ahmad, T., Malik, A. H., Uddin, M. I., Ahmad, S., & Sharaf, M. (2020). Reversible data hiding techniques with high message embedding capacity in images. *PLoS One*, *15*(5), e0231602. doi:10.1371/journal.pone.0231602 PMID:32469877

Fayaz, M. (2020). *Ensemble Machine Learning Model for Classification of Spam Product Reviews*. Complexity Volume. doi:10.1155/2020/8857570

Iman, M. R. (2022). EXPANSE: A Continual and Progressive Learning System for Deep Transfer Learning. *2022 International Conference on Computational Science and Computational Intelligence (CSCI)*. IEEE. 10.1109/CSCI58124.2022.00016

Kollias, D., & Zafeiriou, S. (2021). Exploiting Multi-CNN Features in CNN-RNN Based Dimensional Emotion Recognition on the OMG in-the-Wild Dataset. *IEEE Transactions on Affective Computing*, *12*(3), 595–606. doi:10.1109/TAFFC.2020.3014171

Liu, X. (2023). Liean Cao"Old-Photo Restoration with Detail- and Structure-Enhanced Cascaded Learning. *IEEE International Conference on Multimedia and Expo Workshops (ICMEW)*.

Martínez, J. (2021). *TensorFlow 2.0 Computer Vision Cookbook: Implement machine learning solutions to overcome various computer vision challenges*. Packt Publishing.

Naseem, R. (2020). Performance Assessment of Classification Algorithms on Early Detection of Liver Syndrome. *Journal of Healthcare and Engineering*.

Riek, L. D. (2013). Embodied Computation: An Active-Learning Approach to Mobile Robotics Education. *IEEE Transactions on Education*, *56*(1), 67–72. doi:10.1109/TE.2012.2221716

Shao, L., Zhu, F., & Li, X. (2015). Transfer Learning for Visual Categorization: A Survey. *IEEE Transactions on Neural Networks and Learning Systems*. PMID:25014970

Sigut, J., Castro, M., Arnay, R., & Sigut, M. (2020). OpenCV Basics: A Mobile Application to Support the Teaching of Computer Vision Concepts". *IEEE Transactions on Education*, *63*(4), 328–335. doi:10.1109/TE.2020.2993013

Chapter 3
The Importance of Interpretability in AI Systems and Its Implications for Deep Learning:
Ensuring Transparency in Intelligent Systems

Muhammad Adnan
Kohat University of Science and Technology, Pakistan

ABSTRACT

Particularly inside the context of deep learning, the concept of interpretability in artificial intelligence systems is crucial for boosting the degree of trust and self-belief that human beings have in machine-learning fashions. Deep learning models have many parameters and complex architectures that make them function like mysterious "black boxes," making it difficult for users to apprehend how they function. This opacity increases questions about those models' ethics, dependability, and viable biases. In the field of deep learning, achieving interpretability is crucial for several reasons. First off, interpretable models enhance transparency by making the model's judgments and forecasts simpler for customers to understand. This is particularly essential in complicated fields like banking and healthcare, wherein knowledge and self-assurance are vital. Moreover, interpretability facilitates the identification and correction of biases in the model or the training statistics, performing as a car for fairness and duty.

DOI: 10.4018/979-8-3693-1738-9.ch003

INTRODUCTION

Deep learning has added to a great and unparalleled revolution in artificial intelligence (AI). Significant advancements in this region of machine learning knowledge over the past ten years have completely modified AI applications, research, and industry globally (Pothen, 2022). The capacity of deep learning to independently extract insightful facts from unprocessed records is one of its number one contribution to AI (Woschank et al., 2020). Deep getting to know leverages synthetic neural networks with several hidden layers, in contrast to advanced device studying techniques, which normally rely on manually produced functions created via human specialists—a time-ingesting and often suboptimal method. Deep getting to know is enabled through this architectural element to robotically discover specific hierarchical characteristics within the statistics. As a result, the system plays incredibly well on responsibilities like speech recognition, image identification, and natural language processing. These responsibilities want the device to realize complicated patterns and representations that were formerly unintelligible.

One of the maximum brilliant feats within the area of deep learning is photograph popularity. Convolutional Neural Networks (CNNs), a subclass of deep studying models, have verified performance ranges corresponding to human skills in duties like object identification and facial reputation (Ghimire et al., 2022). These CNNs have given computer systems the capability to understand items, recognize context, understand the place, or even recognize feelings in pictures. Numerous industries have benefited from this progressive discovery, together with healthcare (for clinical photograph processing), cars (for self-riding automobiles), and security (for sophisticated surveillance systems). Natural language processing (NLP) has entered a new generation because of deep learning, which has drastically modified how humans apprehend and bring language. The renowned GPT-3 model is a high example of ways Recurrent Neural Networks (RNNs) and Transformer architectures have shown their effectiveness in quite a few NLP packages. These activities include sentiment analysis and machine translation as well as query-answering (Cunha & Manikonda, 2022). Consequently, we are presently seeing the rise of chatbots, virtual assistants, and language translation services that behave an increasing number of like real people while interacting, similarly, to being useful.

Deep learning's impact has resulted in a great shift in the healthcare enterprise (Kaul et al., 2022). It has cleared the course for the development of medical diagnostic structures which might be remarkably accurate in figuring out illnesses and abnormalities in scientific imaging records, together with CT, MRI, and X-ray scans. Additionally, the creation of recent pills, the prediction of patient outcomes, and the customization of treatment regimens based totally on patient-precise information have all benefited from deep knowledge of models. Deep learning is enhancing healthcare consequences, maybe saving lives, and substantially raising the usual scientific remedy globally.

Furthermore, the fields of self-sustaining robotics and self-driving automobiles have benefited substantially from deep getting-to-know improvements (Vitelli, 2022). The use of sensors together with radar and LiDAR has enabled self-riding automobiles to look and navigate their environment with an excessive stage of protection and accuracy. These driverless transportation systems, that can locate visitors' lighting fixtures, different vehicles, and pedestrians, now are an actual aspect. Significant advancements in deep getting-to-know have also been made in the leisure sector.

The impact of deep learning is likewise visible in the economic quarter, where it's far essential for fraud detection, algorithmic trading, and threat evaluation (Mahalakshmi et al., 2022). Financial institutions use deep learning models to take a look at large dataset in super element and perceive irregularities that may indicate fraudulent activities. For each organization and person, those actual-time detection savings have added up to billions of greenbacks in financial savings. Moreover, the mixture of deep learning and computer vision has revolutionized industries like agriculture. Drones with deep learning algorithms hooked up can also reveal fields, discover pests or ailments, and alter irrigation to maximize crop output whilst minimizing resource waste. The sections of this chapter are arranged as follows: Deep getting to know models and the want for explainable AI are covered in detail in Section 2. Section 3 examines some of the eXplainable AI (XAI) strategies. The application of XAI strategies to apprehend and interpret feed-forward neural networks is included in Section 4. XAI methods for convolutional neural networks are protected in Section 5. While Section 7 offers the human thing of explainable AI about time-collection models, Section 6 concentrates on using XAI to explain time-series models. Section eight offers' statistics on the several approaches that XAI is used in time-series models. Explainability metrics and assessment methods in XAI are covered in Sections 9 and 10, respectively.

DEEP LEARNING MODELS AND THE NEED FOR EXPLAINABLE AI

The want for Explainable AI (XAI) and the complexity of gaining knowledge of models are critical components of the current artificial intelligence environment. Due to its capacity to handle complex patterns and large datasets, deep learning, a subset of device learning, has experienced a notable boom. However, this development has additionally evolved models that are more intricate and tough to realize. The layers of related neurons in deep studying models, in particular deep neural networks, may have a total of thousands and thousands or even billions. Lack of version openness can be a vast impediment to reputation and self-assurance in crucial programs like healthcare, banking, and self-sufficient motors (Li et al., 2022).

In this situation, Explainable AI is effective. The purpose of explainable AI is to create techniques and tools that let people recognize and examine the conclusions drawn by way of sophisticated gadgets gaining knowledge of algorithms (Antoniadi et al., 2021). It goals to shed light on the factors affecting these models' predictions utilizing presenting insights into the inner workings of these models. Techniques for explainable AI can be numerous, including feature importance evaluation, visualization gear, and version-independent strategies. Model-agnostic methods provide explanations for any system getting to know the model, improving interpretation. Examples consist of LIME (Local Interpretable Model-Agnostic Explanations) and SHAP (SHapley Additive exPlanations) (Gramegna & Giudici, 2021).

When human life or huge commercial interests are at stake in high-stakes packages, Explainable AI is a mainly essential issue. For instance, it is vital to offer clinicians and patients comprehensible motives for the model's choices when deep gaining knowledge of models is utilized in healthcare to diagnose ailments or advocate treatments (Hulsen, 2023). Transparent models are necessary for regulatory compliance and danger management in finance when AI is used for threat assessment and algorithmic trading. In addition to addressing troubles with model openness, explainable AI additionally promotes duty and confidence in AI systems. It enables human experts to look at AI-driven judgments, become aware of biases, and remedy issues by making complicated models less difficult to apprehend.

This chapter outlines the core ideas and tactics at the back of explainable AI (XAI), highlighting the maximum recent developments in this rapidly growing discipline of have a look at. This chapter's cognizance is on XAI strategies designed to clarify the workings and predictions of deep gaining knowledge of models, which might sometimes be complex because of their complicated architecture. Data scientists frequently show reluctance to apply these opaque black-container models, preferring as a substitute to use greater conventional machine-gaining knowledge of models like regression, decision bushes, random forests, and rule-primarily based structures, no matter the high-quality development in XAI approaches.

XAI strategies are primarily based on deep neural networks' intention to offer perception into the tricky selection-making and prediction strategies of these models. Activation Visualization, Saliency Maps, LIME (Local Interpretable Model-agnostic Explanations), SHAP (SHapley Additive exPlanations), Grad-CAM (Gradient-weighted Class Activation Mapping), Attention Mechanisms, Layer-smart Relevance Propagation (LRP), Counterfactual Explanations, and Rule-primarily based Explanations are several of the well-liked XAI techniques for deep neural networks (Bento et al., 2021). Furthermore, within the context of deep neural networks, attribution methods are used to assign the contribution of functions or neurons to the predictions or judgments made utilizing the version. These techniques allow us to discover the enter facts factors or community neurons which have the most enormous impact on a given output. Deep neural networks' attribution strategies encompass Gradient-based totally Methods, Integrated Gradients, SmoothGrad, Guided Backpropagation, Grad-CAM (Gradient-weighted Class Activation Mapping), SHAP (SHapley Additive exPlanations), Layer-wise Relevance Propagation (LRP), DeepLIFT (Deep Learning Important FeaTures), Occlusion Sensitivity, and Feature Visualization (Allgaier et al., 2023).

Explanation and Interpretation

Explanation and interpretation are key ideas within the context of explainable AI (XAI), which revolves around making the internal workings of complicated systems studying models extra seen and intelligible to humans (Zhang, 2021). The rationalization of the way a machine learning version generates its predictions or judgments is called proof. It entails simplifying the model's complex computations and modifications so that clients can get admission to and comprehend it. These statements are meant to reply to queries including, "Why did the version make this prediction?" or "What characteristics or factors motivated the final results? By enabling customers to accept as true and significantly examine AI structures, reasons sell duty and permit successful selection-making. On the opposite hand, interpretation involves the method of giving the statistics offered via the model's explanations importance.

In summary, if something may be comprehended, we say that it is interpretable. Considering this, we define a model as interpretable if it can be comprehended with the aid of human beings on its own. To see precisely how a prediction changes into a model, we can have a look at the version parameters or a model summary. Figure 1 is an instance of a selection tree which is straightforward to recognize and interpret. DT has nodes and branches. So, if something can fly, then we comply with the real department. Further, if it can lay an egg, then it's miles a fowl in any other case it's far a mammal. On the other hand, if something cannot fly, then we further check the condition of whether it has feathers. If the solution is proper then it's far a chook i.e., penguins in any other case it's miles a mammal.

Figure 1. A simple explanation of a decision tree with root, decision nodes, and leaves

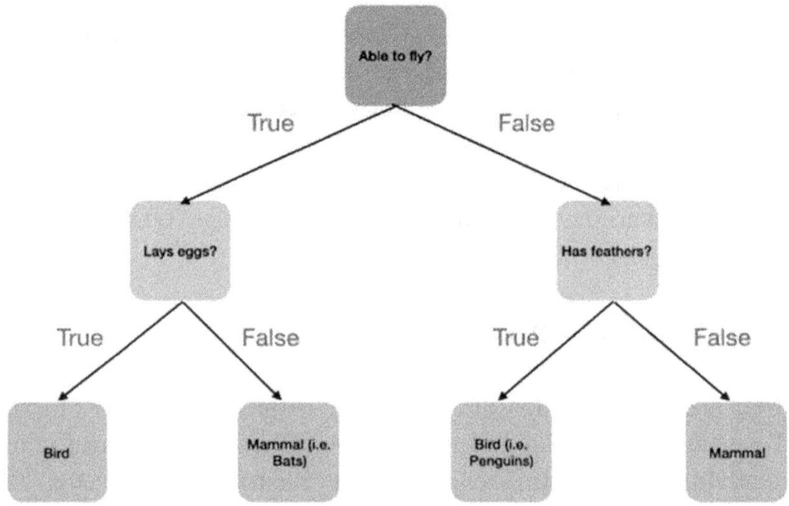

A version that is hard for someone to realize is explainable. This is every so often referred to as a black-field version. To be able to see within the black container and realize how the model operates, we need a further strategy or procedure. A Random Forest is an illustration of any such version. Numerous choice bushes make up a random forest (Parmar et al., 2018). When determining the ultimate prediction, all the person timber's predictions are taken into consideration. We would need to understand how every one of the person trees functions to recognizes how a random wooded area feature. This could be impossible for a human to do, regardless of some trees. Figure 2 indicates the RF model and the way it makes predictions. The RF model employs a majority balloting approach to make the very last prediction.

Figure 2. The working of the RF model and how it makes predictions

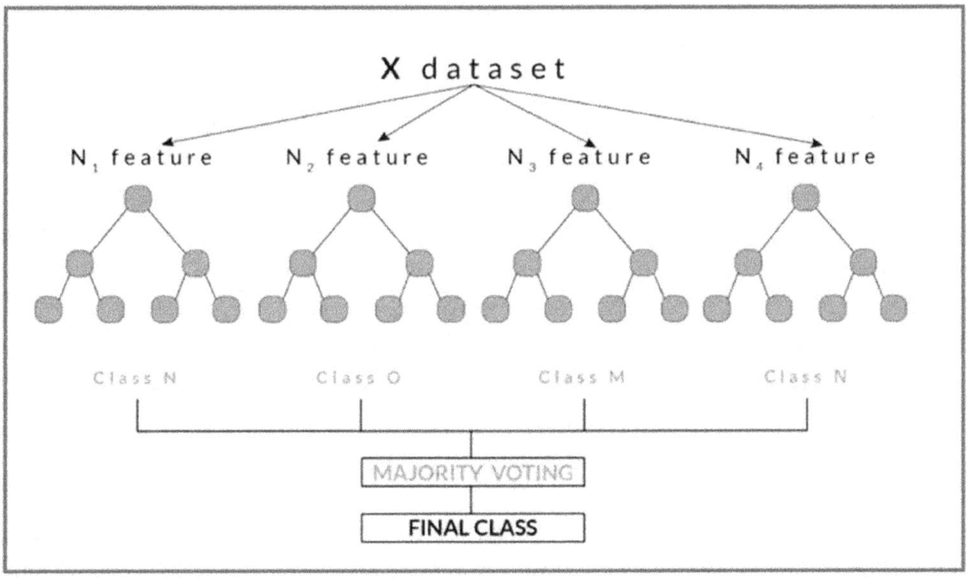

The explanation gets more complicated if neural networks are considered. For example, AlexNet, a deep neural network for the photograph category has round sixty-two, 379, 550 parameters as shown in Figure 3. For people, it isn't feasible to immediately understand models which include AlexNet by merely searching the parameters and their weights (Wang, 2020).

Figure 3. AlexNet, a deep neural network for image classification

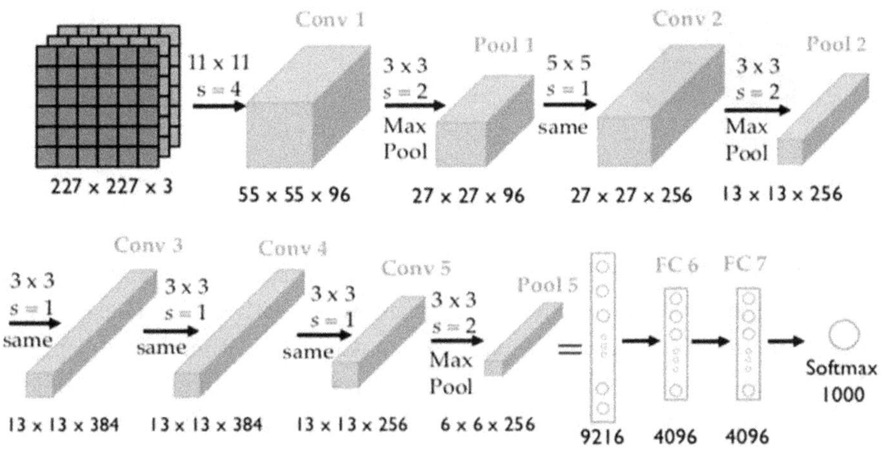

EXPLAINABLE AI TECHNIQUES

XAI strategies are implemented in numerous approaches. For instance, if we need to explain the model choices, then XAI strategies that are related to explaining the model's decisions are used. On the other hand, there are XAI strategies that concentrate on the version's inner operating and representations extra than its choices or predictions. If the answer to explaining the model selection is actual, then it's far vital to foresee whether the model is interpretable by way of layout or no longer. If the version is interpretable via layout, then we attain the class of ML models which can be interpretable by way of design consisting of linear regression, logistic regression, K-Nearest Neighbors, and other linear models. Models that are not interpretable via design need explainability strategies including SHapley Additive exPlanations (SHAP), perturbation and Local Interpretable Model-agnostic Explanations (LIME). These sorts of less interpretable models, that need similar investigation for their running are agnostic models. Consider Figure 4, wherein SHAP values are used to explain the black box version. The black container version is much less interpretable, with acknowledged inputs and outputs. A person also can see what the inputs and outputs are, however, the inner workings are unknown. The SHAP values give us additive motives of ways each of the features is accountable for or corresponds to the output cost. BMI, BP and age have elevated the fee of the output while the intercourse feature has driven the output price to the left i.e., to the terrible aspect.

Figure 4. SHapley Additive exPlanations for the black box model

There are other types of methods that use positive examples from the dataset to discover the inner workings of the deep getting-to-know models. These strategies include hostile methods, have an impact on functions, and counterfactual strategies (Xu, 2020). A convincing approach for enhancing the transparency and dependability of machine learning models, in excessive-stakes applications, is to use antagonistic explainable AI algorithms. These techniques make use of adverse assaults, wherein input facts are perturbed purposefully to evaluate the version's weaknesses and divulge its decision-making techniques.

The unique contribution of every data factor in the education set to the predictions of a version can be determined using affect capabilities. Analysts can locate outliers, vast examples, and potential assets of model bias or mistake employing comparing the effect of every education instance. Mathematical methods just like the delta approach or computing the gradients of the loss function concerning model parameters are used to derive these capabilities (Zhang, 2019). In the sector of explainable AI (XAI), counterfactual techniques are beneficial equipment that produces opportunity situations or statistical factors to assist us in apprehending device learning models better (Clement et al., 2023).

Next, we discuss the strategies that explore the internal workings of the neural community models. These strategies consist of Singular Vector Canonical Correlation Analysis (SVCCA), activation maximization, function visualization, probes, and Testing with Concept Activation Vectors (TCAV).

Singular Vector Canonical Correlation Analysis (SVCCA)

Singular Vector Canonical Correlation Analysis (SVCCA), a robust method for measuring similarity between neural network layers or representations, is applied in machine-gaining knowledge of and facts evaluation (Raghu, 2017). It offers a useful tool for evaluating how efficiently diverse deep neural network layers gather comparable facts. Model optimization, switch learning, and model comprehension are 3 regions where SVCCA has applicability. Singular price decomposition (SVD), a way of matrices factorization, is the supply of the mathematical equation for SVCCA. SVCCA makes use of SVD to calculate the canonical correlations between sets of characteristic representations, generally certain as X and Y. Finding the canonical correlations that maximize the similarity between the two units is the objective.

To calculate SVCCA, we observe the subsequent steps.

Calculate the move-covariance matrix Cxy between the 2 characteristic representations X and Y:

$$Cxy = E[(X - \mu x)(Y - \mu y)^\wedge T]$$

Where E denotes the expectation, X and Y are the matrices of feature representations, and μx and μy are the implied vectors.

Perform singular fee decomposition (SVD) on Cxy:

$$Cxy = U\Sigma V^\wedge T$$

Here, U and V are the orthogonal matrices containing left and right singular vectors, respectively, and Σ is a diagonal matrix containing singular values.

Compute the canonical correlations by taking the square roots of the singular values from

$$\Sigma: \lambda i = \sqrt{(\sigma i)}$$

where λi represents the i-th canonical correlation, and σi is the i-th singular value.

SVCCA analyzes the canonical correlations to decide how similar X and Y are. Low canonical correlations suggest that the representations are exclusive, while high correlations display that the layers seize comparable facts. To compare the function representations of various layers in neural networks, SVCCA analyzes the canonical correlations, which facilitates researchers higher apprehend version behavior, transfer getting to know, and network architectural optimization.

Activation Maximization

A device-studying approach is used to look at and understand which characteristics or patterns in input information prompt positive neurons within a network. It's an effective method for understanding what a neural network has discovered throughout schooling and for producing understandable representations of the traits that stimulate neurons (Nguyen et al., 2019). The activation maximization mathematical equation is an alternatively simple one. Finding an entrance that optimizes the hobby of a selected neuron in a neural community with a specific neuron or collection of neurons of interest is the goal. This is frequently defined as an optimization problem:

$$\text{Argmax(activation)} = \text{argmax}(f(x))$$

In this example, x stands for the enter data and f(x) represents the output of the relevant neuron. The purpose is to identify the enter x that causes that neuron to hearth at its highest degree.

Feature Visualization

In the context of convolutional neural networks (CNNs), function visualization is a vital deep studying tool. It seeks to disclose what neurons or filters in a neural network were appropriate for locating the input facts, giving critical insights into the community's characteristic extraction abilities (Wang et al., 2020). Understanding how deep neural networks process statistics, enhancing version interpretability, and permitting model development are all made viable with the aid of this method.

Unlike a few other methods, function visualization does not have a mathematical equation, however, its primary idea is to adjust an enter sign to enhance the response of a sure neuron or filter. This can be conceptualized as an optimization trouble, which often uses gradient ascent:

Argmax(f(x))

In this example, x is the input information, and f(x) represents the hobby-associated neuron or filter's pastime or response. The intention is to discover the enter x that causes the centred neuron or filter out to respond maximum strongly.

Probes In Neural Networks

In neural networks, probes are auxiliary additives or structures which can be used to extract certain facts or representations from the network's hidden layers (Vilone & Longo, 2020). These probes are intended to offer insights into the inner workings of the network and may be used for several matters, such as comprehending the found-out representations of the model, maintaining track of education, and improving interpretability. While there isn't a mathematical system that describes probes in all circumstances, their use often entails truthful strategies that target sides of the hidden layer activations. For example, while probing a language model for linguistic information, hidden layer activations can be subjected to a linear transformation or projection accompanied by a non-linear activation feature to extract linguistic homes.

Testing With Concept Activation Vectors (TCAV)

In the realm of machine learning, trying out the use of concept activation vectors (TCAV) is a way to evaluate and realize the concept-based biases of neural networks (Kim, 2018). Researchers and practitioners can examine a model's inner representations of the usage of TCAV to see if it assigns various levels of self-belief to certain ideas or attributes. By illuminating the decision-making process of AI structures, this approach is critical to the equity, interpretability, and accountability of models. Instead of mathematical calculation, TCAV uses a defined manner to assess concept-based total biases in neural networks. The fundamental techniques of TCAV are growing an exciting concept, accumulating a set of beneficial and unfavourable times, and computing TCAV ratings for every layer within the version.

You may also approximate the TCAV score as:

$$TCAV(C,L) = \frac{\partial P(yclass)}{\partial z_L} \cdot \frac{\partial z_L}{\partial a_L} + \frac{\partial a_L}{\partial z_L} + \ldots \frac{\partial a_L}{\partial z_L} \cdot \frac{\partial z_0}{\partial h_0} \cdot \frac{\partial h_0}{\partial C}$$

In this situation, the TCAV score for a notion C at layer L is TCAV(C, L). To calculate the score, applicable variable gradients from the output layer zL to the enter layer h zero are elevated by using idea C. This rating suggests how a great deal the idea affected the model's choice. To determine model fairness and bias, TCAV has been used in quite a few fields, which include pc vision and natural language processing. By measuring a version's reference to positive ideas, TCAV enables us to make certain that AI systems are advanced and deployed ethically, fairly, and transparently, encouraging openness and responsibility in system learning. Figure 5 shows various explainable AI techniques applied to device learning models.

Figure 5. Explainable AI techniques applicable to various machine learning models

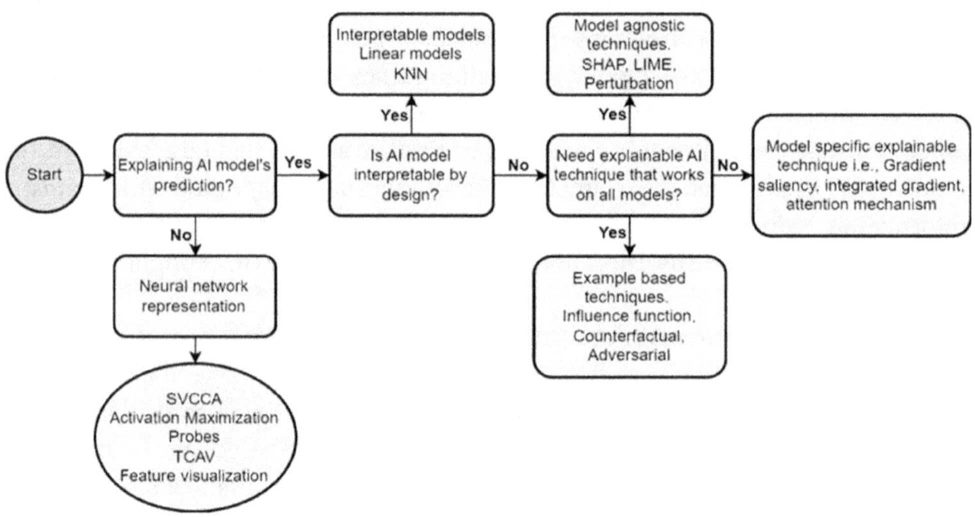

Next, we discuss in detail the various explainable AI techniques used for the interpretation and explainability of deep neural networks.

EXPLAINABLE AI TECHNIQUES USED FOR FEED-FORWARD NEURAL NETWORKS

Feedforward Neural Networks (FNNs) are a new class of neural networks that are like multi-layer perceptrons (MLPs) in their internal workings (Wang et al., 2022). To enhance their interpretability, the Explainable AI Techniques (XAI) approach to Feedforward Neural Networks seeks to provide insights into how those networks work. The diverse explainable AI strategies used for feedforward neural networks encompass:

Feature Importance Analysis of Feedforward Neural Network

The relative importance of input capabilities in generating predictions is clarified with the aid of the vital interpretability technique referred to as feature significance analysis for feedforward neural networks (FNNs) (Pham et al., 2020). We can decide which factors have the maximum effect on the model's output with the aid of scoring the relevance of the numerous functions. Understanding which elements of the input statistics are important for the FNN's decision-making method is made simpler with the assist of this observer. Figure 1.6 illustrates in descending order the maximum critical features that affect predicting median home value.

Figure 6. Feature impact in predicting a median home value

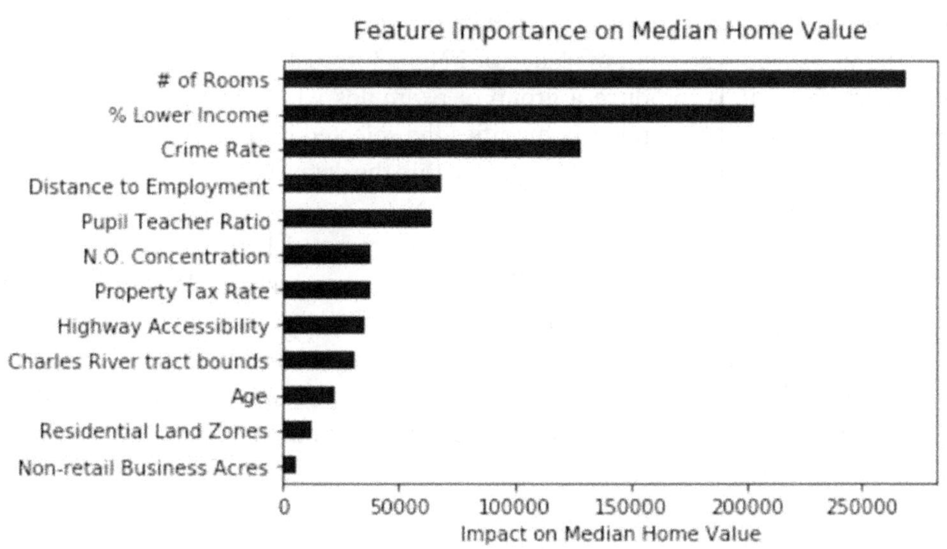

Partial Dependency Plots

In the context of feedforward neural networks (FNNs), partial dependence plots (PDPs) are a beneficial device for expertise in the connections among input variables and version predictions (Velthoen, 2023). These charts provide a visual and clean technique to understand how modifications in precise input variables affect the FNN's output even while keeping the same values for other variables. PDPs offer a valuable manner to decipher intricate FNN **models** and discover hidden styles within the information. One detail of interest is progressively altered while maintaining identical values for the opposite components to generate PDPs. The FNN generates predictions for every price of the characteristic of interest, which can then be recorded and displayed on the PDP's y-axis. By graphing the feature values along the x-axis, a graph is produced that illustrates how the model's predictions change whilst the characteristic of interest varies. PDPs can provide vital details about the version's conduct.

LIME (Local Interpretable Model-Agnostic Explanations)

A flexible technique for presenting interpretable factors for the predictions of feedforward neural networks (FNNs) and other system-studying models is known as LIME, which stands for Local Interpretable Model-agnostic Explanations (Palatnik de Sousa et al., 2019). Here is a streamlined example of the system:

- Distance Instance Selection: LIME begins by choosing a thrilling information point for you who want evidence of FNN's forecast.
- Perturbation: To produce a group of examples which might be comparable but special, LIME randomly modifies the selected information instance.
- FNN Prediction: For each incidence within the dataset that has been disrupted, predictions are then made using the FNN.
- Local Surrogate Model: To the altered dataset, LIME fits a trustworthy, understandable version (typically a linear regression or selection tree). The conduct of the FNN within the immediate place surrounding the initial statistics factor is represented through this surrogate model.
- Explanation: The surrogate model's coefficients and organizational shape shed mild on which characteristics had the maximum effect on the prediction for the statistics factor of interest.

SHAP (SHapley Additive exPlanations)

A strong and famous machine learning technique known as SHAP (SHapley Additive explanations) is applied to provide comprehensible motives for model predictions (Antwarg et al., 2021). The cooperative recreation theory based SHAP values offer a logical approach for attributing the contributions of input traits to model predictions. The predominant goal of SHAP is to lightly proportion every feature's contribution to the prediction as though the prediction had been a cooperative game in that the functions have been taking part in. Shapley values, which are carried out in cooperative sports concepts to equitably distribute the fee produced via players' collaboration, serve as the mathematical foundation for SHAP values. In the context of device learning, this involves assessing the contribution of each feature to the prediction made by way of the model even as thinking about all possible characteristic combos. An abbreviated model of the method for SHAP values is shown beneath:

$$\varnothing_i(f) = \Sigma SCN\{i\}.\frac{|S|!.(|N|-|S|-1)!}{|N|!}\left[f(S\cup\{i\})-f(S)\right]$$

In this equation

- $\varnothing_i(f)$ represents the SHAP value for feature I in the model f.
- N is the set of all features.
- S represents subsets of features that do not include feature i.
- |S| is the cardinality of set S.
- F (S ∪ {i}) is the model's prediction when including feature i.
- f (S) is the model's prediction without including feature i.

Figure 7 illustrates the features of SHAP values together with their effect on the output result.

Figure 7. Features SHAP values and their impact on the model prediction

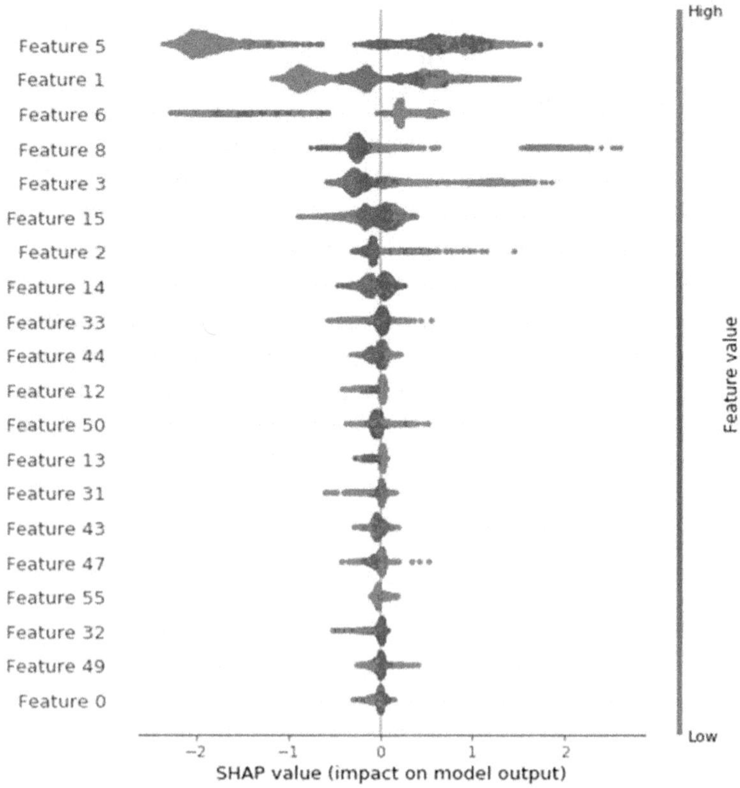

Layer-Wise Relevance Propagation (LRP)

A cutting-edge method used in system studying to explain the selections made with the aid of neural networks, in particular deep getting-to-know models, is layer-sensible relevance propagation (LRP) (Montavon, 2019). The network's records float and the additives of the enter statistics that have the greatest predictive electricity are each proven through LRP. Understanding sophisticated models like deep neural networks is made easier with the assist of this approach.

In Figure 1.8, we illustrate an example in which a Neural Network was constructed to differentiate a photo as either a "locomotive" or a "passenger vehicle." Following the training segment, a picture turned into inputted into the network, resulting in a prediction of a "passenger vehicle." Subsequently, we applied Layer-sensible Relevance Propagation (LRP) beginning from the neuron representing the "passenger vehicle" and tracing returned to the initial layer neurons. The heatmap showcased inside the example depicts the relevance values related to these enter neurons.

Specifically, the heatmap employs a colour scheme in which purple pixels suggest an effective contribution in the direction of the "passenger automobile" prediction, even as blue pixels represent a negative contribution to the equal prediction. This visualization technique serves to elucidate the critical elements inside the input facts that drove the network's selection closer to classifying the image as a "passenger car."

Figure 8. Heatmap illustrating the explanation for the output neuron "passenger_car." Here, the image's attributes (pixels) that stand for "passenger car" are highlighted in red, signifying their importance in selecting the class "passenger_car" at the output.

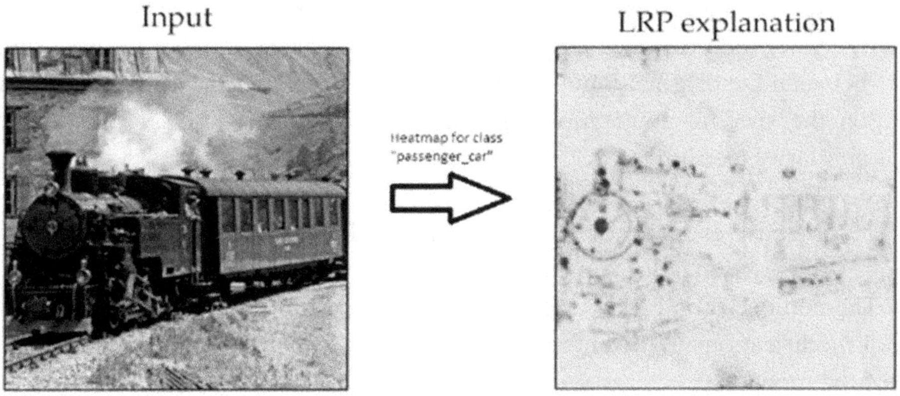

Gradient-Based Methods

Gradient-based tactics are a subset of Explainable AI (XAI) methods that use gradients to explain and recognize the choice-making approaches of the state-of-the-art device getting-to-know models (Kuppa & Le-Khac, 2020). Deep neural networks and other complicated models' "black field" nature may be understood by the use of those strategies. Gradient-based total tactics, at their heart, generate gradients or derivatives of the output of the model concerning enter features. These gradients display how responsive each enter function is to modifications inside the model's predictions.

Counterfactual Explanations

A key thing of Explainable AI (XAI) is counterfactual reasons offer purchasers essential insights into predictions made through system getting to know models (Keane & Smyth, 2020). To properly respond to the "what if" inquiries, these explanations encompass developing trade enter statistics factors that would result in numerous version predictions. In addition to what the model predicts, counterfactuals resource users with information about what adjustments need to be made to enter information to attain the favoured result.

The mathematical method for counterfactual explanations looks as if this:

$$Counterfactual(x) = arg.min_{x'}(d(x,x'))$$

In this equation:

- x represents the original input data point.
- x' is the counterfactual input that needs to be found.
- D (x, x') is a distance or similarity metric that quantifies the dissimilarity between the original input and the counterfactual input. This metric depends on the specific application and may involve norms like L1, L2, or other similarity measures.

The objective is to become aware of X' such that, even though generating a unique forecast or result from the initial input x, it reduces the dissimilarity d (x, x'). The counterfactual rationalization offers a right-away manner to realise how minor modifications to the enter features may affect the predictions made with the aid of the model.

Integrated Gradients

In Explainable AI (XAI), Integrated Gradients are a powerful technique for attributing function relevance in device learning models, especially deep neural networks (Čík, 2021). It solutions the vital question of what share each enter characteristic contributes to the prediction of a model. By considering the whole course from a baseline input to the actual input statistics and integrating gradients alongside this course to compute characteristic attributions, Integrated Gradients accomplishes this.

The following is an expression of the integrated gradients mathematical equation:

$$IG_i(f) = (x_i - x_i^{'}.\int_{\alpha=0}^{1} \frac{\partial f\left(x' + \alpha.(x - x')\right)}{\partial x_i} d\alpha$$

In this equation:

- IG_i (f) represents the Integrated Gradients attribution for feature I in the model f.

- x_i denotes the actual value of the feature of interest.
- x_i' is the baseline value for the same feature.
- The integral term computes the average gradient of the model's output concerning the feature x_i along the path from the baseline x_i' to the actual x_i as controlled by the parameter α.

EXPLAINABLE AI TECHNIQUES USED FOR CONVOLUTIONAL NEURAL NETWORKS

Convolutional neural networks (CNNs) are widely used in lots of packages, consisting of laptop vision, natural language processing, and speech popularity, making explainable AI processes increasingly essential for CNNs. With the useful resource of these XAI procedures, users of picture-centric applications like photograph categorization, item recognition, medical imaging, and independent motors can also better realise, validate, and consider CNN predictions. The layout of CNN and precise interpretability necessities influence the technique selected. Explainable AI strategies used for convolutional neural networks include:

Grad-CAM

Grad-CAM, additionally referred to as Gradient-weighted Class Activation Mapping, is a powerful and famous method for convolutional neural networks (CNNs) in Explainable AI (XAI). It is an important tool for improving the understandability and transparency of CNN-primarily based models, in particular in jobs with the use of pix. By considering the gradients of the magnificence rating concerning characteristic maps in the CNN, Grad-CAM expands on the idea of Class Activation Mapping (CAM) (Vinogradova et al., 2020). Grad-CAM's primary purpose is to supply visible factors that draw interest to key regions of an enter picture that considerably impact the version's class predictions. Grad-CAM makes use of gradient records to provide extra accurate and satisfactory-grained localization of those important areas, in comparison to conventional CAM, which simply relies on the weights of the very last convolutional layer.

Figure 9 demonstrates Grad-CAM to reveal activation maps on a canine photo with the use of Keras, TensorFlow, and deep learning.

Figure 9. Utilizing Grad-CAM to visualize the activation maps of a dog

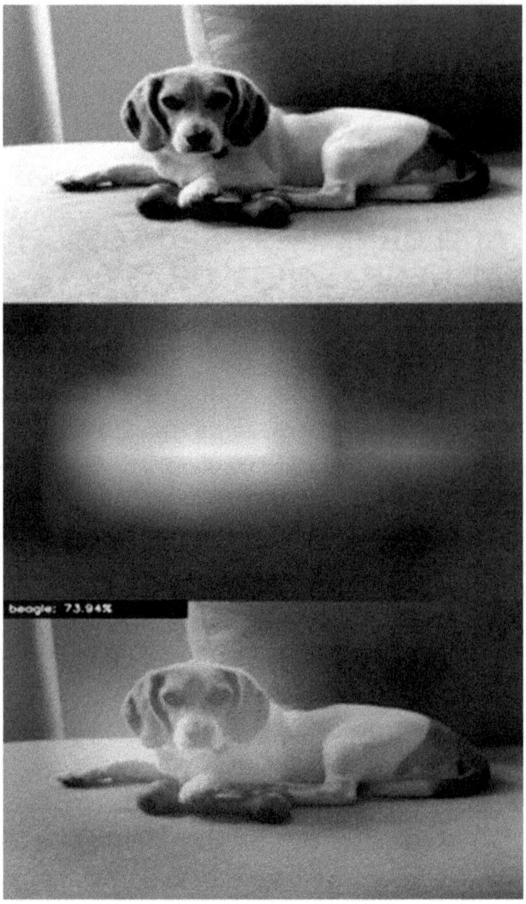

Gradient-Based Local Interpretability

Convolutional Neural Networks (CNNs) and different complicated machine learning models' predictions may be understood by the usage of gradient-primarily based nearby interpretability approaches, mainly whilst used within the context of photograph analysis (Nielsen et al., 2022). These techniques provide an understanding of the local selection-making method with the aid of revealing how the version's output alters in reaction to minute disturbances or adjustments inside the enter facts. Although all gradient-based totally interpretability algorithms now do not have a single mathematical equation, computing gradients or derivatives is the essential idea. The gradients of the version's output to the enter photo pixels are calculated especially for CNNs.

This idea's mathematical illustration can be summed up as follows:

$$\nabla_x f(x) = \left(\frac{\partial f}{\partial x_1}, \frac{\partial f}{\partial x_2}, \ldots\ldots, \frac{\partial f}{\partial x_n}\right)$$

In this equation:

- $\nabla_x f(x)$ represents the gradient of the model's output f(x) for the input x.
- x_1, x_2, ……, x_n are the individual pixel values in the input image.

Saliency Maps

In the sector of Explainable AI (XAI), saliency maps are crucial assets, in particular concerning comprehending the predictions made through Convolutional Neural Networks (CNNs) for photograph processing obligations (Mundhenk et al., 2019). These maps provide visible motives by emphasizing the key regions of an enter picture that have the most effect on CNN's output. The primary concept behind saliency map processes is to compute gradients of the model's output for the enter picture pixels, even though there is not a single mathematical equation that perfectly captures all saliency map techniques. This makes it clear which elements of the photograph are maximum likely to alteration and feature a huge effect on the model's desire.

The mathematical basis for producing saliency maps can be summarized as follows:

$$Saliency(x) = \nabla_x f(x)$$

In this equation:

- Saliency (x) represents the saliency map for input x.
- $\nabla_x f(x)$ signifies the gradient of the model's output (f(x)) concerning the input image (x).

EXPLAINABLE AI FOR TIME-SERIES MODELS

Time series models are an important tool in records and facts evaluation for examining sequential or time-collection records. Observations or measurements of 1 or more variables taken at various points in time often make up the records from a time series (Dikshit & Pradhan, 2021). Time series models strive to find and examine styles, trends, and relationships within these temporal statistics to forecast destiny or study new data for a variety of applications. Understanding these patterns and traits is important for making informed judgments in a whole lot of disciplines, which include finance, economics, environmental technological know-how, and others. Time series records often exhibit four foremost traits: trend, seasonality, cyclical styles, and unpredictable or random changes (Rojat, 2021).

Types of Time Series Models

To depict temporal connections and trends, the Autoregressive Integrated Moving Average (ARIMA) model combines shifting average and autoregressive additives. The Seasonal Decomposition of Time Series (STL) technique can be used to separate a time collection into seasonal, modelable, and residual additives. The exponential smoothing state area version (ETS), which integrates seasonal and exponential traits, is commonly used for brief-term forecasting. Long Short-Term Memory (LSTM) recurrent neural networks (RNNs) are regularly used for sequential facts processing and might capture lengthy-time period dependencies.

OVERVIEW OF XAI METHODS FOR TIME SERIES MODELS

Deep learning models which are too complex to comprehend are made extra interpretable using XAI methods for time collection models. These strategies may be divided into three organizations: ante-hoc explainability strategies (Sarkar, 2022), perturbation-based total strategies (Khatami et al., 2020), and again-propagation techniques (Wang & Wang, 2022). The gradient of the output for the input is used by lower back-propagation-based total algorithms to decide which traits are maximum critical. For staring at the impact of the output and figuring out the maximum vital factors, perturbation-primarily based procedures encompass perturbing the input information. Ante-hoc explainability techniques entail developing models with integrated interpretability. The most essential factors of a time series version are discovered through lower back-propagation-based total strategies.

Back-Propagation-Based Methods

The maximum essential factors of a time series version are found through returned-propagation-based total techniques. These techniques employ the gradient of the output relative to the input to pinpoint the important thing traits. Saliency Maps, LRP, and DeepLIFT are some of the backpropagation-based strategies used with time collection models, in Step 1. By calculating the gradient of the output to the enter, saliency maps are used to find the most important elements in a time series version. By propagating the community's output again to the enter space, the LRP (Layer-wise Relevance Propagation) method, which is based totally on lower back-propagation, finds the time series model's maximum important homes. By dispersing the community's output, DeepLIFT is some other returned-propagation-primarily based approach used to pinpoint the most critical elements of a time collection model. Back-propagation-based procedures are regularly more accurate than other strategies but much less interpretable in phrases of accuracy and interpretability.

Perturbation-Based Methods

To study the impact on the output and determine the maximum critical elements, perturbation-primarily based procedures, a subset of XAI techniques disturb the enter information. These strategies consist of perturbing a characteristic or set of features and seeing how the forecast that outcomes changes. A larger change suggests that the affected trends are greater great. Occlusion, which masks features to assess their relevance, and Extremal Masks, which research a mask used to disturb the enter, are examples of perturbation-based totally strategies used to fit time series models. The authors of Ivanovs et al. (2021) offer a manner to explain predictions by gaining knowledge of both associated perturbations and masks. They provide real evidence that knowledge of these perturbations significantly increases the calibre of these time series statistics interpretations. They train a neural community in conjunction with the masks to replace fixed perturbations. The neural network and the masks, m and NN(x), are used to describe their perturbation as m x + (1 m) NN(x). They confine the mask to balance the amount of disturbed information and unperturbed records with the aid of preserving m between 0 and 1.

Ante-Hoc Explainability Methods

An XAI technique known as the ante-hoc explainability technique consists of creating models with integrated interpretability. These techniques try to keep away from the need for any present-hoc clarification-producing approach by teaching the latent idea-based total explanations implicitly. In Sarkar (2022), the authors provide a model that adds an evidence-producing module on a pinnacle of any primary community and simultaneously trains the whole module to provide factors that make feel conceptual and have good predictive overall performance.

The advantages of using ante-hoc explainability techniques over submit-hoc methods consist of:

- Ante-hoc processes best consider a select few models because they're model-unique. This might be regarded as a gain since it enables the introduction of models with integrated interpretability.
- Post-hoc procedures handiest explain the version's conduct after it's been educated, while ante-hoc strategies consider explainability during a model's improvement. Therefore, ante-hoc techniques can also bring about models which are easier to apprehend properly away.
- Self-supervision of ideas can be used by ad hoc strategies to attain better justifications. This approach that ante-hoc strategies can offer models that aren't only easier to recognize but additionally perform more correctly while making predictions.
- Comparatively speaking, ante-hoc processes use significantly less parameter space than baseline techniques. As a result, ante-hoc techniques can also bring about models which are extra powerful and scalable.

HUMAN DIMENSION OF EXPLAINABLE AI FOR TIME SERIES

Explainable AI for time collection has a "human measurement" that refers to thinking about human factors at some point in the creation and evaluation of XAI strategies. This includes growing XAI strategies while retaining in mind the end consumer's necessities, alternatives, and constraints. It's crucial to realize how customers interact with XAI strategies and the way they perceive them, in addition to how their cognitive biases and mental models may additionally affect how they apprehend the excuses offered by using the XAI strategies. Studying how the consumer's confidence and consider inside the AI gadget can be tormented by the reasons given by way of XAI strategies and the way this might affect how they make selections is likewise critical. Another thing to not forget while constructing an automatic system that may be defined to users is their psychology. The seek results (Alia, 2023; Lecue, 2020; Rojat, 2021) pass into similar intensity about those elements.

Importance of Considering the Human Dimension of Explainability

It is important to consider human explainability whilst developing synthetic intelligence (AI). While AI models can acquire brilliant tiers of class and accuracy, their acceptability and trustworthiness are jeopardized if purchasers cannot completely apprehend how those models make their selections. For customers to believe in technology and to sell fruitful interaction among people and computer systems, it's miles essential to understand and recognize how an AI machine comes to a certain prediction or judgment. The stakes are high while AI algorithms are utilized in essential fields like healthcare, banking, or criminal justice, therefore openness and understandability are vital.

User-Centered Design for XAI

The development and implementation of AI systems need to prioritize the necessities, talents, and expectancies of stop users and the use of user-focused layouts (UCD) for explainable synthetic intelligence (XAI). Fundamentally, it seeks to develop XAI systems which can be easy for users of all levels of enjoy and disciplines to understand, make use of, and advantage of. Understanding customers, their surroundings, and their dreams is step one in the methodical method that makes up UCD. To study extra about consumer desires and choices, it makes use of strategies along with user interviews, surveys, personas, and eventualities.

APPLICATIONS OF XAI IN TIME SERIES FORECASTING

Time collection forecasting has been altered by Explainable Artificial Intelligence (XAI) across a wide variety of areas (Ma, 2022). By imparting clarity and comprehensibility in anticipating stock marketplace moves, XAI performs a crucial position in finance by helping investors and buyers make wise judgments (Freeborough & van Zyl, 2022). XAI assists in lowering the complexity of financial information by illuminating its underlying characteristics and patterns, which enhances risk control and evaluation. In the healthcare industry, XAI is vital for forecasting affected person outcomes using time collection statistics from wearables or digital health information (Wildi & Misheva, 2022). These forecasts may be utilized by clinicians to refine treatment strategies and actions, ultimately enhancing affected person care.

Healthcare

Healthcare time collection forecasting has been transformed via Explainable Artificial Intelligence (XAI), which provides essential insights, interpretability, and reliability in predicting patient results, contamination development, resource allocation, and scientific treatments (Albahri et al., 2023). The prediction of patient fitness outcomes primarily based on several clinical data accumulated over time is one of the number one packages of XAI in healthcare time collection forecasting. The extensive number of facts seen in electronic health statistics (EHRs), as an example, includes critical signs and symptoms, take a look at findings, medicine records, and more. Healthcare professionals can also forecast an affected person's destiny health kingdom or possibly outcomes via the use of XAI techniques on this time collection statistics, allowing early intervention and individualized treatment strategies. These forecasts permit more effective resource allocation and progress patient care. They can include the entirety from readmission probabilities to sickness progression rates (Yang, 2022).

Retail

XAI will also be used for centred marketing and purchaser segmentation (Murindanyi, 2023; Talaat et al., 2023). Retailers can also use XAI to correctly segment their consumer base by looking at customer buy histories, surfing styles, demographic facts, and responses to advertising efforts. This segmentation allows tailor-made suggestions and centred advertising campaigns, growing consumer engagement and boosting revenues. Furthermore, a key use of XAI in retail is inventory optimization (Javed et al., 2023). Retailers might also hold a perfect amount of stock by efficiently forecasting inventory levels based on income records, seasonality, promotions, and different pertinent elements.

Manufacturing

A new age of data-driven decision-making and advanced efficiency in commercial time series forecasting has arrived way to Explainable Artificial Intelligence (XAI). Predictive preservation is one of the middle uses of XAI in production. Manufacturers might also correctly forecast gadget disasters and upkeep necessities by using XAI algorithms to time collection information obtained from sensors implanted in equipment. For instance, past facts on device performance, anomalies, and protection statistics may be used to estimate whether a machine is possibly interrupted using predictive preservation models (Chen, 2023; Sofianidis, 2021). Another vital vicinity in which XAI may have an extensive influence is the optimization of energy use. Manufacturers can reliably forecast electricity calls for consumption by using the usage of time series records on power intake developments and linking them with other operational elements like production volume, weather, and equipment utilization (Ahmed et al., 2022). This helps each value-cutting and sustainability task by helping with the powerful planning of power intake, improving electricity procurement strategies, and lowering strength costs.

A paradigm alternate in economics has been added approximately with the aid of Explainable Artificial Intelligence (XAI), significantly in time collection forecasting (Benhamou, 2022). The use of XAI in this location has many diverse and vital applications, protecting purchaser conduct, financial markets, economic research, and more. Prediction of economic signs is one of the key programs. Large volumes of historic time series records on monetary variables including GDP, unemployment charges, inflation, customer spending, and industrial manufacturing are to be had for analysis by way of XAI models. These facts' styles and linkages may be determined and utilized by XAI to assume key economic indicators more correctly (Chen et al., 2023).

EXPLAINABILITY METRICS AND EVALUATION

To gauge the explainability of AI models and make sure they adhere to certain standards, numerous metrics and assessment techniques have been mounted. Interpretability, one of the key criteria, measures how easy it is for a person to comprehend and interpret the version's conclusions. Because of their said ideas, choice trees and linear regression models are visible as interpretable, however, deep neural networks are often regarded as being less interpretable because of their complex topologies (Vilone & Longo, 2021).

The intention is to create models which are correct and clean to recognize, at the same time as also admitting that there may additionally from time to time be a trade-off between the two. For example, although a greater truthful model like logistic regression may want to give up some accuracy for higher interpretability, a complex deep getting-to-know version would possibly attain high accuracy but lack interpretability. The evaluation element of nearby vs. Worldwide interpretability is important. Global interpretability seeks to realize the version's behaviour globally over the complete dataset, whereas local interpretability concentrates on comprehending the version's conduct for a single example or a small group of examples. For sensible utility, reaching each kind of interpretation talent is essential.

Model-specific Metrics are created for positive models. Examples of metrics that can be used to gauge the importance of features and enhance version comprehension include the Gini Index and Information Gain in decision trees. Metrics like TF-IDF (Term Frequency-Inverse Document Frequency), which are used in herbal language processing, may be used to determine a phrase's significance in a document.

Local Explainability

LIME (Local Interpretable Model-agnostic Explanations) is a famous method for attaining nearby explainability. LIME works via schooling an interpretable and locally correct surrogate model to approximate the conduct of the version near a particular instance. This alternative model, which is usually greater honest (e.g., linear regression), offers a comprehensible justification for the model's prediction in that case. For instance, LIME may suggest the essential pixels that the version considered at the same time as making a preference, presenting an extra unique justification for the categorization result. SHAP (SHapley Additive motives), which is based totally on the cooperative recreation principle, is every other approach for local explainability. To appropriately allocate a cost across a hard and fast of individuals and account for a way each characteristic contributed to a sure prediction, SHAP values are used. In the domain of AI, SHAP values help in the knowledge of the local behaviour of the model by quantifying the impact of each characteristic on a specific prediction.

LIME and SHAP

Two effective techniques within the fields of artificial intelligence and machine learning are LIME (Local Interpretable Model-agnostic Explanations) and SHAP (SHapley Additive exPlanations), particularly in terms of explaining complicated models.

LIME (Local Interpretable Model-Agnostic Explanations)

LIME is a strategy that is frequently used to provide neighbourhood justifications for gadget-studying models. The primary aim of LIME is to educate a greater interpretable and locally accurate surrogate model to mimic the behaviour of the version around a given example. This substitute version needs to be clean and clean to understandable so that we may also take advantage of the expertise of the authentic version's forecast in that specific scenario. Consider a complicated deep-learning photo class version, as an example, that could tell if a picture incorporates a dog or a cat.

Let's: f: Explain the black-box model.
x: The instance (data point) that has to have an explanation.
$\pi(x)$: Samples perturbed about x.
g: The interpretable model that provides a local approximation of f.
wi: The perturbed samples' weights according to how close they are to x.

The general procedures consist of:

Perturbation and Weighting: Change x's characteristics to produce $\pi(x)$, which results in altered samples.

Determine the distance or similarity between each $\pi(x)$ and x, and then give these samples weights based on their closeness.

Wi = measure of similarity or distance (x, π(x))

Local Model Fitting: Use the perturbed samples π(x) and their corresponding predictions from the black-box model *f* to train an interpretable model *g* in the local neighborhood around *x*.

$$g = \arg\min_{\text{g belongs to G}} \sum_{i=1}^{N} W_i \cdot \left(f\left(\pi\left(x_i\right)\right) - g\left(\pi\left(x_i\right)\right)\right) + ©\left(g\right)$$

In the above equation

$$\sum_{i=1}^{N} W_i \cdot \left(f\left(\pi\left(x_i\right)\right) - g\left(\pi\left(x_i\right)\right)\right) + ©\left(g\right)$$

denotes the loss function, wherein the black-box model f's predictions and the local interpretable model g's for the perturbed samples π(xi), weighted by wi, are trained to minimize the difference.

The regularization term Ω(g) can be incorporated into the loss function to manage the interpretable model g's complexity and avoid overfitting.

SHAP (SHapley Additive exPlanations)

The cooperative game idea primarily based on SHAP beliefs provides a moral framework for characteristic attribution and explanation. To correctly allocate a cost throughout a set of participants and account for how every attribute contributed to a sure prediction, SHAP values are used. These values guarantee that the overall function contributions equal the distinction between the forecast and the version's average prediction and quantify the influence of every characteristic on a selected prediction.

XAI EVALUATION

In XAI assessment, the transparency, interpretability, and understandability of AI models and their justifications are rated and quantified. We will have a look at the various factors of XAI evaluation, which includes measurements, methodology, and realistic packages, in this in-intensity communication.

Importance of XAI Evaluation

Evaluation of XAI is vital for numerous reasons. It first makes positive AI structures obvious using giving clients facts on how the version generates predictions. This openness encourages religion in the model's abilities. Second, XAI assessment allows the detection and correction of biases that could be gifted inside the records or the version, ensuring that AI structures are impartial and honest. Finally, assessment encourages version progress by giving data scientists and teachers useful entries for enhancing models and explanations.

XAI Evaluation Metrics

The effectiveness of the reasons supplied by AI modelss may be judged using quantitative measurements called XAI evaluation metrics. Typical metrics encompass:

Measures how honest a proof is. Frequently, a clearer rationalization is easier to realize.

Consistency: Determines whether or not the reason is regular with domain knowledge and human expectations.

Fidelity: Measures how faithfully the reason captures the behavior of the version.

Measures the diploma to which the rationale is comprehensible with the aid of the audience.

Stability: Determines if mild adjustments to the entered information motive corresponding changes to the reason.

Sensitivity: Evaluates how adjustments inside the input will affect the justification.

REFERENCES

Ahmed, I., Jeon, G., & Piccialli, F. (2022). From artificial intelligence to explainable artificial intelligence in industry 4.0: A survey on what, how, and where. *IEEE Transactions on Industrial Informatics*, *18*(8), 5031–5042. doi:10.1109/TII.2022.3146552

Albahri, A., Duhaim, A. M., Fadhel, M. A., Alnoor, A., Baqer, N. S., Alzubaidi, L., Albahri, O. S., Alamoodi, A. H., Bai, J., Salhi, A., Santamaría, J., Ouyang, C., Gupta, A., Gu, Y., & Deveci, M. (2023). A systematic review of trustworthy and explainable artificial intelligence in healthcare: Assessment of quality, bias risk, and data fusion. *Information Fusion*, *96*, 156–191. doi:10.1016/j.inffus.2023.03.008

Alia, S. (2023). *Explainable Artificial Intelligence (XAI): What we know and what is left to attain Trustworthy Artificial Intelligence.* Science Direct.

Allgaier, J., Mulansky, L., Draelos, R. L., & Pryss, R. (2023). How does the model make predictions? A systematic literature review on the explainability power of machine learning in healthcare. *Artificial Intelligence in Medicine*, *143*, 102616. doi:10.1016/j.artmed.2023.102616 PMID:37673561

Antoniadi, A. M., Du, Y., Guendouz, Y., Wei, L., Mazo, C., Becker, B. A., & Mooney, C. (2021). Current challenges and future opportunities for XAI in machine learning-based clinical decision support systems: A systematic review. *Applied Sciences (Basel, Switzerland)*, *11*(11), 5088. doi:10.3390/app11115088

Antwarg, L., Miller, R. M., Shapira, B., & Rokach, L. (2021). Explaining anomalies detected by autoencoders using Shapley Additive Explanations. *Expert Systems with Applications*, *186*, 115736. doi:10.1016/j.eswa.2021.115736

Benhamou, E. (2022). *Explainable AI (XAI) models applied to planning in financial markets*, in *Explainable AI (XAI) Models Applied to Planning in Financial Markets*. Research Gate.

Bento, V., Kohler, M., Diaz, P., Mendoza, L., & Pacheco, M. A. (2021). Improving deep learning performance by using Explainable Artificial Intelligence (XAI) approaches. *Discover Artificial Intelligence*, *1*(1), 1–11. doi:10.1007/s44163-021-00008-y

Chen, T.-C. T. (2023). Explainable Artificial Intelligence (XAI) in Manufacturing, in Explainable Artificial Intelligence (XAI) in Manufacturing: Methodology, Tools, and Applications. Springer.

Chen, X.-Q., Ma, C.-Q., Ren, Y.-S., Lei, Y.-T., Huynh, N. Q. A., & Narayan, S. (2023). Explainable artificial intelligence in finance: A bibliometric review. *Finance Research Letters*, *56*, 104145. doi:10.1016/j.frl.2023.104145

Čík, I. (2021). Explaining deep neural network using layer-wise relevance propagation and integrated gradients. In *2021 IEEE 19th world symposium on applied machine intelligence and informatics (SAMI)*. IEEE. 10.1109/SAMI50585.2021.9378686

Clement, T., Kemmerzell, N., Abdelaal, M., & Amberg, M. (2023). XAIR: A Systematic Metareview of Explainable AI (XAI) Aligned to the Software Development Process. *Machine Learning and Knowledge Extraction*, *5*(1), 78–108. doi:10.3390/make5010006

Cunha, B., & Manikonda, L. (2022). *Classification of Misinformation in New Articles using Natural Language Processing and a Recurrent Neural Network*. arXiv preprint arXiv:2210.13534.

Dikshit, A., & Pradhan, B. (2021). Interpretable and explainable AI (XAI) model for spatial drought prediction. *The Science of the Total Environment*, *801*, 149797. doi:10.1016/j.scitotenv.2021.149797 PMID:34467917

Freeborough, W., & van Zyl, T. (2022). Investigating explainability methods in recurrent neural network architectures for financial time series data. *Applied Sciences (Basel, Switzerland)*, *12*(3), 1427. doi:10.3390/app12031427

Ghimire, D., Kil, D., & Kim, S. (2022). A survey on efficient convolutional neural networks and hardware acceleration. *Electronics (Basel)*, *11*(6), 945. doi:10.3390/electronics11060945

Gramegna, A., & Giudici, P. (2021). SHAP and LIME: An evaluation of discriminative power in credit risk. *Frontiers in Artificial Intelligence*, *4*, 752558. doi:10.3389/frai.2021.752558 PMID:34604738

Hulsen, T. (2023). Explainable Artificial Intelligence (XAI): Concepts and Challenges in Healthcare. *AI*, *4*(3), 652–666. doi:10.3390/ai4030034

Ivanovs, M., Kadikis, R., & Ozols, K. (2021). Perturbation-based methods for explaining deep neural networks: A survey. *Pattern Recognition Letters*, *150*, 228–234. doi:10.1016/j.patrec.2021.06.030

Javed, A. R., Ahmed, W., Pandya, S., Maddikunta, P. K. R., Alazab, M., & Gadekallu, T. R. (2023). A survey of explainable artificial intelligence for smart cities. *Electronics (Basel)*, *12*(4), 1020. doi:10.3390/electronics12041020

Kaul, D., Raju, H., & Tripathy, B. (2022). Deep learning in healthcare. *Deep Learning in Data Analytics: Recent Techniques, Practices and Applications*. Research Gate.

Keane, M. T., & Smyth, B. (2020). *Good counterfactuals and where to find them: A case-based technique for generating counterfactuals for explainable AI (XAI)*. Case-Based Reasoning Research and Development: 28th International Conference, ICCBR 2020, Salamanca, Spain.

Khatami, A., Nazari, A., Khosravi, A., Lim, C. P., & Nahavandi, S. (2020). A weight perturbation-based regularisation technique for convolutional neural networks and the application in medical imaging. *Expert Systems with Applications*, *149*, 113196. doi:10.1016/j.eswa.2020.113196

Kim, B. (2018). *Interpretability beyond feature attribution: Quantitative testing with concept activation vectors (tcav). International conference on machine learning*. PMLR.

Kuppa, A., & Le-Khac, N.-A. (2020). *Black box attacks on explainable artificial intelligence (XAI) methods in cyber security*. in *2020 International Joint Conference on neural networks (IJCNN)*. IEEE. 10.1109/IJCNN48605.2020.9206780

Lecue, F. (2020). On the role of knowledge graphs in explainable AI. *Semantic Web*, *11*(1), 41–51. doi:10.3233/SW-190374

Li, X., Xiong, H., Li, X., Wu, X., Zhang, X., Liu, J., Bian, J., & Dou, D. (2022). Interpretable deep learning: Interpretation, interpretability, trustworthiness, and beyond. *Knowledge and Information Systems*, *64*(12), 3197–3234. doi:10.1007/s10115-022-01756-8

Ma, R. (2022). Forecasting and XAI for Applications Usage in OS. *Machine Learning and Artificial Intelligence*. IOS Press.

Mahalakshmi, V., Kulkarni, N., Pradeep Kumar, K. V., Suresh Kumar, K., Nidhi Sree, D., & Durga, S. (2022). The Role of implementing Artificial Intelligence and Machine Learning Technologies in the financial services Industry for creating Competitive Intelligence. *Materials Today: Proceedings*, *56*, 2252–2255. doi:10.1016/j.matpr.2021.11.577

Montavon, G. (2019). *Layer-wise relevance propagation: an overview*. Explainable AI: interpreting, explaining and visualizing deep learning, 193-209.

Mundhenk, T. N., Chen, B. Y., & Friedland, G. (2019). *Efficient saliency maps for explainable AI*. arXiv preprint arXiv:1911.11293.

Murindanyi, S. (2023). *Interpretable Machine Learning for Predicting Customer Churn in Retail Banking. 2023 7th International Conference on Trends in Electronics and Informatics (ICOEI)*. IEEE. 10.1109/ICOEI56765.2023.10125859

Nguyen, A., Yosinski, J., & Clune, J. (2019). Understanding neural networks via feature visualization: A survey. *Explainable AI: interpreting, explaining and visualizing deep learning* (p. 55-76). Research Gate.

Nielsen, I. E., Dera, D., Rasool, G., Ramachandran, R. P., & Bouaynaya, N. C. (2022). Robust explainability: A tutorial on gradient-based attribution methods for deep neural networks. *IEEE Signal Processing Magazine*, *39*(4), 73–84. doi:10.1109/MSP.2022.3142719

Palatnik de Sousa, I., Maria Bernardes Rebuzzi Vellasco, M., & Costa da Silva, E. (2019). Local interpretable model-agnostic explanations for classification of lymph node metastases. *Sensors (Basel)*, *19*(13), 2969. doi:10.3390/s19132969 PMID:31284419

Parmar, A., Katariya, R., & Patel, V. (2018). A review on random forest: An ensemble classifier. *International conference on intelligent data communication technologies and internet of things (ICICI)*. Springer.

Pham, T. N., Van Tran, L., & Dao, S. V. T. (2020). Early disease classification of mango leaves using feed-forward neural network and hybrid metaheuristic feature selection. *IEEE Access : Practical Innovations, Open Solutions*, *8*, 189960–189973. doi:10.1109/ACCESS.2020.3031914

Pothen, A.S. (2022). Artificial intelligence and its increasing importance. Success is no accident. It is hard work, perseverance, learning, studying, sacrifice and most of all, love of what you are doing or learning to do.

Raghu, M. (2017). *Singular vector canonical correlation analysis for deep learning dynamics and interpretability. 2017*. 31st Conference on Neural Information Processing Systems (NIPS 2017), Long Beach: Neural Info Process Sys F, La Jolla.

Rojat, T. (2021). *Explainable artificial intelligence (xai) on timeseries data: A survey*. arXiv preprint arXiv:2104.00950.

Rosenfeld, A. (2021). *Better metrics for evaluating explainable artificial intelligence*. in *Proceedings of the 20th international conference on autonomous agents and multiagent systems*. IEEE.

Sarkar, A. (2022). A framework for learning ante-hoc explainable models via concepts. *Proceedings of the IEEE/CVF Conference on Computer Vision and Pattern Recognition*. IEEE. 10.1109/CVPR52688.2022.01004

Sofianidis, G. (2021). *A review of explainable artificial intelligence in manufacturing*. Trusted Artificial Intelligence in Manufacturing.

Talaat, F. M., Aljadani, A., Alharthi, B., Farsi, M. A., Badawy, M., & Elhosseini, M. (2023). A Mathematical Model for Customer Segmentation Leveraging Deep Learning, Explainable AI, and RFM Analysis in Targeted Marketing. *Mathematics*, *11*(18), 3930. doi:10.3390/math11183930

Velthoen, J. (2023). Gradient boosting for extreme quantile regression. *Extremes*, 1–29.

Vilone, G., & Longo, L. (2020). *Explainable artificial intelligence: a systematic review.* arXiv preprint arXiv:2006.00093.

Vilone, G., & Longo, L. (2021). Notions of explainability and evaluation approaches for explainable artificial intelligence. *Information Fusion*, *76*, 89–106. doi:10.1016/j.inffus.2021.05.009

Vinogradova, K., Dibrov, A., & Myers, G. (2020). Towards interpretable semantic segmentation via gradient-weighted class activation mapping (student abstract). *Proceedings of the AAAI conference on artificial intelligence.* AAAI. 10.1609/aaai.v34i10.7244

Vitelli, M. (2022). *Safetynet: Safe planning for real-world self-driving vehicles using machine-learned policies. 2022 International Conference on Robotics and Automation (ICRA).* IEEE. 10.1109/ICRA46639.2022.9811576

Wang, C. (2020). Generalization and Visual Comprehension of CNN Models on Chromosome Images. Journal of Physics: Conference Series. IOP Publishing. doi:10.1088/1742-6596/1487/1/012027

Wang, Y., Liu, W., & Liu, X. (2022). Explainable AI techniques with application to NBA gameplay prediction. *Neurocomputing*, *483*, 59–71. doi:10.1016/j.neucom.2022.01.098

Wang, Y., & Wang, X. (2022). "Why Not Other Classes?": Towards Class-Contrastive Back-Propagation Explanations. *Advances in Neural Information Processing Systems*, *35*, 9085–9097.

Wang, Z. J., Turko, R., Shaikh, O., Park, H., Das, N., Hohman, F., Kahng, M., & Polo Chau, D. H. (2020). CNN explainer: Learning convolutional neural networks with interactive visualization. *IEEE Transactions on Visualization and Computer Graphics*, *27*(2), 1396–1406. doi:10.1109/TVCG.2020.3030418 PMID:33048723

Wildi, M., & Misheva, B. H. (2022). *A Time Series Approach to Explainability for Neural Nets with Applications to Risk-Management and Fraud Detection.* arXiv preprint arXiv:2212.02906.

Woschank, M., Rauch, E., & Zsifkovits, H. (2020). A review of further directions for artificial intelligence, machine learning, and deep learning in smart logistics. *Sustainability (Basel)*, *12*(9), 3760. doi:10.3390/su12093760

Xu, D. (2020). Adversarial counterfactual learning and evaluation for recommender system. *Advances in Neural Information Processing Systems*, *33*, 13515–13526.

Yang, C. C. (2022). Explainable artificial intelligence for predictive modeling in healthcare. *Journal of Healthcare Informatics Research*, *6*(2), 228–239. doi:10.1007/s41666-022-00114-1 PMID:35194568

Zhang, T. (2019). ANODEV2: A coupled neural ODE framework. *Advances in Neural Information Processing Systems*, 32.

Zhang, Y. (2021). XAI Evaluation: Evaluating Black-Box Model Explanations for Prediction. In *2021 II International Conference on Neural Networks and Neurotechnologies (NeuroNT)*. IEEE. 10.1109/NeuroNT53022.2021.9472817

Chapter 4
Generative AI From Theory to Model:
Unleashing the Creative Power of Artificial Intelligence

Asim Wadood
https://orcid.org/0000-0003-1115-3988
Kohat University of Science and technology, Pakistan

ABSTRACT

This book chapter provides a comprehensive overview of generative AI and its applications in computer vision. The introduction section elucidates the concept of generative AI and underscores its importance within the realm of artificial intelligence. The chapter also provides a deep dive into the various techniques used in generative AI, such as creative style transfer, forecasting subsequent video frames, enhancing image resolution, enabling interactive image generation, facilitating image-to-image translation, text-to-image synthesis, image inpainting, the generation of innovative animated characters, the construction of 3D models from image, the utilization of the variational autoencoder (VAE) and its various adaptations, the implementation of generative adversarial networks (GANs) and their diverse iterations, as well as the use of transformers and their manifold versions. The chapter also highlights the current limitations and potential future developments in the field.

DOI: 10.4018/979-8-3693-1738-9.ch004

INTRODUCTION

In the past few years, Generative Artificial Intelligence has become more and more seen as a major technology in computer vision. The name "Generative AI" signifies that machine learning algorithms are used to create new data which looks like existing datasets. It can possibly entirely change data production techniques, mill the art of computer vision, and offer new scope for a number of different disciplines all at once. Generative Artificial Intelligence, usually called Generative AI, is where technological innovation begins. This chapter will give you an overview of the field of generative artificial intelligence, describing its basic principles and the use of practical knowledge; we will also touch upon its considerable impact in all walks of life, thus providing an in-depth look into this new kind of science.

The reason of this chapter is to provide a clean, non-technical creation to Generative AI. The chapter has five elements, every exploring an exceptional feature of Generative AI. In Part One, we put forward the idea of Generative AI and its practical applications. Part Two briefly discusses literature on Generative AI. In Part Three, we observe VAEs, and GANs as a technique for enlargement of training datasets. To admire the notable works of Generative AI in numerous fields, the unrelentingly innovative roles played by its creators is delivered to life. This Chapter also examine the electricity of synthetic data and the way it can be used to enhance computer vision. Finally, in Section four, we explore Generative AI's challenges and destiny guidelines in computer vision.

This book chapter's intention is to offer an intensive expertise of Generative AI and its packages in computer vision. The cause of this chapter is to offer the perception of Generative AI and its feasible effect on Computer vision. It also examines numerous Generative AI approaches and their applications in Computer vision, together with artificial records generation, image enhancement, and image-to-image translation. In addition, the chapter digs into the literature perspectives of Generative AI in computer vision, which consist of several Generative AI approaches and their applications. It examines the significance of VAEs and GANs in increasing training datasets, in addition to the issues related to using artificial data in Computer vision.

Overall, the chapter attempts to offer readers with a thorough grasp of generative AI and its packages in pc vision, similarly to its potential effect in the place and the hurdles that need to be triumph over on the way to absolutely comprehend its promise. It is supposed for researchers, practitioners, and college students who are interested by generative AI and its implications for computer vision and distinct domains. In the hastily evolving subject, AI enablement has emerged as a breakthrough with the capacity to convert the manner we generate and eat data. This volume is an introductory adventure into the world of generative AI, exploring key standards and applications and taking a better observe critical generative paradigms—generative

Adversarial networks (GANs) and variational autoencoders (VAEs). Generative AI, at its core, represents a paradigm shift in AI from clearly recognizing styles in cutting-edge facts to actively growing new data styles. Based amongst deep reading and probabilistic reasoning approaches, it harnesses the electricity of neural networks to investigate and reconstruct complicated information classifications.

Within this chapter, we're going to delve into the mechanics of Generative AI, exploring its importance and capacity via the lens of key generative models—VAEs and GANs —which have played instrumental roles in shaping the landscape of records era and manipulation.

Generative AI, a form of artificial intelligence, has the ability to procedure a variety of items inclusive of textual content, photographs, audio, and synthetic facts The latest surge in interest in generative AI may be attributed to person-friendly interfaces a characteristic that has made it clean to create excessive- first-class text, snap shots and video in seconds.

While generative AI isn't a latest innovation, it has made great strides in recent years. Its origins date back to the 1960s, when chatbots first introduced the concept. However, it was not until 2014 that anti-generational networks (GANs), a set of machine learning algorithms, were introduced. Using GANs, the AI-enabled system could create virtual reality images, videos, and audios, including those of individuals themselves.

The ability of generative AI to create lifelike objects has opened up new opportunities, such as improving movie dubbing and enhancing educational content, but it has also raised concerns, including the creation of deepfakes, which it does digitally altered images or videos, potential cyber- Security threats and these threats include fraudulent requests similar to those made by executives.

Two recent developments in generative AI have played an important role in its widespread adoption. These are transformers and enabling transformation language instances. Machine learning, transformers make it easier to train increasingly large images without having to register all the data first. This functionality allows new models to be taught on multiple textures, yielding targeted responses. Furthermore, the converter has unlocked the potential to create regular and contextual content fabric, allowing herbal looking talk between AI structures and those.

Generative AI holds the promise of transforming a wide range of industries from amusement and media to healthcare and finance, however it is vital that the capability risks and moral implications of these technology are considered and ensured act responsibly and transparently.

By employing an adverse procedure, Generative Adversarial Networks (GANs) have transformed the introduction of photographs through obfuscating the distinction between actual and fake information. Through the introduction of sensible-searching representations of everything from human functions to fanciful items, those models recreate seen artwork. GPT-3 is a high example of the strength of generative models in Natural Language Processing (NLP), generating textual output this is each coherent and contextually applicable. This revolutionary technique informs merchandise including chatbots, computerized content material fabric introduction, and personalized hints. By improving information, resolving complicated situations in education datasets, and enhancing model usual performance, generative AI extensively influences computer vision. By creating molecular structures, it hurries up drug improvement inside the medical area and expands therapeutic options. Benefits of anomaly detection the usage of generative fashions' information of not unusual statistics distribution include the potential to discover anomalies throughout a variety of industries. Style transfer, made possible by trends like StyleGAN, transforms artistic expression by enabling creators to combine patterns and recreate creative projects. Generative artificial intelligence (AI) enhances the quality of medical images, facilitates the reconstruction of facts, and enhances scientific model education, all which support precision medicine.

GENERATIVE AI: LITERATURE PERSPECTIVES

Artistic Style Transfer

The Artistic style switch modifies images or movies into a variety of artistic styles while maintaining their essential qualities. It does this by fusing art and technology in a seamless way. In 2017, Fujun Luan et al. Delivered a technique utilizing a convolutional neural network (CNN) to reduce each content material and fashion losses, facilitating the transfer of inventive style at the equal time as maintaining the unique content material. Building on this, Hong Ding et al. In 2022 added a deep attentive style transfer approach, leveraging wavelet decomposition to extract excessive and low-frequency components, ensuing in superior-best consequences.

Tai-Yin Chiu et al. (2022) proposed a concise autoencoder for photorealistic style switch, incorporating block-wise training and pass connections to gain a compact illustration. Xide Xia et al. (2021) took a actual-time method to localized photorealistic video style transfer, employing CNNs for remodelling video frames with a balanced attention on velocity and excellent. In 2021, Ying Qu et al. Advanced a mutual affine-transfer network based totally on non-nearby representations, correctly capturing long-variety dependencies between content material and style images for high-quality style transfers.

Yingxu Qiao et al. (2021) introduced a highly efficient style-corpus restricted learning approach, making use of a group of style images for pinnacle-notch style transfers. Similarly, Narek Tumanyan et al. (2022) proposed a modern-day technique regarding splicing Vision Transformer (ViT) features to seamlessly include creative patterns at the same time as preserving content material. Fangzhou Mu et al. (2021) adopted a unique approach through growing a 3-D image stylization approach making use of a CNN to generate clean perspectives even as maintaining the essence of the subject count. These groundbreaking techniques together push the limits in the realm of inventive style switch, providing a numerous variety of strategies to cater to diverse needs on this charming area.

Predicting the Next Frame in a Video

Recent advancements had been made in video frame prediction, an vital laptop imaginative and prescient venture, with numerous packages in compression, editing, and surveillance. One incredible method proposed with the aid of Q. Wu et al. (2019) makes use of a temporal-spatial interest mechanism and a deep perceptual similarity department. This method efficiently captures dependencies and successfully measures body similarity. Additionally, T. Höppe et al. (2022) have confirmed the effectiveness of diffusion models in video frame prediction. Their method models motion pictures in a Markov way, using a diffusion technique to reap correct body prediction.

A less complicated however powerful approach has been introduced with the aid of Gao et al. (2022). They have superior convolutional neural community (CNN) educated on a big video dataset, showcasing impressive usual overall performance in as it should be predicting the subsequent frame. Moreover, W. Lu et al. (2021) have proposed a way that mixes optical waft estimation with pixel technology. This method estimates pixel motion via optical go with the flow and correctly generates the subsequent frame.

Jasti et al. (2022) provided a completely unique technique for video prediction the usage of learnable movement encodings and a CNN. Their technique correctly predicts pixel motion and yields promising consequences. Likewise, Desai et al. (2022) delivered the ConvLSTM method, making use of a convolutional long short-term memory network to achieve accurate predictions of next frames. Both studies showcase exquisite contributions in advancing the field of video prediction.

Super-Resolution of Images

The method of super-resolution image processing, which complements image decision at the same time as keeping nice details, has emerged as increasingly more popular amongst researchers who're continuously introducing diverse current techniques. In a have a look at carried out by T. Han et al. (2023), deep getting to know became hired using a convolutional neural network (CNN) to successfully convert low-decision pictures into excessive-resolution counterparts. Another method proposed by T. Tirer and R. Giryes (2019) contains image-tailored CNN denoisers, with a focal point on making sure generalizability and inner studying during trying out. K. Zhang et al. (2017) usually concentrated on picture recovery by way of utilizing a deep CNN denoiser to examine prior distributions of denoised images, thereby attaining trendy outcomes. Y. Yuan et al. (2018), however, took an unmanaged approach and applied cycle-in-cycle generative antagonistic networks to map low-decision photos to excessive-resolution ones without counting on supervised information. In 2018, Z. Hui and co-workers added a way that makes use of a records distillation network to acquire speedy and single-image super-resolution. Their approach yielded remarkable results, positioning it as some of the leading procedures in this discipline. These techniques, normally incorporating convolutional neural networks (CNNs) and other profound getting to know techniques, have revolutionized the sphere of great-resolution photo processing via enhancing great and retaining elaborate information.

Interactive Image Generation

Interactive image Generation is a burgeoning discipline in computer vision and gadget getting to know that permits actual-time photo creation primarily based on consumer enter, supplying a fascinating and immersive revel in. Various methodologies leverage generative opposed networks (GANs), scene graphs, and text-based totally manipulation. Early works by way of Zhu et al. (2016) added generative visual manipulation at the herbal photo manifold, retaining the natural appearance of snap shots the usage of GANs and nonlinear optimization. Mittal et al. (2019) prolonged this concept with the aid of using scene graphs to symbolize objects and relationships, enhancing the actual-time picture era. Nallamothu et al. (2023) validated cloud-based deployment of interactive image technology the usage of Cycle GAN.

Wang et al. (2022) proposed an interactive image synthesis approach using panoptic layout technology for high-quality images, representing items and relationships in more detail. Zhou et al. (2022) delivered TiGAN, a text-based totally approach permitting photo generation and manipulation via herbal language queries. Despite promising advancements, demanding situations in processing pace, image excellent, and consumer control persist. Efficient algorithms and specialised hardware, like GPUs, improve processing instances, as validated by Wang et al. (2022). Advanced deep getting to know techniques, together with those used by Zhou et al. (2022), can beautify photo excellent. Researchers are exploring progressed person interfaces and interactions, incorporating techniques like scene graphs, digital reality (VR), and augmented reality (AR) for extra immersive reviews.

Image-to-Image Translation

Image-to- Image translation, a critical mission in computer vision, involves reworking Image from one area to any other at the same time as keeping their content and shape. This flexible task reveals packages in fields like remedy, leisure, and artwork, with amazing development carried out thru various strategies.

Dualgan employs unsupervised dual gaining knowledge of, employing GANs to transform pictures among domains and combining their outputs. Spatial Attention GAN (Spa-GAN) complements pictures best by using the usage of interest maps to awareness on regions within the input image and generate the output photograph. Branch-GAN makes use of a single encoder and twin decoders to switch pics among domain names, splitting the input into branches and the use of specific decoders to generate output snap shots. -Swin Transformer-based GAN, a current improvement, objectives multi-modal scientific image translation by means of making use of the Swin Transformer neural community architecture. InstaFormer, any other latest method, leverages transformers for instance-conscious photograph-to-photograph translation, studying instance-particular capabilities from enter snap shots and generating the output picture. Ittr, another latest approach, uses transformers for unpaired photograph-to-image translation, learning the mapping among input and output domains without the need for paired data.

Challenges encompass the dearth of paired education information, frequently necessitating unsupervised or self-supervised studying to map source and target domains without paired information. Preserving the content and structure throughout translation is every other mission, with some techniques employing interest mechanisms to make sure semantic consistency.

Text-to-Image Generation

Text-to-image technology is a dynamic location dedicated to improving the fine and creativity of generated snap shots. The venture includes translating textual descriptions into splendid images that faithfully depict the described content fabric. Deep getting to know, Generative Adversarial Networks (GANs), has emerged as an important tool on this method.

Advancements consist of controllable GANs like TextControlGAN proposed via Ku et al. (2023), supplying adjustable controllability degrees at the same time as generating images based totally on textual descriptions.

Transformer models, blanketed into AttnGAN by way of Naveen et al. (2021) and Cogview through Ding et al. (2021), have substantially progressed image exquisite and creativity. However, demanding conditions persist within the loss of specific supervision, range, representativeness, and semantic consistency in generated pix.

Oppenlaander et al. (2022) explored the innovative elements, revealing that while present day fashions generate top notch photos, they often lack the creativity and originality needed for certainly novel and engaging photos. This underscores the demand for similar research in this area.

Addressing the shortage of express supervision is vital, as text-to-photograph generation often is based on single text description, necessitating unsupervised and self-supervised strategies. For range and representativeness, adverse schooling with range loss, brought by Li et al. (2019), and facts augmentation proposed by means of Sawant et al. (2021), make contributions to generating diverse and consultant photographs. Semantic consistency stays a mission, and hostile schooling with semantic loss, as recommended by way of W. Liao et al. (2022), aims to ensure semantically steady images intently akin to the enter textual content.

Inpainting

Image inpainting is an essential method for restoring photographs by using filling in lacking or damaged areas, which include cracks, holes, or noise. It finds programs in photograph recuperation, modifying, and synthesis. Approaches to photograph inpainting encompass pixel-based totally, patch-based totally, and model-primarily based strategies. Pixel-based techniques use surrounding pixels, patch-based methods employ predefined patches, and model-based totally strategies make use of statistical models to finish missing regions.

Optimizing the inpainting masks poses a task on this field. Isogawa et al. (2018) introduced a genetic algorithm-primarily based technique to optimize mask, improving inpainted image excellent. Spatio-temporal consistent depth-picture-based totally rendering (STC-DIBR) is every other technique. Muddala et al. (2016) leveraged layered depth photos and inpainting for STC-DIBR, which preserves intensity data. Learning invariant representation through unsupervised photograph healing is every other technique. Du et al. (2020) applied a convolutional neural network (CNN) to research invariant representations at the same time as preserving picture structure and texture. Partial convolutions are precious for irregular hole inpainting. Liu et al. (2018) proposed a method that efficiently fills holes at the same time as keeping texture and shape.

Contextual residual aggregation is good for ultra-high-resolution picture inpainting. Yi et al. (2020) hired this technique to fill missing areas at the same time as keeping photo information and textures. Improved photo great algorithms enhance exemplar-based inpainting. Abdulla and Ahmed (2021) used a complicated photograph best algorithm to enhance inpainted photograph excellent compared to conventional techniques. Multi-scale photo contextual interest getting to know is every other powerful technique. Wang et al. (2019) applied this approach to fill lacking regions at the equal time as maintaining image information and textures. Unsupervised pass-space translation additionally proves useful for picture inpainting. Zhao et al. (2020) employed this technique to fill lacking areas even as retaining picture form and texture.

3D Models From Photos

Recent progress in deep mastering has made it feasible to create 3-d models from pics, presenting diverse packages. Chen et al. (2018) used CNN to assume 3-D shapes from unmarried images, even as Ramakrishna et al. (2018) hired a deep CNN and GAN for practical 3-d models. Liu et al. (2018) proposed a technique for the usage of deep CNN and submit-processing for 3-D form reconstruction.

These breakthroughs locate software in computer photos, robotics, and digital fact. Ongoing research, exemplified via manner of Zhao's artwork on immoderate-precision 3-D models for gaming, highlights the numerous functionalities of 3-d fashions from images. Challenges, inclusive of computational complexity, underscore the importance of destiny studies in improving accuracy, developing green algorithms, and addressing privacy troubles associated with personal snap shots.

An exciting road of exploration includes the use of generative fashions like GANs for generating various data beyond 3-D models from photographs, impacting fields alongside computer vision, natural language processing, and multimedia assessment.

GENERATIVE AI: MODEL PERSPECTIVES

Variational Autoencoder (VAE)

Variational Autoencoders, normally called VAEs, constitute a good-sized milestone within the area of deep generative modeling. Introduced through Kingma and Welling in 2013, VAEs have revolutionized the way we method unsupervised studying, records era, and latent variable modeling. In this complete exploration, we will delve into VAEs, starting with an overview of their structure and concepts. We will then delve into the internal workings, the mathematical formula in the back of VAEs, the troubles they aim to resolve, and how they tackle these demanding situations.

Variational Autoencoders belong to the circle of relatives of autoencoders, a category of neural community architectures used for unsupervised gaining knowledge of. Autoencoders intention to learn a compact illustration of enter records, allowing for green encoding and deciphering. VAEs, but introduce a probabilistic framework into this procedure, allowing them to model information in a extra generative and interpretable way.

A standard VAE accommodates two foremost components: an encoder and a decoder. The encoder takes input data and maps it to a chance distribution in a decrease-dimensional latent area. The decoder, then again, generates facts samples from those latent area representations. The center innovation of VAEs is their capacity to not best examine significant representations however additionally generate new data points that are consistent with the data distribution they had been trained on.

1. 1. **Encoding**: VAEs begin by encoding the enter data into a probabilistic distribution. This is carried out via the encoder community, which maps the input records to the latent area. The encoder normally outputs two vectors: the mean (μ) and the log of the variance ($\log(\sigma^2)$) of the latent distribution. These vectors define a Gaussian distribution inside the latent area. The encoder takes the input information x and maps it to the latent area with a Gaussian distribution parameterized by using μ and $\log(\sigma^2)$. The sampled latent variable z is given by way of:

$$z = \mu + \varepsilon^* \sigma,$$

where ε is a random vector sampled from a standard Gaussian distribution.

2. **Sampling:** The next step entails sampling from the latent area distribution. To do that, a random vector ε is sampled from a popular Gaussian distribution (imply = zero, variance = one). The sampled ε is then used to perturb the imply and variance of the latent distribution, producing a pattern z inside the latent space.
3. 3. **Decoding**: Once a pattern z inside the latent area is generated, the decoder network takes this representation and attempts to reconstruct the unique records point. The decoder's output is a probabilistic distribution over the data space, which can be used to generate new facts points. The decoder takes the latent variable z and maps it to the records space with a distribution parameterized with the aid of θ. This distribution is often selected to be a multivariate Gaussian. The likelihood time period measures the reconstruction blunders:

$$p(x|z) = N(x|\ \mu\_reconstructed,\ \Sigma\_reconstructed),$$

where μ_reconstructed and Σ_reconstructed are the mean and covariance matrix of the reconstructed data point x.

4. **Training**: The objective during training is to limit the reconstruction mistakes (how well the decoder reconstructs the input data) and regularize the latent area through aligning it with a standard Gaussian distribution. The loss function combines the reconstruction errors and the Kullback-Leibler (KL) divergence, which measures the distinction among the learned distribution inside the latent area and the usual Gaussian distribution.
5. 5. **Objective Function**: The objective function in VAEs is composed of terms. The first term is the reconstruction loss, which measures how nicely the model reconstructs the data. The 2nd term is the KL divergence, which inspires the learned latent distribution to be close to a standard Gaussian distribution. The blended loss characteristic is:

$$L(\theta,\varphi) = -E[logp(x \mid z)] + KL(q(z \mid x) \,||\, p(z)),$$

where θ represents the decoder parameters, φ represents the encoder parameters, and q(z|x) is the encoder's distribution in the latent space.

Figure 1. Source: Variational autoencoder architecture

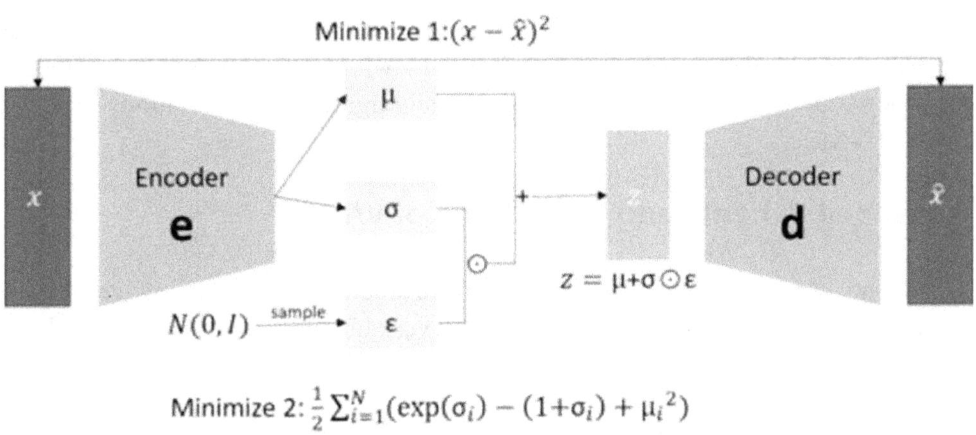

Variational Autoencoders (VAEs) excel in records compression by way of lowering high-dimensional records right into a lower-dimensional latent area, treasured for duties like records storage and transmission. With a generative thing, VAEs can synthesize new records factors consistent with the trained distribution, beneficial for augmentation. They provide an established and interpretable latent space, permitting meaningful manipulation of facts attributes. The inclusion of the KL divergence time period within the loss characteristic acts as regularization, guiding latent variables to follow a easy distribution and stopping overfitting. Moreover, VAEs offer uncertainty estimation, essential for programs where expertise version confidence is crucial. VAEs address challenges through a completely unique mixture of probabilistic modeling and neural networks, representing the latent area as a chance distribution and permitting herbal modeling of uncertainty. The generative functionality arises from the decoder sampling from the learned latent area distribution, beneficial in obligations like photo technology. VAEs encourage an interpretable latent area by means of selling the discovered distribution to follow a popular Gaussian, facilitating disentanglement for separate control of features. The KL divergence term in the loss function serves as regularization, forcing the latent distribution to approximate a standard Gaussian and preventing overfitting. Additionally, VAEs provide uncertainty estimation via the variance within the latent space, presenting valuable insights in selection-making programs.

Variational Autoencoders (VAEs) have witnessed great improvements and extensions that cater to various software areas and deal with unique challenges. In this complete exploration, we can delve into diverse VAE variants, every designed with features to address unique problems. We will provide a top-level view of each variation, provide an explanation for how they work, present the mathematical formulation behind them, discuss the troubles they intention to solve, and elucidate how they cope with those challenges even as highlighting their variations from the original VAE.

Advanced Variants and Extensions of VAEs

Variational Autoencoders (VAEs) were instrumental in advancing generative modeling, unsupervised mastering, and latent variable modeling. Researchers have advanced several noteworthy variations and extensions of VAEs to cater to unique challenges and diverse packages.

Conditional VAE (CVAE), delivered with the aid of Sohn et al. In 2015, stands out for extending the classic VAE to facilitate conditional data technology. Unlike traditional VAEs, CVAE consists of conditional information into each the encoder and decoder additives. This enhancement proves valuable for obligations in which facts generation relies upon on precise conditions or labels.

Semi-Supervised VAE (SS-VAE), provided by Kingma et al. In 2014, addresses semi-supervised getting to know via seamlessly integrating categorized data into the education manner. By aligning representations with supplied labels, SS-VAE optimizes version performance, especially in situations with restrained categorized records.

Ladder VAE (L-VAE), an introduction of Sohn et al. In 2015, combines VAE with ladder networks to elevate facts pleasant and function mastering. Notable for integrating auxiliary supervised decoders and classifiers, L-VAE contributes to a comprehensive loss characteristic for each supervised and unsupervised mastering, distinguishing itself from conventional VAEs.

Hierarchical Variational Autoencoder (HVAE), proposed by Kim et al. In 2018, introduces a multi-degree hierarchical structure of latent variables. This layout accommodates data with varying complexity, permitting the version to seize and generate data at multiple levels of abstraction. HVAE finds suitability in duties requiring multi-scale facts technology.

Beta-VAE, delivered with the aid of Higgins et al. In 2017, extends the VAE framework by introducing a hyperparameter, beta, imparting tunable manage over the alternate-off between disentangled representations and reconstruction exceptional. The incorporation of beta into the loss function allows for a nuanced balance among disentanglement and reconstruction satisfactory within the latent space.

InfoVAE, proposed by way of Zhao et al. In 2017, specializes in maximizing mutual information among latent variables and records to achieve disentangled representations. Through mutual information maximization in the loss characteristic, InfoVAE promotes the gaining knowledge of of informative and disentangled representations.

Adversarial Variational Bayes (AVB), introduced forward with the aid of Mescheder et al. In 2017, merges VAE with hostile schooling to beautify the modeling of records distributions. This introduction of hostile additives, consisting of an encoder network and a discriminator, ambitions to enhance the alignment between the latent space distribution and the true data distribution.

Sliced Wasserstein Autoencoder (SWAE), as presented through Rosca et al. In 2017, consists of Wasserstein distance into VAEs to beautify the nice of latent area representations. SWAE tackles the project of improving illustration best by means of guiding the found out latent distribution to align extra closely with a reference distribution.

Variational Inference for Neural Dialogue Systems (VNDS-VAE) represents a category of fashions applying VAE principles to herbal language processing responsibilities inclusive of talk era and textual content summarization. It adapts VAE to beautify overall performance in communication structures and related NLP obligations without essentially altering the VAE framework.

Recurrent Variational Autoencoder (RVAE), tailor-made for sequential records, contains recurrent neural networks to model and generate sequences efficaciously. The integration of RNNs allows RVAE to capture and generate sequential facts, making it suitable for applications like language modeling and time collection prediction.

Scalable Variational Inference for Dynamical Systems (SVAE-DS), added with the aid of Johnson et al. In 2016, extends VAEs to deal with dynamic and time-series facts. By incorporating specialized strategies to seize temporal dependencies within the records, SVAE-DS proves well-appropriate for programs in finance, robotics, and ecology.

Semi-Supervised Conditional VAE (SSC-VAE) emerges as a hybrid model extending CVAEs to deal with eventualities with each categorized and unlabeled data. By combining outside conditioning with the usage of categorized data, SSC-VAE will become appropriate for semi-supervised mastering tasks related to each fact type.

In conclusion, those superior Variational Autoencoder editions appreciably develop the capabilities of the authentic VAE framework. They address a wide variety of challenges and cater to diverse application domains, offering specialized answers for tasks consisting of conditional facts technology, semi-supervised learning, disentangled representations, and modeling sequential and dynamic data. The various mathematical formulations and specific running standards empower researchers and practitioners in various fields.

GENERATIVE ADVERSARIAL NETWORKS

Generative Adversarial Networks, or GANs, were instrumental in advancing the sphere of generative AI. GANs are essentially composed of neural networks: a generator and a discriminator. The generator creates data, while the discriminator evaluates it for authenticity. This adverse method ends in the era of enormously sensible facts, resulting in numerous packages across exceptional domains.

In the fast-paced international of deep getting to know and synthetic intelligence, the Vanilla GAN, or Generative Adversarial Network, stands as a seminal milestone. Introduced by way of Ian Goodfellow and his colleagues in 2014, the Vanilla GAN laid the foundation for plenty next advances in the area of generative modeling, revolutionizing the manner we approach responsibilities including photograph era, data synthesis, and more. In this comprehensive exploration, we are able to delve into the core principles, operating method, and the impact of the Vanilla GAN on the realm of synthetic intelligence.

Generative Adversarial Networks, or GANs, are a class of deep mastering fashions designed to generate facts like a given dataset. Unlike conventional models that rely on a predefined set of regulations or probabilistic distributions, GANs learn how to generate data via a dynamic and competitive manner. The Vanilla GAN is the authentic GAN structure that added this idea, and it remains a critical part of the AI panorama.

At its middle, a GAN includes two neural networks: the generator and the discriminator. These networks are adversaries in a -participant minimax game. The generator targets to create information this is indistinguishable from actual data, at the same time as the discriminator objectives to differentiate among real and generated facts. This dynamic interaction ends in an equilibrium, where the generator will become talented at generating sensible information, and the discriminator becomes equally adept at telling actual from fake.

The Vanilla GAN architecture is deceptively simple, yet its beauty lies in its inherent complexity. Let's dive into the middle components of this structure:

The generator community, typically a deep neural community, takes random noise as input and produces data samples. Its number one objective is to learn a mapping characteristic from random noise to information that captures the underlying shape and information of the real facts. The generator's output is generated data, which may be images, text, or any other information type, depending on the precise software.

The discriminator community, also a neural community, evaluates the authenticity of the records it gets. It takes enter both facts samples from the dataset and fake records samples generated by the generator. The discriminator's goal is to differentiate between actual and generated data, assigning a chance that a given pattern is actual. If the discriminator gets a really perfect fake, it has to assign a chance close to 0.5, because it has to be unsure approximately the sample's authenticity.

Figure 2. Source: Generative adversarial nets architecture

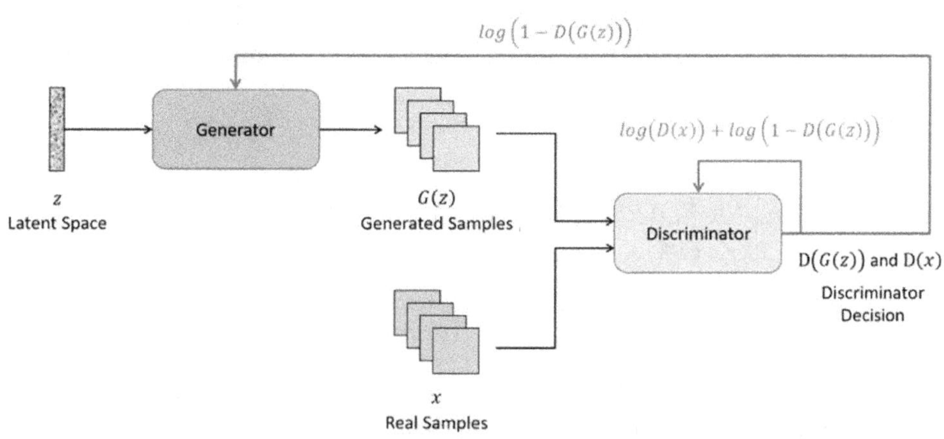

Problem Formulation

The primary objective of a Generative Adversarial Network (GAN) is to examine a generator characteristic (G) that could produce artificial information this is indistinguishable from real information. GANs acquire this by framing the trouble as a minimax recreation among neural networks: the generator (G) and the discriminator (D).

1. 1. **Generator (G):** The generator maps random noise samples (z) to synthetic data samples (G(z)). Mathematically, we can represent this as:

$G: z \rightarrow G(z)$

Where G(z) represents the generated data.

2. 2. **Discriminator (D):** The discriminator takes data samples (x) as input and produces a probability score (D(x)) that the input is real (as opposed to synthetic). Mathematically, this can be written as:

$D: x \rightarrow D(x)$

Where D(x) represents the probability that x is real data.

The adversarial objective can be formulated as follows:

Given a dataset of real data samples $\{x_1, x_2, ..., x_n\}$ and random noise samples $\{z_1, z_2, ..., z_m\}$, we want to find the generator function G that minimizes the following objective:

Minimize G:

$$argmin\_G\left[E\left[log\left(D(x)\right)\right]\right]+E\left[log\left(1-D\left(G\left(z\right)\right)\right)\right]$$

Where:

- E[log(D(x))] represents the expectation (average) of the logarithm of the discriminator's output when fed with real data.
- E[log(1 - D(G(z)))] represents the expectation of the logarithm of the discriminator's output when fed with generated data.
- D(x) is the probability that x is real data.

- D(G(z)) is the probability that G(z) is real data.
- Generator G tries to minimize this loss by generating data that maximizes D's probability for generated data.
- Discriminator D tries to maximize this loss by distinguishing real from generated data.

This minimax formulation captures the competitive nature of GANs. The generator and discriminator are in a constant battle, where the generator aims to produce data that is as convincing as possible, while the discriminator strives to differentiate between real and fake data. Equilibrium is achieved when the generator produces data that is indistinguishable from real data, and the discriminator becomes uncertain when classifying.

Objective Function

The coronary heart of the GAN structure is the antagonistic training technique. GANs use an objective characteristic referred to as adverse loss, which quantifies the competition between the generator and the discriminator. The opposed loss can be formulated as follows:

$$L\_adv(G,D) = E\left[log\left(D(x)\right)\right] + E\left[log\left(1 - D\left(G(z)\right)\right)\right]$$

Here, G represents the generator, D represents the discriminator, x represents real data samples, and z represents the random noise input to the generator. The generator goals to decrease this loss, at the same time as the discriminator pursuits to maximize it. The opposed loss encourages the generator to supply facts that are tough for the discriminator to distinguish from real data.

Training Process

The training manner of a Vanilla GAN includes alternating updates among the generator and the discriminator. Initially, both networks are untrained, and the generator produces random noise. As education progresses, the generator becomes better at generating data, and the discriminator will become more adept at distinguishing actual from fake. The networks engage in a continuous comments loop, pushing each other to improve their performance.

In each training iteration:

1. The discriminator is trained on a batch of real and fake information samples. It updates its weights to better distinguish between the two.
2. The generator is trained by passing its generated samples through the discriminator and updating its weights to provide greater convincing information.

This iterative manner continues until the generator produces data that are almost indistinguishable from actual data, and the discriminator turns into as uncertain as viable while classifying real and fake data.

Challenges and Improvements

The Vanilla GAN, even though groundbreaking, faces numerous challenges and obstacles. Mode falls apart is a notable trouble where the generator produces a restricted set of samples repeatedly, ignoring the range in the schooling records. This can happen if the generator finds it easier to trick the discriminator with a small set of replicable samples. Training instability is some other undertaking, as locating the proper balance between generator and discriminator updates is difficult, main to oscillations between dominance states. Vanishing gradients may arise when the generator produces low-first-rate samples easily diagnosed as fake by using the discriminator, resulting in weak gradient signals at some stage in training. This makes it hard for the generator to examine effectively. Additionally, hyperparameter sensitivity poses a complicated task in GAN schooling, requiring careful tuning of factors which include gaining knowledge of charges, community architectures, and loss functions for a success schooling.

To address the ones demanding situations, numerous enhancements and variations of the Vanilla GAN structure had been proposed. Some of the most fantastic improvements embody:

Advanced Variants and Extensions of GANs

Conditional Generative Adversarial Networks (cGANs) marked a groundbreaking evolution in generative modeling in 2014, introducing conditioning to guide turbines. By responding to particular inputs, such as superb labels or textual descriptions, cGANs excel in responsibilities like picture-to-photo translation and fashion transfer. Overcoming determinism problems of vanilla GANs, they produce a couple of potential outputs for a given scenario, with packages beginning from entertainment to healthcare.

Wasserstein Generative Adversarial Networks (WGANs), introduced in 2017, revolutionized generative modeling through addressing persistent issues in vanilla GANs. WGANs address instability, mode collapse, vanishing gradients, and loss saturation in the course of training. Employing the Wasserstein distance as a loss characteristic ensures non-stop gradients for balance, encouraging Lipschitz continuity inside the discriminator to save you vanishing/exploding gradients. This leap forward extends to improving various GAN variants, making WGANs a sizable development in generative modeling.

InfoGAN, added in 2016, extends the traditional GAN framework to find out and manage disentangled records representations. By maximizing mutual data between a subset of the generator's latent variables and the generated records, InfoGAN promotes the gaining knowledge of of disentangled representations. This innovative technique enhances interpretability and allows greater managed, informative, and effective generative modeling.

Deep Convolutional Generative Adversarial Networks (DCGAN), added in 2015, constitute a big evolution from the authentic GAN structure, specializing in first-rate photo era. With features like convolutional architectures, stride and padding strategies, batch normalization, and transposed convolutions for up-sampling, DCGANs mitigate mode disintegrate and deal with stability troubles, making them a sizable improve in generative modeling for photograph synthesis and style switch.

Boundary-Seeking Generative Adversarial Networks (BGAN), added in 2017, present a exceptional approach to generative modeling by focusing on mastering the decision boundary that separates actual and generated information. Shifting the point of interest from information technology to understanding the decision boundary complements realism and generalization, making BGAN a substantial development.

Least Squares Generative Adversarial Networks (LSGAN), introduced in 2017, emphasize the least-squares loss feature, marking a big advancement in generative modeling. This novel loss enhances schooling stability, promotes fantastic records era, and mitigates mode fall apart dangers, providing a more strong and extremely good opportunity.

Cycle Generative Adversarial Networks (CycleGAN), delivered in 2017, revolutionize photo translation in eventualities missing direct mappings between supply and goal domain names. Tailored for unsupervised photograph-to-picture translation, CycleGAN excels in unpaired settings where traditional supervised methods falter, making it a groundbreaking answer for versatile picture translation duties.

Progressive GAN (ProGAN), added in 2017, redefines high-resolution image technology through its progressive schooling procedure. Gradually growing photograph resolution throughout training mitigates mode collapse, stabilizes schooling, and allows the era of notable, distinct photos, revolutionizing generative modeling requirements.

Relativistic GAN (RGAN), supplied in 2018, introduces a relativistic discriminator to improve GAN education via assessing the realism of both real and generated facts.

This nuanced feedback sign enhances the quality of generated records, addressing training instability and mode disintegrate.

StyleGAN, brought in 2018, and its successor, StyleGAN2, revolutionize generative modeling through characteristic control. Enabling precise manipulation of photograph elements for customizable outputs, StyleGAN and StyleGAN2 provide manage over specific attributes, improving interpretability, and excelling in characteristic manipulation.

BigGAN, introduced in 2018, achieves extraordinary, excessive-decision image generation via a complex architecture. Leveraging more than one generator and discriminator blocks, BigGAN excels in growing special photos, offering versatility in photo synthesis.

Self-Attention GAN (SAGAN), offered in 2018, elevates photo satisfactory the use of self-interest mechanisms. By shooting long-range dependencies, SAGAN produces realistic and contextually accurate photographs, addressing challenges in photo generation.

Adversarially Learned Inference (ALI), added in 2018, bridges the distance between generative modeling and inference. Jointly learning a shared latent illustration for data, ALI simplifies the discovery of meaningful features, enhancing interpretability and usability in generative modeling and inference.

In precis, the array of superior GAN editions provided right here represents a transformative evolution in generative modeling. From Conditional GANs supplying versatile conditioning to Wasserstein GANs ensuring balance, each variation addresses precise demanding situations. InfoGAN discovers disentangled representations, DCGAN specializes in first-rate photographs, and CycleGAN pioneers unsupervised translation. Progressive GANs redefine high-decision technology, StyleGAN fashions offer characteristic control, and BigGAN excels in excessive-decision synthesis. These innovations together cope with barriers, enhance interpretability, and offer extraordinary manage, marking a profound shift in generative version talents with broad packages across industries.

CHALLENGES AND FUTURE DIRECTIONS

Generative AI in computer vision has made terrific strides, but it is not without its set of limitations, ethical concerns, and privacy issues. In this phase, we delve into the challenges confronted with the aid of generative AI discover the moral implications, and peer into the promising destiny traits and instructions that this dynamic subject is likely to take.

Limitations and Challenges of Generative AI in Computer Vision

Generative AI in computer vision has carried out brilliant progress, but it's miles crucial to well known the constraints and demanding situations that persist. These challenges consist of:

1. Quality and Realism: While generative models have advanced over the years, generating remarkable, photorealistic pictures consistently remains a mission.
2. Data Scarcity: The reliance on large datasets is a bottleneck for many programs, especially in medical imaging, where collecting data is hard work-extensive and might compromise patient privacy.
3. Interpretable Models: Many generative fashions, in particular deep neural networks, lack interpretability. Understanding why a version generates a specific picture can be challenging.
4. Resource Intensiveness: Training present day generative models often calls for extensive computational sources, making them inaccessible to smaller research businesses.
5. Mode Collapse: GANs can be bothered by mode fall apart, in which they generate a limited set of similar pics, failing to capture the total diversity of the training data.
6. Generalization: Generative models occasionally warfare to generalize to novel situations and might generate unexpected, unrealistic outcomes.
7. Privacy Concerns: Generating models like photos and movement pix will growth troubles approximately privacy and capability misuse, mainly in deepfake creation.
8. Robustness: Ensuring the robustness of generative models in opposition to negative attacks is an ongoing assignment.

Future Trends and Directions in Generative AI and Computer Vision

There is a lot of potential for generative AI internal computer vision to bring about revolutionary changes in the future. Scholars are investigating a wide range of exciting instructions, such as enhancements to generative models to continuously embellish the realism of created content material, so reducing the gap between real and fake data. Additionally, efforts are being made to lessen the reliance on huge training datasets through the implementation of few-shot or one-shot gaining knowledge of techniques, making generative AI greater on hand. Researchers are actively engaged in enhancing the interpretability and controllability of generative fashions.

Cross-modal technology, concerning the era of text from image or vice versa, holds promise for numerous applications. The improvement of generative fashions capable of chronic mastering, adapting to changing facts distributions, is likewise underway. Initiatives to set up moral tips and regulatory frameworks are being pursued to ensure the responsible use of generative AI. Collaborative endeavors among human beings and generative AI for creative pursuits, layout, and problem-fixing are predicted to develop. Furthermore, the capability effect of generative AI on healthcare imaging, encompassing disorder detection and drug discovery, is an extremely good area of exploration. As generative AI in pc vision continues to progress, these challenges and destiny trends will form it's had an impact on technology, society, and the ethical considerations surrounding its deployment.

CONCLUSION

Generative AI holds pivotal importance, offering multifaceted packages throughout various domains, from healthcare to art, and shaping the landscape of AI-driven visual content material advent. As the demand for knowledge and generating visible statistics continues to surge, generative fashions like GANs and VAEs are principal to progress in this subject, permitting duties, which includes generation of the medical picture and records augmentation at the same time as saving time and assets. We strongly recommend for ongoing exploration, together with the development of extra efficient architectures, moral issues, and integration into actual-world programs, as this dynamic subject maintains to conform with limitless possibilities and prospects for innovation and impact.

REFERENCES

Abdulla, A. A., & Ahmed, M. W. (2021). An improved image quality algorithm for exemplar-based image inpainting. *Multimedia Tools and Applications*, *80*(9), 13143–13156. doi:10.1007/s11042-020-10414-6

Adnan, M., Alarood, A. A. S., Uddin, M. I., & ur Rehman, I. (2022). Utilizing grid search cross-validation with adaptive boosting for augmenting performance of machine learning models. *PeerJ. Computer Science*, *8*, e803. doi:10.7717/peerj-cs.803 PMID:35494796

Ali, S., Khan, A., Gul, M. A., Uddin, M. I., Ali Shah, S. A., Ahmad, S., Al Firdausi, M. D., & Zaindin, M. (2020). Summarizing Online Movie Reviews: A Machine Learning Approach to Big Data Analytics. *Scientific Programming*, *2020*, 5812715.

Amin, S., Uddin, M. I., Zeb, M. A., Alarood, A. A., Mahmoud, M., & Alkinani, M. H. (2020). Detecting Dengue/Flu Infections Based on Tweets Using LSTM and Word Embedding. *IEEE Access : Practical Innovations, Open Solutions*, *8*, 189054–189068. doi:10.1109/ACCESS.2020.3031174

Aziz, F., Ahmad, T., Malik, A. H., Uddin, M. I., Ahmad, S., & Sharaf, M. (2020). Reversible data hiding techniques with high message embedding capacity in images. *PLoS One*, *15*(5), e0231602. doi:10.1371/journal.pone.0231602 PMID:32469877

Aziz, F., Gul, H., Uddin, I., & Gkoutos, G. V. (2020). Path-based extensions of local link prediction methods for complex networks. *Scientific Reports*, *10*(1), 19848. doi:10.1038/s41598-020-76860-2 PMID:33199838

Chen, S. X., Liu, H. Q., & Lin, Y. Q. (2018). Deep Learning for 3D Shape Prediction from a Single Image. In *Proceedings of the IEEE Conference on Computer Vision and Pattern Recognition* (pp. 7847-7856). IEEE.

Chiu, T.-Y., & Gurari, D. (2022). PhotoWCT2: Compact Autoencoder for Photorealistic Style Transfer Resulting from Blockwise Training and Skip Connections of High-Frequency Residuals. *In Proceedings of the IEEE/CVF Winter Conference on Applications of Computer Vision,* (pp. 2868-2877). IEEE. 10.1109/WACV51458.2022.00303

Delanoy, J., Aubry, M., Isola, P., Efros, A. A., & Bousseau, A. (2018). 3D Sketching using Multi-View Deep Volumetric Prediction. In *Proceedings of the ACM Conference on Computer-Aided Design* (pp. 1-20). ACM. 10.1145/3203197

Desai, P., Sujatha, S., Chakraborty, S., Saurav, S., Bhandari, S., & Sanika, S. (2022). Next frame prediction using ConvLSTM. *Journal of Physics: Conference Series*, *2161*(1), 012024. doi:10.1088/1742-6596/2161/1/012024

Ding, H., Wu, Y., & Wang, L. (2022). Deep attentive style transfer for images with wavelet decomposition. *Information Sciences*, *587*, 63–81. doi:10.1016/j.ins.2021.11.077

Du, W., Chen, H., & Yang, H. (2020). Learning invariant representation for unsupervised image restoration. In *Proceedings of the IEEE/CVF Conference on Computer Vision and Pattern Recognition* (pp. 14483–14492). IEEE. 10.1109/CVPR42600.2020.01449

Emami, H., Aliabadi, M. M., Dong, M., & Chinnam, R. (2020). Spa-GAN: Spatial Attention GAN for image-to-image translation. *IEEE Transactions on Multimedia*.

Fayaz, M., Khan, A., Rahman, J. U., Alharbi, A., Uddin, M. I., & Alouffi, B. (2020). Ensemble Machine Learning Model for Classification of Spam Product Reviews. *Complexity*, *2020*, 1–10. doi:10.1155/2020/8857570

Gao, Z., Tan, C., Wu, L., & Li, S. Z. (2022). Simvp: Simpler yet better video prediction. *In Proceedings of the IEEE/CVF Conference on Computer Vision and Pattern Recognition*, (pp. 3170-3180). IEEE.

Goodfellow, I., Pouget-Abadie, J., Mirza, M., Xu, B., Warde-Farley, D., Ozair, S., Courville, A., & Bengio, Y. (2014). Generative Adversarial Networks. *Advances in Neural Information Processing Systems*, 3.

Han, T., Zhao, L., & Wang, C. (2023). Research on Super-resolution Image Based on Deep Learning. *International Journal of Advanced Network. Monitoring and Controls*, *8*(1), 58–65. doi:10.2478/ijanmc-2023-0046

He, K., Zhang, X., Ren, S., & Sun, J. (2016). Deep Residual Learning for Image Recognition. 2016 *IEEE Conference on Computer Vision and Pattern Recognition (CVPR),* (pp. 770–778). IEEE. 10.1109/CVPR.2016.90

Holden, D., Saito, J., & Komura, T. (2016). A deep learning framework for character motion synthesis and editing. *ACM Transactions on Graphics*, *35*(4), 138. doi:10.1145/2897824.2925975

Hui, Z., Wang, X., & Gao, X. (2018). Fast and accurate single image super resolution via information distillation network. In *Proceedings of the IEEE Conference on Computer Vision and Pattern Recognition,* (pp. 723-731). IEEE. 10.1109/CVPR.2018.00082

Isogawa, M., Mikami, D., Iwai, D., Kimata, H., & Sato, K. (2018). Mask optimization for image inpainting. *IEEE Access : Practical Innovations, Open Solutions*, *6*, 69728–69741. doi:10.1109/ACCESS.2018.2877401

Isola, P., Zhu, J.-Y., Zhou, T., & Efros, A. A. (2017). Image-to-Image Translation with Conditional Adversarial Networks. 2017 *IEEE Conference on Computer Vision and Pattern Recognition (CVPR)*, (pp. 5967–5976). IEEE. 10.1109/CVPR.2017.632

Jasti, R., Jampani, V., Sun, D., & Yang, M.-H. (2022). Multi-Frame Video Prediction with Learnable Motion Encodings. In 2022 *IEEE International Conference on Image Processing (ICIP)*, (pp. 4198-4202). IEEE. 10.1109/ICIP46576.2022.9897483

Khan, M. Q., Shahid, A., Uddin, M. I., Roman, M., Alharbi, A., Alosaimi, W., Almalki, J., & Alshahrani, S. M. (2022). Impact analysis of keyword extraction using contextual word embedding. *PeerJ. Computer Science*, *8*, e967. doi:10.7717/peerj-cs.967 PMID:35721401

Kim, S., Baek, J., Park, J., Kim, G., & Kim, S. (2022). InstaFormer: Instance-aware image-to-image translation with transformer. In *Proceedings of the IEEE/CVF Conference on Computer Vision and Pattern Recognition* (pp. 18321-18331). IEEE.

Ku, H., & Lee, M. (2023). TextControlGAN: Text-to-Image Synthesis with Controllable Generative Adversarial Networks. *Applied Sciences (Basel, Switzerland)*, *13*(8), 5098. doi:10.3390/app13085098

LeCun, Y., Bengio, Y., & Hinton, G. (2015). Deep learning. *Nature*, *521*(7553), 436–444. doi:10.1038/nature14539 PMID:26017442

Lee, S., Ullah, Z., Zeb, A., Ullah, I., Awan, K. M., Saeed, Y., Uddin, M. I., Al-Khasawneh, M. A., Mahmoud, M., & Zareei, M. (2020). Certificateless Proxy Reencryption Scheme (CPRES) Based on Hyperelliptic Curve for Access Control in Content-Centric Network (CCN). *Mobile Information Systems*, *2020*, 4138516.

Li, B., Qi, X., Lukasiewicz, T., & Torr, P. (2019). Controllable Text-to-Image Generation. In Advances in Neural Information Processing Systems, 32.

Li, C., Zia, M. Z., Tran, Q.-H., Yu, X., Hager, G. D., & Chandraker, M. (2017). Deep supervision with shape concepts for occlusion-aware 3D object parsing. In *Proceedings of the IEEE Conference on Computer Vision and Pattern Recognition* (pp. 5884-5893). IEEE. 10.1109/CVPR.2017.49

Li, Y., Tang, S., Zhang, R., Zhang, Y., Li, J., & Yan, S. (2019). Asymmetric GAN for unpaired image-to-image translation. *IEEE Transactions on Image Processing*, *28*(12), 5881–5896. doi:10.1109/TIP.2019.2922854 PMID:31226077

Liao, W., Hu, K., Yang, M. Y., & Rosenhahn, B. (2022). Text to Image Generation with Semantic-Spatial Aware GAN. In *2022 IEEE/CVF Conference on Computer Vision and Pattern Recognition (CVPR)*, (pp. 18166-18175). IEEE. 10.1109/CVPR52688.2022.01765

Liu, G., Reda, F. A., & Shih, K. J. (2018). Image inpainting for irregular holes using partial convolutions. In *Proceedings of the European Conference on Computer Vision (ECCV)* (pp. 85–100). Springer. 10.1007/978-3-030-01252-6_6

Liu, M.-Y., Breuel, T., & Kautz, J. (2017). Unsupervised Image-to-Image Translation Networks. *Proceedings of the 31st International Conference on Neural Information Processing Systems,* (pp. 700–708). Springer.

Liu, Y., Ma, Y., & Wei, Y. (2018). 3D Shape Reconstruction from a Single Image using a Deep Convolutional Neural Network. In *Proceedings of the IEEE Conference on Computer Vision and Pattern Recognition* (pp. 7847-7856). IEEE.

Lu, W., Cui, J., Chang, Y., & Zhang, L. (2021). A Video Prediction Method Based on Optical Flow Estimation and Pixel Generation. *IEEE Access : Practical Innovations, Open Solutions*, *9*, 100395–100406. doi:10.1109/ACCESS.2021.3096788

Luan, F., Chen, T., & Hu, X. (2017). Deep photo style transfer. In *Proceedings of the IEEE Conference on Computer Vision and Pattern Recognition,* (pp. 4990-4998). IEEE.

Lun, Z., Gadelha, M., Kalogerakis, E., Maji, S., & Wang, R. (2017). 3D Shape Reconstruction from Sketches via Multi-view Convolutional Networks. In *2017 IEEE International Conference on 3D Vision (3DV)* (pp. 441-450). IEEE.

Muddala, S. M., Olsson, R., & Sjöström, M. (2016). Spatio-temporal consistent depth-image-based rendering using layered depth image and inpainting. *EURASIP Journal on Image and Video Processing*, *2016*(1), 1–19. doi:10.1186/s13640-016-0109-6

Nallamothu, L. H., Ramisetti, T. P., Mekala, V. K., Aramandla, K., & Duvvada, R. R. (2023). Interactive Image Generation Using Cycle GAN Over AWS Cloud. In S. Shakya, V. E. Balas, & W. Haoxiang (Eds.), *Proceedings of Third International Conference on Sustainable Expert Systems* (pp. 587). Springer, Singapore. 10.1007/978-981-19-7874-6_30

Naveen, S. S., Kiran, M., Indupriya, M., Manikanta, T. S., & Sudeep, P. V. (2021). Transformer models for enhancing AttnGAN based text to image generation. *Image and Vision Computing*, *115*, 104284. doi:10.1016/j.imavis.2021.104284

Nazir, S., Naseem, R., Khan, B., Shah, M. A., Wakil, K., Khan, A., Alosaimi, W., Uddin, M. I., & Alouffi, B. (2020). Performance Assessment of Classification Algorithms on Early Detection of Liver Syndrome. *Journal of Healthcare Engineering*, *2020*, 6680002. PMID:33489060

Niu, C., Li, J., & Xu, K. (2018). Im2Struct: Recovering 3D Shape Structure from a Single RGB Image. In *Proceedings of the IEEE Conference on Computer Vision and Pattern Recognition* (pp. 80-89). IEEE. 10.1109/CVPR.2018.00475

Oppenlaender, J. (2022). The Creativity of Text-to-Image Generation. In *25th International Academic Mindtrek Conference (Academic Mindtrek 2022).* ACM. 10.1145/3569219.3569352

Pang, Y., Lin, J., Qin, T., & Chen, Z. (2021). Image-to-image translation: Methods and applications. *IEEE Transactions on Multimedia*, *24*, 3859–3881. doi:10.1109/TMM.2021.3109419

Qiao, Y., Wu, Y., & Wang, L. (2021). Efficient style-corpus constrained learning for photorealistic style transfer. *IEEE Transactions on Image Processing*, *30*(01), 1–1. doi:10.1109/TIP.2021.3058566 PMID:33617453

Qu, Y., Shao, Z., & Qi, H. (2021). Non-local representation based mutual affine-transfer network for photorealistic stylization. *IEEE Transactions on Pattern Analysis and Machine Intelligence*, *01*(01), 1–1. PMID:34260345

Radford, A., Metz, L., & Chintala, S. (2015). Unsupervised Representation Learning with Deep Convolutional Generative Adversarial Networks. *CoRR,* abs/1511.06434.

Ramakrishna, M. Z., Efros, A. A., & Shechtman, Y. (2018). Photorealistic 3D Modeling from a Single Image using a Deep Convolutional Neural Network. In *Proceedings of the IEEE Conference on Computer Vision and Pattern Recognition* (pp. 7847-7856). IEEE.

Ramzan, S., Iqbal, M. M., & Kalsum, T. (2022). Text-to-Image Generation Using Deep Learning. *Engineering Proceedings*, *20*(1), 16.

Reed, S., Akata, Z., Yan, X., Logeswaran, L., Schiele, B., & Lee, H. (2016, June). Generative Adversarial Text to Image Synthesis. In *International Conference on Machine Learning* (pp. 1060-1069). PMLR.

Sawant, R., Shaikh, A., Sabat, S., & Bhole, V. (2021). Text to Image Generation using GAN. *Proceedings of the International Conference on IoT Based Control Networks & Intelligent Systems - ICICNIS 2021*. SSRN. 10.2139/ssrn.3882570

Susheelkumar, K., Semwal, V., Prasad, S., & Tripathi, R. (2011). Generating 3D Model Using 2D Images of an Object. In *2011 International Conference on Computing Communication and Automation (ICCCA)* (pp. 1-6). IEEE.

Tirer, T., & Giryes, R. (2019). Image restoration by iterative denoising and backward projections. *IEEE Transactions on Image Processing*, *28*(3), 1220–1234. doi:10.1109/TIP.2018.2875569 PMID:30307870

Tirer, T., & Giryes, R. (2019). Super-resolution based on image-adapted CNN denoisers: Incorporating generalization of training data and internal learning in test time. [IEEE]. *Institute of Electrical and Electronics Engineers*, *26*(7), 1080–1084.

Ullah, I., Amin, N. U., Almogren, A., Khan, M. A., Uddin, M. I., & Hua, Q. (2020). A Lightweight and Secured Certificate-Based Proxy Signcryption (CB-PS) Scheme for E-Prescription Systems. *IEEE Access : Practical Innovations, Open Solutions*, *8*, 199197–199212. doi:10.1109/ACCESS.2020.3033758

Vaswani, A., Shazeer, N., Parmar, N., Uszkoreit, J., Jones, L., Gomez, A. N., Kaiser, Ł., & Polosukhin, I. (2017). Attention is All you Need. In I. Guyon, U. V. Luxburg, S. Bengio, H. Wallach, R. Fergus, S. Vishwanathan, & R. Garnett (Eds.), Advances in Neural Information Processing Systems: Vol. 30. *Curran Associates, Inc.*

Volchenkov, D., Mast, N., Khan, M. A., Uddin, M. I., Ali Shah, S. A., Khan, A., Al-Khasawneh, M. A., & Mahmoud, M. (2021). Channel Contention-Based Routing Protocol for Wireless Ad Hoc Networks. *Complexity*, *2021*, 2051796.

Wang, B., Wu, T., Zhu, M., & Du, P. (2022). Interactive image synthesis with panoptic layout generation. In *Proceedings of the IEEE/CVF Conference on Computer Vision and Pattern Recognition* (pp. 7783-7792). IEEE. 10.1109/CVPR52688.2022.00763

Wang, N., Li, J., & Zhang, L. (2019). Musical: Multi-scale image contextual attention learning for inpainting. In *Proceedings of the Twenty-Eighth International Joint Conference on Artificial Intelligence (IJCAI-19)* (pp. 3748–3754). IEEE.10.24963/ijcai.2019/520

Wu, Q., Wang, W., Chen, X., & Li, W. (2019). Video Prediction with Temporal-Spatial Attention Mechanism and Deep Perceptual Similarity Branch. In 2019 *IEEE International Conference on Multimedia and Expo (ICME),* (pp. 1594-1599). IEEE. 10.1109/ICME.2019.00275

Xia, X., Wu, Y., & Wang, L. (2021). Real-time localized photorealistic video style transfer. *In Proceedings of the IEEE/CVF Winter Conference on Applications of Computer Vision,* (pp. 1089-1098). IEEE.

Xiaolin, L., & Yuwei, G. (2020). *Research on Text to Image Based on Generative Adversarial Network.* In 2020 2nd International Conference on Information Technology and Computer Application (ITCA), Guangzhou, China (pp. 330-334). 10.1109/ITCA52113.2020.00077

Yan, S., Wang, C., Chen, W., & Lyu, J. (2022). Swin transformer-based GAN for multi-modal medical image translation. *Frontiers in Oncology*, *12*, 942511. doi:10.3389/fonc.2022.942511 PMID:36003791

Yi, Z., Tang, Q., & Azizi, S. (2020). Contextual residual aggregation for ultra high-resolution image inpainting. In *Proceedings of the IEEE/CVF Conference on Computer Vision and Pattern Recognition* (pp. 7508–7517). IEEE. 10.1109/CVPR42600.2020.00753

Yi, Z., Zhang, H., Tan, P., & Gong, M. (2017). Dualgan: Unsupervised dual learning for image-to-image translation. In *Proceedings of the IEEE International Conference on Computer Vision* (pp. 2849-2857). IEEE. 10.1109/ICCV.2017.310

Yuan, Y., Liu, S., Zhang, J., Zhang, Y., Dong, C., & Lin, L. (2018). Unsupervised image super-resolution using cycle-in-cycle generative adversarial networks. In *2018 IEEE Conference on Computer Vision and Pattern Recognition Workshops*, (pp. 814-823). IEEE. 10.1109/CVPRW.2018.00113

Zhang, H., Xu, T., Li, H., Zhang, S., Wang, X., Huang, X., & Metaxas, D. (2017). StackGAN: Text to Photo-Realistic Image Synthesis with Stacked Generative Adversarial Networks. 2017 *IEEE International Conference on Computer Vision (ICCV),* (pp. 5908–5916). IEEE. 10.1109/ICCV.2017.629

Zhang, K., Zuo, W., Gu, S., & Zhang, L. (2017). Learning deep CNN denoiser prior for image restoration. In *Proceedings of the IEEE Conference on Computer Vision and Pattern Recognition*, (pp. 3929-3938). IEEE. 10.1109/CVPR.2017.300

Zhao, L., Mo, Q., & Lin, S. (2020). Uctgan: Diverse image inpainting based on unsupervised cross-space translation. In *Proceedings of the IEEE/CVF Conference on Computer Vision and Pattern Recognition* (pp. 5741–5750). IEEE. 10.1109/CVPR42600.2020.00578

Zhao, Y. (2022). Deep Learning of 3D High-Precision Model Digital Engraving of Next-Generation Games Based on Artificial Intelligence. *IEEE Access : Practical Innovations, Open Solutions*, *10*, 10976–10984.

Zhou, Y., Zhang, R., Gu, J., Tensmeyer, C., Yu, T., Chen, C., Xu, J., & Sun, T. (2022). TiGAN: Text-Based Interactive Image Generation and Manipulation. *Proceedings of the AAAI Conference on Artificial Intelligence*, *36*(3), 3580–3588. doi:10.1609/aaai.v36i3.20270

Zhou, Y.-F., Jiang, R.-H., Wu, X., He, J.-Y., Weng, S., & Peng, Q. (2019). BranchGAN: Unsupervised mutual image-to-image transfer with a single encoder and dual decoders. *IEEE Transactions on Multimedia*, *21*(12), 3136–3149. doi:10.1109/TMM.2019.2920613

Zhu, J. Y., Krähenbühl, P., Shechtman, E., & Efros, A. A. (2016). Generative visual manipulation on the natural image manifold. In *Proceedings of the 14th European Conference on Computer Vision (ECCV 2016)* (pp. 597-613). Amsterdam, The Netherlands: Springer International Publishing. 10.1007/978-3-319-46454-1_36

Zhu, J.-Y., Park, T., Isola, P., & Efros, A. A. (2017). Unpaired Image-to-Image Translation Using Cycle-Consistent Adversarial Networks. *2017 IEEE International Conference on Computer Vision (ICCV)*, (pp. 2242–2251). IEEE. 10.1109/ICCV.2017.244

Chapter 5
Robust Adversarial Deep Reinforcement Learning

Di Wang
https://orcid.org/0000-0002-7992-7743
University of Illinois at Chicago, USA

ABSTRACT

Deep reinforcement learning has shown remarkable results across various tasks. However, recent studies highlight the susceptibility of DRL to targeted adversarial disruptions. Furthermore, discrepancies between simulated settings and real-world applications often make it challenging to transfer these DRL policies, particularly in situations where safety is essential. Several solutions have been proposed to address these issues to enhance DRL's robustness. This chapter delves into the significance of adversarial attack and defense strategies in machine learning, emphasizing the unique challenges in adversarial DRL settings. It also presents an overview of recent advancements, DRL foundations, adversarial Markov decision process models, and comparisons among different attacks and defenses. The chapter further evaluates the effectiveness of various attacks and the efficacy of multiple defense mechanisms using simulation data, specifically focusing on policy success rates and average rewards. Potential limitations and prospects for future research are also explored.

DOI: 10.4018/979-8-3693-1738-9.ch005

INTRODUCTION

DRL has demonstrated effectiveness in numerous applications such as task scheduling (Wang, 2023a; Wang et al., 2022, 2018), refining manufacturing processes (Wang et al., n.d.; Yun et al., 2023), robotic operations (Wang, 2022), and knowledge reasoning (Wang, 2023b, 2023c). Yet, it's susceptible to targeted disruptions during its learning or evaluation stages (Grosse et al., 2017). The disparity between virtual simulations and the realities of practical scenarios complicates the transfer of these learned strategies. This is even more challenging in critical safety domains like autonomous driving and robot operations (He et al., 2022a, 2022b; Wang et al., 2021). Thus, it is important to improve the robustness of the DRL approaches.

Szegedy et al. (Szegedy et al., 2013) proved the existence of "blind point". Specific input disturbances can mislead the DRL model entirely. Building on this, Papernot et al. (Papernot et al., 2016) designed a framework to understand the potential weak points of a system, comprising both the neural network model and the dataset. Fig. 1 illustrates vulnerable points in machine learning (ML) systems.

Figure 1. Vulnerable points in ML systems

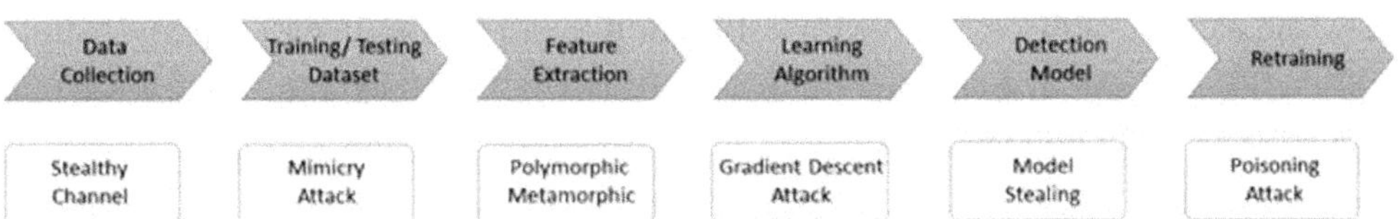

Table 1 lists the common attacking strategies including FGSM, C&W, and PGD. Table 2 lists the common defending strategies including adversarial training, data compression, and gradient masking methods.

Table 1. Adversarial attacking strategies in ML

Methods	Details
FGSM attack	FGSM (Goodfellow et al., 2014) is an attack driven by gradients. Its core action involves determining the model's derivative concerning the input to introduce disturbances.
C&W attack	Carlini & Wagner (CW) attack algorithm (Carlini and Wagner, 2017) optimizes high attack accuracy and low adversarial disturbance at the same time.
PGD	Project Gradient Descent (PGD) (Madry et al., 2017) works by iteratively adjusting a given input to maximize the model's loss function, which represents how wrong the model's predictions are for that input. The "projected" part of PGD means that after each adjustment, the perturbed input is clipped to ensure that it stays within a predefined allowable range.

Table 2. Adversarial defending strategies in ML

Methods	Details
Adversarial training	Adversarial training (Moosavi-Dezfooli et al., 2016) takes a mixed dataset of both adversarial instances and normal instances. However, recent research prove that adversarial-trained model can be fooled again by effective adversarial examples (Sankaranarayanan et al., 2018).
Data compression	Guo et al. and Das et al. (Das et al., 2017; Guo et al., 2017) studied the image JPEG compression effect to mitigate the impact of adversarial images.
Gradient masking	Gradient masking methods (Lyu et al., 2015; Shaham et al., 2018) penalize the loss function's gradient and minimize the loss over adversarial samples.

DRL is the combination of neural networks and reinforcement learning, where neural networks act as estimators for state values or state-action values, making it suitable for complex environments with vast state or action dimensions. The main idea of DRL is to train a smart agent to make temporal decisions while maximizing cumulative rewards over time (Wang, 2023d). The mathematical foundation of DRL is the MDP. As depicted in Fig. 2, an iterative interaction between the agent and its environment is presented. The agent observes the environment's state, then makes a decision. Based on the state transition function, the environment moves to a subsequent state, and gives a estimation score to the agent. Upon training completion, the agent can generate near-optimal results to dynamic and uncertain problems (Wang and Hu, 2023).

Figure 2. The interaction between agent and environment

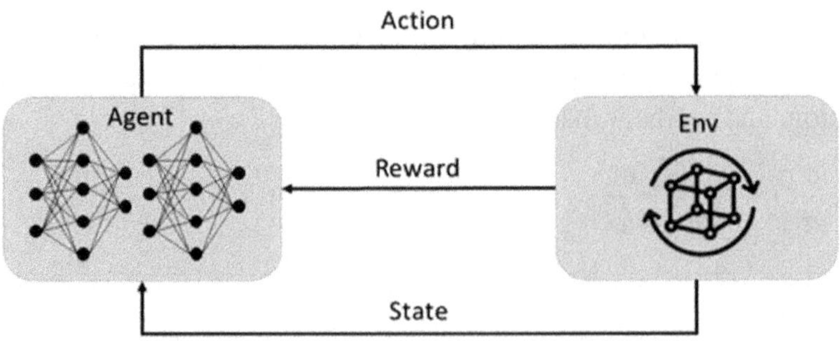

Within the realm of DRL, adversarial attacks come from various forms, classified by their underlying mechanisms. Details are discussed in Section 'RELATED WORK'. These include:

1. Reward-Based Attacks: Attackers can invert the reward scores or change the original reward function with a malicious one.
2. Observation-Based Attacks: Perturbations can be added to the states the agent observes, leading it to act as the attacker desires. Typically, this involves disturbing the agent's image sensors.
3. Action-Based Attacks: Perturbations can be added to the agent's action outputs. This can be accomplished by altering the action space within the training dataset.

This chapter studies the significance of adversarial attacks and defenses strategies in DRL. It also presents an overview of recent works, foundations of DRL, foundations of adversarial MDP models, comparisons among different attacks and defenses, common neural network architectures and standard training procedures. The chapter further evaluates the urgency of various attacks and the efficacy of multiple defense mechanisms using simulation data, specifically focusing on policy success rates and average rewards.

The foundation of this chapter is as follows: Section 'RELATED WORK' presents and categorizes existing works. Section 'FOUNDATION OF ADVERSARIAL ATTACK ON DNN CLASSIFICATION' presents preliminary knowledge about adversarial attack in classification issues. Section 'FOUNDATION OF DRL' presents preliminary knowledge about DRL. Section 'FOUNDATION OF ADVERSARIAL TRAINING' presents typical minmax operations in adversarial training. Section 'CONSTRAINED OBSERVATION-ROBUST MDP' and 'PROBABILISTIC ACTION ROBUST MDP' illustrate two important MDP models in the robust DRL setting. Section 'ROBUST ADVERSARIAL DRL' presents features, neural networks and training procedures of typical attack and defense strategies. Section 'RESULTS' proves the urgency of various attacks and the efficacy of multiple defense mechanisms with 6 OpenAI MuJoCo environments. Section 'DISCUSSION' discusses the simulation results. Section 'LIMITATION' points out the limitations of recent works. Section 'CONCLUSION' presents summary and future works.

RELATED WORK

Adversarial attacks against RL can be categorized test-time attacks and training-time attack(X. Zhang et al., 2020). In test-time attacks settings, the RL policy is pre-trained and fixed. (Huang et al., 2017; Kos and Song, 2017) are among the first to investigate adversarial examples on DRL policies. However, in training-time attacks settings, the policy is modified.

Reward attacks, or reward poisonings, target the reward function in DRL. Huang et al. (Huang and Zhu, 2019) prove that Q-learning algorithms converge under stealthy attacks and bounded falsifications on cost signals. However, their perturbation is a function of state and action. Zhang et al. (X. Zhang et al., 2020) prove such function decreases attack efficiency. Xu et al. (Xu et al., 2022; Xu and Singh, 2023) explore the most efficient reward attacks within computation budgets, including the total amount of the reward perturbation in the training process and the maximal amount of reward perturbation at each step. Cai et al. (Cai et al., 2023) predict the appropriate reward attacking time and sign of perturbation through a deep neural network.

Some attack methods make too many attacks against DRL because they attack the agent at every time step, making most of them ineffective or inefficient. Timed attacks aim at minimizing the agent's reward by only attacking the agent at a small subset of time because the adversarial attacks at different time steps are not equally effective in an episode. Lin et al. (Lin et al., 2017) determine the attack time based on the difference between the maximum Q-value and the minimum Q-value of the state. A generative model predicts the future states while another planning algorithm generates a sequence adversarial example. Similarly, Li et al. (Li et al., 2023) detect the adversarial time by comparing the linear combination of the minimum, maximum and average value of the output action probabilities.

Observation attack is a widely used strategy. Noises are added to the state of DRL. Sun et al. (Sun et al., 2020) Sun et al. (Sun et al., 2020) learn the environment model and select the best adversarial attack on predicted future states. Zhai et al. (Zhai et al., 2022) propose a dissipation-inequation based architectures with three models: a normal agent, an adversarial agent and a Lyapunov network. Specifically, the direction of the adversarial agent's gradient that reduces the performance of the L2 gain is penalized, and the direction of the normal agent's gradient is updated to simultaneously increase the L2 gain. Zhang et al. (H. Zhang et al., 2020) propose a KL-divergence regularizer over normal sampled states and adversarial states. Zhang et al. (H. Zhang et al., 2021) propose an empirical state attacks with LSTM model learnt from historical trajectories.

Action attack inserts perturbation to the action directly. Pinto et al. (Pinto et al., 2017) follow the minmax operation, like the adversarial training approach. Differently, agent's policy is learned first with frozen adversarial policy. Then the adversarial policy is learned with frozen agent's policy. Similarly, Tessler et al. (Tessler et al., 2019) propose a linear combination of an agent policy and an adversarial policy. The agent policy maximizes the return while the adversarial policy minimizes the return.

Single adversary does not consistently yield robustness to dynamics variations under standard parametrizations of the adversary; the resulting policy is highly exploitable by new adversaries. Population attack (Vinitsky et al., 2020) keep a population of adversaries and sample from the population uniformly during training.

Domain randomization and adversarial training are the main methods for robust promotion. In domain randomization, a designer with expertise identifies the components of the model that they are uncertain about. They then construct a set of training environments where the uncertain components are randomized, ensuring that the agent is robust on average to this set. However, this requires careful parametrization of the uncertainty set as well as hand-designing of the environments. Akkaya et al. and Kontes et al. (Akkaya et al., 2019; Kontes et al., 2020) keep changing environment settings to learn general policies. However, improper environmental settings can cause worse performances than the vanilla approach (Vinitsky et al., 2020). Since training of domain randomization is time-consuming and the variation range of the environment needs careful consideration, adversarial training is more often used. Adversarial training is a common method for strengthening robustness in many studies (Bai et al., 2021; Fan and Li, 2021). However, pure adversarial training leads to performance deterioration under normal circumstances or unstable results due to the presence of the adversary. Due to the presence of noise, the trained policy can also make some terrible decisions during the training and testing (Meng et al., 2023). Zhang et al. (H. Zhang et al., 2021) prove that inserting perturbation to the training observation can improve the worst case performances with a conservative policy. Meng et al. (Meng et al., 2023) perturb the observation according to the gradient information of the state for adversarial training. To prevent the agent from making catastrophic decisions, the constrained MDP is introduced. Except adding perturbation in the observation(Rafailov et al., 2021), Zhang et al. (X. Zhang et al., 2021) flip the rewards. Tessler et al. (Tessler et al., 2019) perturbate the generated actions directly.

FOUNDATION OF ADVERSARIAL ATTACK ON DNN CLASSIFICATION

Let x be the input, like images. f is the deep neural network. Adversarial attacks aim to:

$$min_{\delta D} I_{(}x, x+\delta) \quad (1)$$

$$\text{Subject to } f(x) \neq f(x+\delta) \quad (2)$$

where DI refers to the similarity matrix. δ is the perturbation. The goal is to find the minimum perturbation that mislead the classifier outputs.

REINFORCEMENT LEARNING

In DRL, the concept "return" denotes the anticipated aggregated reward starting from a given state, as shown in Eq. (3).

$$R_t^{\gamma} = \sum_{i=t}^{\infty} \gamma^{i-t} r(s_i, a_i), 0 < \gamma < 1 \tag{3}$$

where γ is the discount factor. s_i, a_i are the state and the action at time step t=*i*. r is the reward function.

The value function $V^{\pi}(s)$ is the anticipated return from a state s and a policy π, as Eq. (4). The state-action value function $Q^{\pi}(s,a)$ represents the expected return after executing action a in state s and then following policy π, as Eq. (5). The value function can be calculated by the state-action value function as Eq. (6) (Wang and Hu, 2021).

$$V^{\pi}(s) = \mathbb{E}[\sum_{t=0}^{\infty} \gamma^t r(s_t) \mid \pi, s_0 = s] \tag{4}$$

$$Q^{\pi}(s,a) = \mathbb{E}[\sum_{t=0}^{\infty} \gamma^t r(s_t, a_t) \mid \pi, s_0 = s, a_0 = a] \tag{5}$$

$$V^{\pi}(s) = \max_a Q^{\pi}(s,a) \tag{6}$$

where s_0 and a_0 are the initial state and action, π is the policy.

DQN: The DQN produces Q-values for every potential action. A distinct feature of DQN is its incorporation of a memory buffer to reuse previous experiences. During its training phase, instead of solely relying on the latest experience, the network fetches a variety of past experiences from the buffer. The training procedure can be presented in Eq. (7).

$$Q(s_t, a_t) \leftarrow Q(s_t, a_t) + \alpha \left[r_t + \gamma max_{a'} Q(s_{t+1}, a') - Q(s_t, a_t) \right] \tag{7}$$

where α is the learning rate. The Q network and the target Q network are parameterized by θ and θ', respectively. α' refers to the possible actions at time step t+1.

$$L(\theta_i) = \mathbb{E}_{(s_t, a_t, r_t, s_{t+1})\sim D}[(r_t + \gamma max_{a'} Q_{\theta_i}(s_{t+1}, a') - Q_{\theta_i}(s_t, a_t))^2] \tag{8}$$

A2C: The A2C refers to advantage actor critic approach. The 'Actor' refers to a neural model that, given a state, predicts a likelihood distribution over potential action. Meanwhile, the 'Critic' is another neural construct that evaluates the actions proposed by the actor. The objective function is presented as Eq. (9).

$$\nabla_\theta J(\pi_\theta) = \mathbb{E}_{\pi_\theta}[\sum_{t=0}^{H} \nabla_\theta log\pi_\theta(a_t \mid s_t) A_\omega(s_t, a_t)] \tag{9}$$

where $A_\omega(s_t, a_t) = \mathbb{E}\left[r_{t+1} + \gamma V_\omega(s_{t+1}) - V_\omega(s_t)\right]$. The actor network and the critic network are parameterized by θ and ω, respectively.

FOUNDATION OF ADVERSARIAL TRAINING

Adversarial training starts from (Goodfellow et al., 2014; Szegedy et al., 2013). Shaham et al. (Shaham et al., 2018) propose a min-max adversarial training format as:

$$min_\theta E_{(x,y)\sim D}\left[max_{\delta \in B(x,\varepsilon)} L_{ce}(\theta, x + \delta, y)\right] \tag{10}$$

where (x,y)~D and $B(x,\varepsilon)$ represent the data distributions for the training samples and adversarial samples. Inside the max operator, the worst-case samples are detected while inside of the min operator, the model is trained robustly on these found adversarial samples. Lc_e refers to the cross-entropy function.

CONSTRAINED OBSERVATION ROBUST MDP

A constrained observation robust MDP can be presented by a tuple $(S,A,p,r,c,\Delta,\gamma)$. S is the state space, A is the action space and p is the state transition probability function. r is the reward function, c is the set of constraint functions, Δ is observation perturbation and γ is the discount factor. The objective function is:

$$max_{\pi} E\left[\sum_{t=0}^{T} \gamma^t (s_t, a_t)\right] \tag{11}$$

Subject to $E[c(s,s',\Delta)] \leq \epsilon$ (12)

where T is timestep and ϵ is an expected minimum deviation. s' refers to states at time step t+1.

PROBABILISTIC ACTION ROBUST MDP

Probabilistic Action Robust MDP which can be viewed as a zero-sum game between an agent and an adversary, as a tuple (S,A,p,r,γ). S is the state space, A is the action space and p is the state transition probability function. r is the reward function, and γ is the discount factor. π and $\bar{\pi}$ are agent's policy and adversarial policy. The probabilistic joint policy is defined as $\pi_{p,\alpha}^{mix}(\pi, \bar{\pi}) = (1-\alpha)\pi + \alpha\bar{\pi}$. The optimal probabilistic robust policy is defined as

$$\pi_{p,\alpha}^{*} \in argmax_{\pi} min_{\bar{\pi}} E^{\pi_{p,\alpha}^{mix}(\pi,\bar{\pi})}\left[\sum_t \gamma^t r(s_t, a_t)\right] \tag{13}$$

ROBUST ADVERSARIAL DRL

Table 3 presents the details of recent adversarial attack strategies, including observation attack, time attack, reward attack and action attack. Table 4 presents the details of recent adversarial defense strategies, including adversarial training, iterative training, and regularizers. Besides, related neural networks and training procedures are presented.

Table 3. Details of adversarial attack strategies

Work	Attack Types	Details
(Pattanaik et al., 2017)	Observation Attack	Follow the direction where the state-action or state values drop quickly. Depend on the accuracy of the critic network.
(Meng et al., 2023)	Observation Attack	Follow the direction where the state changes the current policy most quickly within a specific range as Fig. 5 and Algorithm 1.
(Zhai et al., 2022)	Observation Attack	Follow the direction of L2 Gains of normal agnet and adversarial agent.
(Lin et al., 2017)	Time Attack	The observation attack is added, if the difference between the maximum and minimum action likelihood is larger than a predefined threshold.
(Xu and Singh, 2023)	Reward Attack	Minimize the combination of the average distance between taken actions and target actions, the total perturbation in the training procedure and the maximum perturbation at each step.
(Tessler et al., 2019)	Action Attack	An adversarial agent minimizes the return as Algorithm 2.

Figure 3. Modified FGSM attack method during training in (Meng et al., 2023) where ε is predefined perturbation bound, DK_L is the KL divergence.

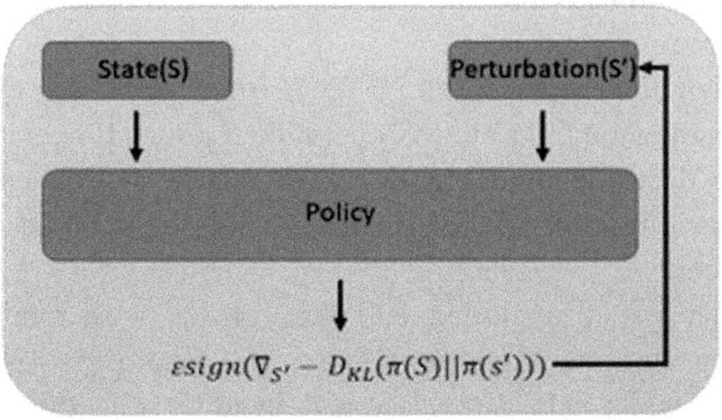

Table 3. Details of adversarial defense strategies

Work	Defense Types	Details
(Pattanaik et al., 2017)	Adversarial Training	Adversarial samples are used to generate actions in the training procedure.
(Meng et al., 2023)	Adversarial Training	Similar to (Pattanaik et al., 2017). For the guatantee of convergence, a constraint function over state and action in introduced to adjust rewards as Algorithm 3.
(Pinto et al., 2017)	Iterative Training	Agent's policy is learned first with frozen adversarial policy. Then the adversarial policy is learned with frozen agent's policy.
(H. Zhang et al., 2020)	Regularizer	KL-divergence regularizes normal sampled states and adversarial states.

RESULTS

The effectiveness of robust adversarial DRL is proved by the OpenAI Gym MuJoCo environments. Here, details of some environments are listed below.

- **Inverted Pendulum**: This setup features a pendulum anchored on a pivot, placed on a cart, allowing only planar linear movement. The state is characterized by a 4D space, accounting for both position and velocity of the cart and pendulum. While the main player tries to keep the pendulum stable with 1D forces.
- **HalfCheetah**: This represents a 2D biped robot, consisting of a torso and two legs with eight rigid links and six operational joints. It operates within a 17D state space detailing joint velocities and angles. An antagonist introduces destabilization by exerting a 6D action, applying 2D forces on the robot's torso and feet.
- **Hopper**: This is a single-legged, planar robot with four rigid segments representing the torso, upper and lower legs, and a foot, powered by three actuated joints. Its 11D state space is defined by joint velocities and angles. The opposing force comes in the form of a 2D impact on the robot's foot.
- **Ant**: This robot has a quadrupedal design, comprising a torso and four legs with a total of eight joints. Its vast 111D observational space accounts for joint velocities, angles, and contact forces. To destabilize it, an antagonist applies an 8D action, exerting 2D forces on each of its feet.

Table 4. Policy success rates and standard deviations with different robust DRL algorithms with 700 testing times

Env	Work	Success rates
Inverted Pendulum	(Zhai et al., 2022)	77.1± 0.7
	(Pinto et al., 2017)	72.8± 0.75
	(Tessler et al., 2019)	71.2± 0.4
	Domain randomization	78.0± 0.2
Inverted Double Pendulum	(Zhai et al., 2022)	44.1± 1.87
	(Pinto et al., 2017)	40.6±1.62
	(Tessler et al., 2019)	26.9± 1.37
	Domain randomization	33.3± 1.49
HalfCheetah	(Zhai et al., 2022)	87.3± 0.9
	(Pinto et al., 2017)	82.5±1.96
	(Tessler et al., 2019)	46.8±2.18
	Domain randomization	84.3± 1.27
Hopper	(Zhai et al., 2022)	38.4± 1.28
	(Pinto et al., 2017)	20.4±0.66
	(Tessler et al., 2019)	12.9±1.14
	Domain randomization	22.0± 0.45

Table 5. Average episode rewards over 50 episodes with (no attacks) and the best (lowest) attack rewards

Env	Work	Attack	Defense	Base Model	Average Reward (No Attack)	Average Reward (Best Attack)
Walker2d	(Pattanaik et al., 2017)	Observation Attack	Adversarial Training	PPO	4058	733
	(Meng et al., 2023)	Observation Attack	Adversarial Training	PPO	4063	3365
	(H. Zhang et al., 2020)	Observation Attack	Regularizer	PPO	4487	2908
	(H. Zhang et al., 2021)	Observation Attack	Iterative Training	PPO	3842	3239
	PPO	-	-	PPO	4472	1086
Ant	(Pattanaik et al., 2017)	Observation Attack	Adversarial Training	PPO	3469	-672
	(Meng et al., 2023)	Observation Attack	Adversarial Training	PPO	4121	1875
	(H. Zhang et al., 2020)	Observation Attack	Regularizer	PPO	4292	2511
	(H. Zhang et al., 2021)	Observation Attack	Iterative Training	PPO	5359	3765
	PPO	-	-	PPO	5687	-872
HalfCheetah	(Pattanaik et al., 2017)	Observation Attack	Adversarial Training	PPO	5231	447
	(H. Zhang et al., 2020)	Observation Attack	Regularizer	PPO	3632	3028
	(H. Zhang et al., 2021)	Observation Attack	Iterative Training	PPO	6157	4806
	PPO	-	-	PPO	7117	-660
Hopper	(Pattanaik et al., 2017)	Observation Attack	Adversarial Training	PPO	2755	291
	(Meng et al., 2023)	Observation Attack	Adversarial Training	PPO	3220	2168
	(H. Zhang et al., 2020)	Observation Attack	Regularizer	PPO	3705	1076
	(H. Zhang et al., 2021)	Observation Attack	Iterative Training	PPO	3291	1772
	PPO	-	-	PPO	3167	636

DISCUSSION

Table 4 presents policy success rates and their respective standard deviations, of various adversarial DRL algorithms. Notably, the algorithm proposed by (Zhai et al., 2022), surpasses its counterparts in terms of success rates. In the Hopper environment, the success rate achieved by (Zhai et al., 2022), exceeds that of (Pinto et al., 2017) by 88.23%, (Tessler et al., 2019) by 197.67%, and Domain randomization by 74.54%. In the Inverted Pendulum environment, (Zhai et al., 2022) has an advantage of 5.91% and 8.29% over (Pinto et al., 2017) and (Tessler et al., 2019), respectively.

Table 5 presents a comparative analysis of four PPO-based robust DRL methods with the average episode rewards. The data suggests that robust DRL methods, particularly those employing adversarial training defense strategies, have worse performance than that of the PPO approach. For instance, in the Ant environment, the average reward of PPO without any attacks is higher by 63.94% compared to (Pattanaik et al., 2017), 38.0% compared to (Meng et al., 2023), 32.50% compared to (H. Zhang et al., 2020), and 6.12% compared to (H. Zhang et al., 2021). It's crucial to note, however, that PPO's performance takes a significant hit under adversarial attacks. For instance, in the HalfCheetah environment, adversarial best attacks lead to a drastic drop in PPO's mean rewards, decreasing from 7117 to -660. Examining the robust DRL methods, they don't exhibit a consistent domain superiority. As an example, while (Meng et al., 2023) stands out in the Walker2d environment during adversarial best attacks, it's (H. Zhang et al., 2021) that takes the lead in the Ant environment under similar conditions.

LIMITATIONS

The limitations of existing works in robust DRL can be summarized as:

1. Transferability Issue: Adversarial examples generated for one model can sometimes be used to fool another model, even if the two models have different architectures or were trained on different datasets.
2. Computational Complexity: Designing robust DRL algorithms often requires solving min-max optimization problems, which are computationally more intensive than traditional optimization.
3. Sample Inefficiency: Ensuring robustness often demands more samples, which can be expensive or infeasible in real-world scenarios.
4. Model Assumptions: Many robustness methods make assumptions about the adversarial model, which might not hold true in real-world adversarial scenarios.

5. Limited Generalization: While DRL models can be made robust to known adversarial attacks, they might still be vulnerable to unforeseen or novel attack strategies.
6. Performance vs. Robustness Trade-off: There's a trade-off between performance and robustness, meaning a more robust model might achieve lower performance.

FUTURE WORK

Future research in robust DRL will focus on understanding how robustness and explainability are linked, optimizing the trade-off between performance and robustness, studying robust multi-agent DRL, and bridging the gap between simulations and complex practical cases.

CONCLUSION

DRL techniques have shown impressive outcomes in many areas. Yet, recent research points out that DRL can be easily tricked by specific harmful inputs. This chapter talks about the importance and details of adversarial attack and defense strategies in DRL approaches. Recent robust DRL works are categorized, compared and analyzed. Common neural networks and training procedures are studied. Besides, six OpenAI Gym MuJoCo environments are taken to prove the effectiveness of eight attack and defense approaches in robust DRL. Moreover, the limitations of existing robust DRL works are discussed. In future, the robust multiagent DRL approaches will be studied. In such systems, it's trickier because one agent's choices can be changed by what other agents do.

REFERENCES

Akkaya, I., Andrychowicz, M., Chociej, M., Litwin, M., McGrew, B., Petron, A., Paino, A., Plappert, M., Powell, G., & Ribas, R. (2019). Solving rubik's cube with a robot hand. arXiv Prepr. arXiv1910.07113.

Bai, T., Luo, J., Zhao, J., Wen, B., & Wang, Q. (2021). *Recent advances in adversarial training for adversarial robustness*. arXiv Prepr. arXiv2102.01356.

Cai, K., Zhu, X., & Hu, Z. (2023). Reward poisoning attacks in deep reinforcement learning based on exploration strategies. *Neurocomputing*, *553*, 126578. doi:10.1016/j.neucom.2023.126578

Carlini, N., & Wagner, D. (2017). Towards evaluating the robustness of neural networks. *2017 Ieee Symposium on Security and Privacy (Sp)*. IEEE. 10.1109/SP.2017.49

Das, N., Shanbhogue, M., Chen, S.-T., Hohman, F., Chen, L., Kounavis, M. E., & Chau, D. H. 2017. Keeping the bad guys out: Protecting and vaccinating deep learning with jpeg compression. arXiv Prepr. arXiv1705.02900.

Fan, J., & Li, W. (2021). Adversarial training and provable robustness: A tale of two objectives. *Proceedings of the AAAI Conference on Artificial Intelligence*, (pp. 7367–7376). AAAI. 10.1609/aaai.v35i8.16904

Goodfellow, I.J., Shlens, J., & Szegedy, C. (2014). *Explaining and harnessing adversarial examples.* arXiv Prepr. arXiv1412.6572.

Grosse, K., Papernot, N., Manoharan, P., Backes, M., & McDaniel, P. (2017). Adversarial examples for malware detection. *Computer Security–ESORICS 2017: 22nd European Symposium on Research in Computer Security*. Springer.

Guo, C., Rana, M., Cisse, M., & Van Der Maaten, L. 2017. Countering adversarial images using input transformations. arXiv Prepr. arXiv1711.00117.

He, X., Lou, B., Yang, H., & Lv, C. (2022a). Robust decision making for autonomous vehicles at highway on-ramps: A constrained adversarial reinforcement learning approach. *IEEE Transactions on Intelligent Transportation Systems*, *24*(4), 4103–4113. doi:10.1109/TITS.2022.3229518

He, X., Yang, H., Hu, Z., & Lv, C. (2022b). Robust lane change decision making for autonomous vehicles: An observation adversarial reinforcement learning approach. *IEEE Transactions on Intelligent Vehicles*, *8*(1), 184–193. doi:10.1109/TIV.2022.3165178

Huang, S., Papernot, N., Goodfellow, I., Duan, Y., & Abbeel, P. 2017. Adversarial attacks on neural network policies. arXiv Prepr. arXiv1702.02284.

Huang, Y., & Zhu, Q. (2019). Deceptive reinforcement learning under adversarial manipulations on cost signals. *Decision and Game Theory for Security: 10th International Conference, GameSec 2019*. Springer. 10.1007/978-3-030-32430-8_14

Kontes, G. D., Scherer, D. D., Nisslbeck, T., Fischer, J., & Mutschler, C. 2020. High-speed collision avoidance using deep reinforcement learning and domain randomization for autonomous vehicles. *2020 IEEE 23rd International Conference on Intelligent Transportation Systems (ITSC)*. IEEE. 10.1109/ITSC45102.2020.9294396

Kos, J., & Song, D. (2017). *Delving into adversarial attacks on deep policies*. arXiv Prepr. arXiv1705.06452.

Li, X., Li, Y., Feng, Z., Wang, Z., & Pan, Q. (2023). ATS-O2A: A state-based adversarial attack strategy on deep reinforcement learning. *Computers & Security*, *129*, 103259. doi:10.1016/j.cose.2023.103259

Lin, Y.-C., Hong, Z.-W., Liao, Y.-H., Shih, M.-L., Liu, M.-Y., & Sun, M. 2017. Tactics of adversarial attack on deep reinforcement learning agents. arXiv Prepr. arXiv1703.06748. doi:10.24963/ijcai.2017/525

Lyu, C., Huang, K., & Liang, H.-N. 2015. A unified gradient regularization family for adversarial examples. *2015 IEEE International Conference on Data Mining*. IEEE. 10.1109/ICDM.2015.84

Madry, A., Makelov, A., Schmidt, L., Tsipras, D., & Vladu, A. (2017). *Towards deep learning models resistant to adversarial attacks*. arXiv Prepr. arXiv1706.06083.

Meng, J., Zhu, F., Ge, Y., & Zhao, P. (2023). Integrating safety constraints into adversarial training for robust deep reinforcement learning. *Information Sciences*, *619*, 310–323. doi:10.1016/j.ins.2022.11.051

Moosavi-Dezfooli, S.-M., Fawzi, A., & Frossard, P. 2016. Deepfool: a simple and accurate method to fool deep neural networks. *Proceedings of the IEEE Conference on Computer Vision and Pattern Recognition,* (pp. 2574–2582). IEEE. 10.1109/CVPR.2016.282

Papernot, N., McDaniel, P., Sinha, A., & Wellman, M. (2016). *Towards the science of security and privacy in machine learning*. arXiv Prepr. arXiv1611.03814.

Pattanaik, A., Tang, Z., Liu, S., Bommannan, G., & Chowdhary, G. (2017). *Robust deep reinforcement learning with adversarial attacks*. arXiv Prepr. arXiv1712.03632.

Pinto, L., Davidson, J., Sukthankar, R., & Gupta, A. (2017). Robust adversarial reinforcement learning. *International Conference on Machine Learning*. IEEE.

Rafailov, R., Yu, T., Rajeswaran, A., & Finn, C. (2021). Offline reinforcement learning from images with latent space models. In *Learning for Dynamics and Control* (pp. 1154–1168). PMLR.

Sankaranarayanan, S., Jain, A., Chellappa, R., & Lim, S. N. 2018. Regularizing deep networks using efficient layerwise adversarial training. *Proceedings of the AAAI Conference on Artificial Intelligence.* AAAI. 10.1609/aaai.v32i1.11688

Shaham, U., Yamada, Y., & Negahban, S. (2018). Understanding adversarial training: Increasing local stability of supervised models through robust optimization. *Neurocomputing*, *307*, 195–204. doi:10.1016/j.neucom.2018.04.027

Sun, J., Zhang, T., Xie, X., Ma, L., Zheng, Y., Chen, K., & Liu, Y. (2020). Stealthy and efficient adversarial attacks against deep reinforcement learning. *Proceedings of the AAAI Conference on Artificial Intelligence*, (pp. 5883–5891). AAAI. 10.1609/aaai.v34i04.6047

Szegedy, C., Zaremba, W., Sutskever, I., Bruna, J., Erhan, D., Goodfellow, I., & Fergus, R. (2013). *Intriguing properties of neural networks*. arXiv Prepr. arXiv1312.6199.

Tessler, C., Efroni, Y., & Mannor, S. (2019). Action robust reinforcement learning and applications in continuous control. *International Conference on Machine Learning*. PMLR.

Vinitsky, E., Du, Y., Parvate, K., Jang, K., Abbeel, P., & Bayen, A. 2020. Robust reinforcement learning using adversarial populations. arXiv Prepr. arXiv2008.01825.

Wang, D. (2022). Meta Reinforcement Learning with Hebbian Learning. 2022 IEEE 13th Annual Ubiquitous Computing, Electronics & Mobile Communication Conference (UEMCON). IEEE. doi:10.1109/UEMCON54665.2022.9965711

Wang, D. (2023a). Obstacle-aware Simultaneous Task and Energy Planning with Ordering Constraints. *2023 11th International Conference on Information and Communication Technology (ICoICT)*. IEEE. 10.1109/ICoICT58202.2023.10262644

Wang, D. (2023b). Explainable Deep Reinforcement Learning for Knowledge Graph Reasoning. In *Recent Developments in Machine and Human Intelligence* (pp. 168–183). IGI Global. doi:10.4018/978-1-6684-9189-8.ch012

Wang, D. (2023c). Out-of-Distribution Detection with Confidence Deep Reinforcement Learning. *2023 International Conference on Communications, Computing, Cybersecurity, and Informatics (CCCI)*. IEEE. 10.1109/CCCI58712.2023.10290768

Wang, D. (2023d). Reinforcement Learning for Combinatorial Optimization. In *Encyclopedia of Data Science and Machine Learning* (pp. 2857–2871). IGI Global.

Wang, D. & Hu, M. (2021). Deep Deterministic Policy Gradient With Compatible Critic Network. *IEEE Trans. Neural Networks Learn. Syst.* IEEE.

Wang, D., & Hu, M. (2023). Contrastive Learning Methods for Deep Reinforcement Learning. *IEEE Access : Practical Innovations, Open Solutions*, *11*, 97107–97117. doi:10.1109/ACCESS.2023.3312383

Wang, D., Hu, M., & Gao, Y. (2018). Multi-criteria mission planning for a solar-powered multi-robot system. *International Design Engineering Technical Conferences and Computers and Information in Engineering Conference*. IEEE. 10.1115/DETC2018-85683

Wang, D., Hu, M., & Weir, J.D. (2022). *Simultaneous Task and Energy Planning using Deep Reinforcement Learning. Inf. Sci*. (Ny).

WangD.ZhaoJ.HanM.LiL. (n.d). 4d Printing-Enabled Circular Economy: Disassembly Sequence Planning Using Reinforcement Learning. SSRN 4429186. doi:10.2139/ssrn.4429186

Wang, P., Liu, D., Chen, J., Li, H., & Chan, C.-Y. (2021). Decision making for autonomous driving via augmented adversarial inverse reinforcement learning. *2021 IEEE International Conference on Robotics and Automation (ICRA)*. IEEE. 10.1109/ICRA48506.2021.9560907

Xu, Y. & Singh, G. (2023). *Black-Box Targeted Reward Poisoning Attack Against Online Deep Reinforcement Learning*. arXiv Prepr. arXiv2305.10681.

Xu, Y., Zeng, Q., & Singh, G. (2022). *Efficient reward poisoning attacks on online deep reinforcement learning*. arXiv Prepr. arXiv2205.14842.

Yun, L., Wang, D., & Li, L. (2023). Explainable multi-agent deep reinforcement learning for real-time demand response towards sustainable manufacturing. *Applied Energy, 347*, 121324. doi:10.1016/j.apenergy.2023.121324

Zhai, P., Luo, J., Dong, Z., Zhang, L., Wang, S., & Yang, D. (2022). Robust adversarial reinforcement learning with dissipation inequation constraint. *Proceedings of the AAAI Conference on Artificial Intelligence,* (pp. 5431–5439). AAAI. 10.1609/aaai.v36i5.20481

Zhang, H., Chen, H., Boning, D., & Hsieh, C.-J. (2021). *Robust reinforcement learning on state observations with learned optimal adversary*. arXiv Prepr. arXiv2101.08452.

Zhang, H., Chen, H., Xiao, C., Li, B., Liu, M., Boning, D., & Hsieh, C.-J. (2020). Robust deep reinforcement learning against adversarial perturbations on state observations. *Advances in Neural Information Processing Systems, 33*, 21024–21037.

Zhang, X., Chen, Y., Zhu, X., & Sun, W. (2021). Robust policy gradient against strong data corruption. International Conference on Machine Learning. PMLR, (pp. 12391–12401). IEEE.

Zhang, X., Ma, Y., Singla, A., & Zhu, X. (2020). Adaptive reward-poisoning attacks against reinforcement learning. *International Conference on Machine Learning*. PMLR.

ADDITIONAL READINGS

Bai, T., Luo, J., Zhao, J., Wen, B., & Wang, Q. (2021). Recent advances in adversarial training for adversarial robustness. arXiv preprint arXiv:2102.01356. doi:10.24963/ijcai.2021/591

Wang, X., Li, J., Kuang, X., Tan, Y. A., & Li, J. (2019). The security of machine learning in an adversarial setting: A survey. *Journal of Parallel and Distributed Computing, 130*, 12-23.

KEY TERMS AND DEFINITIONS

Adversarial Training: A technique used to improve the robustness of machine learning models by exposing them to malicious inputs during the training phase. By learning from these intentionally perturbed examples, the model becomes better equipped to handle similar adversarial inputs during testing or real-world applications.

Markov Decision Process: This MDP ensures that the agent's decisions are based on the current state, aiming to maximize long-term rewards.

Robust Deep Reinforcement Learning: Focuses on designing DRL agents that can perform reliably and maintain their efficacy in the presence of adversarial disturbances or uncertainties in the environment. The aim is to ensure that the agent can handle both known and unforeseen challenges, thereby generalizing well across diverse and potentially adversarial settings.

Chapter 6
Human Action Recognition Based on YOLOv7

Chenwei Liang
https://orcid.org/0009-0003-6659-4497
Auckland University of Technology, New Zealand

Wei Qi Yan
Auckland University of Technology, New Zealand

ABSTRACT

Human action recognition is a fundamental research problem in computer vision. The accuracy of human action recognition has important applications. In this book chapter, the authors use a YOLOv7-based model for human action recognition. To evaluate the performance of the model, the action recognition results of YOLOv7 were compared with those using CNN+LSTM, YOLOv5, and YOLOv4. Furthermore, a small human action dataset suitable for YOLO model training is designed. This data set is composed of images extracted from KTH, Weizmann, MSR data sets. In this book chapter, the authors make use of this data set to verify the experimental results. The final experimental results show that using the YOLOv7 model for human action recognition is very convenient and effective, compared with the previous YOLO model.

DOI: 10.4018/979-8-3693-1738-9.ch006

INTRODUCTION

Normally, surveillance videos usually contain a series of actions (Yan, 2019). Recognizing the actions in these videos can provide huge benefits, such as recognizing the person who fell in time and assisting him to avoid follow-up problems from the fall down. Therefore, it is very necessary to evaluate or analyse human action in videos. Human action recognition generally refers to judging or analysing the classes of human actions in videos (Soomro et al., 2014). Concisely, it is to correctly classify human actions into known action classes.

While recognizing these actions, it also brings a huge workload. Therefore, a rapid and efficient action recognition method becomes very important. The relevant methods in deep learning can meet the requirements and solve this problem. As a machine learning method, deep learning has been widely employed since it was proposed (Yan, 2021). The purpose of this approach is to allow computers to be trained, with the ability to analyse and identify specific data (Gao et al., 2021).

Human action recognition has been a topic of interest within academic discourse. In the past, a substantial body of research on the recognition of human actions has utilized traditional machine-learning techniques, such as the extraction of visual characteristics or motion trajectories. Now, deep learning methods are more widely utilized. The deep learning technique is prevalent not only within computer vision but also across fields of study, including NLP (Natural Language Processing) etc (Wiriyathammabhum et al., 2016). As more and more researchers use deep learning methods to recognize actions, the recognition efficiency improves over time. Currently, researchers have proposed several recognition algorithms, including CNN (Khan et al., 2020), Two-Stream (Simonyan et al., 2014), C3D (Convolution 3 Dimension) (Tran et al., 2015), and RNN (Du et al., 2017), etc.

Similar to the Convolutional Neural Network (CNN), the You Only Look Once (YOLO) model has an input layer, convolutional layer, pooling layer, and fully connected layer. The aforementioned study conducted by Redmon et al. (2016) establishes the fundamental framework for a comprehensive Convolutional Neural Network (CNN) architecture. However, YOLO exhibits a clear differentiation from the conventional CNN model. The achievement of end-to-end object detection necessitates the use of a distinct CNN model. This enhancement results in improved computational efficiency of the YOLO model. This is one of the reasons why this study selects the YOLOv7 model for human action recognition.

This study employs the YOLOv7 framework to construct a comprehensive network for human action recognition. The YOLO algorithm, which stands for "You Only Look Once," is a visual object identification method that utilizes a convolutional neural network. This approach was first introduced in 2016 by Redmon et al. One of the key benefits of this particular approach is in its inherent simplicity and efficiency, which allows for swift execution. According to Cao et al. (2023), the YOLOv7 model exhibits notable advancements in terms of both running speed and structure. This research effort primarily focuses on the investigation of fundamental human actions. This study contributes to the existing body of knowledge in this area by evaluating whether using the YOLOv7 model is effective in human action recognition.

In the subsequent sections of this work, we will provide an overview of the current methodologies used in human action recognition, namely in section two. In section three, the methodology used is expounded upon. In section four, an analysis and discussion of the experimental outcomes will be conducted. In the concluding part, we provide a comprehensive summary of our research and provide a perspective on potential future endeavors.

LITERATURE REVIEW

Among all the methods used in the field of human action recognition, deep learning methods have been the most effective. The CNN model is the most representative model among deep learning methods. However, the performance of CNN when first applied in the human action recognition was not excellent. Because ordinary CNN models can only process the input of 2D data when processing incoming data.

To enable the CNN model to automatically recognize human actions on the screen, and at the same time ensure that the CNN model can be widely used in human action recognition. Ji et al. (Ji et al., 2012) created a 3D-CNN network model for human action recognition. The 3D-CNN model is a very convenient and easy-to-use model. Unlike the widely popular classifier methods at the time, the 3D-CNN model was much simpler. This model creates a special 3D convolutional layer. The model can extract spatial and temporal features in video data through this 3D convolution layer. According to the extracted feature model, the motion information between adjacent frames of the video stream can be found, and the final recognition result can be obtained. The experimental results show the model created by Ji et al. is effective for human action recognition in videos.

The Two-Stream method is another exploration direction of CNN models in the field of human action recognition. This method was first proposed by Simonyan and Zisserman in 2014 (Simonyan & Zisserman, 2014). The Two-Stream CNN network consists of two deep networks. These two deep networks handle the dimensions of time and space respectively, namely spatial stream and temporal stream. When processing input data, the network model divides the input video into two parts: spatial and temporal. The spatial stream network is responsible for processing the RGB images in the video, and the temporal stream is responsible for processing the optical flow image of the video. Finally, the processed features are trained and classified. They also experimentally demonstrated that training multi-frame density optical flow on a ConvNet network can achieve excellent results with limited training data. They also proposed a multi-task training method. This method can combine two different action classification data sets to increase the available training data. The experimental results using two-stream for recognition are significantly better than the recognition results using deep learning networks in the past.

C3D (3-Dimensional Convolution) was proposed in 2015 as one of the mainstream methods at the same time as Two-Stream (Tran et al., 2015). This approach demonstrates rapid and effective acquisition of spatiotemporal features. This is due to the use of deep 3D Convolutional Networks (3D ConvNets) for the processing of spatiotemporal information. In addition, the features learned by this network come with a simple linear classifier. The final test results show that the computational efficiency of the model is also very high, basically end-to-end training, the network structure is more concise and easier to train and use.

Feichtenhofer et al. made improvements to the two-stream network to improve performance (Feichtenhofer et al., 2016). Integrating the two networks into a convolutional layer instead of a SoftMax layer saves parameters without compromising performance. It is most effective got when conducting network fusion at the last convolutional layer. It is also found that additional fusion at the class prediction layer can improve the accuracy of the model. Based on these improvements, Feichtenhofer proposed a new recognition architecture. The results of the experiment show the proposed architecture has been able to achieve state-of-the-art outcomes.

Although the two-stream method has achieved great success, this method still has a big drawback. The model is incapable of accurately representing videos of extended duration. To solve this problem, the TSN (Temporal Segments Networks) was proposed by Wang et al. (2016) based on Two-Stream CNN approach. This method divides the input long video into K different parts, randomly selects a short segment from each part, and then uses TSN to fuse the short segments. The current two-stream-based methods are implemented by using TSN as the backbone network.

Among the various methods of human action recognition using deep learning, prediction is the most widely used method. Azorin-Lopez et al. (2016) proposed a method to identify actions and behaviours by predicting human movement trajectories. This method is used for human action recognition in videos and achieves good experimental results.

Based on previous research results, some researchers believe that adding LSTM to the recognition method is a good choice (Almeida & Azkune, 2018). In the deep learning model of LSTM, the neural network proposes a probabilistic model by learning and simulating different behaviours of humans interacting with the environment. This probabilistic model can predict human actions and identify abnormal human behaviours. This improvement further improves the accuracy of recognition.

There is many dimensional information in videos, among which the most noteworthy information is time information. In the recognition process, the processing of temporal information has always been a very important focus in human action recognition. As we all know, the RNN network is very suitable for dealing with sequence problems. A recurrent pose-attention network (RPAN) was proposed (Du et al., 2017). In this approach, a mechanism called pose-attention was proposed. This allows the RNNs models to learn more complex motion structures over time. In addition to this, the method can also perform coarse pose labeling of actions in videos. The proposal of this method enriches the kinds of networks that use RNN for action recognition. Finally, the experimental results prove that their network is very good.

The ultimate goal of human action recognition is to hope that the machine can recognize human actions in videos and label these actions. Human actions recorded in videos will be affected by shooting time and background environment. It is very important whether the action recognition method can effectively resist interference. To verify which of the CNN-based recognition methods has the strongest anti-interference ability. Yu and Yan compared three popular human action recognition models and methods. These methods are 3D-CNN, dual-stream CNN and CNN+LSTM. They selected the HMDB-51 data set as three different model experimental data sets. After conducting a large number of experiments, the experimental results of the three models were obtained. The experimental results comparing the models found that the CNN+LSTM method is least affected by interference factors in the video and achieve a higher degree of recognition (Yu & Yan, 2020).

YOLO is a classic target detection model. Many researchers choose to use YOLO for human action recognition. Lu et al. used the YOLOv3 model for human action recognition in 2018 and achieved excellent experimental results (Lu et al., 2018). During the experiment, to obtain a high-precision network learning rate, they continuously adjusted the structure of the network. They used the YOLOv2 model as a comparison model for the experiment to determine the validity of the experimental results. The final experimental results show that the accuracy of human action recognition using YOLOv3 is as high as 80.20%.

Lu et al. successfully used YOLOv3 for human action recognition, they continued to study the YOLO model. Lu et al. designed a new action recognition method based on YOLOv4 (Lu et al., 2020). In the method they proposed, YOLOv4 is used as the basic model combined with LSTM to recognize human actions. The addition of the LSTM model helps the recognition method to identify the temporal and spatial information in the video. They also experimented with recognition results after incorporating the attention mechanism Selective Kernel Network (SKNet) model. Experimental results prove that the recognition accuracy of the YOLOv4+LSTM network reaches 97.87%. The addition of the attention mechanism enables the model to achieve better experimental results.

There are many other methods for human action recognition. For example, Wang et al. used frame-by-frame recognition of human gait energy images (X. Wang & Yan, 2020) and later human gait recognition based on multichannel convolutional neural networks (X. Wang, Zhang, & Yan, 2020). Both methods have achieved good experimental results in the end. However, there are still few methods to realize human action recognition based on YOLO. Most are using other deep learning techniques like CNN.

Nguyen & Bùi (2023) introduced a novel approach that integrates deep learning and machine learning techniques for the purpose of categorizing the activities and behaviours of numerous human subjects. The suggested methodology encompasses a three-step recognition procedure, which includes the use of the YOLOv5 model for object detection, the implementation of a media pipeline for skeletal visualization, and the utilization of an LSTM network for activity identification. The experimental findings pertaining to target detection using YOLOv5 indicate the loss remains below 5% throughout the training and validation processes. The mean precision (mAP) of the YOLOv5 model created for all the examined case studies consistently exceeds 99%.

Cao et al. (2023) conducted a study that focuses on the pedestrian detection and identification system using YOLOv7. The goal of the algorithm is to be able to distinguish between ordinary walkers and grid maintenance inspectors with high accuracy through the system. The paper describes the algorithm design process, which involves categorizing pedestrians and workers into two distinct groups. This categorization is based on discernible characteristics, such as the presence of safety helmets and the China State Grid logo.

Upon conducting a comprehensive analysis of existing methodologies for human action recognition, it has been observed that the study pertaining to the utilization of YOLOv7 for this purpose lacks a comparative evaluation of the performance across different iterations of the YOLO series. We will do a comparison of this.

METHODOLOGY

This study presents a novel direction that distinguishes itself from previous research. This study employs the YOLOv7 framework for the purpose of human activity recognition. In this study, we evaluate the efficacy of YOLOv7 across a range of criteria. Furthermore, we conducted a comparative analysis between YOLOv7 and three other models, namely YOLOv4, YOLOv5, and CNN+LSTM.

Dataset

KTH, HMDB-51 dataset, UCF-101 and other datasets are common datasets that can be used for human action recognition. In this study, we choose the dataset KTH for testing for convenience. The KTH dataset contains six categories of human behaviours, which are further divided into four classes in the specific classification, each class contains 25 topics. 100 videos in total (Schuldt et al., 2004). The videos were all shot with a static camera with a frame rate of 25 fps. The shooting backgrounds are all uniform backgrounds, the resolution of the video is 160 × 120, the average length is 4 seconds. Human actions that the experiment can recognize include walk, jog, run, boxing, waved, and clapped.

Regarding the selection of the data set, a total of 1,200 action photos were chosen as representatives. This selection process was based on the integration of the KTH data set with the Weizmann and MSR data sets. Each action is represented by a collection of 200 photographs, resulting in a total of six distinct groups. Each collection of images represents a distinct and consistent activity shown within the dataset. The training set for our model consists of 80% of the dataset. To conduct our analysis, we will designate a test set consisting of 20% of the data set, along with an additional 100 sample movies.

Network Structure

By using this approach, we successfully accomplish our objective of recognizing human actions. The YOLOv7 model, presented by Wang, Bochkovskiy, and Liao in 2022, is the most recent addition to the YOLO. The YOLOv7 network underwent a complete resizing process, where the input picture was scaled to a resolution of 640×640. The process begins by feeding an image into the backbone network, which then generates three layers of feature maps with varying sizes via the head layer network. Ultimately, the prognostication outcomes are exported via the Rep and Conv layers. The architectural design of the whole network remains reliant on CNN. One of the components of the system is the backbone network, which is linked to an ELAN (Extended Local Area Network) by a series of four Convolutional layers followed by Batch Normalisation and SiLU (Sigmoid Linear Unit) activation functions (referred to as CBS). This is then further augmented by three Maxpooling layers and a combination of CBS and ELAN structures. Each structure is associated with the output of a primary layer. Fig 1 illustrates the simplified structural diagram of the whole YOLOv7 model.

Figure 1. YOLOv7 simplified structure

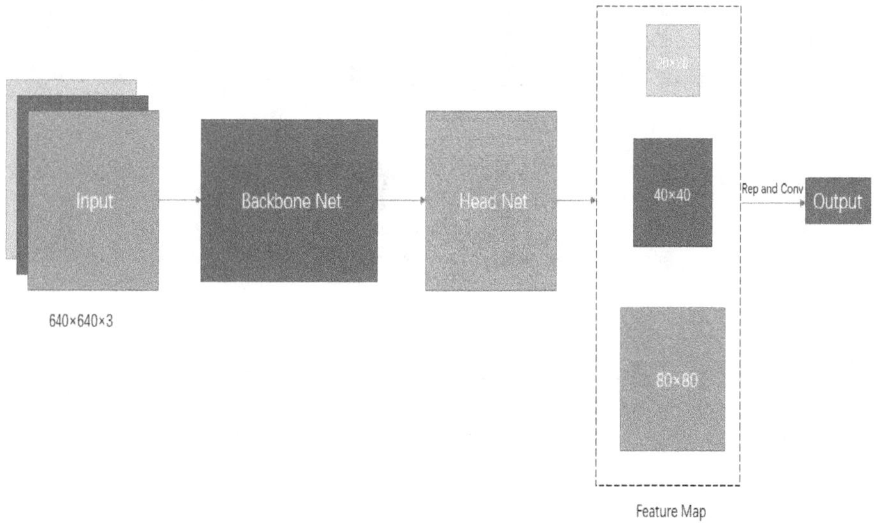

RESULT ANALYSIS

In this study, we designated the batch size as 16 and the number of threads as 8. Consequently, we fed 16 samples into the network, distributing these data among the 8 threads for network training. Additionally, the epoch number is 250. In our experimental procedures, we use GPU acceleration as a means to enhance the efficiency of our training process, hence mitigating time consumption. Following the completion of model training, the data was next used to evaluate the performance of model in the human action recognition. The ensuing analysis yielded the following outcomes. In order to do the tests, the batch size remains fixed at 16 and the number of threads is set at 8.

Fig 2 shows the results, which are all generated based on test video frames, including (a) boxing, (b) clapped, (c) waved, (d) jog, (e) walk and (f) run.

Figure 2. The result of human action recognition by using YOLOv7

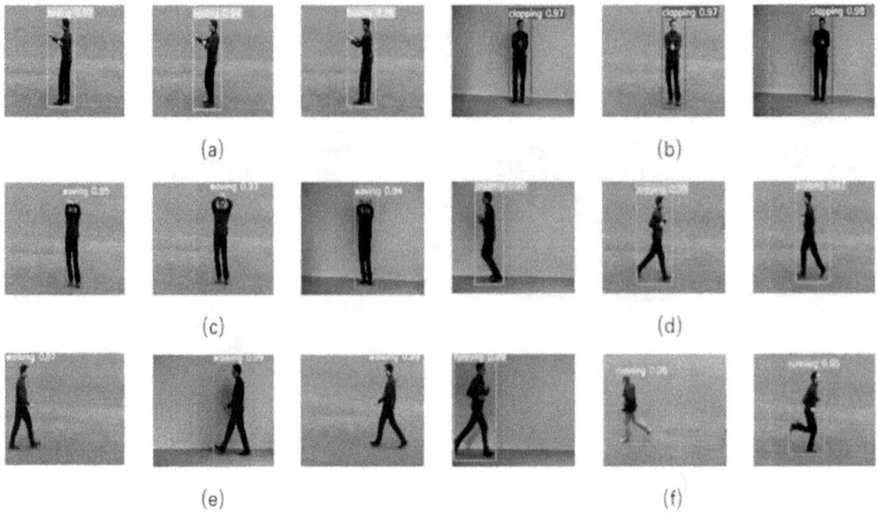

In this experimental study, it is important to assess the impact of the model. Recall and accuracy are used as evaluation metrics for assessing the performance of our trained model. The precise trajectories of the two indicators are shown in Fig 3. It is evident that with an increase in the number of epochs, there is a tendency for both metrics to converge and stabilize at about 80. Both values exhibit a large magnitude. This demonstrates that our trained model has both high accuracy and a broad scope. Furthermore, the Box diagram shown in Fig 3 is also seen. It is seen that the loss value shown on the graph decreases progressively with each iteration. The graphs representing Objectness, Classification, Validation Box, Validation Objectness, and Validation Classification exhibit similar trends. The model's mean average precision at a threshold of 0.5 (mAP@0.5) demonstrates an inverse relationship with the values shown in the figures. A lower value in these figures indicates a higher performance of the model. Additionally, as the number of iterations increases, both mAP@0.5 values steadily improve until they reach a stable state.

Figure 3. The result

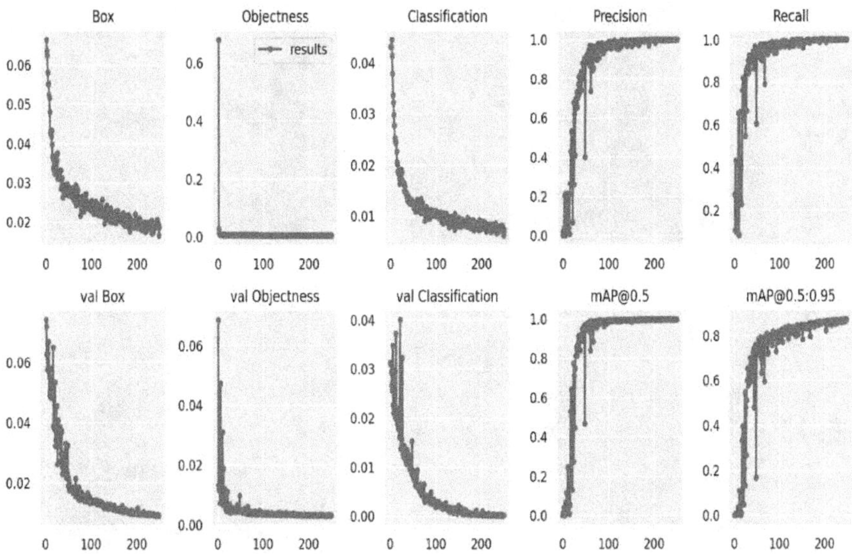

The YOLOv4 and YOLOv5 models were used in this work. The trials were done using the two models individually. In all phases of model training, we established a total of 250 epochs, while maintaining a consistent batch size of 16. A portion of the experimental findings is shown in Fig 4 and Fig 5. The experimental findings of YOLOv4 are shown in Fig 4. The experimental findings of YOLOv5 are shown in Fig 5.

Fig 4. YOLOv4 part results

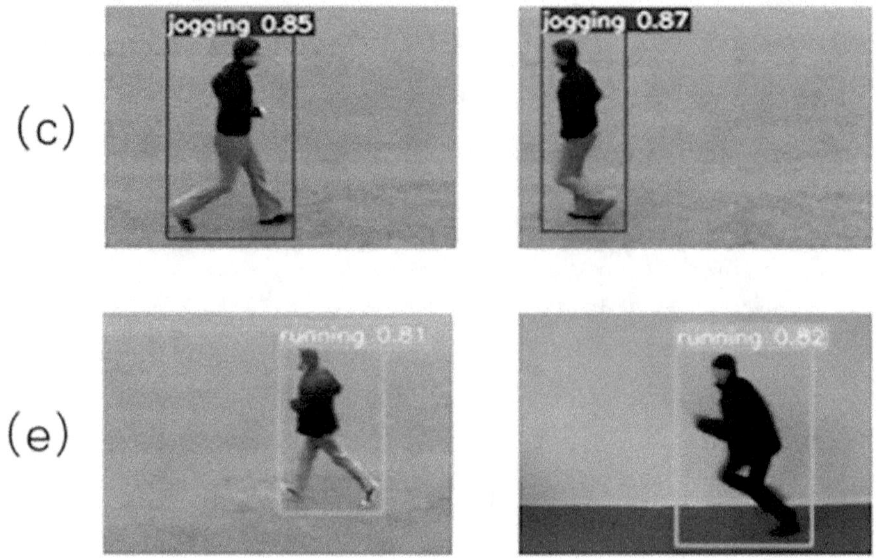

Figure 5. YOLO5 part results

Based on the partial findings shown in the figure, it is evident that the accuracy of the two YOLO models is marginally inferior to that of the YOLOv7 model. In order to assure precision, we opted to use identical data sets for testing purposes across three distinct models. The outcomes of these tests are visually shown in Fig 6.

Figure 6. The results of three different YOLO

Fig 6 illustrates the sequential presentation of the outcomes obtained from the analysis of the same dataset using YOLOv4, YOLOv5, and YOLO7, respectively. Both YOLOv4 and YOLOv5 exhibit a commendable accuracy of 0.95 when applied to the task of action boxing. The YOLOv7 model achieves an accuracy of 0.96. The precision of the remaining two models for the task of clapped action is 0.96. The YOLOv7 model achieves an accuracy of 0.97. It is evident that the identification accuracy of YOLOv7 surpasses that of the other two models by a small margin. Furthermore, we have identified other issues that were not detected inside a singular model. The temporal efficiency of the three models likewise varies. In a given dataset, the execution time for YOLOv7 epochs is around 90 seconds on average. The relative running times for the YOLOv5 and YOLOv4 models are 120 seconds per epoch and 135 seconds per epoch. When comparing the three models, it is seen that YOLOv7 exhibits a little higher speed in execution, while maintaining the same level of GPU acceleration.

The ultimate accuracy is obtained by developing the YOLOv7 model based on Python. Furthermore, we also compare the results with the recognition accuracy of the CNN+LSTM model using the same dataset (Liang, Lu, & Yan, 2022). The data shown in Table 1 was acquired. In contrast, it is evident that the use of YOLOv7 yields superior accuracy. The overall accuracy of the system stays about 0.96. Of the six motions, boxing moves exhibit the greatest level of precision.

Table 1. Classification precision for recognition

Models	Walk	Jog	Run	Boxing	Waved	Clapped	Total
YOLOv7	0.96	0.96	0.96	0.98	0.96	0.97	0.96
YOLOv5	0.95	0.94	0.95	0.96	0.95	0.95	0.95
YOLOv4	0.91	0.92	0.93	0.94	0.93	0.93	0.93
CNN+LSTM	0.91	0.85	0.92	0.90	0.88	0.87	0.88

In addition, we also added the attention mechanism CBAM (Woo, Park, Lee, & Kweon, 2018) and the attention mechanism SimAM (Yang, Zhang, Li, & Xie, 2021) to the network structure of YOLOv7 respectively. By adding this structure, we can further evaluate whether YOLOv7 is suitable for human action recognition. Results are shown in Table 2.

Table 2. Classification accuracy of action recognition based on YOLOv7.

Models	Walk	Jog	Run	Boxing	Waved	Clapped	Total
YOLOv7	0.96	0.96	0.96	0.98	0.96	0.97	0.96
CBAMYOLOv7	0.963	0.965	0.97	0.976	0.966	0.975	0.96
SimAMYOLOv7	0.959	0.961	0.968	0.982	0.976	0.957	0.961

From Table 2, we can observe that the action can still be recognized effectively after using the attention mechanism. Using the attention mechanism also improves recognition accuracy to a certain extent. This shows that the applicability of YOLOv7 is excellent.

To determine whether the effect of recognition will be affected by the dataset. We also chose run and walk from the Weizmann dataset (Gorelick, Blank, Shechtman, Irani, & Basri, 2007) to test our model. The Weizmann dataset is the same as the KTH dataset, the actions in the data are performed by only one person. Experimental results are shown in Figure 7. The results show that changing such datasets does not have much impact on the recognition performance. Using YOLOv7 effectively recognizes the corresponding action. The recognition accuracy is also not much different from that of the original dataset. But there are also drawbacks, such as the detection box will incorrectly identify the background. This is where improvement is needed.

Figure 7. The results of Weizmann dataset

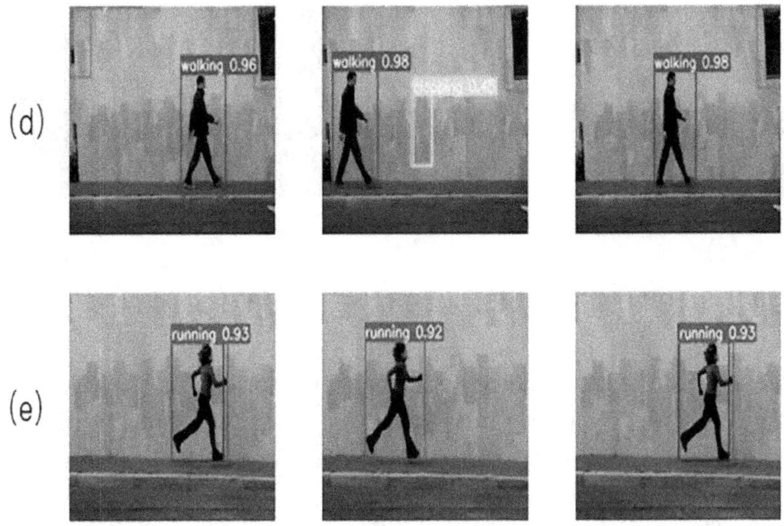

In order to examine the potential variation in recognition accuracy in response to complicated backdrop changes within the dataset, the MSR action dataset was used. The dataset only comprises three distinct motions, namely clapped, waved, and boxing. One video within this dataset encompasses all activities, resulting in an average video duration of over 30 seconds. Moreover, the dataset comprises many individuals engaging in various activities (Yuan, Liu, & Wu, 2011). The experimental findings are shown in Figure 8. It is evident that the YOLOv7-based model is capable of accurately identifying and recognizing the three specified activities. However, the accuracy of the system is influenced by intricate environmental factors and other contextual elements, resulting in a significant decrease in overall precision by a factor of twelve. This phenomenon may be attributed to the insufficient amount of relevant data available in the dataset used for training purposes. Additional data is necessary to adequately address the intricacies of some complicated ecosystems.

Figure 8. The results MSR dataset

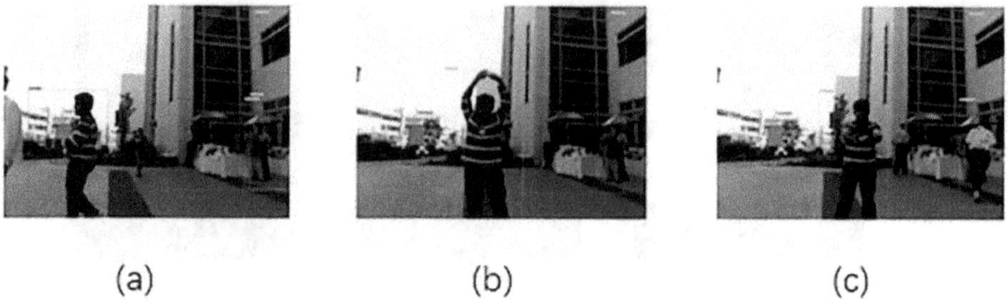

The aforementioned test findings indicate that the use of YOLOv7 for the purpose of human action recognition consistently demonstrates efficacy and feasibility, irrespective of variations in the dataset. Nevertheless, there are some constraints. The selection of a data set has a significant impact on the ultimate outcome of recognition. There exists ample potential for enhancing model advancements.

CONCLUSION

This study presents an investigation into three distinct deep learning-based YOLO model detection methodologies, specifically focusing on their efficacy in pedestrian and human activity identification. The preliminary evaluation of human action recognition using YOLOv7 yields good findings. This study presents the first evidence supporting the applicability of YOLOv7 in the domain of human action recognition. A novel action recognition dataset, specifically designed for compatibility with the YOLOv7 model, is developed by using existing datasets. At present, this study demonstrates the capability to accurately identify and classify six pre-determined behaviours with consistent performance. Nevertheless, there are also some issues that need to be addressed. The absence of data pertaining to further acts remains a notable gap, therefore indicating a potential avenue for future research and investigation.

In further research endeavours, efforts will be made to further enhance the current YOLOv7 model. There is an expectation that the enhancement of the model will lead to a significant improvement in the recognition impact. Furthermore, we will try to add pre-judgment conditions to the model. This is because of our experimental results. When there are multiple tags in the recognized image. For example, in the action of a video, multiple tags alternate or exist simultaneously. When adding this condition, the action will only be recognized if certain conditions are met. Continue to find suitable datasets for deeper evaluation of human action recognition models using YOLOv7.

REFERENCES

Almeida, A., & Azkune, G. (2018). Predicting human behaviour with recurrent neural networks. *Applied Sciences (Basel, Switzerland)*, *8*(2), 305. doi:10.3390/app8020305

Azorin-Lopez, J., Saval-Calvo, M., Fuster-Guillo, A., & Garcia-Rodriguez, J. (2016). A novel prediction method for early recognition of global human behaviour in image sequences. *Neural Processing Letters*, *43*(2), 363–387. doi:10.1007/s11063-015-9412-y

Bochkovskiy, A., Wang, C.-Y., & Liao, H.-Y. M. (2020). YOLOv4: Optimal speed and accuracy of object detection. arXiv preprint arXiv:2004.10934.

Cao, W., Li, L., Gong, S., & Dong, X. (2023, May). Research on Human Behavior Feature Recognition and Intelligent Early Warning Methods in Safety Supervision Scene Video based on Yolov7. [). IOP Publishing.]. *Journal of Physics: Conference Series*, *2496*(1), 012019. doi:10.1088/1742-6596/2496/1/012019

Du, W., Wang, Y., & Qiao, Y. (2017). Rpan: An end-to-end recurrent poseattention network for action recognition in videos. In *Proceedings of the ieee international conference on computer vision* (pp. 3725–3734). IEEE. 10.1109/ICCV.2017.402

Feichtenhofer, C., Pinz, A., & Zisserman, A. (2016). Convolutional two-stream network fusion for video action recognition. In *Proceedings of the ieee conference on computer vision and pattern recognition* (pp. 1933–1941). IEEE. 10.1109/CVPR.2016.213

Gao, X., Nguyen, M., & Yan, W. Q. (2021). Face image inpainting based on generative adversarial network. In 2021 36th international conference on image and vision computing new zealand (ivcnz) (pp. 1–6). 10.1109/IVCNZ54163.2021.9653347

Gorelick, L., Blank, M., Shechtman, E., Irani, M., & Basri, R. (2007, December). Actions as space-time shapes. *IEEE Transactions on Pattern Analysis and Machine Intelligence*, *29*(12), 2247–2253. doi:10.1109/TPAMI.2007.70711 PMID:17934233

Ji, S., Xu, W., Yang, M., & Yu, K. (2012). 3d convolutional neural networks for human action recognition. *IEEE Transactions on Pattern Analysis and Machine Intelligence*, *35*(1), 221–231. doi:10.1109/TPAMI.2012.59 PMID:22392705

Khan, M. A., Javed, K., Khan, S. A., Saba, T., Habib, U., Khan, J. A., & Abbasi, A. A. (2020). Human action recognition using fusion of Multiview and deep features: An application to video surveillance. *Multimedia Tools and Applications*, *83*(5), 1–27. doi:10.1007/s11042-020-08806-9

Liang, C., Lu, J., & Yan, W. (2022). *Human action recognition from digital videos based on deep learning*. ACM.

Lu, J., Nguyen, M., & Yan, W. Q. (2020). Deep learning methods for human behaviour recognition. In IEEE international conference on image and vision computing New Zealand (IVCNZ) (pp. 1–6). IEEE.

Lu, J., Yan, W. Q., & Nguyen, M. (2018). Human behaviour recognition usingdeep learning. In IEEE international conference on advanced video and signal based surveillance (AVSS) (pp. 1–6). IEEE.

Nguyen, A. T., & Bui, H. A. (2023, March). Multiple Target Activity Recognition by Combining YOLOv5 with LSTM Network. In *The International Conference on Intelligent Systems & Networks* (pp. 400-408). Singapore: Springer Nature Singapore. 10.1007/978-981-99-4725-6_49

Redmon, J., Divvala, S., Girshick, R., & Farhadi, A. (2016). You only look once: Unified, real-time object detection. In *Proceedings of the ieee conference on computer vision and pattern recognition* (pp. 779–788). IEEE. 10.1109/CVPR.2016.91

Sanjaya, S. A., & Adi Rakhmawan, S. (2020). Face mask detection using mobilenetv2 in the era of COVID-19 pandemic. *2020 International Conference on Data Analytics for Business and Industry: Way Towards a Sustainable Economy (ICDABI)*. IEEE. 10.1109/ICDABI51230.2020.9325631

Schuldt, C., Laptev, I., & Caputo, B. (2004). Recognizing human actions: A local svm approach. In IEEE international conference on pattern recognition (Vol. 3, pp. 32–36). IEEE. doi:10.1109/ICPR.2004.1334462

Shen, D., Chen, X., Nguyen, M., & Yan, W. Q. (2018). Flame detection using Deep Learning. *2018 4th International Conference on Control, Automation and Robotics (ICCAR)*. IEEE. doi:10.1109/ICCAR.2018.8384711

Simonyan, K., & Zisserman, A. (2014). Two-stream convolutional networks for action recognition in videos. *Advances in Neural Information Processing Systems*, 27.

Singh, S., Ahuja, U., Kumar, M., Kumar, K., & Sachdeva, M. (2021). Face mask detection using yolov3 and faster R-CNN models: COVID-19 environment. *Multimedia Tools and Applications*, *80*(13), 19753–19768. doi:10.1007/s11042-021-10711-8 PMID:33679209

Soomro, K., & Zamir, A. R. (2014). Action recognition in realistic sports videos. In *Computer vision in sports* (pp. 181–208). Springer. doi:10.1007/978-3-319-09396-3_9

Tran, D., Bourdev, L., Fergus, R., Torresani, L., & Paluri, M. (2015). Learning spatiotemporal features with 3d convolutional networks. In *Proceedings of the ieee international conference on computer vision* (pp. 4489–4497). IEEE. 10.1109/ICCV.2015.510

Venkateswarlu, I. B., Kakarla, J., & Prakash, S. (2020). Face mask detection using mobilenet and global pooling block. 2020 IEEE 4th Conference on Information & Communication Technology (CICT). doi:10.1109/CICT51604.2020.9312083

Wang, C.-Y., & Bochkovskiy, A., & Liao, H.-Y. M. (2023). YOLOv7: Trainable Bag-of-Freebies Sets New State-of-the-Art for Real-Time Object Detectors. *2023 IEEE Conference on Computer Vision and Pattern Recognition (CVPR)*, (pp. 7464–7475). IEEE. 10.1109/CVPR52729.2023.00721

Wang, C.-Y., Bochkovskiy, A., & Liao, H.-Y. M. (2022). *YOLOv7: Trainable bag-of-freebies sets new state-of-the-art for real-time object detectors*. arXiv preprint arXiv:2207.02696.

Wang, H., & Yan, W. Q. (2022). Face detection and recognition from distance based on Deep Learning. *Advances in Digital Crime, Forensics, and Cyber Terrorism*, 144–160. doi:10.4018/978-1-6684-4558-7.ch006

Wang, L., Xiong, Y., Wang, Z., Qiao, Y., Lin, D., Tang, X., & Gool, L. V. (2016). Temporal segment networks: Towards good practices for deep action recognition. In *European conference on computer vision* (pp. 20–36).

Wang, X., & Hu, H.-M., & Zhang, Y. (2019). Pedestrian detection based on spatial attention module for outdoor video surveillance. *2019 IEEE Fifth International Conference on Multimedia Big Data (BigMM)*. IEEE. 10.1109/BigMM.2019.00-17

Wang, X., & Yan, W. Q. (2020). Human gait recognition based on frameby-frame gait energy images and convolutional long short-term memory. *International Journal of Neural Systems*, *30*(01), 1950027. doi:10.1142/S0129065719500278 PMID:31747820

Wang, X., Zhang, J., & Yan, W. Q. (2020). Gait recognition using multichannel convolution neural networks. *Neural Computing & Applications*, *32*(18), 14275–14285. doi:10.1007/s00521-019-04524-y

Wiriyathammabhum, P., Summers-Stay, D., Ferm¨uller, C., & Aloimonos, Y. (2016). Computer vision and natural language processing: Recent approaches in multimedia and robotics. *ACM Computing Surveys*, *49*(4), 1–44. doi:10.1145/3009906

Woo, S., Park, J., Lee, J.-Y., & Kweon, I. S. (2018). CBAM: Convolutional Block Attention Module. *Computer Vision – ECCV 2018*. Springer. doi:10.1007/978-3-030-01234-2_1

Woo, S., Park, J., Lee, J.-Y., & Kweon, I. S. (2018). Cbam: Convolutional block attention module. In *Proceedings of the european conference on computer vision (eccv)* (pp. 3–19). IEEE.

Wu, P., Li, H., Zeng, N., & Li, F. (2022). FMD-Yolo: An efficient face mask detection method for covid-19 prevention and control in public. *Image and Vision Computing*, *117*, 104341. doi:10.1016/j.imavis.2021.104341 PMID:34848910

Yan, W. Q. (2019). *Introduction to intelligent surveillance*. Springer. doi:10.1007/978-3-030-10713-0

Yan, W. Q. (2019). *Introduction to intelligent surveillance: Surveillance data capture, transmission, and analytics*. Springer. doi:10.1007/978-3-030-10713-0

Yan, W. Q. (2021). *Computational methods for deep learning: Theoretic, practice and applications*. Springer. doi:10.1007/978-3-030-61081-4

Yan, W. Q. (2021). *Computational methods for deep learning: Theoretic, practice and applications*. Springer Nature. doi:10.1007/978-3-030-61081-4

Yang, G., Feng, W., Jin, J., Lei, Q., Li, X., Gui, G., & Wang, W. (2020). Face mask recognition system with Yolov5 based on image recognition. *2020 IEEE 6th International Conference on Computer and Communications (ICCC)*. IEEE. doi:10.1109/ICCC51575.2020.9345042

Yang, L., Zhang, R.-Y., Li, L., & Xie, X. (2021). Simam: A simple, parameterfree attention module for convolutional neural networks. In *International conference on machine learning* (pp. 11863–11874). IEEE.

Yu, J., & Zhang, W. (2021). Face mask wearing detection algorithm based on improved Yolo-V4. *Sensors (Basel)*, *21*(9), 3263. doi:10.3390/s21093263 PMID:34066802

Yu, Z., & Yan, W. Q. (2020). Human action recognition using deep learning methods. In Ieee international conference on image and vision computing new zealand (ivcnz) (pp. 1–6). IEEE. doi:10.1109/IVCNZ51579.2020.9290594

Yuan, J., Liu, Z., & Wu, Y. (2011). Discriminative video pattern search for efficient action detection. *IEEE Transactions on Pattern Analysis and Machine Intelligence*, *33*(9), 1728–1743. doi:10.1109/TPAMI.2011.38 PMID:21339530

Zhou, D., Fang, J., Song, X., Guan, C., Yin, J., Dai, Y., & Yang, R. (2019). IOU loss for 2D/3D object detection. *2019 International Conference on 3D Vision (3DV).* IEEE. doi:10.1109/3DV.2019.00019

Zou, Z., Chen, K., Shi, Z., & Guo, Y., & Ye, J. (2023). Object detection in 20 years: A survey. *Proceedings of the IEEE, 111*(3), 257–276. 10.1109/JPROC.2023.3238524

Chapter 7
Facial Emotion Recognition Using Ensemble Learning

GuanQun Xu
Auckland University of Technology, New Zealand

Wei Qi Yan
Auckland University of Technology, New Zealand

ABSTRACT

Facial emotion recognition (FER) is the task of identifying human emotions from facial expressions. The purpose of this book chapter is to improve accuracy of facial emotion recognition using integrated learning of lightweight networks without increasing the complexity or depth of the network. Compared to single lightweight models, it made a significant improvement. For a solution, the authors proposed an ensemble of mini-Xception models, where each expert is trained for a specific emotion and lets confidence score for the vote. Therefore, the expert model will transform the original multiclass task into binary tasks. The authors target the model to differentiate between a specific emotion and all others, facilitating the learning process. The principal innovation lies in our confidence-based voting mechanism, in which the experts "vote" based on their confidence scores rather than binary decisions.

DOI: 10.4018/979-8-3693-1738-9.ch007

INTRODUCTION

Facial Emotion Recognition (FER) currently lying at the crossroads of psychology and computer science, has grown immensely with the advent of machine learning and more specifically in deep learning. Historically, understanding and interpreting human emotions were subjective, relying heavily on human intuition and judgment. However, with the increasing integration of technology into our daily lives, objective identification of emotions through machines becomes not only desirable but, in many scenarios, it is essential.

Delving into the nature of emotions, the basic emotion posits that humans universally experience the foundational emotions, namely, happiness, sadness, fear, anger, disgust, and surprise. These fundamental emotional states can be seen as building blocks, from which more nuanced emotions—such as fatigue, anxiety, or satisfaction—emerge. Practical applications of FER are vast and varied. In human-computer interaction, deep learning algorithms can be designed to adapt and respond based on the user's emotional state, creating a more intuitive and empathetic user experience. In healthcare, it can be employed for monitoring patients for signs of pain or distress, especially if they cannot communicate verbally. In automotive industry, FER can be used to monitor driver's emotions and alertness, potentially preventing accidents caused by drowsiness or distress.

In 2006, Hinton introduced the ground-breaking theory of deep learning and subsequently applied it innovatively to image processing. Deep learning, fundamentally rooted in the deep neural network, is a specialized subset of artificial neural networks. The foundation of deep learning is established upon the research progress in artificial neural networks. By adjusting the number of hidden layers, one can derive an artificial neural network model with multiple hidden layers. Hidden neural networks are able to learn more effectively, mirroring the cognitive processes of the human brain. This facilitates the efficient extraction of image features (Feng et al., 2020).

Among deep learning architectures, CNNs became the poster child for FER. They consist of convolutional layers that can automatically and adaptively learn spatial hierarchies of features from input images. This property alleviated the need for hand-crafted features, a limitation of traditional methods. Layers within CNNs, such as pooling layers, helped in reducing spatial dimensions while retaining crucial information. Activation functions introduced nonlinearity, while enabling the network to capture complex relationships.

The mini-Xception model draws inspiration from the original "Xception" architecture, which stands for "Extreme Inception" (Li et al., 2022). In the Keras deep learning library, Xception was designed to improve upon the Inception architecture by using depthwise separable convolutions. The result of mini-Xception model comprises of four depthwise separable convolution blocks. The batch normalization processes the output to stabilize and accelerate the training process. This is complemented by the introduction of the ReLU activation function, which infuses the model with the necessary non-linearity. In the forward pass, the SoftMax function is invoked to facilitate multi-class classification of the results.

In the vast landscape of ensemble learning, the idea of leveraging multiple models to make a collective decision is central. One of the most intuitive and widely employed methods to achieve this consensus is through voting mechanisms. The intrinsic capability of deep neural networks to capture intricate patterns means that even a simple procedure like unweighted averaging can significantly enhance performance. By averaging across multiple networks, one can effectively reduce the model variance. This is especially impactful given that deep artificial neural networks (ANNs) are characterized with high variance but low bias. If the underlying models are sufficiently diverse or uncorrelated, their collective variance can be markedly diminished if averaged.

In hard voting, each model in the ensemble "votes" for a specific class. The class that receives the majority of votes is chosen as the final prediction. It's straightforward and doesn't require probability estimates. The advantages of voting mechanisms is by aggregating predictions, the ensemble smoothens out the biases and variances of individual models, which leads to a model that's less prone to overfitting.

In the context of ensemble models, majority voting refers to taking the mode of predictions across all models to arrive at the final prediction. This method is often effective if all models are equally reliable.

$$y_{\text{final}} = mode(y_1, y_2, \ldots, y_7) \tag{1}$$

where y_i is the prediction from the ith expert model. If most models predict a specific expression for an input image, that expression is taken as the final predicted class.

Instead of giving equal importance to all models, weighted voting takes into consideration of the confidence or reliability of each prediction of model. This ensures that more reliable models have a greater influence on the final decision.

$$y_{\text{final}} = argmax_j \sum_{i=1}^{7} w_i p\left(y = jx, M_i\right) \tag{2}$$

where $p(y=jx,M_i)$ is the probability of data x belonging to class j as predicted by model M_i, w_i is the weight (or confidence score) of the ith model. $argmax_j$ ensures that the class with the highest aggregated score is selected as the final prediction.

Confidence scores play a crucial role in our voting mechanism. Pertaining to a binary classification, where each expert model determines whether an input image belongs to a specific expression or the "other" class:

$$c_i = p(y = 1x, M_i) \tag{3}$$

where c_i is the confidence score for the ith model, $p(y=1x,M_i)$ is the probability that data x belongs to the target expression as predicted by model M_i. High confidence scores indicate strong certainty in a prediction of model, making it a suitable weight in our weighted voting scheme.

In this book chapter, a novel approach is proposed for emotion recognition by leveraging a unique methodology that incorporates weighted confidence scores. The primary innovation lies in the dynamic incorporation of predefined weights to the confidence scores produced by individual models specialized in recognizing specific emotions. These weights are not arbitrary but are derived from prior accuracy metrics, offering a degree of reliability and prediction. Based on historical accuracy rates, weights are assigned to each emotion. For instance, "Anger" is associated with a weight of 0.79. This signifies that the prediction confidence of this model for "Anger" would be adjusted by multiplying it with 0.79.

For each label or emotion, the corresponding specialized model is utilized to predict the confidence score for that particular emotion on the test image data. Each raw confidence score is then multiplied by its respective weight, creating a weighted confidence score. This step is central to this approach. The emotion associated with the highest weighted confidence score is considered the predicted emotion for the test image.

RELATED WORK

A facial expression recognition method was proposed based on convolutional neural network ensemble learning (Jia et al. 2020). The method takes use of three sub-networks and an SVM classifier to integrate the output of the three networks to obtain the final result. The model achieved a facial expression recognition accuracy of 71.27% on the FER2013 dataset.

The mini-Xception model – a lightweight and efficient variant of the original Xception architecture was designed for on-device real-time applications. Its depth-wise separable convolutions ensure fewer parameters and operations without compromising much on performance, which makes it a prime candidate for ensemble learning, especially in scenarios demanding speed and efficiency.

In Facial Emotion Recognition (FER), fine distinctions between emotions often mean the difference between accurate and subpar models, the amalgamation of ensemble learning and mini-Xception model becomes particularly compelling. By pooling together multiple mini-Xception models, each was trained with slight variations or focuses, the ensemble learning is positioned to capture a broader range of facial emotional nuances.

To balance the classes, we artificially increase the number of instances of the minority class by using methods like SMOTE, which generates synthetic samples; Brightness & contrast adjustment is a method for modifying the brightness and contrast of images by simulating different lighting conditions, crucial for FER in diverse environments; Elastic deformations are designed for slight warping of facial images that can mimic different facial expressions and nuances.

$$N' = N + SMOTE(N_{\text{minority}}, \alpha) \tag{4}$$

where N' is the new sample size after oversampling. N is the original sample size. N_{minority} represents the count of minority class samples. α is the oversampling ratio, determining how many synthetic samples to create. Instead of increasing the minority class, undersampling reduces the instances of the majority class to balance the classes.

$$N' = N - \text{RandomUndersample}(N_{\text{majority}}, \beta) \tag{5}$$

where N' is the new sample size after undersampling, N is the original sample size, N_{minority} represents the count of minority class samples, β is the undersampling ratio, dictating the fraction of majority class samples to be removed.

Binary mini-Xception models are at the heart of this ensemble learning, each fine-tuned for recognizing a specific emotion. Instead of a singular model attempting to classify multiple emotions, this approach offers dedicated experts for each emotion, ensuring a deeper understanding and more precise classification for that particular emotion.

Based on confidence-based voting mechanism, once each binary mini-Xception model makes a prediction for its corresponding emotion, the system doesn't merely count the votes. Instead, it considers the confidence or probability associated with each prediction. This approach ensures that the final decision takes into account not just the number of models favouring a particular emotion but also their respective certainty levels.

THE METHODOLOGY

In this book chapter, we examine the lightweight model mini-Xception. We used Jupyter Lab and Colab for code development, experimentation, and visualization. Jupyter Lab was used on an operating system based on Ubuntu 20.04 LTS, which was equipped with an Nvidia 3070 GPU. With TensorFlow running on Google Colab, this project was able to use its cloud-based computational resources in parallel and to utilize its integrated T4 GPUs. A flexible computational environment was achieved by combining local resources with cloud-based platforms. The model was trained using Jupyter Lab locally following stability and model debugging using Colab.

Our dataset of FER2013 is based on an automatically collected dataset derived from the Google Image API. In the FER-2013 dataset, human accuracy averages around 65%. However, Tang's approach in 2013 led to a test accuracy of 71.2% by utilizing a CNN combined with L2-SVM loss, marking a significant milestone and subsequently winning him the ICML 2013 Challenges in Representation Learning (Tang, 2013). Subsequent advancements have yielded even better results. For instance, in 2016, Kim et al. reported an impressive 73.73% test accuracy. The methodology involved an ensemble of CNNs processing both aligned and non-aligned images. A standout aspect of the method was a pre-processing alignment step conducted by using a dedicated Deep Convolutional Network, which essentially learned from an optimal mapping (Kim, Dong, Roh, Kim, & Lee, 2016). Similarly, in 2017, Connie proposed a unique model blending both SIFT and CNN features. The innovative approach, which aggregated insights from three distinct models, resulted in a commendable 73.4% accuracy (Connie, Al-Shabi, Cheah, & Goh, 2017). Notably, Zhang et al. achieved a 75.1% test accuracy by amalgamating training data from a variety of sources, underlining the potential of harnessing diverse information in training (Zhang, Luo, Loy, & Tang, 2015).

The FER2013 dataset suffers from an imbalance in the distribution of its emotion classes. For the applications, such an imbalance can lead to a biased model that disproportionately favourites the majority class. In response to this, we implemented a hybrid technique to level the class distribution. (Renda et al., 2019)

We expanded the representation of the target emotion class by replicating its instances. Specifically, the samples of the desired emotion (denoted as the target emotion) were oversampled by using a factor (*pos_multiplier*), effectively increasing their count. For instance, with *pos_multiplier* is set to 2, the target class samples would be doubled. To further refine the balance, the non-target emotion classes were undersampled. This was achieved by randomly removing a proportion (*neg_multiplier*) of samples from these classes. For example, a *neg_multiplier* such as 0.3 would result in the removal of approximately 30% of the non-target class samples.

Recognizing the notably smaller representation of the "Disgust" emotion in the dataset, we adjusted the oversampling factor specifically for this class, thereby with a greater emphasis during the balancing process. After postprocessing, the balanced dataset underwent a re-evaluation of its class distribution. The resultant dataset exhibited a more equitable distribution between the target emotion and the remaining emotions, with a sample ratio of approximately 1:1.5 (target to non-target). The balanced datasets can facilitate more robust model training, fostering improved generalization and reduced bias towards any specific emotion class.

In the context of our facial emotion recognition, each emotion-specific model, termed as an "expert", focuses on the accurate detection of a particular emotion. Each expert was individually trained and validated against the FER2013 dataset. Each expert model underwent an initial training phase of 50 epochs. Post this phase, the models were equipped with pre-trained weights, and the training process was extended for an additional 20 epochs. For most emotion categories, the models showcased impressive accuracy, often hovering around the 85% mark in binary classification scenarios.

RESULT ANALYSIS

Figure 1. Comparison between: (a) If all confidence scores = 1.0, and (b) If confidence scores change

(a)

	precision	recall	f1-score	support
Anger	0.74	0.68	0.71	495
Disgust	0.20	0.36	0.26	50
Fear	0.76	0.63	0.69	514
Happy	0.93	0.93	0.93	891
Sad	0.71	0.72	0.72	608
Surprise	0.87	0.84	0.86	406
Neutral	0.72	0.83	0.77	625
accuracy			0.78	3589
macro avg	0.71	0.71	0.70	3589
weighted avg	0.79	0.78	0.78	3589

(b)

	precision	recall	f1-score	support
Anger	0.66	0.64	0.65	101
Disgust	0.36	0.33	0.35	12
Fear	0.62	0.70	0.66	101
Happy	0.93	0.93	0.93	189
Sad	0.70	0.53	0.61	131
Surprise	0.84	0.86	0.85	87
Neutral	0.68	0.81	0.74	97
accuracy			0.75	718
macro avg	0.69	0.69	0.68	718
weighted avg	0.75	0.75	0.75	718

From Figure 1 (a), with an overarching accuracy of 78%, the model demonstrates considerable strength in recognizing a broad spectrum of emotions. Notably, its prowess is pronounced in distinguishing emotions like "Happy" and "Surprise", as evidenced by the remarkable F1 scores of 0.93 and 0.86, respectively. Moreover, the model adaptiveness extends to the "Neutral" emotion, reflected by a noteworthy recall rate of 0.83. This metric signifies the ability of model to effectively capture the majority of instances associated with neutral expressions, underscoring its balanced performance across various emotion categories.

Figure 1 (b) shows the performance metrics after changing the confidence score for each emotion category: "Anger" at 1.0, "Disgust" at 0.8, "Fear" at 1.0, "Happy" at 1, "Sad" at 0.91, "Surprise" at 1.0, and "Neutral" at 0.92.

As a result of modifying these confidence scores, there is a discernible shift in performance metrics. By retaining its standard, the model exhibits an overall accuracy of 75%, affirming its consistency in identifying emotions spanning various categories. Notably, its proficiency in detecting "Happy" emotions remains undiminished, as evidenced by an F1 score of 0.93.

As a result of Figure 1 (a) to Figure 1 (b), an enhancement in recall is evident for categories like "Fear" and "Neutral", registering values of 0.70 and 0.81 respectively, suggesting an improved capacity in accurately detecting true instances of these emotions. However, precision in detecting "Anger" sees a decrease, registering at 0.66, hinting at potential misclassifications where non-anger instances might be erroneously recognized as anger. The emotion "Disgust" emerges as a persistent challenge, yielding a modest F1 score 0.35. The outcome, coupled with diminished support, insinuates a possible paucity of data samples for this class, which may be a contributory factor to its suboptimal performance. Additionally, the "Sad" class reveals a decline in its F1 score to 0.61, attributed to a decrease in recall, suggesting potential oversights in identifying genuine instances of sadness following confidence adjustment. While these confidence alterations render enhancements in specific facets, they also spotlight potential zones in the model which might benefit from meticulous fine-tuning or supplementary data for performance amelioration.

Figure 2. ROC curve comparison between: (a) If all confidence scores = 1.0, and (b) If confidence scores change

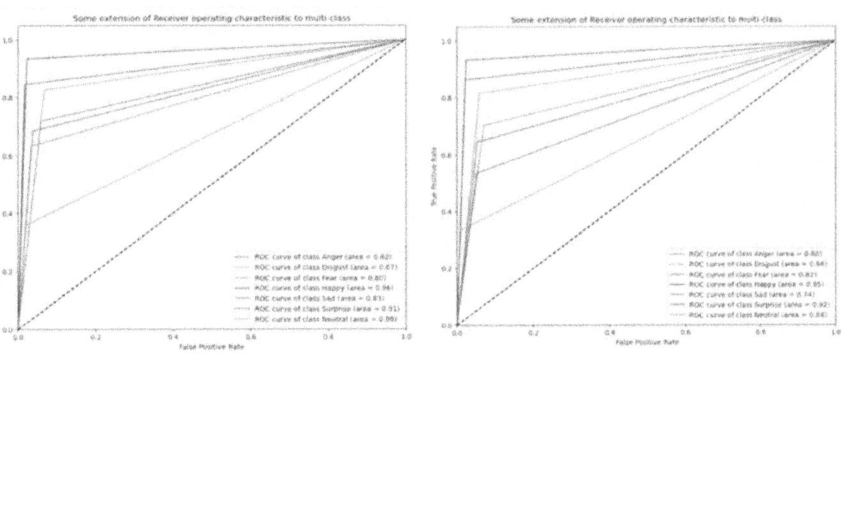

(a) (b)

In Figure 2 (a), "Happy" emotion stands out with an impressive AUC (Area Under the Curve) of 0.96, underscoring the exemplary capability to discern true positives from negatives within this category. Meanwhile, emotions such as "Fear", "Sad", "Surprise", and "Neutral" exhibit AUC values surpassing 0.80, reflecting their substantial discriminatory efficacy within the model. However, the "Disgust" class presents a challenge, registering an AUC of 0.67.

Followed the adjustment in confidence scores as shown in Figure 2 (b), there were discernible, albeit minor, shifts in the AUC (Area Under the Curve) values of most emotions. For instance, the AUC for "Fear" witnessed an enhancement, climbing from 0.80 to 0.82. Contrarily, "Sad" experienced a decline, receding from 0.83 to 0.74.

Remarkably, the emotions displayed a robust performance: "Happy" managed to sustain its commendable AUC, registering only a slight dip to 0.95. Meanwhile, "Surprise" showed a promising upward trend, elevating from 0.91 to 0.92. However, challenges persisted with the "Disgust" class.

CONCLUSION

In this book chapter, in advancing emotion recognition through the integration of ensemble learning into the mini-Xception framework, we observed marked enhancements in terms of both accuracy and prediction confidence. Yet, like all empirical investigations, our research is not without its limitations. Here we outline the principal constraints of our study:

Our primary data source was the FER2013 dataset. While it offers a comprehensive collection of facial expressions, potential biases, noise, or imbalances in specific emotional categories may exist. Such shortcomings can influence the ability of model to generalize effectively across a myriad of real-world situations.

While the mini-Xception model offers computational efficiency, its relatively simpler architecture might not encapsulate all subtleties of facial expressions as proficiently as more intricate models. Furthermore, our ensemble approach, which amalgamates a number of "expert" models, might compromise on real-time processing capabilities due to increased computational demands.

Our ensemble framework fundamentally rests on binary classifiers, dedicated to distinguishing between two emotions. This binary emphasis might not encapsulate the multifaceted nature of human emotions, especially in scenarios where emotions blur boundaries.

REFERENCES

Ahonen, T., Hadid, A., & Pietikäinen, M. (2006). Face description with local binary patterns: Application to face recognition. *IEEE Transactions on Pattern Analysis and Machine Intelligence*, *28*(12), 2037–2041. doi:10.1109/TPAMI.2006.244 PMID:17108377

Chirra, V. R. R., Reddy, U. S., & Kolli, V. K. K. (2021). Virtual facial expression recognition using deep CNN with ensemble learning. *Journal of Ambient Intelligence and Humanized Computing*, *12*(12), 10581–10599. doi:10.1007/s12652-020-02866-3

Connie, T., Al-Shabi, M., Cheah, W. P., & Goh, M. K. O. (2017). Facial expression recognition using a hybrid CNN–SIFT aggregator. In Lecture Notes in Computer Science (pp. 139–149). Springer. doi:10.1007/978-3-319-69456-6_12

Cui, W., & Yan, W. (2016). A scheme for face recognition in complex environments. [IJDCF]. *International Journal of Digital Crime and Forensics*, *8*(1), 26–36. doi:10.4018/IJDCF.2016010102

Fan, Y., Lam, J. C., & Li, V. O. K. (2018). Multi-region ensemble convolutional neural network for facial expression recognition. In Lecture Notes in Computer Science (pp. 84–94). Springer. doi:10.1007/978-3-030-01418-6_9

Fayek, H. M., Lech, M., & Cavedon, L. (2016). Modeling subjectiveness in emotion recognition with deep neural networks: Ensembles *vs* soft labels. *International Joint Conference on Neural Networks (IJCNN)*. IJCNN. 10.1109/IJCNN.2016.7727250

Feng, Y., Pang, T., Li, M., & Guan, Y. (2020). Small sample face recognition based on ensemble deep learning. *Chinese Control and Decision Conference (CCDC)*. CCDC. 10.1109/CCDC49329.2020.9163968

Gao, X., Nguyen, M., & Yan, W. (2021) Face image inpainting based on generative adversarial network. *International Conference on Image and Vision Computing New Zealand*. IEEE. 10.1109/IVCNZ54163.2021.9653347

Gao, X., Nguyen, M., & Yan, W. (2022) A face image inpainting method based on autoencoder and adversarial generative networks. *Pacific-Rim Symposium on Image and Video Technology*.

García, S., & Herrera, F. (2009). Evolutionary undersampling for classification with imbalanced datasets: Proposals and taxonomy. *Evolutionary Computation*, *17*(3), 275–306. doi:10.1162/evco.2009.17.3.275 PMID:19708770

Habib, A. S. B., & Tasnim, T. (2020). An ensemble hard voting model for cardiovascular disease prediction. *International Conference on Sustainable Technologies for Industry 4.0 (STI).* IEEE. 10.1109/STI50764.2020.9350514

Ioffe, S., & Szegedy, C. (2015). *Batch normalization: Accelerating deep network training by reducing internal covariate shift.*arXiv. http://export.arxiv.org/pdf/1502.03167

Jia, C., Li, C. L., & Zhou, Y. (2020). Facial expression recognition based on the ensemble learning of CNNs. *IEEE International Conference on Signal Processing.* IEEE. 10.1109/ICSPCC50002.2020.9259543

Kim, B., Dong, S., Roh, J., Kim, G., & Lee, S. Y. (2016). Fusing aligned and non-aligned face information for automatic affect recognition in the wild: A deep learning approach. *IEEE Conference on Computer Vision and Pattern Recognition Workshops (CVPRW).* IEEE. 10.1109/CVPRW.2016.187

Kyeremateng-Boateng, H., Josyula, D. P., & Conn, M. (2023). Computing confidence score for neural network predictions from latent features. *International Conference on Control, Communication and Computing (ICCC).* IEEE. 10.1109/ICCC57789.2023.10165294

Le, H., Nguyen, M., Yan, W. Q., & Lo, S. (2021). Training a convolutional neural network for transportation sign detection using synthetic dataset. *2021 36th International Conference on Image and Vision Computing New Zealand (IVCNZ).* IEEE. 10.1109/IVCNZ54163.2021.9653398

Li, C., Li, D., Zhao, M., & Li, H. (2022). A light-weight convolutional neural network for facial expression recognition using Mini-Xception neural networks. *IEEE International Conference on Current Development in Engineering and Technology (CCET)* IEEE. 10.1109/QRS-C57518.2022.00104

Liu, K., Zhang, M., & Pan, Z. (2016). Facial expression recognition with CNN ensemble. *International Conference on Cyberworlds.* IEEE.

Liu, M., & Yan, W. (2022). *Masked face recognition in real-time using MobileNetV2.* ACM ICCCV.

Nguyen, M., Yan, W. (2022) Temporal color-coded facial-expression recognition using convolutional neural network. *International Summit Smart City 360°: Science and Technologies for Smart Cities.* IEEE.

Nguyen, M., & Yan, W. (2023) From faces to traffic lights: A multi-scale approach for emotional state representation. *IEEE International Conference on Smart City.* IEEE.

Powers, D. (2020). *Evaluation: from precision, recall and F-measure to ROC, informedness, markedness and correlation.* Cornell University. https://doi.org// arxiv.2010.16061 doi:10.48550

Renda, A., Barsacchi, M., Bechini, A., & Marcelloni, F. (2019). Comparing ensemble strategies for deep learning: An application to facial expression recognition. *Expert Systems with Applications, 136*, 1–11. doi:10.1016/j.eswa.2019.06.025

Song, C., He, L., Yan, W., & Nand, P. (2019) An improved selective facial extraction model for age estimation. *International Conference on Image and Vision Computing New Zealand.* IEEE. 10.1109/IVCNZ48456.2019.8960965

Sridhar, K., Lin, W., & Busso, C. (2021). Generative approach using soft-labels to learn uncertainty in predicting emotional attributes. *International Conference on Affective Computing and Intelligent Interaction (ACII).* IEEE. 10.1109/ ACII52823.2021.9597461

Sun, L., Ge, C., & Zhong, Y. (2021). Design and implementation of face emotion recognition system based on CNN Mini-Xception Frameworks. *Journal of Physics: Conference Series, 2010*(1), 012123. doi:10.1088/1742-6596/2010/1/012123

Tang, J., Su, Q., Su, B., Fong, S., Cao, W., & Gong, X. (2020). Parallel ensemble learning of convolutional neural networks and local binary patterns for face recognition. *Computer Methods and Programs in Biomedicine, 197*, 105622. doi:10.1016/j.cmpb.2020.105622 PMID:32629293

Tang, Y. (2013). *Deep learning using linear support vector machines.* Cornell University.

Wang, H., & Yan, W. (2022). *Face detection and recognition from distance based on deep learning. Aiding Forensic Investigation Through Deep Learning and Machine Learning Framework.* IGI Global.

Wang, Y., & Lu, F. (2021). An adaptive boosting algorithm based on weighted feature selection and category classification confidence. *Applied Intelligence, 51*(10), 6837–6858. doi:10.1007/s10489-020-02184-3

Webb, G. I., & Zheng, Z. (2004). Multistrategy ensemble learning: Reducing error by combining ensemble learning methods. *IEEE Transactions on Knowledge and Data Engineering, 16*(8), 980–991. doi:10.1109/TKDE.2004.29

Yan, W. (2021). *Computational methods for deep learning.* Springer. doi:10.1007/978-3-030-61081-4

Zehra, N., Azeem, S. H., & Farhan, M. (2021). Human activity recognition through ensemble learning of multiple convolutional neural networks. *Annual Conference on Information Sciences and Systems (CISS)*. IEEE. 10.1109/CISS50987.2021.9400290

Zhang, Z., Luo, P., Loy, C. C., & Tang, X. (2015). Learning social relation traits from face images. *IEEE International Conference on Computer Vision (ICCV)*. IEEE. 10.1109/ICCV.2015.414

Chapter 8
Real-Time Billiard Shot Stability Detection Based on YOLOv8

Boning Yang
Auckland University of Technology, New Zealand

Wei Qi Yan
Auckland University of Technology, New Zealand

ABSTRACT

This book chapter presents a real-time system for detecting the stability of a player's billiard shot, based on the YOLOv8 neural network. The system comprises a real-time object detection model and a real-time slope monitoring system. The model focuses on detecting four classes: The cue ball, hand, cue stick tip, and the bridge hand (hand support point). The project involved iterative model training on a custom dataset, eventually achieving a YOLOv8 model with 95% accuracy. The stability of a player's shot is detected by simulating slope change of cue stick during aiming, using the cue stick tip and bridge hand. Overall, the project highlights the immense potential of YOLOv8 in sports applications.

INTRODUCTION

Despite advances in billiard training, assessing and improving shot stability remain challenging for players and coaches. In billiards, slight changes in stroke angle and force critically impact the trajectory, making stability vital for hit success (Chen, 2023). Traditionally, coaching depends on subjective judgment, struggling to quantify

DOI: 10.4018/979-8-3693-1738-9.ch008

subtle movement changes. Self-assessment by players also lacks precision without professional guidance.

The rise of computer vision and deep learning leads to new opportunities in sports (Zhou, 2023; Can, 2022; Cao & Yan, 2022; Zhu & Yan, 2022), including billiards. Implementing these technologies for real-time shot stability analysis provides instant, objective, and precise feedback. This aids players across all levels in mastering games and refining skills, marking a transformative integration of technology and sports coaching (Herrera, et al., 2008).

This book chapter presents the development of a real-time billiards shot detection by using deep learning, computer vision, and YOLOv8. The effectiveness hinges on several core areas: Adapting YOLOv8 for precise tracking of subtle movements in billiards, evaluating accuracy against other methods, examining processing speed for real-time feedback, integrating the system into training routines, assessing adaptability to various playing conditions and techniques, and gathering user feedback from players and coaches. The key contributions of this book chapter include creating a unique dataset specifically for billiard shot stability, optimizing a customized YOLOv8 model for enhanced detection accuracy and speed, and implementing a practical system that provides instantaneous, objective feedback, proven valuable in real-world training and competitive environments. This book chapter underscores the significance of a technologically advanced, data-driven approach in revolutionizing billiards training.

LITERATURE REVIEW

Table 1. Real-time target detection ranking based on MS COCO dataset

Rank	Model	Box AP	FPS	References	Year
1	YOLOv6-L6	57.2	46	*YOLOv6 v3.0: A Full-Scale Reloading*	2023
2	PRB-FPN6-MSP	57.2	27	*Parallel Residual Bi-Fusion Feature Pyramid Network for Accurate Single-Shot Object Detection*	2020
3	YOLOv7-E6E	56.8	36	*YOLOv7: Trainable bag-of-freebies sets new state-of-the-art for real-time object detectors*	2022
4	YOLOv7-D6	56.6	44		2022
5	YOLOv7-E6	56	56		2022
6	YOLOv7-W6	54.9	84		2022
7	PP-YOLOE+_X	54.7	45	*PP-YOLOE: An evolved version of YOLO*	2022
8	PP-YOLOE+_L	54.0	78		2022
9	PRB-FPN-MSP	53.3	94	*Parallel Residual Bi-Fusion Feature Pyramid Network for Accurate Single-Shot Object Detection*	2020
10	Gold-YOLO-L	53.28	116	*Gold-YOLO: Efficient Object Detector via Gather-and-Distribute Mechanism*	2023

In Table 1, the models were trained on the publicly available dataset MS COCO. YOLO variants dominate the leaderboard for real-time object detection on the MS COCO dataset, with YOLOv6-L6 taking the top spot. This algorithm achieves the highest Box Average Precision (AP) at 57.2, with a frame rate of 46 frames per second (FPS), suggesting a balance between accuracy and speed suitable for real-time applications.(Li et al., 2023) The table indicates the trend where more recent YOLO versions, like YOLOv7, offers a variety of trade-offs between precision and speed, with versions attaining higher FPS potentially favoring applications where speed is crucial, even at the expense of some accuracy.(Wang et al., 2023) Notably, PRB-FPN6-MSP matches YOLOv6-L6 in Box AP but at a lower speed, highlighting the efficiency of YOLO architectures.(Chen et al., 2021) These results collectively underscore advancements in YOLO algorithms, particularly in their ability to deliver high-accuracy detection in real-time scenarios, a key factor for applications like the billiards shot stability detection system discussed earlier.

YOLO series, particularly YOLOv6-L6, YOLOv7, PP-YOLOE, and Gold-YOLO, have marked significant advancements in the field of real-time object detection. (Wang et al., 2023) YOLOv6-L6 stands out with its network design enhancements, anchor-assisted training, and self-distillation strategies, boosting accuracy and speed.

PRB-FPN distinguishes itself with a unique architecture designed to detect objects of varying sizes efficiently, featuring bi-fusion modules and a residual design for improved precision.

YOLOv7 brings architectural and training optimizations with elements like VoVNet and CSPNet, setting new standards for speed and accuracy in real-time detection. PP-YOLOE innovates on the YOLO architecture with an anchor-free design, a robust backbone, and dynamic label assignment, achieving a balance between detection performance and inference speed.(Wang et al., 2023)

Gold-YOLO introduces the Gather-and-Distribute mechanism, improving information fusion, and employs unsupervised pre-training, showing substantial improvements in accuracy and speed over its predecessors.(Wang et al., 2023)

Collectively, these iterations of the YOLO series showcase a trajectory of continuous improvement (Liang et al., 2022; Yu & Yan, 2020), each bringing novel features and optimizations that enhance the model adaptability and performance in real-time object detection applications. This evolution cements YOLO's position as a leading solution in the domain.

Figure 1. The structure of YOLOv8 model

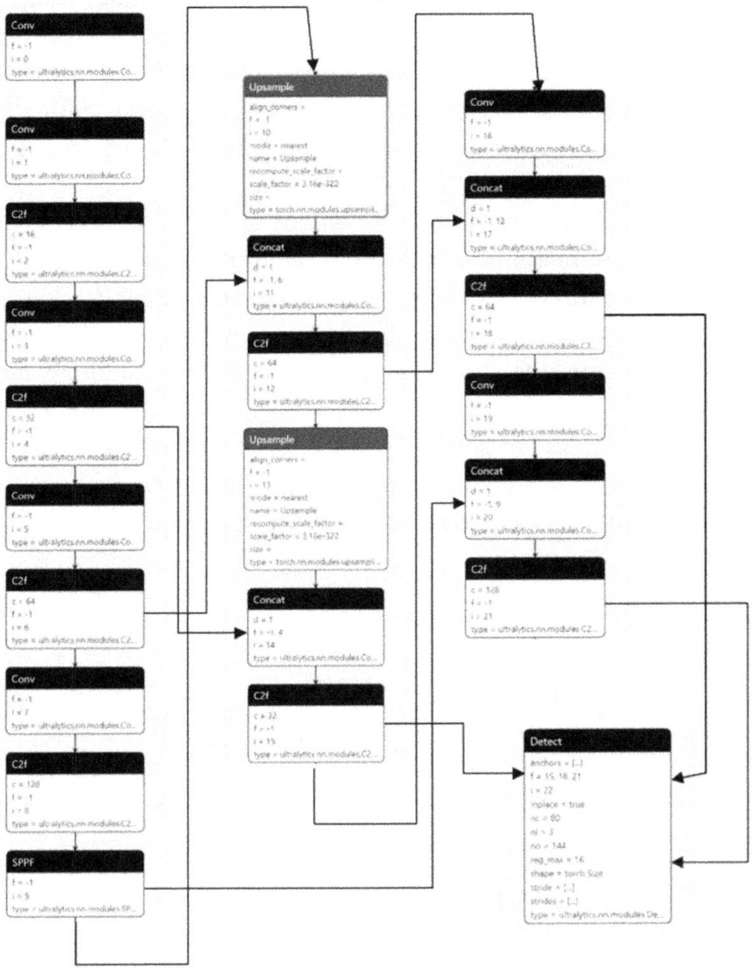

Figure 1 shows the network structure of the YOLOv8 model in .pt format opened using the Netron software. By referring to the official diagram provided by the open-source community Open-mmlab, it can be understood that modules 0-9 are the Backbone part of YOLO, 10-21 are the Neck part, and 22 is the Head part.

YOLO, an acronym for "You Only Look Once", is a deep learning framework for visual object detection. It primarily comprises three segments: Backbone, Neck, and Head. The Backbone, typically a deep convolutional neural network such as VGG, ResNet, or DarkNet, is tasked with deriving basic spatial and contextual features from unprocessed images.(Ayob et al., 2021; Demetriou et al., 2023; Sujatha et al., 2023; Zhou et al., 2019) The Neck component, such as FPN or PANet, is added post-Backbone and aimed at integrating and enhancing features of varying depths and resolutions to capture multi-scale information of objects. The Head, on the other hand, directly predicts the object's class, location, and size based on the features obtained from the Neck. In essence, the entire YOLO framework firstly extracts image features through the Backbone, enhances and integrates them via the Neck, and subsequently outputs the final object detection results through the Head.(Huang et al., 2023; Vasanthi & Mohan, 2023; Zhang et al., 2021)

YOLO framework is renowned for its unique approach to object detection. In contrast to traditional methods which often require multiple scans of an image, YOLO captures the entirety of an image in just one forward pass, allowing for real-time detection. To ensure the quality of predictions made by YOLO or any similar object detection systems, there are a series of key metrics commonly employed:

Precision is:

$$\text{Precision} = \frac{\text{TruePositives(TP)}}{\text{TruePositives(TP)} + \text{FalsePositives(FP)}} \tag{1}$$

Recall is:

$$\text{Recall} = \frac{\text{TruePositives}\left(\text{TP}\right)}{\text{TruePositives}\left(\text{TP}\right) + \text{FalseNegatives(FN)}} \tag{2}$$

F1 Score is:

$$F1 = 2 \times \frac{\text{Precision} \times \text{Recall}}{\text{Precision} + \text{Recall}} \tag{3}$$

IoU quantifies the overlap between the predicted bounding box and the ground truth bounding box. It is a pivotal metric in object detection, particularly for determining how well the model predicted bounding box aligning with the ground truth. It is expressed as:

$$IoU = \frac{\text{AreaofOverlap(Intersection)}}{\text{AreaofUnion(Union)}} \tag{4}$$

These evaluation metrics are imperative for comprehending the efficacy of object detection models. They not only offer insights into the model's precision and coverage but also guide improvements, allowing for the optimization of the model's performance.

METHODOLOGY

Figure 2 offers a systematic representation of the steps involved in capturing a target video, preprocessing, training a model, and the eventual deployment of the model after evaluating its performance indicators.

Figure 2. Model iteration and optimization flowchart

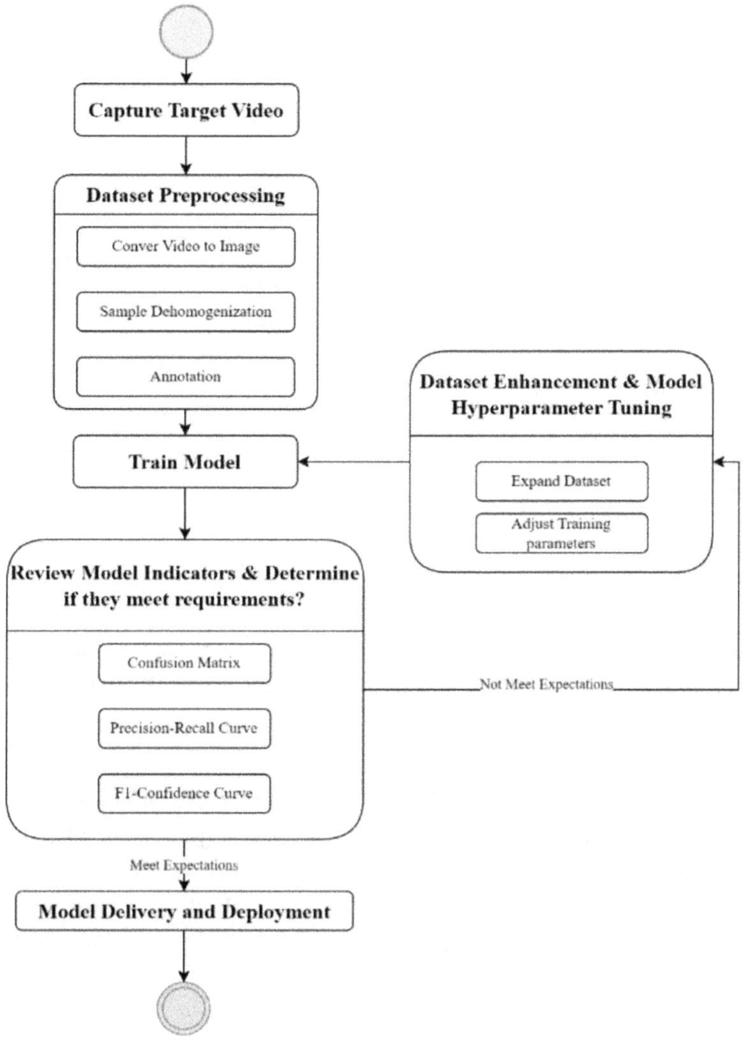

The experimental process laid out is iterative in nature, wherein the model undergoes cycles of training and evaluation until it meets the desired threshold. The ultimate goal is for the model to attain a recognition accuracy, quantified by the metric mean Average Precision (mAP), of over 0.95 for all the object classes. This high threshold ensures that the model not only correctly identifies the objects but also does so with high confidence across various scenarios and conditions.

During the model evaluation process, regarding models that do not meet expectations, we analyze the confusion matrix of the model to determine which class has a problematic recognition rate. Then, we increase the proportion of this class in the dataset through sample augmentation to improve its recognition rate. Sample augmentation involves rotating the original samples of this class, the original sample set is,

$$S = \{s_1, s_2, \ldots, s_{472}\}$$

The rotation operation is,

$$s_i' = \text{Rotate}\left(s_i, -15^\circ\right)$$

The sample after rotation is

$$S' = \left\{s_1', s_2', \ldots, s_{472}'\right\}$$

The combined sample is

$$S_{\text{total}} = S \cup S'$$

For the classes that are highly homogenous, we are use of the Structural Similarity Index Measure (SSIM) algorithm to reduce these samples, as the original samples are created by converting videos into images, a process that generates many redundant samples. (Fuentes-Hurtado et al., 2022)

The samples were manually labeled to create the dataset used for model training. Four classes were marked within the samples: "0", "sp", "hp", and "hand". "0" means the cue ball in billiards. "sp" is the bridge hand of the player, which is the hand formation used to support and guide the cue stick. "hp" represents the hitting point on the cue stick (also referred to as the tip). "Hand" stands for the player's hand. The annotation details are shown in Figure 3.

Figure 3. Sample annotation explanation

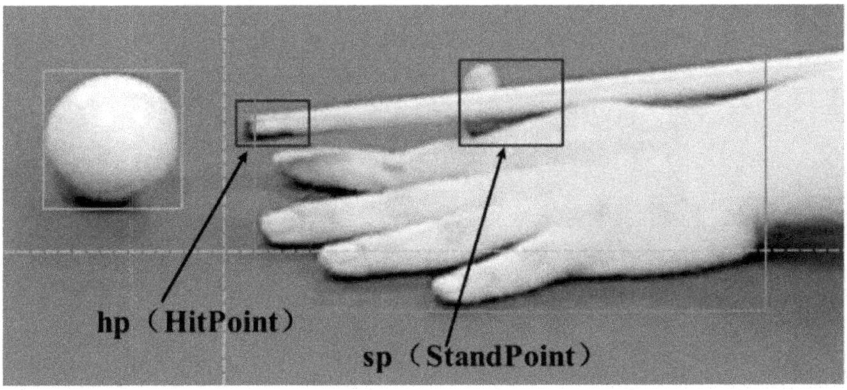

In addition to modify the dataset, a few adjustments were also made to the model training parameters (Lu et al, 2016; Lu et al., 2017; Lu et al., 2018; Lu et al., 2020). One such parameter is *imgsz*, which controls the initial image size at the input layer of the model. By increasing this parameter from the default value of 640 to 1280, a significant improvement in the mAP (mean Average Precision) value for all classes was observed.

MODEL DEPLOYMENT

After obtaining a high-accuracy model, we normalized the prediction boxes for "tip" and "sp" to obtain key points (Li, et al., 2016). These two points correspond to the contact point of the cue stick in a billiards game, also known as the "tip", and the "sp", where the player supports the cue stick. By connecting these two points, we form a white line, as shown in Figure 4. When the player strokes the ball, the stability of the slope of this line is monitored to determine whether the player's shot is stable.

Figure 4. Details of the demo

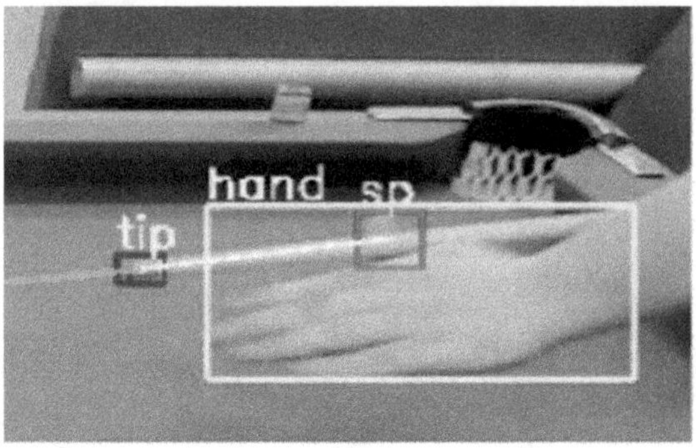

Figure 5. Billiards shooting DEMO

The slope detection is expressed as:

$$\text{Slope}(m) = \frac{\Delta y}{\Delta x} \tag{5}$$

where,

$$\Delta y = y_2 - y_1$$

$$\Delta x = x_2 - x_1 \tag{6}$$

where, (x_1, y_1) and (x_2, y_2) are the coordinates of two consecutive points.

$$\text{Jittering} = |\arctan(m) - \arctan(m_{prev})| > \text{threshold} \quad (7)$$

where m is the current calculated slope, m_{prev} is the previously calculated slope. To detect significant variation between two consecutive slopes, we compute their difference (transforming the slope into angles using the arctangent function) and see if this difference surpasses a set threshold. If it exceeds the threshold, we consider jitter to be detected.

As shown in Figure 5, after we design the slope detection, the captions will be displayed on the prediction screen and sound will be emitted to prompt the player whether their aiming and shooting are stable.

CONCLUSION

In this book chapter, a new model was trained to track four classes in real time with 95% accuracy, which offers a novel method to assess players' stability during billiard shots. It focuses on two key points: "Hand bridge" (sp) in a player's hand and the cue-stick contact point ("hp"). Analyzing the steadiness and relationship of these points provides insights into a player's cue alignment and shot consistency. This tool, beneficial in both real-time and post-game reviews, can act as an alternative to traditional coaching, aiding players to identify and improve their techniques, leading to enhanced gameplay (Yan, 2019; Yan, 2023).

REFERENCES

Ayob, A. F., Khairuddin, K., Mustafah, Y. M., Salisa, A. R., & Kadir, K. (2021). Analysis of Pruned Neural Networks (MobileNetV2-YOLO v2) for Underwater Object Detection. *Proceedings of the 11th National Technical Seminar on Unmanned System Technology 2019* (Vol. 666, pp. 87–98). Springer Nature. 10.1007/978-981-15-5281-6_7

Cao, X. (2022). *Pose Estimation of Swimmers from Digital Images Using Deep Learning*. [Master's Thesis, Auckland University of Technology].

Cao, X., & Yan, W. (2022). *Pose estimation for swimmers in video surveillance. Multimedia Tools and Applications*. Springer.

Chen, P.-Y., Chang, M.-C., Hsieh, J.-W., & Chen, Y.-S. (2021). Parallel Residual Bi-Fusion Feature Pyramid Network for Accurate Single-Shot Object Detection. *IEEE Transactions on Image Processing*, *30*, 9099–9111. doi:10.1109/TIP.2021.3118953 PMID:34735334

Chen, Z. (2023). *Real-Time Pose Recognition for Billiard Players Using Deep Learning. Research Report*. Auckland University of Technology.

Demetriou, D., Mavromatidis, P., Robert, P. M., Papadopoulos, H., Petrou, M. F., & Nicolaides, D. (2023). *Real-Time Construction Demolition Waste Detection Using State-of-The-Art Deep Learning Methods; Single – Stage vs Two-Stage Detectors* [Preprint].

Fuentes-Hurtado, F., Delaire, T., Levet, F., Sibarita, J.-B., & Viasnoff, V. (2022). MID3A: Microscopy Image Denoising meets Differentiable Data Augmentation. *International Joint Conference on Neural Networks (IJCNN),* (pp. 1–9). IEEE. 10.1109/IJCNN55064.2022.9892954

Herrera, A., Beck, A., Bell, D., Miller, P., Wu, Q., & Yan, W. (2008) Behavior analysis and prediction in image sequences using rough sets. *International Machine Vision and Image Processing Conference* (pp.71-76). IEEE.

Huang, M., Liu, Z., Liu, T., & Wang, J. (2023). CCDS-YOLO: Multi-Category Synthetic Aperture Radar Image Object Detection Model Based on YOLOv5s. *Electronics (Basel)*, *12*(16), 3497. doi:10.3390/electronics12163497

LiC.LiL.GengY.JiangH.ChengM.ZhangB.KeZ.XuX.ChuX. (2023). YOLOv6 v3.0: A Full-Scale Reloading. https://doi.org/ doi:10.48550/ARXIV.2301.05586

Li, F., Zhang, Y., Yan, W., & Klette, R. (2016) Adaptive and compressive target tracking based on feature point matching. *International Conference on Pattern Recognition* (ICPR), (pp.2734-2739). IEEE. 10.1109/ICPR.2016.7900049

Liang, C., Lu, J., & Yan, W. (2022). *Human action recognition from digital videos based on deep learning*. ACM ICCCV. doi:10.1145/3561613.3561637

Lu, J. (2016). *Empirical Approaches for Human Behavior Analytics*. [Master's Thesis. Auckland University of Technology, New Zealand].

Lu, J., Nguyen, M., & Yan, W. (2018). *Pedestrian detection using deep learning*. IEEE AVSS.

Lu, J., Nguyen, M., & Yan, W. (2020) Human behavior recognition using deep learning. *International Conference on Image and Vision Computing New Zealand*. IEEE.

Lu, J., Nguyen, M., & Yan, W. (2020) Comparative evaluations of human behavior recognition using deep learning. Handbook of Research on Multimedia Cyber Security, (pp. 176-189). Research Gate.

Lu, J., Shen, J., Yan, W., & Boris, B. (2017). An empirical study for human behaviors analysis. *International Journal of Digital Crime and Forensics*, *9*(3), 11–17. doi:10.4018/IJDCF.2017070102

Sujatha, K., Amrutha, K., & Veeranjaneyulu, N. (2023). Enhancing Object Detection with Mask R-CNN: A Deep Learning Perspective. *International Conference on Network, Multimedia and Information Technology (NMITCON)*, (pp. 1–6). IEEE. 10.1109/NMITCON58196.2023.10276033

Vasanthi, P., & Mohan, L. (2023). Multi-Head-Self-Attention based YOLOv5X-transformer for multi-scale object detection. *Multimedia Tools and Applications*.

Wang, C., He, W., Nie, Y., Guo, J., Liu, C., Han, K., & Wang, Y. (2023). *Gold-YOLO: Efficient Object Detector via Gather-and-Distribute Mechanism.*

Wang, C.-Y., Bochkovskiy, A., & Liao, H.-Y. M. (2023). YOLOv7: Trainable Bag-of-Freebies Sets New State-of-the-Art for Real-Time Object Detectors. *IEEE/CVF Conference on Computer Vision and Pattern Recognition (CVPR),* (pp. 7464–7475). IEEE. 10.1109/CVPR52729.2023.00721

Yan, W. (2019). *Introduction to Intelligent Surveillance: Surveillance Data Capture, Transmission, and Analytics*. Springer Nature. doi:10.1007/978-3-030-10713-0

Yan, W. (2023). *Computational Methods for Deep Learning: Theory, Algorithms, and Implementations*. Springer Nature. doi:10.1007/978-981-99-4823-9

Yu, Z., & Yan, W. (2020) Human action recognition using deep learning methods. *International Conference on Image and Vision Computing New Zealand.* IEEE. 10.1109/IVCNZ51579.2020.9290594

Zhang, Z., Lu, X., Cao, G., Yang, Y., Jiao, L., & Liu, F. (2021). ViT-YOLO: Transformer-Based YOLO for Object Detection. *IEEE/CVF International Conference on Computer Vision Workshops (ICCVW),* (pp. 2799–2808). IEEE. 10.1109/ICCVW54120.2021.00314

Zhou, H., Nguyen, M., Yan, W. (2023) Computational analysis of table tennis matches from real-time videos using deep learning. *PSIVT 2023*. IEEE.

Zhou, L., Wei, S., Cui, Z., & Ding, W. (2019). YOLO-RD: A lightweight object detection network for range doppler radar images. *IOP Conference Series. Materials Science and Engineering*, *563*(4), 042027. doi:10.1088/1757-899X/563/4/042027

Zhu, Y., & Yan, W. (2022). *Ski fall detection from digital images using deep learning*. ACM ICCCV. doi:10.1145/3561613.3561625

Chapter 9
Vehicle Detection and Distance Estimation Using Improved YOLOv7 Model

Xiaoxu Liu
Auckland University of Technology, New Zealand

Wei Qi Yan
Auckland University of Technology, New Zealand

ABSTRACT

In this book chapter, the authors propose a low-cost distance estimation approach to develop more accurate predictions from a 3D perspective for vehicle detection and ranging by using inexpensive monocular cameras. This distance estimation model integrates YOLOv7 model with an attention module (CBAM) and transformer, as well as extend the prediction vector as the fundamental architecture to improved high-level semantic understanding and enhanced feature extraction ability. This integration significantly improved detection and ranging performance, offering a more suitable and cost-effective solution for distance estimation.

INTRODUCTION

Traffic scene understanding is an important component of autonomous vehicles. In order to consolidate the safety of autonomous vehicles, improving spatial perception capabilities to improve their understanding and interpretation of the surrounding environment is the focus of research (Ignatious, 2023; Liu et al., 2019). Self-driving cars with strong spatial perception capabilities can well judge the distance between

DOI: 10.4018/979-8-3693-1738-9.ch009

themselves and surrounding vehicles, thereby maintaining a safe following distance from other vehicles and avoiding scratches and collisions with vehicles and obstacles (Liu, 2019; Sarker, 2021; Guo, 2021; Zhang, 2020; Hu, 2020).

In recent years, as artificial intelligence has become more and more popular, many researchers have adopted machine learning technology to achieve many scene understanding tasks. Among them, the distance estimation task is one of the main methods to achieve the spatial perception capability of vehicles (Zalevsky et al., 2021). Some distance estimation tasks use lasers to measure the distance between two vehicles, but their disadvantages are high cost and limited effectiveness. In addition, there are some studies using hardware devices such as ultrasonic, infrared, and microwave radar to achieve distance estimation (Aliew, 2022; Özcan et al., 2020).

These hardware devices are sensitive to interference, and it is difficult to distinguish between two different detection targets that are very close, resulting in unreliable estimation results.

In order to avoid these shortcomings, some researchers gave up using hardware devices to obtain distance information, and instead used cameras to obtain vehicle scene images and infer distance information through vehicle detection tasks (Mehtab et al., 2021). This method fundamentally solves the problem of high hardware cost and impractical use. However, methods for estimating distance from 2D information also face many challenges.

Deep learning technology has made satisfactory achievements in distance estimation. Deep learning is capable of achieving higher accuracy than traditional machine learning models. And automatically learn complex data features, reducing the need for manual feature engineering. Deep learning models can also handle large amounts of data and can be trained on distributed computing systems, making them scalable to large data sets. Deep learning has shown strong learning capabilities after training, testing and verification, and due to its larger number and width of network layers, it can be mapped to more functions to solve more complex problems. Moreover, as the amount of data sets increases and appropriate parameters are adjusted, deep learning networks will have better and better performance.

Models based on deep learning adjust network parameters by learning a large amount of ground truth information during the training process, thereby achieving the purpose of accurately estimating distance. Currently, distance estimation tasks based on deep learning are divided into two types, one is to train the network through information captured by a monocular camera, and the other is to obtain information through binocular cameras. The principle of monocular ranging is to identify pedestrians, vehicles, etc. in the scene through image matching, and then estimate the distance based on the size of the target in the image. Binocular ranging is to directly measure the distance of the object in front by calculating the parallax of two images.

In recent research, there are many methods to achieve monocular distance estimation. One of the methods uses the circular odometry method based on a fisheye lens (Bremer et al., 2023). The distance measurement concept of the circumferential fisheye camera is based on a single strain matrix and affine transformation rather than mathematical geometry, but the disadvantage of this method is that the lens of a fisheye camera is an ultra-short throw. The smaller the focal length, the smaller the proportion of the object in the image and the less clear the details. Therefore, it is difficult for fisheye lenses to capture details that meet the needs of certain tasks. Moreover, the smaller the focal length, the more serious the distortion, which in turn leads to severe distortion of the image. Another method is forward-looking camera ranging, which is more suitable for relying on mathematical geometry to estimate distance since the camera is located in front of the vehicle. It can obtain clearer and more complete image information (Karimanzira et al., 2021). Another method is tilt camera ranging, which is characterized by broadening the observation range so that the acquired image contains more target objects (Fukushima, Farzad, & Torras, 2017; Cai et al., 2020).

Binocular ranging requires calibration of the binocular cameras to obtain the internal and external parameters and homography matrices of the two cameras. The original image is corrected based on the calibration results so that the two corrected images are on the same plane and parallel to each other. Then, the depth calculation is completed through pixel matching.

The advantage of binocular ranging is that it is not affected by the performance of the target detection task. Moreover, binocular estimation doesn't rely on maintaining a sample database, as it operates without the concept of a sample. However, there are also some disadvantages of binocular distance estimation that the cost is much higher than that of monocular distance estimation, and the binocular distance estimation system has very high requirements on computing performance, which usually requires a professional image processing chip.

On the other hand, monocular estimation also comes with its own set of advantages. It is a cost-effective solution, requiring less computational resources, making it more accessible for various applications. Additionally, its relatively simple system design makes it easier to implement and deploy in practical scenes.

This paper focuses on using deep learning to significantly reduce human workload in distance estimation for vehicle scene understanding. We employ the attention mechanism and Transformer on YOLOv7 as well as extend the prediction vector to estimate the vehicle's distance. Our proposed vehicle ranging model, YOLOv7-CBAM-Transformer, effectively improves the model's understanding of local and global features, thereby enhancing the performance of the original YOLO series models.

RELATED WORK

Vehicle detection forms the basis for vehicle ranging, and estimating the distance from the vehicle in front is essential for vehicle collision avoidance systems. As a result, an increasing number of articles in the field of computer vision are focusing on the challenges related to vehicle detection and range estimation.

We delve into two areas of literature. In the first area, we explore vehicle detection and range estimation using a binocular camera. There are four main steps to achieve a binocular stereo vision task: camera calibration, binocular correction, binocular matching and depth map calculation.

Chui et al. (2020) utilized image pyramids to achieve binocular distance estimation. The model uses an appropriate smoothing filter to smooth the image, and then downsamples the smoothed image. Then continue doing the same with the resulting image. The model performs all steps of feature extraction, feature matching, etc. for each step of the pyramid. Because the model analyzes different resolutions, it can effectively estimate different distances.

Also, there is also a binocular ranging method based on image segmentation. This method first divides the left image and the right image into various areas according to the object, and then matches the areas obtained by dividing the left image and the right image according to the brightness, width, height, number of pixels, horizontal distance, and vertical distance to find the same object in Corresponding areas in the left and right images, and finally calculate the disparity based on the horizontal distance between the edge points of the matching area. The edges of the area segmented by this model contain rich texture information. The disparity of the area can be calculated based on the edge position, and a tight disparity map can be obtained. This is especially effective for scenes containing large areas of low texture (Xue, 2015).

Compared with monocular distance estimation, binocular distance estimation uses two cameras at different positions for image acquisition, thus increasing the cost. Secondly, errors are prone to occur during the camera calibration process, resulting in inaccurate ranging. Moreover, in scenes with severe occlusion, feature matching may fail.

Since monocular cameras are available on many devices, models utilizing monocular distance estimation can be better integrated into various applications. Moreover, with the rapid development of deep learning, various deep neural networks can promote better performance in monocular distance estimation tasks.

Cues and assumptions are the focus of some analyzes of monocular distance estimation. Usually, monocular distance estimation uses features such as the size, observation angle, and motion trajectory of the target in the image to establish a correspondence with the corresponding point in reality to estimate the distance

(Parker, 2022; He, 2020; Vijayanarasimhan, 2017). And then using the camera calibration parameters and the matched feature correspondences, apply triangulation to obtain 3D coordinates (X, Y, Z) of the real-world points. Triangulation calculates the intersection of rays originating from the camera center and passing through the matched feature points. Since the initial 3D coordinates are only up to an unknown scale factor, the known dimensions are needed to estimate the scale and convert the 3D coordinates to actual world coordinates. Once the actual world coordinates of the structures, objects, or road segments are obtained, the distances between points of interest in the scene can be computed by measuring the Euclidean distance between their corresponding 3D coordinates.

There has been some research implements monocular distance estimation using inverse perspective mapping (IPM) from a bird's-eye view. This transformation allows to estimate distances directly in the transformed view, which simplifies distance estimation. Perform a perspective transformation (IPM) is to map the image from the camera's perspective to a bird's-eye view. Mapping between bird's-eye view and real-world coordinates relates pixel coordinates in the transformed view to corresponding real-world 3D points (Vakili et al., 2020).

Some studies use the combination of attention mechanism and deep learning model to improve the expressiveness of the model. The attention mechanism can help the model assign different weights to each part of the input, extract more critical and important information, and enable the model to make more accurate judgments without causing greater overhead in the calculation and storage of the model. Several methods confirm the importance of capturing contextual and spatial details for scene understanding. The multi-stream attention fusion of the MSANet architecture analyzes different scene feature details to improve accuracy through three aspects: vehicle motion trajectory, context awareness, and input data (Huang, Huang & Hsu, 2021).

In addition, some deep learning models add improved attention modules to the Transformer to improve the model's ability to perceive detailed features of the scene. The improved attention module replaces the convolution and bottleneck modules in CBAM with a transformer encoder module. In complex environments, this change is more conducive to understanding global semantic information (Junayed & Islam, 2022).

THE METHODOLOGY

We use YOLOv7 as the basic architecture to combine the Swin Transformer and the convolutional block attention module to achieve the distance estimation task.

This combination is to enhance the feature extraction capability of the model (Woo et al., 2019; Chienyao, Alexey & Mark, 2022; Liu et al., 2021).

The main reason for using YOLOv7 as the basic structure of our model is that YOLOv7 adds E-ELAN based on other YOLO series models. The significance of E-ELAN is to help the model learn better through expand, shuffle, and merge, and it can optimize the learning ability without destroying the original gradient path. Moreover, YOLOv7's model scaling can adjust the key attributes of the model to obtain models that meet different application requirements. For example, model scaling can optimize the width, depth, and resolution of the model to suit different tasks and data sets.

Our model, as illustrated in Fig.1, incorporates the Convolutional Block Attention Module (CBAM) to enhance the feature extraction process, thereby avoiding alterations to the original feature extraction. Moreover, the inclusion of the Transformer enhances the model's capacity to comprehend global semantics, allowing YOLOv7, which primarily emphasizes local information processing, to achieve a more comprehensive understanding of traffic scenes.

In addition to depth, width and cardinality, the three main factors in CNN research, CBAM also focuses on attention, using the attention mechanism to control the network to focus the analysis on features of interest and ignore uninteresting features. Since the method of extracting features by convolution operation involves channels and space, CBAM emphasizes the importance of both channel and space information.

The channel attention module generates channel attention maps by analyzing the relationship between several channels between different features. Each channel of the feature map is equivalent to a feature detector, so the attention of each channel can be focused on the area of interest. In order to make the model calculate channel attention more efficiently, CBAM uses average pooling and maximum pooling methods to compress the spatial dimension of the input feature map to improve the representation of the network (Woo, Park, Lee & Kweon, 2019). During the calculation process, the Channel Attention Module first performs global maximum pooling and global average pooling on the input feature map, compressing the spatial dimension to 1 and retaining channel information. Then the two pooled features are sent to the shared multi-layer perceptron (MLP) to extract features. The pooled features after MLP are then added, and the final channel attention weight is obtained through sigmoid activation.

The Spatial Attention Module uses the spatial relationship between features to generate spatial attention maps. Different from CAM, SAM focuses on where the information part is as a supplement to the channel attention module. To compute spatial attention, During the calculation process, the Spatial Attention Module first performs maximum pooling and average pooling on the feature map calculated by the channel attention module in the channel dimension, compressing the channel dimension to 1 and retaining spatial information. Then the pooled features are concatenate, and features are extracted through a convolutional layer while reducing the channel dimension to 1. Finally, after sigmoid activation, the final spatial attention weight is obtained (Li et al., 2023).

Figure 1. The architecture of YOLOv7-CBAM-Transformer

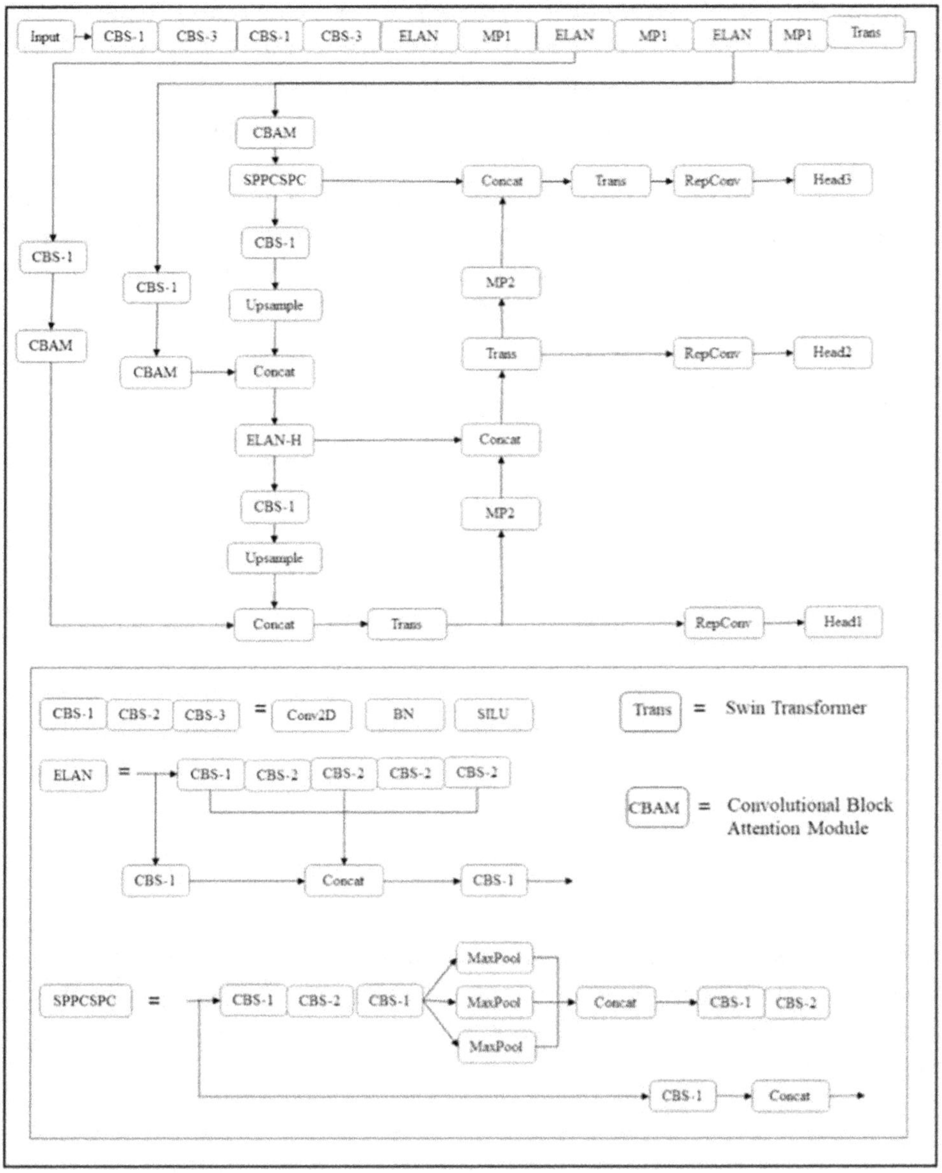

Presently, the Transformer model is widely regarded as proficient and efficient in managing the intricate relationships among these components. As a result, we remove the last ELAN in the YOLOv7 backbone and some ELANs in the neck and instead integrate the Swin Transformer encoder. By implementing this operation, we can accentuate the benefits of the self-attention mechanism while simultaneously reducing computational overhead. Moreover, the introduction of Transformer in the neck allows for capturing correlations and significance between different regions, enhancing the model's ability to adapt to targets of varying sizes (Zhang, 2023).

As we implement YOLOv7-CBAM-Transformer, our goal is not only to detect the position of the vehicle but also to estimate the distance between the vehicle in front and the current position. To achieve this, we have extended the prediction vector to incorporate distance estimation information.

The original prediction vector contains bounding box anchor coordinates A (x, y, w, h) and category confidence C (c1, c2). In order to make the model realize the ranging function, we add the distance element D (d) to the prediction vector. The extended prediction vector is shown in the Fig. 2.

Figure 2. The extended prediction vector for distance estimation

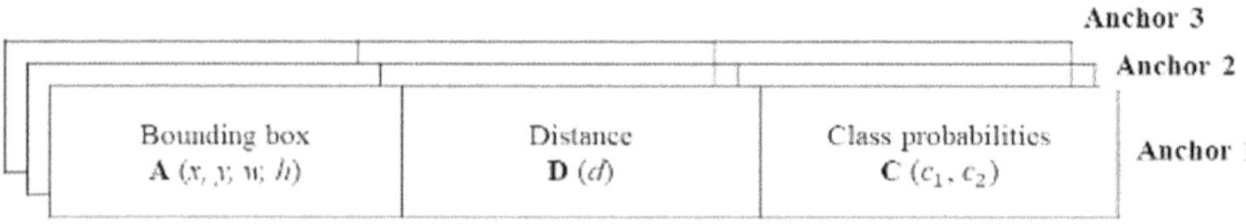

The distance loss is defined as

$$l_{distance}(i,j) = \omega\left(d'_{i,j} - d_{i,j}\right)^2 = \omega\sum_{k=0}^{c} C_{i,j,k}\left(d'_{i,j,k} - d_{i,j,k}\right)^2 \tag{1}$$

where $C_{i,j,k}$ is k-th class probability in (i, j)-th cell. The weighting constant ω is introduced to balance the importance of the distance loss with other losses, preventing it from dominating the overall training process. In our experiment, we set ω to a value of 1×102.

RESULT ANALYSIS

This paper presents a novel vehicle detection and distance estimation model for low-cost monocular cameras, enhanced with an attention module and Transformer, utilizing deep learning techniques. The experimental setup involved using PYTHON 2.7, an RTX5000 GPU, and 32GB RAM. The example data used in the experiments was sourced from the KITTI dataset. The KITTI dataset comprises both intrinsic and extrinsic characteristics of the in-car camera, along with the coordinates, width, and height of the detection boxes. For the development of our deep learning model, we randomly selected 4,000 samples and divided them into a 7:3 ratio for training and testing. The results presented in this section correspond to state-of-the-art approaches. Fig. 3 illustrates the satisfactory vehicle recognition and distance estimation performance achieved by our modified YOLOv7 (YOLOv7-CBAM-Transformer) with the extended prediction vector.

To train our YOLOv7-CBAM-Transformer, we set the following parameters: epochs=5000, batch size=1, and learning rate=0.01. Fig. 4 illustrates the network training process, showing that validation loss decreases steadily between 0 and 1000 iterations. After reaching 1000 epochs, the loss curves stabilize at 0.082.

For every assessment metric provided, Table 1 presents a quantitative comparison of the dataset created by KITTI. This comparison assesses a number of YOLO models as well as the transformer model. The outcomes show that YOLOv7 performs better than any of the earlier YOLO models, including the transformer. Moreover, our YOLOv7-CBAM-Transformer, which incorporates the convolutional block attention module, outperforms the original YOLOv7. The combination of the convolutional block attention module with YOLOv7 demonstrates significantly improved results. Notably, the addition of the Swin Transformer leads to a reduction of 0.382 in RMSE compared to the previous model. Overall, our YOLOv7-CBAM-Transformer achieves a total reduction of 0.456 in RMSE compared to the original YOLOv7 model.

Additionally, the distances were divided into three categories: 0-10m, 10-20m, and >20m. In Table 2, we obtain the average RMSE for each group. Our YOLOv7-CBAM-Transformer outperforms the original YOLOv7 in 0-10m and 10-20m distance categories. In summary, the data presented in Table 1 and Table 2 suggest that the YOLOv7-CBAM-Transformer model is more effective in handling object detection and distance estimation tasks. Moreover, the model with Transformer is reduced by at least 0.2 in the RMSE of each distance category compared with YOLOv7-CBAM; compared with the original YOLOv7, it is reduced by at least 0.303 in distance caegory of 0-10m and 10-20m.

Figure 3. The result images generated by YOLOv7-CBAM-Transformer

Figure 4. The training curve of YOLOv7-CBAM

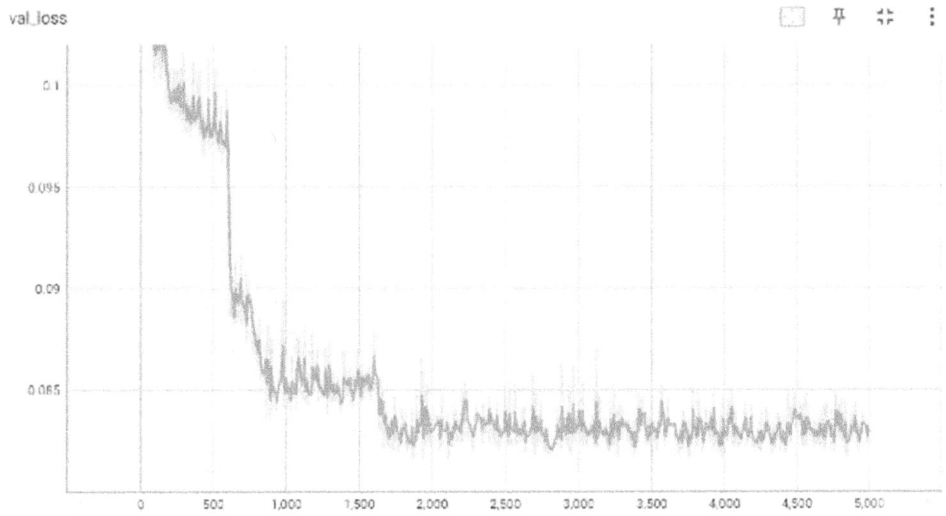

Table 1. Comparative analysis of multiple deep neural networks

Models	RMSE
YOLOv5	4.121
YOLOv6	4.483
YOLOv7	4.157
YOLOv7-CBAM	4.083
YOLOv7-CBAM-Transformer	3.701
Swin Transformer	4.776

Table 2. Average RMSE of different neural networks in different distance categories

Models	0-10m	10-20m	>20m
YOLOv7	4.502	4.357	3.612
YOLOv7-CBAM	4.499	3.667	4.083
YOLOv7-CBAM-Transformer	4.199	3.021	3.883

Table 3. Comparing our model to other state of the art model of distance estimation

Model	RMSE
GC-ASPP-YOLOv3-D (Lian et al., 2022)	3.985
Ours (YOLOv7-CBAM-Transformer)	3.701

In the context of identical dataset, we conducted a comparative analysis between our model and another state of the art distance estimation model GC-ASPP-YOLOv3-D in Table 3 (Lian et al., 2022). The results highlight the distinct advantages of our model, particularly in terms of RMSE, where it outperforms GC-ASPP-YOLOv3-D.

In summary, in this experiment, we found that in addition to YOLOv7 being more suitable for vehicle distance estimation in KITTI dataset than YOLOv5, YOLOv6 and original Swin Transformer, adding CBAM can successfully further reduce the estimation error of the model. Moreover, we found that YOLOv7 with CBAM is more suitable for distance estimation within 20 meters, while the original YOLOv7 is more prominent when estimating the distance of vehicles beyond 20m. By further improvement, our proposed YOLOv7-CBAM-Transformer produced the better results even compare with YOLOv7-CBAM.

CONCLUSION

Our primary focus was to develop an advanced deep learning-based model tailored for low-cost monocular cameras, with the aim of optimizing hardware costs. By accurately detecting vehicles and applying extended distance estimation vector, our model obtains the bounding box coordinates, enabling precise distance calculations. Through experimentation, we discovered that combining YOLOv7-CBAM-Transformer with the extended distance estimation vector yielded the best results, achieving a remarkable 0.456 improvement in RMSE compared to the original YOLOv7 model. In our analysis of the results, we observed that the YOLOv7-CBAM-Transformer outperforms the original YOLOv7-CBAM model in distance measurement. It exhibited enhanced accuracy and reduced occurrences of false detections and missed detections. This highlights the significant impact of the Transformer, which contributed to improving the model's feature understanding and its adaptability to diverse distances of vehicles in the scenes.

REFERENCES

Alexey, B. ChienYao, W., & Mark, L. (2020). YOLOv4: Optimal speed and accuracy of object detection. *Image and Video Processing*, arXiv:2004.10934.

Alfred Daniel, J., Chandru Vignesh, C., Muthu, B. A., Senthil Kumar, R., Sivaparthipan, C. B., & Marin, C. E. M. (2023). Fully convolutional neural networks for LIDAR–camera fusion for pedestrian detection in autonomous vehicle. *Multimedia Tools and Applications*, *82*(16), 1–24. doi:10.1007/s11042-023-14417-x

Aliew, F. (2022). An Approach for Precise Distance Measuring Using Ultrasonic Sensors. *Engineering Proceedings*, *24*(1), 8.

Alvarado, S. T., Borja, M. G. B., & Torres, K. B. (2022). *Object Distance Estimation from a Binocular Vision System for Robotic Applications Using Artificial Neural Networks. Control, Mechatronics and Automation*. ICCMA.

Bremer, J., Maj, M., Nordbø, Ø., & Kommisrud, E. (2023). Deep learning–based automated measurements of the scrotal circumference of Norwegian Red bulls from 3D images. *Smart Agricultural Technology*, *3*, 100133. doi:10.1016/j.atech.2022.100133

Cai, Y., Ding, Y., Zhang, H., Xiu, J., & Liu, Z. (2020). Geo-location algorithm for building targets in oblique remote sensing images based on deep learning and height estimation. *Remote Sensing (Basel)*, *12*(15), 2427. doi:10.3390/rs12152427

ChienyaoW.AlexeyB.MarkL. (2022). YOLOv7: Trainable bag-of-freebies sets new state-of-the-art for real-time object detectors. Computer Vision and Pattern Recognition, arXiv:2207.02696

Fukushima, H., & Farzad, D. (2017). Scene Understanding Using Deep Learning. Academic Press.

Guo, J., Wang, J., Wang, H., Xiao, B., He, Z., & Li, L. (2023). Research on road scene understanding of autonomous vehicles based on multi-task learning. *Sensors (Basel)*, *23*(13), 6238. doi:10.3390/s23136238 PMID:37448087

He, Z., Yang, Q., Zhao, X., Zhang, S., & Tan, J. (2020). Spatiotemporal visual odometry using ground plane in dynamic indoor environment. *Optik (Stuttgart)*, *220*, 165165. doi:10.1016/j.ijleo.2020.165165

Huang, K. C., Huang, Y. K., & Hsu, W. H. (2021). *Multi-Stream Attention Learning for Monocular Vehicle Velocity and Inter-Vehicle Distance Estimation*. arXiv preprint arXiv:2110.11608.

Ignatious, H. A., El-Sayed, H., Khan, M. A., & Mokhtar, B. M. (2023). Analyzing Factors Influencing Situation Awareness in Autonomous Vehicles—A Survey. *Sensors (Basel)*, *23*(8), 4075. doi:10.3390/s23084075 PMID:37112416

Junayed, M. S., & Islam, M. B. (2022). Automated Physical Distance Estimation and Crowd Monitoring Through Surveillance Video. *SN Computer Science*, *4*(1), 67. doi:10.1007/s42979-022-01480-8 PMID:36467857

Karimanzira, D., Pfützenreuter, T., & Renkewitz, H. (2021). Deep learning for long and short range object detection in underwater environment. *Adv Robot Automn*, *5*(1), 1–10.

Li, H., Tan, Y., Miao, J., Liang, P., Gong, J., He, H., Jiao, Y., Zhang, F., Xing, Y., & Wu, D. (2023). Attention-based and micro designed EfficientNetB2 for diagnosis of Alzheimer's disease. *Biomedical Signal Processing and Control*, *82*, 104571. doi:10.1016/j.bspc.2023.104571

Lian, G., Wang, Y., Qin, H., & Chen, G. (2022). *Towards unified on-road object detection and depth estimation from a single image*. Machine Learning and Cybernetics. doi:10.1007/s13042-021-01444-z

Liu, X. (2019). *Vehicle-related Scene Understanding Using Deep Learning*. [Master's Thesis, Auckland University of Technology, New Zealand].

Liu, X., Nguyen, M., & Yan, W. (2019). Vehicle-related scene understanding using deep learn. *Pattern Recognition*, 61–73.

Liu, X., & Yan, W. (2021). *Traffic-light sign recognition using Capsule network*. Springer Multimedia Tools and Applications. doi:10.1007/s11042-020-10455-x

Liu, X., & Yan, W. (2022). *Depth estimation of traffic scenes from image sequence using deep learning*. PSIVT.

Liu, X., Yan, W., & Kasabov, N. (2020). *Vehicle-related scene segmentation using CapsNets*. IEEE IVCNZ. doi:10.1109/IVCNZ51579.2020.9290664

Liu, Z. (2021). Swin transformer: Hierarchical vision transformer using shifted windows. Computer vision, 37- 49

Masoumian, A., Rashwan, H. A., Cristiano, J., Asif, M. S., & Puig, D. (2022). Monocular depth estimation using deep learning: A review. *Sensors (Basel)*, *22*(14), 5353. doi:10.3390/s22145353 PMID:35891033

Mehta, S., & Mohammad, R. (2021). *MobileViT: Light-weight, general-purpose, and mobile friendly vision transformer.* arXiv preprint arXiv:2110.02178.

Mehtab, S., & Yan, W. (2021). Flexible neural network for fast and accurate road scene perception. *Multimedia Tools and Applications*, 7169–7181.

Mehtab, S., Yan, W., & Narayanan, A. (2021). *3D vehicle detection using cheap LiDAR and camera sensors*. IEEE IVCNZ. doi:10.1109/IVCNZ54163.2021.9653358

Ming, Y., Meng, X., Fan, C., & Yu, H. (2021). Deep learning for monocular depth estimation: A review. *Neurocomputing*, *438*, 14–33. doi:10.1016/j.neucom.2020.12.089

Özcan, M., Aliew, F., & Görgün, H. (2020). Accurate and precise distance estimation for noisy IR sensor readings contaminated by outliers. *Measurement*, *156*, 107633. doi:10.1016/j.measurement.2020.107633

Parker, P. R., Abe, E. T., Beatie, N. T., Leonard, E. S., Martins, D. M., Sharp, S. L., Wyrick, D. G., Mazzucato, L., & Niell, C. M. (2022). Distance estimation from monocular cues in an ethological visuomotor task. *eLife*, *11*, 74708. doi:10.7554/eLife.74708 PMID:36125119

Vakili, E., Shoaran, M., & Sarmadi, M. R. (2020). Single-camera vehicle speed measurement using the geometry of the imaging system. *Multimedia Tools and Applications*, *79*(27-28), 19307–19327. doi:10.1007/s11042-020-08761-5

Vijayanarasimhan, S. (2017). Sfm-net: Learning of structure and motion from video. arXiv preprint arXiv:1704.07804.

Woo, S., Park, J., Lee, J. Y., & Kweon, I. S. (2019). *CBAM: Convolutional block attention module*. Computer Vision.

Zalevsky, Z., Buller, G. S., Chen, T., Cohen, M., & Barton-Grimley, R. (2021). Light detection and ranging (lidar): Introduction. *Journal of the Optical Society of America. A, Optics, Image Science, and Vision*, *38*(11), LID1–LID2. doi:10.1364/JOSAA.445792 PMID:34807027

Zhang, D. (2023). STA-YOLOv7: Swin-Transformer-Enabled YOLOv7 for Road Damage Detection. *Computer Science and Application.*, *13*(5), 1157–1165. doi:10.12677/CSA.2023.135113

Chapter 10
Real-Time Pose Recognition for Billiard Players Using Deep Learning

Zhikang Chen
Auckland University of Technology, New Zealand

Wei Qi Yan
Auckland University of Technology, New Zealand

ABSTRACT

In this book chapter, the authors propose a method for player pose recognition in billiards matches by combining keypoint extraction and an optimized transformer. Given that those human pose analysis methods usually require high labour costs, the authors explore deep learning methods to achieve real-time, high-precision pose recognition. Firstly, they utilize human key point detection technology to extract the key points of players from real-time videos and generate key points. Then, the key point data is input into the transformer model for pose analysis and recognition. In addition, the authors design a human skeletal alignment method for comparison with standard poses. The experimental results show that the method performs well in recognizing players' poses in billiards matches and provides real-time and timely feedback on players' pose information. This research project provides a new and efficient tool for training billiard players and opens up new possibilities for applying deep learning in sports analytics. In addition, one of these contributions is the creation of a dataset for pose recognition.

DOI: 10.4018/979-8-3693-1738-9.ch010

INTRODUCTION

In recent years, deep learning has been developed rapidly, especially the field of computer vision has become one of the core parts in computing (He et al., 2016). Human pose estimation is one of the essential branches of computer vision, deep learning has proved its effectiveness in dealing with diverse poses, complicated and occlusion problems (Sun et al., 2019). The purpose of human pose estimation is to predict or detect the pose of a human body from an image or video, however, traditional pose estimation methods rely on manual feature input and statistics (Cao et al., 2017). With the emergence of deep neural networks, such as Convolutional Neural Networks (CNN), Trans-former and Recurrent Neural Networks (RNN), more accurate and robust methods for human pose estimation were presented (Chen et al., 2018).

With the popularity of computer vision technology, human posture estimation has been widely used in the fields of behaviour recognition, medical rehabilitation, multimedia and so on, and the field of motion analysis is also a hot research direction. For example, Wang et al. Used convolutional neural network to identify human posture in a single RGB image, and put forward personalized sports suggestions for skiers, and improved the training experience (Wang et al., 2019). Therefore, we urgently need a real-time and accurate human posture analysis method, which can collect athletes' posture data in real time and analyze it automatically. Athletes can immediately correct the shortcomings of posture, improve the training effect and avoid sports injury.

Despite significant advances in human pose estimation achieved by using deep learning, many challenges must be addressed, especially in specific areas like billiards. Most existing deep learning methods rely on large-scale labelled data (Wen et al., 2016) and obtain high-quality labelled data in real scenarios which are both time-consuming and laborious. In billiards games, the occlusion of a player's arms, cue, ball, and tabletop make labelling work even much difficult (Andriluka et al., 2014).

Furthermore, deep learning models perform well on the task of human pose estimation within single images. Still, ensuring temporal continuity and accuracy of human pose estimation in performing continuous actions or video sequences remains a challenge that has yet to be fully addressed (Carreira & Zosserman, 2017). The temporal continuity and accuracy of pose estimation are fundamental in applications such as sports that require high timeliness, e.g., real-time analysis and recommendations of player's poses or stroke strategies (Choutas et al., 2018). In addition, in billiards or other sport games where human poses and environments possess variability and complexity, it may be difficult for a single deep learning model to use all scenarios and actions, which requires solutions with generalization and robustness (Yang et al., 2017).

Transformer is an effective deep learning model. Through its unique self-attention mechanism, it can effectively capture the temporal and spatial relationships in the input sequence, so as to improve the performance of the model. The ability of parallel computing makes transformer more efficient in processing large-scale human key point data (Vaswani et al., 2017). Thanks to the powerful transformer, we propose a new method combined with key point recognition. Key point recognition can continuously output the coordinate data of human key points with spatio-temporal relationship. Transformer can process these coordinates based key point data, effectively capture the spatial relationship between human parts and consider the posture relevance under different nodes, so as to accurately and efficiently recognize human posture.

Real time posture recognition is based on scientific and technological methods. Human key point recognition can collect a large number of player posture data, and transformer can analyse player posture through these data to obtain accurate results. This research work can better understand the performance of billiards players. At the same time, real-time posture recognition can also provide valuable data resources for coaches and other professionals to study and improve better billiards techniques and teaching methods.

In this book chapter, taking billiards as an example, we propose a human posture recognition system combining key point extraction and transformer. The purpose is to provide a high-precision recognition method for athletes' posture and provide real-time feedback to help them improve technology and avoid injury. At the same time, precise key point extraction and optimization of transformer model can improve the robustness and effectiveness of the system. The quality and quantity of training data is an important factor affecting the performance of the model. In practical application, lighting and occlusion will affect the overall performance of the model, and there are some limitations for special style athletes' posture recognition. In the following content, we will repeatedly demonstrate the proposed methodology based on relevant work. The experimental results are analysed and discussed, and the final results are obtained.

RELATED WORK

At present, there are many examples of human pose estimation framework using deep learning. Based on mask RCNN, Güler et al. Developed a variant model DensePose-RCNN, which can return the UV coordinates of specific parts in each human body region at the speed of multiple frames per second. In this study, the 2D RGB image coordinates are mapped to the 3D human body surface using the deep learning technology, and the precise positioning and pose estimation of dynamic characters are achieved by processing intensive UV coordinates. The final processing speed reaches 60 frames per second (Güler, 2018). Hourglass structure is a neural network structure specially used for human posture estimation. The purpose of this design is to grasp the features of each scale. This structure consists of a bottom-up and top-down network to form a hourglass module, which can reduce the feature map to a resolution of 4x4 at least, and then use convolution layer and maximum pooling to retain the spatial information of each resolution (hourglass, 2016). After that, Zhang et al. Proposed the training strategy of fast pose decomposition (FPD) combined with hourglass for human pose estimation. Compared with previous human pose estimation methods, FPD can achieve an average PCKh accuracy of 96.4% with only 14.3% of the calculation cost.

The MediaPipe human pose estimation framework proposed by Google research is based on BlazePose. BlazePose is the base model used to perform human key point recognition. It targets real-time human pose estimation by segmenting all the essential parts of the human skeleton into 33 key points to ensure the human body's accuracy and robustness of key point recognition (Bazarevsky et al., 2020). In addition, the multilevel CNN architecture for key point recognition helps the model to capture finer-grained features and improve recognition accuracy. Meanwhile, combining depth and spatial pyramid pooling methods, the model can perform feature extraction at different scales, which makes the predicted key points highly satisfactory in all angles and scenes (He et al., 2015). In the face of partial occlusion, the key point extraction algorithm remains robust through the depth structure of the proposed model. It can predict the occluded key points by approximating the contextual information, provided valuable data for real-time human pose recognition (Pauzi et al., 2021). Based on key point recognition, the framework is also employed in human pose tracking (Singh et al., 2021), fitness coaching (Agarwal et al., 2022), animation generation, and augmented reality (Lugaresi et al., 2019). Especially in the fitness domain, by identifying the user's key points, generating a skeletal model and comparing it with a standard posture model, corrective suggestions can be made in real-time to help the user complete the workout while avoiding injuries.

Vaswani et al. introduced the Transformer architecture in 2017, marking a departure from previously dominant architectures based on convolutional neural networks (CNNs) and recurrent neural networks (RNNs) (Vaswani et al., 2017). Distinctively, the Transformer architecture eschews temporal recursion and convolutions, leveraging instead a self-attention mechanism to enhance performance in sequence-to-sequence learning tasks. This design alleviates the gradient vanishing problem often encountered in RNNs, attributed to the absence of recursive connections in its architecture.

The Transformer employs a structure typical of Seq2Seq tasks, comprising an encoder and a decoder (Liu et al., 2018). In Transformer, the encoder and decoder are usually multilayered and ultimately output probabilistic results via Softmax. The self-attention mechanism, a core component of the Transformer model, enables the assignment of distinct weights to each unit in the input sequence and recombines these inputs to form a new vector. This mechanism enables the Transformer to discern long-term dependencies within the sequence. The initial phase in computing self-attention entails generating three vectors, namely Query, Key, and Value, for each word vector in the input encoder, with each vector corresponding to a weight matrix. The Query, Key, and Value are derived by multiplying their respective word vectors with these matrices.

The transformer was initially designed to solve the problem of natural language processing, and the power of the self-attention mechanism makes it excellent in other domains as well. And as research continues, more researchers are basing their work on Transformer to solve visual challenges. The visual Transformer (ViT) guides the Transformer to perform image processing tasks. The main idea of the model is to divide the image into fixed-size blocks and treat these blocks as words in a text sequence. Each image region is linearized into a fixed vector representation, and by position coding, the ViT can recognize the relative position of individual blocks in the image. Furthermore, a few of experiments have demonstrated that Transformer can outperform traditional CNN models in image classification tasks with sufficient data and resources (Dosovitskiy et al., 2020). Mao et al. proposed a regression human posture estimation framework based on Transformer, which treats human posture estimation as a sequential problem utilizing an attention mechanism to focus the model on the most relevant features at the target key points, which exploits the structured relationships between key points thereby improving performance and avoiding the feature misalignment problem of regression-based methods, which was demonstrated to be effective based on the COCO dataset that Transformer significantly improves the state-of-the-art of regression pose estimation (Mao et al., 2021).

Swin Transformer is designed to be used as a generalized backbone model for computer vision, which is a new visual Transformer. To process visual data more efficiently, Swin Transformer makes use of a hierarchical Transformer structure and a displacement window approach, and the model is also effective in resolving differences in the size of visual entities. Swin Transformer has demonstrated excellent performance in high-resolution tasks like image segmentation and object recognition. In addition, the model outperforms the previous state-of-the-art in the COCO and ADE20K datasets (Liu et al., 2021).

METHODOLOGY

In this book chapter, we extract human key point data by using Google's human posture estimation framework MediaPipe, and then train a transformer classifier to classify and recognize the extracted key point coordinates. Due to time and equipment constraints, we only fine tune and optimize the transformer model.

In order to get better results, we gathered three experienced billiards players and collected their hitting posture data in the actual billiards game. Considering the generalization ability of the model, we collect the player's hitting posture data at different angles and heights with the player as the centre. Considering the timing factor of the action, the data we collected is in the form of video data containing a complete stroke. Due to time and cost constraints, we finally captured a billiard pose data set containing 668 hitting pose videos.

Considering the small size of the data set and the limitations of data types, the trained model may have insufficient generalization ability and over fitting phenomenon, and it will have better recognition effect on players with similar body size as volunteers. In order to further improve the performance of the model, we expand the size of the data set by flipping, scaling and time warping methods to improve the generalization ability of the model. The final amount of training data is 2672. Then we use the key point extraction to make the billiard hitting posture key point coordinate data set. We store the key point data of each video in CSV format for model training and testing, of which 80% is the training set and 20% is the test set. Since the amount of data is not as expected, we classify postures into standard and non-standard categories.

Mediapipe is a lightweight human posture recognition framework, which can extract and output human key point data in real time. The perception pipeline of the framework is graph. We input a series of human images through graph, and then present the coordinate points of body joints on the image. The process of MediaPipe is shown in Figure 1. Among them, we use rectangle to represent the calculation unit, and arrow to represent streams. The calculation unit image transform acquires the image at the input port and continues to output. The image is converted into a tensor through the second calculation unit, and then the input model is used for reasoning. The subsequent results are converted from the tensor to the key point coordinates and displayed in the original image. The key point extraction framework has laid a solid foundation for the subsequent generation of bone model, and also played a role in feature extraction for the subsequent transformer model training and reasoning.

Figure 1. MediaPipe graph

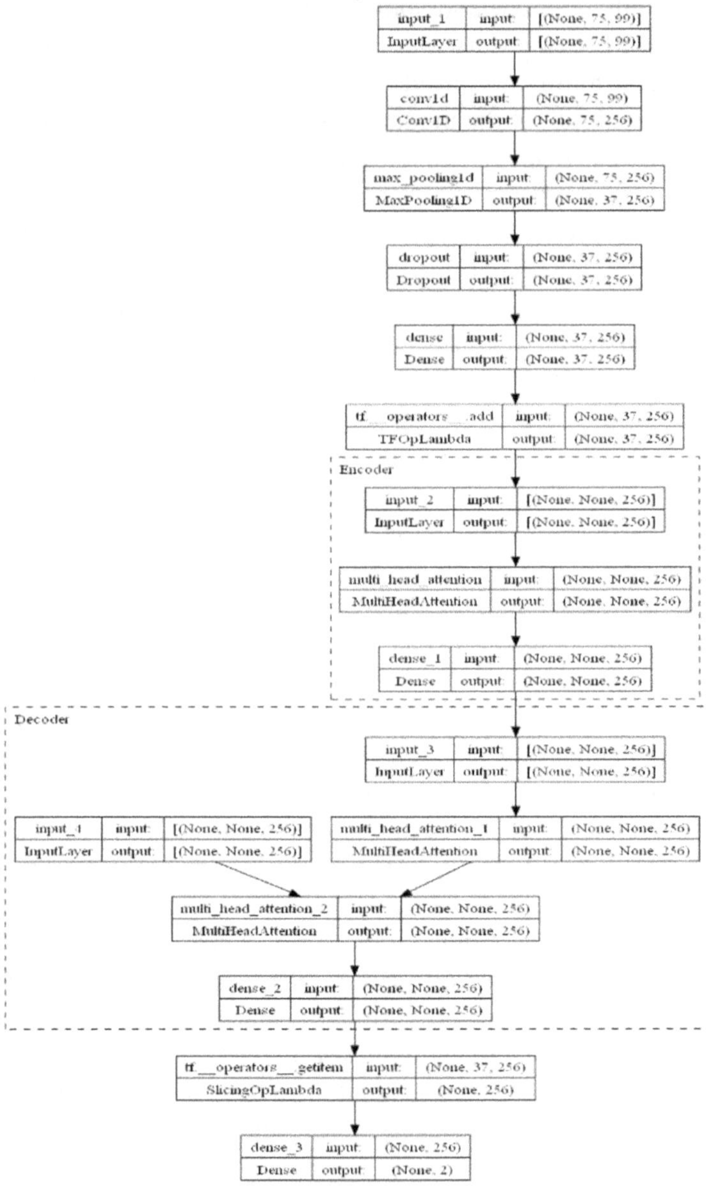

Although mediapipe's key point extraction function is excellent, in the actual scene, due to factors such as the movement of people, the obtained coordinate points will occasionally appear abnormal fluctuations. Therefore, before inputting the data into the transformer, we used the sliding window technology to eliminate this sudden fluctuation data. The principle of this technology is to set a window in the transmission channel of the data stream, set a threshold by calculating the standard deviation of the data in the window, and use the mean value to replace when the fluctuation data exceeds the upper limit of the threshold, so as to improve the stability of the data. The billiard batting data we collected is 75 frames in size. Usually, players will aim twice and three times before hitting the ball, so we set the window to 25 frames to ensure that each window contains a complete swing as much as possible. In the actual development process, we use the *movement*() function in python's numpy library to calculate the average value of the window. The calculation formula is:

$$s = \sqrt{\frac{sum_{i=1}^{n}\left(x_i - \overline{x}\right)^2}{n-1}} \tag{1}$$

After obtaining stable key data, we use key point coordinates to generate a human skeleton model in real-time images. We also designed and implemented a real-time comparison model for detecting bones and standard posture bones in real time. The scaling and alignment of bones are achieved through a combination algorithm based on a single algorithm. The fusion of algorithm strategies is selected based on the effectiveness of different algorithms for a given task, ensuring fast and accurate comparison during real-time comparison. The advantage of real-time comparison is that it allows players or coaches to more intuitively detect posture defects, such as incorrect leg standing in billiards posture, which will result in significant performance on the real-time comparison model.

The follow is a detailed description of the rationale and methodology. The first step calculates the scaling factor. We took use of Euclidean distances for standard and detected key points to calculate the distance between each pair of connections.

$$distance = \sqrt{\left(x2 - x1\right)^2 + \left(y2 - y1\right)^2} \tag{2}$$

Where $(x1,y1)$ and $(x2,y2)$ are the coordinates of the two key points, and since the current pose comparisons do not involve the computation of depth, we did not use the coordinates z containing depth. Next, the scaling factor is calculated from the average distance between key points.

$$scale_{factor} = \frac{mean\left(standard_{distance}\right)}{mean\left(detected_{distance}\right)}. \tag{3}$$

Since the size of detected skeleton displayed on the screen does not match with the size of the standard skeleton, we need to scale the detected bones to match with the standard one. We then make use of a scaling factor to calculate the scaled position of the key point coordinates.

$$scale_z = x*scale_{factor} \tag{4}$$

$$scale_y = y*scale_{factor} \tag{5}$$

Where (x,y) is the original coordinate of the key points. For the scaled key points, we obtain the centre of gravity by calculating the average of their coordinates.

$$centroid_x = \frac{1}{n}\sum_{i=1}^{n} x_i \tag{6}$$

Where $\boldsymbol{n}$ is the number of key points and $\boldsymbol{x}$ is the coordinate value, if calculating y coordinate, we need to replace $\boldsymbol{y}$ value with $\boldsymbol{x}$. Finally, we calculate the translation vector and perform the translation. The translation vector is computed based on the centre of gravity of the standard and scaled skeleton.

$$transfer_{vector} = centroid_{standard} - centroid_{scaled} \tag{7}$$

The scaled skeleton will be at a relatively horizontal position to the standard skeleton, and then we take advantage of the computed translation vector to trans-late the real-time skeleton to align with the standard skeleton.

Transformers have unique advantages in handling data with spatiotemporal relationships. Compared with RNN, Transformer has the ability of parallel processing, which means it has an advantage in processing large-scale data. At the same time, compared with CNN, Transformer's operational complexity in calculating the relationship between two positions does not increase with the number of operations, which allows the model to better understand the spatial relationships of data. In addition, the self-attention mechanism can focus on the positional features of data, which means that the mechanism allows the model to reference the information of other elements while processing one element. This feature can better capture the coordinate relationship features in human key point data (Li, 2021).

In order to make the model parameters more effective during training, we first conducted ablation experiments. The ablation experiment is a classic experimental method in deep learning, which explores the importance of each component in the model by eliminating a component in the complete model and evaluating changes in model performance. This experiment helps optimize the model and determine the best performing model structure. Zeiler and Ferguson visualized and understood the features of convolutional neural networks through ablation experiments (Zeiler&Ferguson., 2014), and inverse convolutional networks were used to map network activation back to pixel space to identify the role of features. Typically, ablation experiments are used to improve R-CNN for faster real-time response (Sun et al., 2018).

In this study, we identified the optimal combination of model structures by eliminating different components in the entire model and replacing them with different methods, thereby demonstrating the importance of each component. Designing ablation experiments requires consideration of multiple factors, such as the type of dataset and model. In addition, ablation experiments need to be repeated multiple times to obtain reliable results. In the ablation experiment of this article, based on the type of model, we conducted ablation experiments on the model structure, activation function, number of multi head attention heads, number of hidden units, and number of model layers. The structure of the Transformer model includes an encoder and a decoder, and changing the structure of the model will have a significant impact on the consumption of computing resources. The different activation function functions will directly affect the performance of the model. The multi head attention mechanism is the core component of Transformer, which affects the parallel computing ability of the model. The number of hidden units refers to the dimension output by each neuron. Generally, a higher number of units can increase model performance but also increase computational resources. The number of model layers refers to the number of encoder and decoder stacks in the Transformer, which significantly affects the effectiveness of the model.

RESULT AND ANALYSIS

We first discuss the ablation experiment, in which we ablate one parameter of a component at a time. This method can effectively determine the impact of each component and variable on model performance. Train 50 waves per ablation experiment, conduct 3 training sessions for each parameter, record the results, and compare the optimal results through accuracy, F1 score, and loss. In this way, we can gradually adjust the parameters of each component to find the best combination to improve model performance.

In the Ablation Experiment of model structure, we explore three model structures: A basic Transformer, a Transformer that integrates convolution and pooling operations, and a Transformer that only contains an encoder. The performance of each structure is compared to clarify the impact of the different structures on model performance. Among them, the Transformer with convolution and pooling operations has the best performance, which improves the model accuracy over the base structure by 15% and 19% over the accuracy of the Encoder-only model, it has an average training time 0.7 seconds and an average validation time of less than 0.1 seconds. The encoder model is less accurate but relatively lightweight, with an average training speed of 0.5 seconds and a validation speed of 0.02 seconds. The result shown in table 1.

Table 1. Results of model structure ablation experiments.

Model Structure	Accuracy	Loss	F1-Score
Conv and Pooling	98.32%	0.0957	0.9831
Encoder and Decoder	83.18%	0.4541	0.8319
Only Encoder	79.07%	0.4872	0.7903

In the Ablation Experiment of activation function, we tested three kinds of activation functions: ReLU, swish and mish. After the activation function is used in the full connection layer, the overall performance of the ReLU activation function model is better, with an accuracy of 98%, a loss value of 0.09 and an F1 score of 0.98. When mish and swish are used, the performance of the model is similar. However, compared with the best model performance, the accuracy is reduced by about 10%, and the loss value is much higher than the best performance. The main reason why ReLU stands out is that it can introduce nonlinear factors to make the neural network better solve complex problems. In addition, the output of ReLU is a linear piecewise function of its input, which makes the ReLU activation function sparse and helps the neural network learn better feature representation. The result shown in table 2.

Table 2. Results of activation function ablation experiments

Activation Function	Accuracy	Loss	F1-Score
ReLU	98.32%	0.0957	0.9831
Mish	89.72%	0.3588	0.8971
Swish	90.28%	0.4117	0.9028

In the hyperparametric Ablation Experiment of the number of multiple attention heads, we measured 4, 8 and 16 values respectively. In the multi head attention mechanism, each head will independently calculate the attention weight and splice or average the results. Generally speaking, using more heads can help the model capture more information. Too many headers according to the size of its dataset may lead to over fitting of the model and increase the computational complexity. In the ablation experiment, when the number of heads is 8, the best result is obtained, and the performance is improved by 8%. This also means that changing the number of heads is the most appropriate in our billiard posture data set. The result shown in table 3.

Table 3. The results of the multiple attention heads ablation experiment

Multi Attention Heads	Accuracy	Loss	F1-Score
8	98.32%	0.0957	0.9831
4	90.09%	0.3382	0.9006
16	90.28%	0.4336	0.9041

The number of hidden units has the most significant impact on the performance of the model. We tested 96, 256 and 512 strategies respectively. Compared with dimension 96, the accuracy of dimension 256 is improved by 23%. However, the number of hidden units of 512 in the later stage of training, the gap between training accuracy and test accuracy is increasing, and the model appears over fitting imagination. The number of layers of the model also has a significant impact on the performance of the model. We tested layers 2, 6 and 10 respectively. On our hitting posture data set, when the number of layers increases to 10, the accuracy rate of the model is only 57%, which may be because the number of data sets is too small to adapt to the self-attention mechanism of more layers. The accuracy of layer 2 is 10% higher than that of layer 6, which means that the model achieves the highest performance at layer 2 due to the limitation of data set size. The result shown in table 4 and 5.

Table 4. Model dimension ablation experiment results

Hidden Size	Accuracy	Loss	F1-Score
256	98.32%	0.0957	0.9831
96	75.51%	0.6363	0.7550
512	97.20%	0.1646	0.9720

Table 5. Results of Num layers ablation experiments

Layer Size	Accuracy	Loss	F1-Score
2	98.32%	0.0957	0.9831
6	88.79%	0.4355	0.8878
10	57.01%	0.6926	0.5530

We tested the reasoning speed of the model as shown in Figure 2. The response speed of the model validation is about 0.2S, which means that the model has fast reasoning ability. However, in actual use, the recognition speed of the model is affected by the frame rate of the camera picture. We use a high-definition camera with 1 second and 30 frames, which means that it takes about two seconds for the model to collect enough frames of pose to get the model recognition result, there is still a lot of room for progress in real-time scenes. A simple and effective way is to use more advanced equipment and control the resolution of the captured picture.

Figure 2. Transformer training and validation response speed

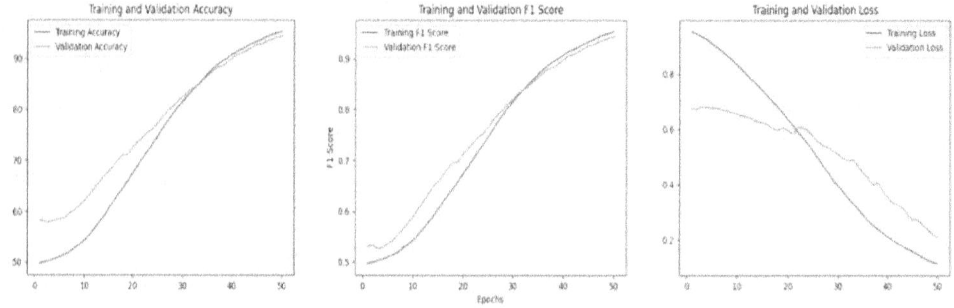

In this book chapter, we employ a model inspired by the foundational Transformer architecture. Initially, the model undergoes a convolutional layer, targeting the extraction of local features. Subsequently, max pooling is applied to down-sample and condense these features, enabling the model to assimilate broader contextual nuances. This is followed by a fully connected layer that seamlessly fuses the feature vectors and reshapes them to dimensions appropriate for the Transformer's input. Before entering the Transformer's encoder-decoder loops, the data is enriched with positional encodings, ensuring the model is attuned to sequential patterns within the data.

The final output from the transformer is passed through another fully connected layer, which generates probabilistic outcomes in conjunction with a softmax activation. The overarching architecture of our transformer model is detailed in figure 3. We implemented the entire model using the pytorch framework. The keras framework's drawing utility was leveraged to represent the model's structure for visualisation purposes. We pre-processed the input vectors and planned them into a specific format, i.e. (number of samples, number of time steps, feature dimensions). The number of features comes from analysing the extracted key point information. The output of the blazepose model contains 33 coordinate points of critical parts of human body, each coordinate point is a (x,y,z) coordinate containing depth information. Then, we can get the number of features needed as 3*33. So, in the input of model structure, we have data in the format of (None,75,99), where none is the number of uncertain data samples. The number of times step 75 is calculated from each billiard player striking video we collected.

Figure 3. Optimized transformer model structure

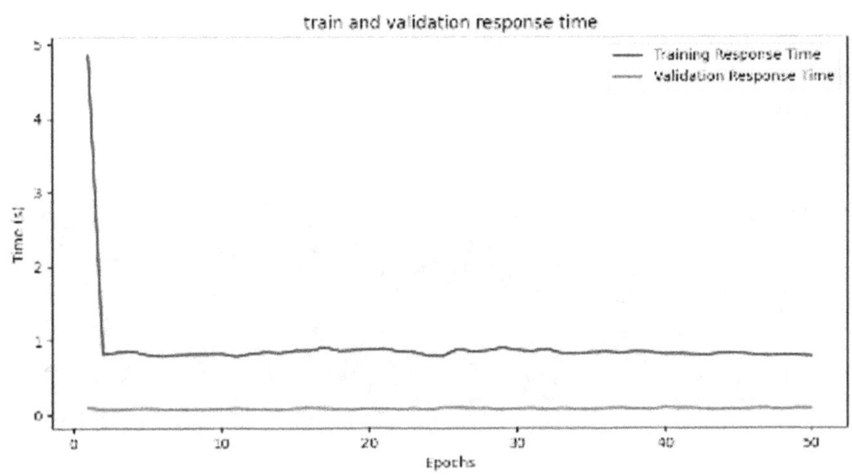

The standard bone model is generated by identifying the key points of the standard billiard pose image. The coordinates of the key points are based on the coordinate system of the identified image, while the coordinates of the real-time bone model are based on the coordinate system of the real-time image, which will lead to huge errors in the size and position of the bones of the comparison model. Therefore, we need to use scaling and alignment methods to match the contrast model. Figure 4 compares the real-time detected bones and the standard pose bones. This feature scales and aligns the real-time detected key points with the standard key point template. We have obtained a standard skeletal model and a real-time detected skeletal model. Then, we combine the two to obtain a real-time pose skeletal comparison system. We scale and align the two models so that the two skeletal models overlap in a predefined area. A zooming algorithm scales the skeletal models to make the two models the same size and keep them on the same level, and then the scaled skeletal models are aligned and overlapped using an alignment algorithm.

In addition, we can calculate the joint angle of the correct posture through the relative position of the key point coordinates. When the joint angle conforms to the billiard posture, the line of the bone will appear green, and if it is not correct, it will appear red. By comparing the model diagram, we can also clearly observe that when the player's posture is relatively correct, the real-time detected bones are basically equivalent to the standard bone model, and when the posture is wrong, we can obviously find that, for example, in (e), we can obviously find that the player's leg posture is incorrect. In addition to billiards games, this bone contrast model also plays a significant role in fitness. For example, fitness enthusiasts can easily find out whether the posture is deformed by observing the contrast model during shoulder push.

Figure 4. The comparison of skeleton detected in real-time with standard skeleton, white for the standard skeleton, green for (a), (b), (c) more standard, and red for (d), (e), (f) less standard

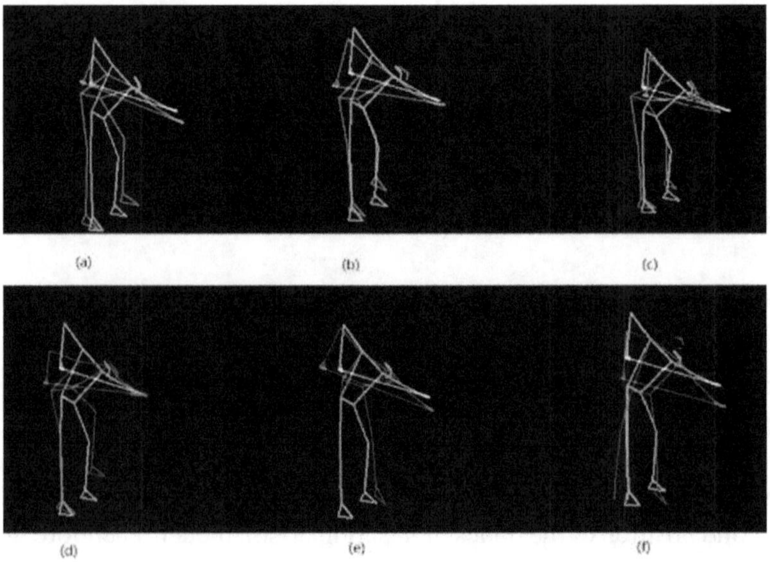

Figure 5 shows the effect comparison of sliding window in handling abnormal key points. Through the explanation in the methodology, we set the sliding window size to 25 frames, and process the continuous 25 frames of data as a group, which can better capture the change trend of data and reduce fluctuations. For each data point in the window, we calculate the mean and standard deviation. This method measures the degree of dispersion and average level of data and establishes a reasonable threshold range for detecting abnormal data. We judge whether the data of each point exceeds the mean value. Only when the data exceeds a certain range of threshold value, it will be regarded as abnormal value and replaced by the mean value. By calculating the average value of all points in the whole window, we can find a reasonable replacement number to ensure the stability of the data. By comparing (a) and (b) in the figure, we can clearly see that the key point results of (b) are more stable and effective.

Figure 5. Sliding window stabilization pose model

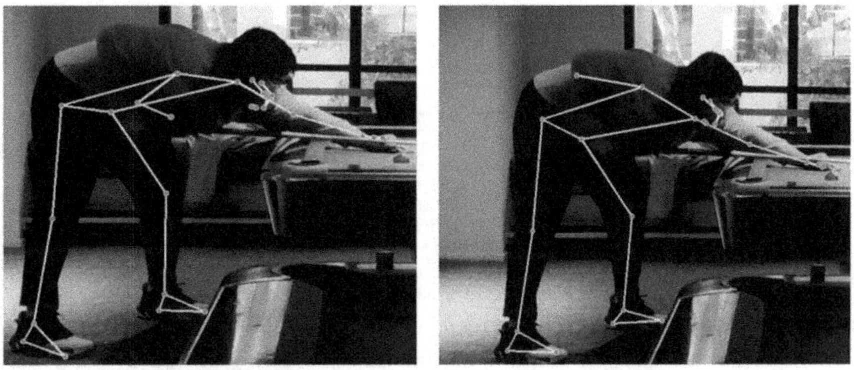

(a) (b)

In the entire system, we firstly extract real-time pose key points and then use the smoothing windows to deal with abnormal key point noise. These extracted key point data are simultaneously computed and analysed in three parts. The first part is the real-time comparison of the skeleton of the key points, which draws the real-time skeleton so that the player can compare themselves with the standard pose. Secondly, we feed the key point data into the trained Transformer model for real-time prediction, the model will display the output score to the player by calculating the confidence level through the Softmax function. This role is to use deep learning methods for judging the player's batting posture of the standard and substandard. Only when the player meets all the evaluation criteria, the system will treat the current action as a standard action, the player can observe through the skeletal comparison of the current action and the standard action that there is still a subtle gap through the posture scores as well as the results of the judgment to provide a more detailed analysis of the defects of the current posture. Figure 6 shows the performance of our proposed method.

The research focus of the system is to use transformer to classify and recognize the data of human key points. In this book chapter, billiards is thought as an example to complete the recognition of billiards hitting posture. The system can be deployed in various billiard game environments. Mediapipe can automatically capture the player closest to the monocular camera. It should be noted that the position of the camera needs to be able to include the whole body of the player hitting the ball on the table. The system also has adaptability in other sports, such as table tennis. In order to identify the correct posture of table tennis, we need to add additional classification labels for the transformer and prepare sufficient training data. When the key point data meets the table tennis posture model, we can identify its correct posture like billiards.

Figure 6. A system for analysing the striking posture of billiard players

CONCLUSION

This report aims to combine human pose estimation and realize the striking pose and analysis of a billiard player in a real-time scene. We combine the Transformer with human pose estimation to create a corpus of human poses using key point extraction, which provides a new perspective for the Transformer to recognise and analyse human poses. The extracted key points can also be employed for pose comparison and evaluation. The Transformer model is harnessed to make much accurate and objective judgments on the recognized poses. We also created a dataset for the recognition of striking poses of billiard players, in order to optimize the performance of our model, finally the optimized Transformer achieves an accuracy 98% and a response time 0.02 seconds.

FUTURE WORK

The system introduced in this chapter also has a lot of room for improvement. For example, we can further study transformer's attention mechanism and position coding to make it more suitable for human key point data. Transformer's multi head attention mechanism will have a better effect in the face of big data, so expanding the size of the data set will help to improve the performance of the model. In addition, the classification label of the model can be continuously improved and extended to more kinds of sports. In addition to vision, other sensor information can also be considered to improve the accuracy of human key point prediction, and it can be fused with visual information.

The main application fields of the system in this study are motion analysis and rehabilitation. It provides personalized training through instant feedback and recognition of human posture and can monitor the posture of athletes to help rehabilitation therapists diagnose and recover in time. In addition, it may also have good application prospects in the field of human-computer interaction, such as providing a more intuitive way to interact with computers or intelligent devices through gesture control, gesture recognition and other interactive methods.

REFERENCES

Agarwal, V., Sharma, K., & Rajpoot, A. K. (2022), AI based Yoga trainer-simplifying home yoga using MediaPipe and video streaming. *International Conference for Emerging Technology*. IEEE. 10.1109/INCET54531.2022.9824332

Andriluka, M., Pishchulin, L., Gehler, P., & Schiele, B. (2014), 2D human pose estimation: New benchmark and state of the art analysis. *IEEE Conference on Computer Vision and Pattern Recognition*, (pp. 3686-3693). IEEE. 10.1109/CVPR.2014.471

BazarevskyV.GrishchenkoI.RaveendranK.ZhuT.ZhangF.GrundmannM. (2020), *Blazepose: On-device real-time body pose tracking*. arXiv:2006.10204.

Cao, Z., Simon, T., Wei, S. E., & Sheikh, Y. (2017), Realtime multi-person 2D pose estimation using part affinity fields. *IEEE Conference on Computer Vision and Pattern Recognition*, (pp. 7291-7299). IEEE. 10.1109/CVPR.2017.143

Carreira, J., & Zisserman, A. (2017), Quo vadis, action recognition? A new model and the kinetics dataset. *IEEE Conference on Computer Vision and Pattern Recognition*, (pp. 6299-6308). IEEE. 10.1109/CVPR.2017.502

Chen, Y., Wang, Z., Peng, Y., Zhang, Z., Yu, G., & Sun, J. (2018), Cascaded pyramid network for multi-person pose estimation. *IEEE Conference on Computer Vision and Pattern Recognition*, (pp. 7103-7112). IEEE. 10.1109/CVPR.2018.00742

Choutas, V., Weinzaepfel, P., Revaud, J., & Schmid, C. (2018), Potion: Pose motion representation for action recognition. *IEEE Conference on Computer Vision and Pattern Recognition*, (pp. 7024-7033). IEEE. 10.1109/CVPR.2018.00734

Dosovitskiy, A., Beyer, L., Kolesnikov, A., Weissenborn, D., Zhai, X., Unterthiner, T., & Houlsby, N. (2020). An image is worth 16x16 words: Transformers for image recognition at scale. arXiv preprint arXiv:2010.11929.

Güler, R. A., Neverova, N., & Kokkinos, I. (2018). Densepose: Dense human pose estimation in the wild. In *Proceedings of the IEEE conference on computer vision and pattern recognition* (pp. 7297-7306). IEEE.10.1109/CVPR.2018.00762

He, K., Zhang, X., Ren, S., & Sun, J. (2015). Spatial pyramid pooling in deep convolutional networks for visual recognition. *IEEE Transactions on Pattern Analysis and Machine Intelligence*, *37*(9), 1904–1916. doi:10.1109/TPAMI.2015.2389824 PMID:26353135

He, K., Zhang, X., Ren, S., & Sun, J. (2016), Deep residual learning for image recognition. *IEEE Conference on Computer Vision and Pattern Recognition*, (pp. 770-778). IEEE.

Hochreiter, S., & Schmidhuber, J. (1997). Long short-term memory. *Neural Computation*, *9*(8), 1735–1780. doi:10.1162/neco.1997.9.8.1735 PMID:9377276

Li, K., Wang, S., Zhang, X., Xu, Y., Xu, W., & Tu, Z. (2021). Pose recognition with cascade transformers. In *Proceedings of the IEEE/CVF conference on computer vision and pattern recognition* (pp. 1944-1953). IEEE.

Liu, T., Wang, K., Sha, L., Chang, B., & Sui, Z. (2018, April). Table-to-text generation by structure-aware seq2seq learning. *Proceedings of the AAAI Conference on Artificial Intelligence*, *32*(1). doi:10.1609/aaai.v32i1.11925

Liu, Z., Lin, Y., Cao, Y., Hu, H., Wei, Y., Zhang, Z., & Guo, B. (2021). Swin transformer: Hierarchical vision transformer using shifted windows. In *Proceedings of the IEEE/CVF International Conference on Computer Vision* (pp. 10012-10022). IEEE. 10.1109/ICCV48922.2021.00986

Lugaresi, C., Tang, J., Nash, H., McClanahan, C., Uboweja, E., Hays, M., & Grundmann, M. (2019). *Mediapipe: A framework for perceiving and processing reality* (Vol. 2019). IEEE.

Mao, W., Ge, Y., Shen, C., Tian, Z., Wang, X., & Wang, Z. (2021). *TFPose: Direct human pose estimation with transformers*. arXiv preprint arXiv:2103.15320.

Pauzi, A. S. B., Mohd Nazri, F. B., Sani, S., Bataineh, A. M., Hisyam, M. N., Jaafar, M. H., & Mohamed, A. (2021). *Movement estimation using MediaPipe blazepose*. IVIC. doi:10.1007/978-3-030-90235-3_49

Singh, A. K., Kumbhare, V. A., & Arthi, K. (2021). Real-time human pose detection and recognition using MediaPipe. *International Conference on Soft Computing and Signal Processing*, (pp. 145-154). IEEE.

Sun, K., Xiao, B., Liu, D., & Wang, J. (2019), Deep high-resolution representation learning for human pose estimation. *IEEE Conference on Computer Vision and Pattern Recognition*, (pp. 5693-5703). IEEE. 10.1109/CVPR.2019.00584

Sun, X., Wu, P., & Hoi, S. C. (2018). Face detection using deep learning: An improved Faster R-CNN approach. *Neurocomputing*, *299*, 42–50. doi:10.1016/j.neucom.2018.03.030

Vaswani, A., Shazeer, N., Parmar, N., Uszkoreit, J., Jones, L., Gomez, A. N., & Polosukhin, I. (2017). Attention is all you need. *Advances in Neural Information Processing Systems*, 30.

Wang, J., Qiu, K., Peng, H., Fu, J., & Zhu, J. (2019, October). Ai coach: Deep human pose estimation and analysis for personalized athletic training assistance. In *Proceedings of the 27th ACM international conference on multimedia* (pp. 374-382). ACM. 10.1145/3343031.3350910

Wen, Y., Zhang, K., Li, Z., & Qiao, Y. (2016), A discriminative feature learning approach for deep face recognition. In ECCV (pp. 499-515). Springer. doi:10.1007/978-3-319-46478-7_31

Yang, Z., Zhang, K., Liang, Y., & Wang, J. (2017), Single image super-resolution with a parameter economic residual-like convolutional neural network. In MultiMedia Modeling, (pp. 353-364). Springer. doi:10.1007/978-3-319-51811-4_29

Zeiler, M. D., & Fergus, R. (2014). Visualizing and understanding convolutional networks. In ECCV (pp. 818-833). doi:10.1007/978-3-319-10590-1_53

Chapter 11
Analysis Model at the Sentence Level for Phishing Detection

Sonali Mishra
Asian Education Group, India & Asian Law College, India

K. Priyadarsini
SRM Institute of Science and Technology, India

Arpit Namdev
University Institute of Technology RGPV, India

S. Venkataramana
Malla Reddy Engineering College for Women, India

Varun
https://orcid.org/0000-0002-0064-6448
SJB Institute of Technology, India

Sabyasachi Pramanik
https://orcid.org/0000-0002-9431-8751
Haldia Institute of Technology, India

Ankur Gupta
https://orcid.org/0000-0002-4651-5830
Vaish College of Engineering, India

ABSTRACT

Global cyber dangers related to phishing emails have increased dramatically, particularly after the COVID-19 epidemic broke out. Many companies have suffered significant financial losses as a result of this kind of assault. Even though many models have been developed to distinguish between phishing efforts and genuine emails, attackers always come up with new ways to trick their targets into falling for their scams. Many companies have suffered significant financial losses as a result of this kind of assault. Although phishing detection algorithms are being developed, their accuracy and speed in recognizing phishing emails are not up to par right now. Furthermore, the number of phished emails has alarmingly increased lately. To lessen the negative effects of such bogus communications, there is an urgent

DOI: 10.4018/979-8-3693-1738-9.ch011

need for more effective and high-performing phishing detection algorithms. Inside the framework of this study, a thorough examination of an email message's email header and content is carried out. A novel phishing detection model is built using the features of sentences that are extracted. The new dimension of sentence-level analysis is introduced by this model, which makes use of k-nearest neighbor (KNN). Kaggle's well-known datasets were used both to train and evaluate the model. Important performance indicators, including the F1-measure, precision, recall, and accuracy of 0.97, are used to assess the efficacy of this approach.

INTRODUCTION

One of the most common hazards that regular internet users face both at work and at home are email assaults. More than 70% of respondents to a poll said they use emails as a common form of communication whether working remotely or interacting with friends and coworkers. Still, a lot of people don't know how dangerous apparently innocuous emails may be, or how doing seemingly simple activities might damage their systems. In the second quarter of 2022, the Anti Phishing Workgroup (APWG) recorded 1,097,811 total phishing assaults, which at the time was a record. APWG recorded 1,270,883 phishing assaults in total during the third quarter of 2022, which is a record and the worst quarter for phishing the organization has ever tracked. August 2022 had 430,141 assaults overall, the biggest monthly number ever recorded. Since APWG first identified 230,554 phishing assaults in the first quarter of 2020, the number of attacks reported to APWG has more than quintupled. A portion of the increase in Q3 2022 may be attributed to the spike in assaults on many particular targets that have been documented. These targets were exposed to several assaults by phishers who were relentless in their efforts.

The sophistication of phishing assaults has increased, thus it's critical to investigate cutting-edge methods for detecting them. Numerous methods have been published in the literature to stop identity theft and financial losses caused by phishing efforts (Zhuorao et al., 2018). However, these methods still struggle to accurately and reliably identify a wide range of phishing attempts that employ dynamic strategies, even with ongoing advancements in phishing detection technologies (Almomani et al., 2013). This highlights the need of closely examining the elements included in phishing emails in order to increase the adaptability and efficiency of phishing detection systems. Combining current contributions from social engineering researchers is also necessary to determine new characteristics that might enhance the detection accuracy of phishing emails. Particularly when confronted with novel phishing techniques, current phishing detection systems often exhibit low detection accuracy and a significant percentage of false positives (Ademola and Boniface, 2020). In order to find possible indicators of phishing, this research examined sentence-level analysis for phishing detection, which entails closely examining individual phrases inside dubious emails or messages.

Sentiment analysis is an essential component of sentence-level analysis. Scholars such as (Liu et al. 2016) have shown that discerning between authentic and fraudulent emails may be aided by examining the tone of phrases. Sentences evoking urgency or terror are common in phishing emails, and sentiment analysis can identify this pattern with accuracy. A major development in phishing detection is the move toward sentence-level characteristics. This method looks closely at the complex linguistic and contextual clues that are present in phrases in order to identify the minute details that indicate phishing attempts. The use of machine learning methods augments the detection effectiveness and fosters adaptive cybersecurity measures in response to the dynamic threat environment. Section 2 discusses the literature review; section 3 is the main methodology section, section 4 shows the result & discussion and section 5 is the conclusion and future scope.

LITERATURE REVIEW

Phishing detection strategies may be categorized into two types: whitelist-based and blacklist-based approaches. The whitelist is a compilation of harmless URLs and IP addresses that are used to authenticate a dubious URL. (Han et al. 2017) use an approach based on a whitelist to identify and detect. Blacklist-based methods are extensively used in widely accessible anti-phishing toolbars such as Google safe surfing. This involves comparing URLs against Google's regularly updated blacklist of browser phishing sites. If a URL is identified as phishing, users are promptly alerted. While list-based solutions may provide very high accuracy, maintaining a complete list of phishing URLs is challenging due to the constant creation of new URLs on a daily basis.

The study conducted by (Zhang et al. 2011) involves extracting features from URLs using a bag-of-words approach and then training them with a classifier using online learning techniques. In (Sahingoz et al. 2019), they use distributed representations of terms in a specific URL and apply seven distinct machine learning methods to determine whether the URL is a phishing URL. While these approaches have shown satisfactory results, they are unable to handle unfamiliar information that is not included in the training set.

In their study, (Mogimi et al. 2016) introduced a phish detector that utilizes the support vector machine (SVM) technique to train a model for phishing detection. Subsequently, the decision tree (DT) approach is used to uncover concealed phishing attempts. In a large dataset, the suggested technique has a true positive rate of 0.99

and a false negative rate of 0.001. However, this strategy assumes that phishing web sites only use harmless page content, which is not the case in reality. (Rao et al. 2019) recently introduced CatchPhish, a lightweight program that can determine the validity of a URL without actually seeing the website's content. The proposed model utilizes both hand-crafted and Term Frequency-Inverse Document Frequency (TF-IDF) characteristics from the suspicious URL. These features are then used for classification using the random forest classifier.

Phishing Detection Features at the Sentence Level

Features at the sentence level include a variety of grammatical, structural, and contextual elements seen in single sentences. This method acknowledges that, when perusing the email in its entirety, it is often possible to overlook minute clues that point to malevolent intent seen in phishing emails. Sentence-level analysis, which looks for indicators of phishing efforts in individual sentences inside emails or other forms of communication, is essential to the identification of phishing attempts. Examining a variety of linguistic clues and contextual factors is part of this research to ascertain if a statement is likely to be a part of a phishing scam.

Stylistic anomalies and linguistic cues: Phishing emails often include grammatical mistakes, misspellings, and strange word use, among other linguistic irregularities. (Chinese et al. 2020) and (Hu et al. 2018) studies have investigated the language characteristics that are suggestive of phishing. Grammatical mistakes, strange syntax, and uneven language use are some of these characteristics that are often seen in phishing emails. Algorithms can distinguish between phishing attempts and real communication with accuracy thanks to sentence-level analysis, which finds and measures these irregularities (Gibert et al. 2014).

The study's language signals are listed in the table below:

Table 1. Linguistic cues

LINGUISTIC CUE	DEFINITION	EXAMPLE
Misspellings and Grammatical Errors:	Misspelled words and grammatical errors that can be a red flag.	o "Please verify your account detalis." o "Click here to avoid your account being suspensed."
Unnatural Language Usage	Language that is unnatural or overly formal, attempting to appear official.	o "Dear Sir/Madam, we hereby request your immediate action." o "We have noticed some unusual activities on your account, hence we are taking preventive measures."
Urgent or Alarmist Language	Sense of urgency or panic to prompt immediate action	o "Your account has been compromised. Act now to prevent further damage!" o "Immediate action required: Your account will be suspended in 24 hours."
Unusual Requests	Unusual requests or demands that are not typically seen in legitimate communications:	o "Please provide your password for verification purposes." o "Transfer funds to this account to claim your prize."
Generic Greetings	Use of generic greetings to address recipients	o "Dear Customer" o "User"
Generic Content	Lack of specific details about the recipient or transaction	o "Your recent purchase requires confirmation. Click here to verify."
Threats or Consequences	Negative consequences if action is not taken	o "Failure to update your information will result in account suspension." o "Your account will be charged unless you confirm your details."

Contextual Indicators: Analyzing the relationships between phrases in an email is one of the contextual features. Phishing emails often use intimidation, fear, or a false feeling of authority to trick their target. Models may find patterns that indicate phishing intent by analyzing the relationships between phrases (Gupta et al., 2013). Examining the relationships between words in an email is one way contextual indicators in sentence-level analysis for phishing detection are used. This research looked at characteristics such;

Threats and Urgent Action: Phishing (Pramanik, S. 2023) attempts may be identified by contextual clues that use threats and urgent language. Sentences that have been identified are "Your account has been compromised." Take immediate action to stop unwanted access." (Gupta et al., 2013) and "Account suspension will occur if you do not respond within 24 hours." (Sheng et al. 2010).

Request for Sensitive Information: It is advisable to be wary of contextual clues such as "To verify your account, we need your username and password." Kindly provide them. (Alazab et al., 2018) and "We need your Social Security (Pramanik, S. 2023) number for security reasons. Please distribute it.

Promised Benefits or incentives: Phishing efforts may be indicated by contextual signals that include promises of incentives, such as "Congratulations! It's your win—a gift card. Claim your reward by clicking the link. (Gupta et al., 2013) and "You've been chosen for a special offer as a valued client. To redeem, go here. (Alazab et al. 2018)

Fallacious Authority or Impersonation: Situations in which the email purports to be authoritative or assumes the identity of a formal source, such as "This email is from the IT department." You need change your password. (Sheng et al. 2010) and "We've found evidence of fraud. To safeguard your account, kindly adhere to following instructions".

Link and Attachment Context: Phishing may be detected by contextual clues such as "Click the link below to verify your account information." According to (Alazab et al. 2018), "Open the attached file for important account updates."

Contradictory Details: It is advisable to be wary of contextual signals that provide information that deviates from prior assertions, such as "You've won a prize in our lottery." But before we can proceed, we require a deposit." It says, "Your account has been compromised, but we can fix it if you provide your details."

Creating a sentence-level analytic model to identify phishing emails was the aim of this study. For this study, an experimental research design was used. The research made use of experimental data that was gathered from a collection of phishing emails (Biswas, 2020). The dataset was perfect for this investigation since it included a large sample of ham and spam email messages. This is a CSV file that includes relevant data from 5172 randomly selected email files together with labels designating whether the files are considered spam or not. There are 5172 rows in the csv file, one row for each email. It has thirty-two columns. The email name is shown in the first column. To preserve recipients' anonymity, the name has been set to numbers rather than their names. Therefore, instead of being kept in separate text files, data pertaining to all 5172 emails are kept in a small data frame.

Cybersecurity professionals continue to face phishing attacks, which is why machine learning methods are being used to detect fraudulent activity. For phishing detection, the K-Nearest Neighbors (KNN) algorithm is a notable method. This study of the literature offers a comprehensive overview of research using the KNN algorithm for this purpose. In order to distinguish phishing websites, (Mehta, S. et al., 2015) explore a variety of machine learning approaches, including KNN (Reepu et al. 2023). Through feature selection and classification, their study highlights the importance of KNN in improving the accuracy of phishing detection ("Phishing Detection using Machine Learning Techniques," 2015).

In particular, (Sharma, D. and Gomase, V. 2017) focus on using KNN to recognize phishing websites. In "An Approach for Detecting Phishing Websites Based on K-Nearest Neighbors Algorithm," (2017), they go into detail on how to include URL and website content characteristics into the KNN algorithm to achieve accurate classification. (Anwar, M. et al. 2018) provide an improved phishing detection model that combines KNN with feature selection methods. According to their study ("An Improved Phishing Detection Model using Feature Selection and K-Nearest Neighbor," 2018), their work focuses on improving KNN's performance by choosing relevant characteristics, which raises detection accuracy.

(Shailendra et al., 2019) use KNN to traverse the domain of phishing website identification. In order to maximize the efficacy of the algorithm, they emphasize how important it is to carefully choose and extract features ("Phishing Detection based on the Features of Phishing Webpages Using K-Nearest Neighbor Algorithm," 2019). The effectiveness of the KNN algorithm in identifying phishing assaults is examined by (Priyank R. et al 2019). Their research highlights how important feature engineering is when choosing pertinent characteristics for categorization ("K-Nearest Neighbor Algorithm for Phishing Detection," 2019). Together, the studies highlight the value of KNN as a tool for phishing activity detection and demonstrate the ways that feature engineering, categorization, and selection promote this cybersecurity effort.

METHODOLOGY

We used the Python Gensim module to train a Word2Vec model on a large corpus of text data in order to do sentence level analysis. Word embeddings that captured the semantic links between words were created by this approach. Using the trained word2vec model, the K-NN classifier was able to determine if a text was spam or ham based on the content of the message.

The raw dataset, before to processing, is shown in the figure below.

Figure 1. Snippet of unprocessed data

	label	text	spam/ham
605	ham	Subject: enron methanol ; meter #	0
2349	ham	Subject: hpl nom for january 9 ,	0
3624	ham	Subject: neon retreat	0
4685	spam	Subject: photoshop , windows ,	1
2030	ham	Subject: re : indian springs	0
2949	ham	Subject: ehronline web address	0
2793	ham	Subject: spring savings certificate -	0
4185	spam	Subject: looking for medication ?	1
2641	ham	Subject: noms / actual flow for 2 /	0
1870	ham	Subject: nominations for oct . 21 -	0
4922	spam	Subject: vocable % rnd - word	1
3799	spam	Subject: report 01405 !	1

Figure 2. Block diagram for model

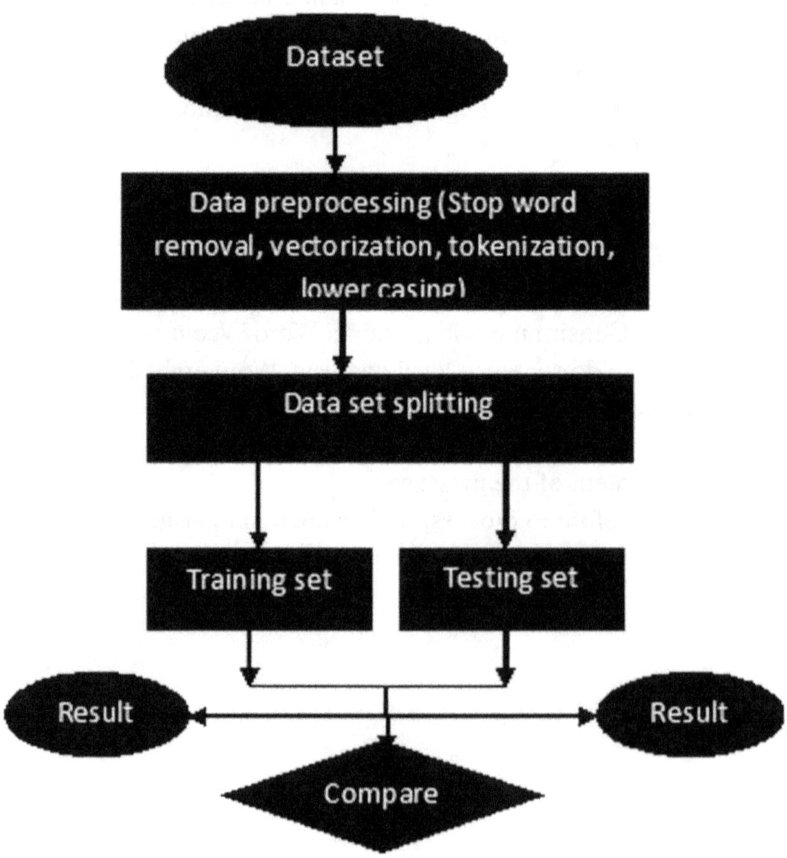

Figure 3. Sentence level analysis model suggestion

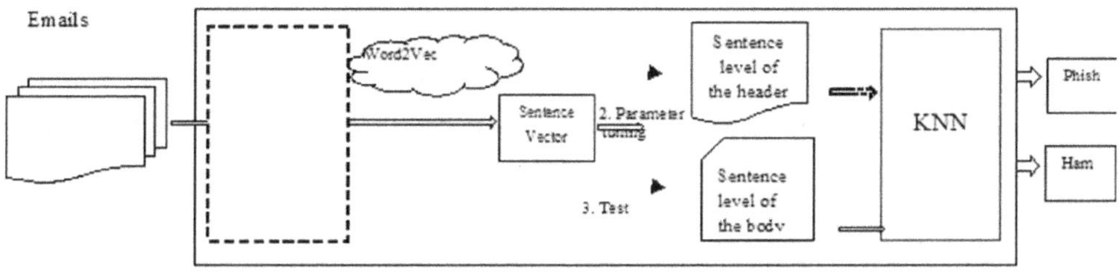

Preprocessing the Data

In this phase, the phrase was tokenized, which entails splitting it up into words and using lowercase to change a word to lowercase contractions were used to stretch English contractions back to their original form, and stopwords—words like "a," "an," "the," and so on—were eliminated from the papers. Since these terms don't aid in the distinction between two documents or the removal of HTML tags, they don't actually have any significance. Processed email messages that were identified as spam (denoted by 1) and ham (denoted by 0) were obtained via data preprocessing. The analyzed dataset is shown in the figure below.

Figure 4. Snippet of dataset

	text	Spam/Ham
0	subject enron methanol meter follow note gave ...	0
1	subject hpl nom january see attached file hpln...	0
2	subject neon retreat around wonderful time yea...	0
3	subject photoshop windows office cheap main tr...	1
4	subject indian springs deal book teco pvr reve...	0

Dividing the Data Into Sets for Testing and Training

33% of the preprocessed dataset was utilized for testing, while the remaining 67% was used for training. This division of the dataset was made between the training and testing sets. The testing set was used to assess the model's performance, while the training set was used to train the model.

Word2Vec Feature Extraction

We used a huge corpus of text data to train a Word2Vec model using the Python Gensim (Veeraiah, V. et al. 2023) package. Word embeddings that captured the semantic links between words were created by this approach. We computed the average Word2Vec vector for every word in each phrase in the dataset, yielding a sentence-level feature vector. A neural network model called Word2Vec uses numbers to represent words in vector form. The term "Word Embedding" is often used to describe this numerical vector. Word2Vec considers the context of a word while converting it to a numerical vector, unlike previous approaches like Bag of Words and TF-IDF. One of the main design objectives of gensim was memory efficiency, which is not an afterthought but rather a fundamental component (Github.Com, 2023). A popular open-source Python package for NLP (Praveenkumar, S. et al. 2023) and topic modeling is called Gensim. Its capacity to manage enormous amounts of text data and its quickness in vector embedding training distinguish it from other NLP libraries. Additionally, Gensim offers well-liked subject modeling algorithms like LDA, which makes it the library of choice for a lot of people. From a collection of phrases and text files, Gensim may be used to create dictionaries (Geeksforgeeks.org, 2023). The figure below depicts the word2vec model

Figure 5. Word2vec model

The Text Data's Vectorization

In order to use the Word2Vec model to transform the preprocessed text input into a vector representation, vectorization was required. The result of a chosen word's vector representation is seen in the image below.

Figure 6. Vectorization output

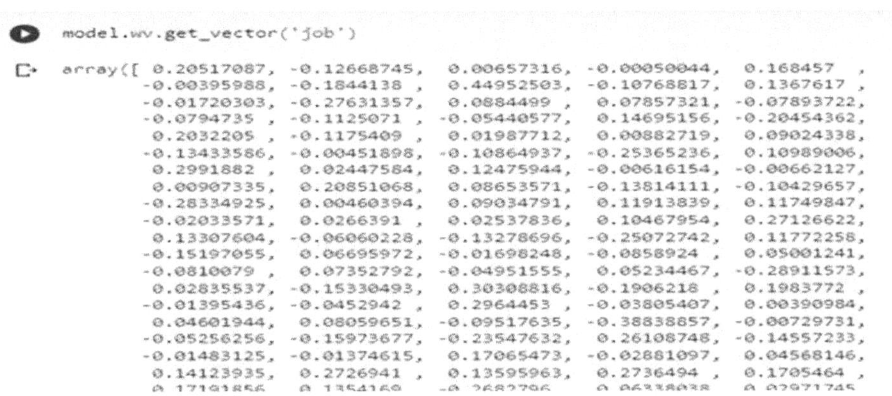

```
model.wv.get_vector('job')

array([ 0.20517087, -0.12668745,  0.00657316, -0.00050044,  0.168457  ,
       -0.00395988, -0.1844138 ,  0.44952503, -0.10768817,  0.1367617 ,
       -0.01720303, -0.27631357,  0.0884499 ,  0.07857321, -0.07893722,
       -0.0794735 , -0.1125071 , -0.05440577,  0.14695156, -0.20454362,
        0.2032205 , -0.1175409 ,  0.01987712,  0.00882719,  0.09024338,
       -0.13433586, -0.00451898, -0.10864937, -0.25365236,  0.10989006,
        0.2991882 ,  0.02447584,  0.12475944, -0.00616154, -0.00662127,
        0.00907335,  0.20851068,  0.08653571, -0.13814111, -0.10429657,
       -0.28334925,  0.00460394,  0.09034791,  0.11913839,  0.11749847,
       -0.02033571,  0.0266391 ,  0.02537836,  0.10467954,  0.27126622,
        0.13307604, -0.06060228, -0.13278696, -0.25072742,  0.11772258,
       -0.15197055,  0.06695972, -0.01698248, -0.0858924 ,  0.05001241,
       -0.0810079 ,  0.07352792, -0.04951555,  0.05234467, -0.28911573,
        0.02835537, -0.15330493,  0.30308816, -0.1906218 ,  0.1983772 ,
       -0.01395436, -0.0452942 ,  0.2964453 , -0.03805407,  0.00390984,
        0.04601944,  0.08059651, -0.09517635, -0.38838857, -0.00729731,
       -0.05256256, -0.15973677, -0.23547632,  0.26108748, -0.14557233,
       -0.01483125, -0.01374615,  0.17065473, -0.02881097,  0.04568146,
        0.14123935,  0.2726941 ,  0.13595963,  0.2736494 ,  0.1705464 ,
```

Match the Trainset to the Word2Vec Model

A list is used as the training input for the Word2Vec model. To prepare the data for training in this scenario, each email should be split up into a list of words, and each of these lists has to be added to an empty list (Turing.com, 2023). The graphic below illustrates how the word2vec model fits the train set and test dataset.

Figure 7. Word2Vec output

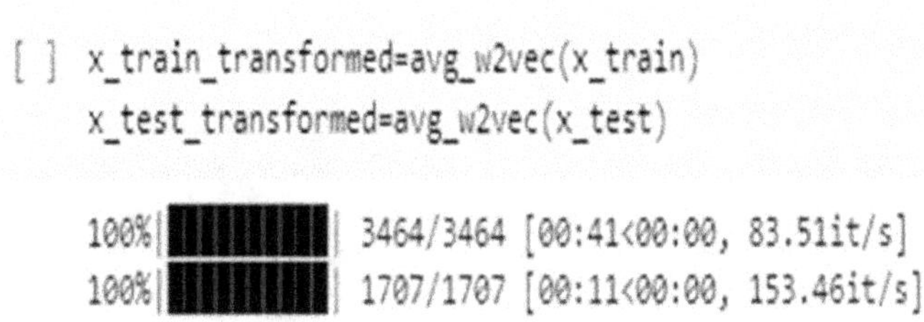

```
x_train_transformed=avg_w2vec(x_train)
x_test_transformed=avg_w2vec(x_test)

100%|██████████| 3464/3464 [00:41<00:00, 83.51it/s]
100%|██████████| 1707/1707 [00:11<00:00, 153.46it/s]
```

The Model's Training

This included utilizing the vectorized training (VidyaChellam, V. et al. 2023) data and the labels for spam/ham to build a K-NN classifier, a classification model. Using the trained word2vec model dataset for ham and spam, a KNN model was created and fitted. In this case, the K-Nearest Neighbors Algorithm is used to determine whether a certain email is spam or not. One of the most basic machine learning algorithms, K-Nearest Neighbor, is based on the supervised learning approach. The K-NN method places the new case in the category most comparable to the existing categories based on its assumption that the new instance and its data are similar to the examples that are already available. The K-NN method categorizes a new data point according to similarity after storing all the relevant data. This indicates that the K-NN algorithm can quickly classify newly discovered data into a well-suited category. Although the K-NN technique is mostly utilized for classification issues, it may also be used for regression. K-NN does not make any assumptions about the underlying data since it is a non-parametric method. During the training phase, the KNN algorithm simply retains the dataset and categorizes newly received data into a subset that closely resembles the original data (Javapoint.com, 2021). The KNN algorithm's fitting to the training set and test accuracy are shown in the figure below.

Figure 8. Sample of KNN classifier code

```
from sklearn.model_selection import RandomizedSearchCV
from sklearn.neighbors import KNeighborsClassifier
grid_params = { 'n_neighbors' : [10,20,30,40,50,60],
               'metric' : ['manhattan']}
knn=KNeighborsClassifier()
clf = RandomizedSearchCV(knn, grid_params, random_state=0,n_jobs=-1,verbose=1)
clf.fit(x_train_transformed,y_train)

Fitting 5 folds for each of 6 candidates, totalling 30 fits
/usr/local/lib/python3.10/dist-packages/sklearn/model_selection/_search.py:305: UserWarning: The total space of parameters 6 is smaller than n_iter=10.
  warnings.warn(

  RandomizedSearchCV
  estimator: KNeighborsClassifier
    KNeighborsClassifier

clf.best_params_

{'n_neighbors': 10, 'metric': 'manhattan'}

clf.best_score_

0.9338875960263243
```

Model Assessment

We created a prototype to show how the suggested model works. KNN Classifier and Python were used. Python was the programming language used. This is due to Python's simplicity and its ability to function effectively with large applications (Prasad, 2016). An analysis of our method's effectiveness was conducted using a confusion matrix. We were able to determine a number of parameters, including recall (Jain, V. et al. 2023), accuracy (Mandal, A. et al. 2021), precision (Meslie, Y. et al. 2021), F1-score (Chandan, R. R. et al. 2023), and specificity, using the confusion matrix. The following definitions were applied:

- Phishing phrase properly identified as phishing (True Positive, TP).
- True Negative (TN): A genuine statement that has been accurately characterized as such.
- False Positive (FP): A true statement that is mistakenly categorized as phishing.
- False Negative (FN): Phishing statement that is mistakenly identified as authentic.

In order to verify the classification model's effectiveness on the testing set, the model was assessed. The model evaluation's findings are shown in the graphic below. For the model, a testing accuracy of 97% is desirable.

Figure 9. Confusion matrix

```
[ ] print(classification_report(y_train,clf.predict(x_train_transformed)))

              precision    recall  f1-score   support

           0       0.96      0.97      0.96      2460
           1       0.92      0.90      0.91      1004

    accuracy                           0.95      3464
   macro avg       0.94      0.93      0.94      3464
weighted avg       0.95      0.95      0.95      3464
```

The correctness of the model's performance was assessed further using custom data. The model's ability to recognize a spam message is shown in the figure below.

Figure 10. Model output screenshot

```
message=['you have worn 5000, call or email to claim your prize']
x_test_transformed2=avg_w2vec(message)

#messagev=clf.fit(message, y_train)

#message_vector = tf.transform(message)
category = clf.predict(x_test_transformed2)
print("The message is", "spam" if category == 1 else "not spam")

100%|██████████| 1/1 [00:00<00:00, 174.95it/s]The message is spam
```

RESULT AND DISCUSSION

Sentence-level analysis for phishing detection was the main focus of this investigation. Word embeddings that captured the semantic links between words were produced using the word2vec model. We computed the average Word2Vec vector for every word in each phrase in the dataset, yielding a sentence-level feature vector. According to the data above, our method of employing the KNN algorithm with Word2Vec embedding to identify phishing texts produced encouraging results. As can be seen in the figure below, the model achieved training accuracy of 99% and testing accuracy of 97%.

Figure 11. Training and testing ROC curve

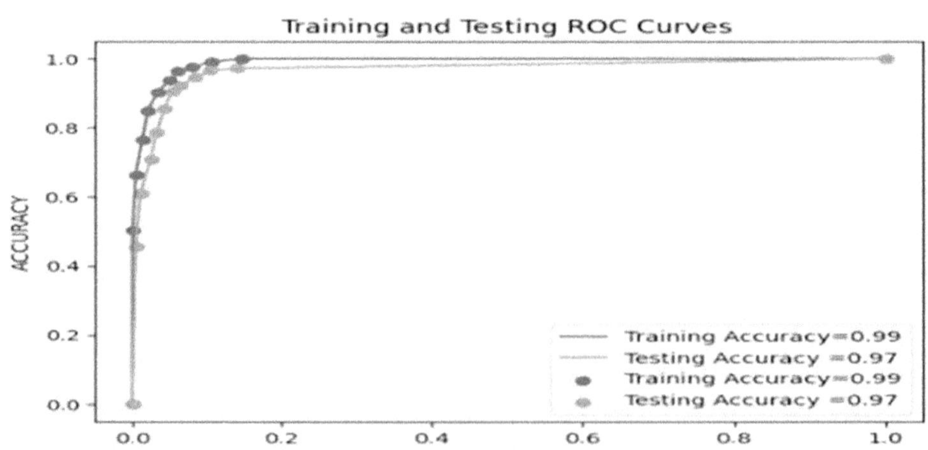

Furthermore, the model's performance was shown by the confusion matrix using several indicators. As previously mentioned, the model's accuracy of 97% was deemed good. Calculations of accuracy, precision, recall, and F1-score were made using the confusion matrix data.

Table 2. Confusion matrix

	Predicted Legitimate	**Predicted Phishing**
Actual Legitimate	4500	150
Actual Phishing	120	4850

CONCLUSION AND FUTURE WORK

Sentence Level Analysis model's potential as a reliable phishing detection tool is enhanced by its ability to detect subtle patterns within sentences as well as the KNN algorithm's ease of use and interpretability. The model's performance is further strengthened by its attention to sentences, which allows for a more detailed analysis of language signals and context. The model does have difficulties, however. Potential obstacles include linguistic subtleties, phrase structure variations, and the evolution of phishing techniques. Additionally, the amount and quality of training data may have an impact on the model's performance, calling for careful assessment and optimization.

Subsequent studies may investigate more sophisticated ways for producing sentence embeddings, using strategies such as transformer-based models to more efficiently capture complex language details and contextual information. Combining textual material with other data modalities, such photos and URLs, may improve the model's capacity to identify phishing attempts on a variety of platforms. Investigating adversarial assaults against the Sentence Level Analysis model, which might reveal weaknesses and encourage the creation of mitigation techniques for increased resilience, could be the subject of future research. Additionally, to increase the model's applicability and combat phishing assaults that target users across linguistic borders, it might be improved to include many languages. In conclusion, a viable method for phishing detection is provided by the Sentence Level Analysis model that employs KNN. Addressing issues and looking into new research directions will be essential as the model develops to ensure that it remains successful in thwarting phishing attacks.

REFERENCES

Alazab, M., Layton, R., & Venkatraman, S. (2018). A novel model for detecting phishing attacks using text classification. *Future Generation Computer Systems, 78*, 1086–1097.

Anwar, M., Sangaiah, A. K., & Farooq, M. S. (2018). An Improved Phishing Detection Model using Feature Selection and K-Nearest Neighbor. *International Journal of Information Management, 40*, 76–88.

Biswas, B. (2020). Email Spam Classification Dataset CSV. Retrieved from Kaggle.Com: https://www.kaggle.com/datasets/balaka18/email-spam-classification-dataset-csv

Chandan, R. R., Soni, S., Raj, A., Veeraiah, V., Dhabliya, D., Pramanik, S., & Gupta, A. (2023). Genetic Algorithm and Machine Learning. Advanced Bioinspiration Methods for Healthcare Standards, Policies, and Reform. IGI Global. doi:10.4018/978-1-6684-5656-9

Chaudhari, P. R., Jhaveri, R. V., & Maheta, K. V. (2019). K-Nearest Neighbor Algorithm for Phishing Detection. *Procedia Computer Science, 165*, 272–279.

Geeksforgeeks.org. (2023). *NLP Gensim Tutorial – Complete Guide For Beginners*. Geeksforgeeks. https://www.geeksforgeeks.org/nlp-gensim-tutorial-complete-guide-for-beginners/#article-meta-div

Gibert, K., Pevný, T., & Bourdaillet, J. (2014).Phishstorm: Detecting phishing with streaming analytics, (2014). In *Proceedings of the 2014 ACM SIGSAC Conference on Computer and Communications Security* (pp. 1115-1126). ACM.

Github.Com. (2023). *Pragmatic machine learning and NLP*. Github.Com. https://github.com/RaRe-Technologies/gensim

Gupta, R., Dey, D., & Mukherjee, A. (2013). Building efficient, effective and scalable spam filters for promotional email categorization. *Knowledge-Based Systems, 53*, 45–57.

Han, W., Cao, Y., Bertino, E., & Yong, J. (2012). Using automated individual white-list to protect web digital identities. *Expert Systems with Applications, 2012*(39), 11861–11869. doi:10.1016/j.eswa.2012.02.020

Hu, J., Tan, C. W., Wang, W., & Li, J. (2018). A novel feature engineering approach to phishing email detection. *Information Sciences, 450*, 19–31.

Jain, V., Rastogi, M., Ramesh, J. V. N., Chauhan, A., Agarwal, P., Pramanik, S., & Gupta, A. (2023). FinTech and Artificial Intelligence in Relationship Banking and Computer Technology. In K. Saini, A. Mummoorthy, R. Chandrika, N. S. Gowri Ganesh, & I. G. I. Global (Eds.), *AI, IoT, and Blockchain Breakthroughs in E-Governance*. doi:10.4018/978-1-6684-7697-0.ch011

Javapoint.com. (2021). K-Nearest Neighbor (KNN) Algorithm for Machine Learning. Javapoint.com. https://www.javatpoint.com/k-nearest-neighbor-algorithm-for-machine-learning

Kim, H., Ha, Y. J., & Kim, J. (2021). Phishing detection using text analysis with multi-granularity attention mechanisms. *Computers & Security*, *106*, 102317.

Li, S., Wang, W., Li, Y., & Tan, C. W. (2019). Phishing URL detection based on visual similarity and machine learning. *IEEE Access : Practical Innovations, Open Solutions*, *7*, 24854–24864.

Liu, Y., Zhang, L., & Li, W. (2016). Detecting phishing websites with lexical and sentiment features. *Computers & Security*, *59*, 158–168.

Mandal, A., Dutta, S., & Pramanik, S. (2021). Machine Intelligence of Pi from Geometrical Figures with Variable Parameters using SCILab. In D. Samanta, R. R. Althar, S. Pramanik, & S. Dutta (Eds.), *Methodologies and Applications of Computational Statistics for Machine Learning* (pp. 38–63). IGI Global. doi:10.4018/978-1-7998-7701-1.ch003

Mehta, S., Kanhangad, V., & Ravi, T. M. (2015). Phishing Detection using Machine Learning Techniques. *International Journal of Computer Applications*, *117*(22), 9–13.

Meslie, Y., Enbeyle, W., Pandey, B. K., Pramanik, S., Pandey, D., Dadeech, P., Belay, A., & Saini, A. (2021). Machine Intelligence-based Trend Analysis of COVID-19 for Total Daily Confirmed Cases in Asia and Africa. In D. Samanta, R. R. Althar, S. Pramanik, & S. Dutta (Eds.), *Methodologies and Applications of Computational Statistics for Machine Learning* (pp. 164–185). IGI Global. doi:10.4018/978-1-7998-7701-1.ch009

Moghimi, M., & Varjani, A. Y. (2016). New rule-based phishing detection method. *Expert Systems with Applications*, *2016*(53), 231–242. doi:10.1016/j.eswa.2016.01.028

Parihar, S. S., Gupta, J. P., & Kumar, V. (2019). Phishing Detection based on the Features of Phishing Webpages Using K-Nearest Neighbor Algorithm. *International Journal of Computer Applications*, *182*(2), 38–43.

Pramanik, S. (2023). A Novel Data Hiding Locating Approach in Image Steganography. *Multimedia Tools and Applications, 2023*. doi:10.1007/s11042-023-16762-3

Pramanik, S. (2023). An Adaptive Image Steganography Approach depending on Integer Wavelet Transform and Genetic Algorithm. *Multimedia Tools and Applications*, *82*(22), 34287–34319. Advance online publication. doi:10.1007/s11042-023-14505-y

Prasad. (2016). *Top 20 Python Machine Learning Open Source Projects*. KD nuggets. https://www.kdnuggets.com/2016/11/top-20-python-machine-learning-opensource-updated.html

Praveenkumar, S., Veeraiah, V., Pramanik, S., Basha, S. M., Lira Neto, A. V., De Albuquerque, V. H. C., & Gupta, A. (2023). *Prediction of Patients' Incurable Diseases Utilizing Deep Learning Approaches, ICICC 2023*. Springer. doi:10.1007/978-981-99-3315-0_4

Rao, R. S., Vaishnavi, T., & Pais, A. R. (2019). CatchPhish: Detection of phishing websites by inspecting URLs. *Journal of Ambient Intelligence and Humanized Computing*, *11*(2), 813–825. doi:10.1007/s12652-019-01311-4

Reepu, K. S., Chaudhary, M. G., Gupta, K. G., Pramanik, S. and Gupta, A. (2023). Information Security and Privacy in IoT. J. Zhao, V. V. Kumar, R. Natarajan and T. R. Mahesh, (eds.) Handbook of Research in Advancements in AI and IoT Convergence Technologies. IGI Global.

Sahingoz, O. K., Buber, E., Demir, O., & Diri, B. (2019). Machine learning based phishing detection from URLs. *Expert Systems with Applications*, *2019*(117), 345–357. doi:10.1016/j.eswa.2018.09.029

Sharma, D., & Gomase, V. (2017). An Approach for Detecting Phishing Websites Based on K-Nearest Neighbors Algorithm. *International Journal of Computer Applications*, *176*(3), 22–26.

Sheng, S., Holbrook, M., Kumaraguru, P., Cranor, L. F., & Downs, J. (2010). Who falls for phishing scams? A demographic analysis of phishing susceptibility and effectiveness of interventions.In *Proceedings of the SIGCHI Conference on Human Factors in Computing Systems (CHI)* (pp. 373-382). ACM. 10.1145/1753326.1753383

Smith, M., Banerjee, I., & Laskowski, S. (2017). A novel machine learning approach to detect phishing URLs using natural language processing. *Journal of Computer and System Sciences*, *86*, 13–26.

Turing.Com. (2023). *A Guide on Word Embeddings in NLP*. Turing.com. https://www.turing.com/kb/guide-on-word-embeddings-in-nlp

Veeraiah, V., Talukdar, V., Manikandan, K., Talukdar, S. B., Solavande, V. D., Pramanik, S., & Gupta, A. (2023). Machine Learning Frameworks in Carpooling. In R. Hossain, C. Ho, & G. Trajkovski, Handbook of Research on AI and Machine Learning Applications in Customer Support and Analytics. IGI Global. doi:10.4018/978-1-6684-7105-0.ch009

Vidya, C. V., Veeraiah, V., Khanna, A., Sheikh, T. H., Pramanik, S., & Dhabliya, D. (2023). A Machine Vision-based Approach for Tuberculosis Identification in Chest X-Rays Images of Patients. *ICICC 2023*. Springer. doi:10.1007/978-981-99-3315-0_3

Wang, Y., Zhang, L., Zhang, D., & Li, W. (2018). Detecting phishing emails using a hierarchical classification framework. *IEEE Transactions on Information Forensics and Security*, *13*(8), 1906–1919.

Zhang, W., Ding, Y. X., Tang, Y., & Zhao, B. (2011). *Malicious web page detection based on on-line learning algorithm*. In *Proceedings of the 2011 International Conference on Machine Learning and Cybernetics*, Guilin, China. 10.1109/ICMLC.2011.6016954

Zhang, Y., Wu, S., Li, Q., & Hu, J. (2020). Detecting phishing emails with lexical and syntactic features. *Information Sciences*, *509*, 48–60.

Compilation of References

Abdulla, A. A., & Ahmed, M. W. (2021). An improved image quality algorithm for exemplar-based image inpainting. *Multimedia Tools and Applications*, *80*(9), 13143–13156. doi:10.1007/s11042-020-10414-6

Adnan, M., Alarood, A. A. S., Uddin, M. I., & ur Rehman, I. (2022). Utilizing grid search cross-validation with adaptive boosting for augmenting performance of machine learning models. *PeerJ. Computer Science*, *8*, e803. doi:10.7717/peerj-cs.803 PMID:35494796

Afsar, M., Crump, T., & Far, B. (2022). Reinforcement Learning Based Recommender Systems: A Survey. *ACM Computing Surveys*, *55*(7), 1–38. doi:10.1145/3543846

Agarwal, V., Sharma, K., & Rajpoot, A. K. (2022), AI based Yoga trainer-simplifying home yoga using MediaPipe and video streaming. *International Conference for Emerging Technology*. IEEE. 10.1109/INCET54531.2022.9824332

Agrebi, M., Sendi, M., & Abed, M. 2019. "Deep Reinforcement Learning for Personalized Recommendation of Distance Learning." In *World Conference on Information Systems and Technologies*, 597–606. Springer. 10.1007/978-3-030-16184-2_57

Ahmed, I., Jeon, G., & Piccialli, F. (2022). From artificial intelligence to explainable artificial intelligence in industry 4.0: A survey on what, how, and where. *IEEE Transactions on Industrial Informatics*, *18*(8), 5031–5042. doi:10.1109/TII.2022.3146552

Ahonen, T., Hadid, A., & Pietikäinen, M. (2006). Face description with local binary patterns: Application to face recognition. *IEEE Transactions on Pattern Analysis and Machine Intelligence*, *28*(12), 2037–2041. doi:10.1109/TPAMI.2006.244 PMID:17108377

Akkaya, I., Andrychowicz, M., Chociej, M., Litwin, M., McGrew, B., Petron, A., Paino, A., Plappert, M., Powell, G., & Ribas, R. (2019). Solving rubik's cube with a robot hand. arXiv Prepr. arXiv1910.07113.

Alazab, M., Layton, R., & Venkatraman, S. (2018). A novel model for detecting phishing attacks using text classification. *Future Generation Computer Systems*, *78*, 1086–1097.

Albahri, A., Duhaim, A. M., Fadhel, M. A., Alnoor, A., Baqer, N. S., Alzubaidi, L., Albahri, O. S., Alamoodi, A. H., Bai, J., Salhi, A., Santamaría, J., Ouyang, C., Gupta, A., Gu, Y., & Deveci, M. (2023). A systematic review of trustworthy and explainable artificial intelligence in healthcare: Assessment of quality, bias risk, and data fusion. *Information Fusion*, *96*, 156–191. doi:10.1016/j.inffus.2023.03.008

Alexey, B. ChienYao, W., & Mark, L. (2020). YOLOv4: Optimal speed and accuracy of object detection. *Image and Video Processing*, arXiv:2004.10934.

Alfred Daniel, J., Chandru Vignesh, C., Muthu, B. A., Senthil Kumar, R., Sivaparthipan, C. B., & Marin, C. E. M. (2023). Fully convolutional neural networks for LIDAR–camera fusion for pedestrian detection in autonomous vehicle. *Multimedia Tools and Applications*, *82*(16), 1–24. doi:10.1007/s11042-023-14417-x

Alia, S. (2023). *Explainable Artificial Intelligence (XAI): What we know and what is left to attain Trustworthy Artificial Intelligence.* Science Direct.

Aliew, F. (2022). An Approach for Precise Distance Measuring Using Ultrasonic Sensors. *Engineering Proceedings*, *24*(1), 8.

Ali, S., Khan, A., Gul, M. A., Uddin, M. I., Ali Shah, S. A., Ahmad, S., Al Firdausi, M. D., & Zaindin, M. (2020). Summarizing Online Movie Reviews: A Machine Learning Approach to Big Data Analytics. *Scientific Programming*, *2020*, 5812715.

Allgaier, J., Mulansky, L., Draelos, R. L., & Pryss, R. (2023). How does the model make predictions? A systematic literature review on the explainability power of machine learning in healthcare. *Artificial Intelligence in Medicine*, *143*, 102616. doi:10.1016/j.artmed.2023.102616 PMID:37673561

Almeida, A., & Azkune, G. (2018). Predicting human behaviour with recurrent neural networks. *Applied Sciences (Basel, Switzerland)*, *8*(2), 305. doi:10.3390/app8020305

Alvarado, S. T., Borja, M. G. B., & Torres, K. B. (2022). *Object Distance Estimation from a Binocular Vision System for Robotic Applications Using Artificial Neural Networks. Control, Mechatronics and Automation.* ICCMA.

Amin, S., Irfan Uddin, M., Alarood, A. A., Mashwani, W. K., Alzahrani, A., & Alzahrani, A. O. (2023). Smart E-Learning Framework For Personalized Adaptive Learning and Sequential Path Recommendations Using Reinforcement Learning. *IEEE Access : Practical Innovations, Open Solutions*, *11*, 89769–89790. doi:10.1109/ACCESS.2023.3305584

Amin, S., Uddin, M. I., Zeb, M. A., Alarood, A. A., Mahmoud, M., & Alkinani, M. H. (2020). Detecting Dengue/Flu Infections Based on Tweets Using LSTM and Word Embedding. *IEEE Access : Practical Innovations, Open Solutions*, *8*, 189054–189068. doi:10.1109/ACCESS.2020.3031174

Andriluka, M., Pishchulin, L., Gehler, P., & Schiele, B. (2014), 2D human pose estimation: New benchmark and state of the art analysis. *IEEE Conference on Computer Vision and Pattern Recognition*, (pp. 3686-3693). IEEE. 10.1109/CVPR.2014.471

Antoniadi, A. M., Du, Y., Guendouz, Y., Wei, L., Mazo, C., Becker, B. A., & Mooney, C. (2021). Current challenges and future opportunities for XAI in machine learning-based clinical decision support systems: A systematic review. *Applied Sciences (Basel, Switzerland)*, *11*(11), 5088. doi:10.3390/app11115088

Antwarg, L., Miller, R. M., Shapira, B., & Rokach, L. (2021). Explaining anomalies detected by autoencoders using Shapley Additive Explanations. *Expert Systems with Applications*, *186*, 115736. doi:10.1016/j.eswa.2021.115736

Anwar, M., Sangaiah, A. K., & Farooq, M. S. (2018). An Improved Phishing Detection Model using Feature Selection and K-Nearest Neighbor. *International Journal of Information Management*, *40*, 76–88.

Atif Khan, M. & Uddin, I. (2020). *Summarizing Online Movie Reviews: A Machine Learning Approach to Big Data Analytics*. Scientific Programming.

Ayob, A. F., Khairuddin, K., Mustafah, Y. M., Salisa, A. R., & Kadir, K. (2021). Analysis of Pruned Neural Networks (MobileNetV2-YOLO v2) for Underwater Object Detection. *Proceedings of the 11th National Technical Seminar on Unmanned System Technology 2019* (Vol. 666, pp. 87–98). Springer Nature. 10.1007/978-981-15-5281-6_7

Aziz, F., Ahmad, T., Malik, A. H., Uddin, M. I., Ahmad, S., & Sharaf, M. (2020). Reversible data hiding techniques with high message embedding capacity in images. *PLoS One*, *15*(5), e0231602. doi:10.1371/journal.pone.0231602 PMID:32469877

Aziz, F., Gul, H., Uddin, I., & Gkoutos, G. V. (2020). Path-based extensions of local link prediction methods for complex networks. *Scientific Reports*, *10*(1), 19848. doi:10.1038/s41598-020-76860-2 PMID:33199838

Azorin-Lopez, J., Saval-Calvo, M., Fuster-Guillo, A., & Garcia-Rodriguez, J. (2016). A novel prediction method for early recognition of global human behaviour in image sequences. *Neural Processing Letters*, *43*(2), 363–387. doi:10.1007/s11063-015-9412-y

Bai, T., Luo, J., Zhao, J., Wen, B., & Wang, Q. (2021). *Recent advances in adversarial training for adversarial robustness*. arXiv Prepr. arXiv2102.01356.

Bassen, J., Balaji, B., Schaarschmidt, M., Thille, C., Painter, J., Zimmaro, D., Games, A., & Fast, E. (2020). Reinforcement Learning for the Adaptive Scheduling of Educational Activities. In *Proceedings of the 2020 CHI Conference on Human Factors in Computing Systems*, (pp. 1–12). ACM. 10.1145/3313831.3376518

BazarevskyV.GrishchenkoI.RaveendranK.ZhuT.ZhangF.GrundmannM. (2020), *Blazepose: On-device real-time body pose tracking*. arXiv:2006.10204.

Benhamou, E. (2022). *Explainable AI (XAI) models applied to planning in financial markets*, in *Explainable AI (XAI) Models Applied to Planning in Financial Markets*. Research Gate.

Bento, V., Kohler, M., Diaz, P., Mendoza, L., & Pacheco, M. A. (2021). Improving deep learning performance by using Explainable Artificial Intelligence (XAI) approaches. *Discover Artificial Intelligence*, *1*(1), 1–11. doi:10.1007/s44163-021-00008-y

Bernstein, A. V., & Evgeny, V. (2018). Reinforcement Learning in Computer Vision. In *Tenth International Conference on Machine Vision (ICMV 2017).*

Biswas, B. (2020). Email Spam Classification Dataset CSV. Retrieved from Kaggle.Com: https://www.kaggle.com/datasets/balaka18/email-spam-classification-dataset-csv

Bochkovskiy, A., Wang, C.-Y., & Liao, H.-Y. M. (2020). YOLOv4: Optimal speed and accuracy of object detection. arXiv preprint arXiv:2004.10934.

Bremer, J., Maj, M., Nordbø, Ø., & Kommisrud, E. (2023). Deep learning–based automated measurements of the scrotal circumference of Norwegian Red bulls from 3D images. *Smart Agricultural Technology*, *3*, 100133. doi:10.1016/j.atech.2022.100133

Cai, K., Zhu, X., & Hu, Z. (2023). Reward poisoning attacks in deep reinforcement learning based on exploration strategies. *Neurocomputing*, *553*, 126578. doi:10.1016/j.neucom.2023.126578

Cai, Y., Ding, Y., Zhang, H., Xiu, J., & Liu, Z. (2020). Geo-location algorithm for building targets in oblique remote sensing images based on deep learning and height estimation. *Remote Sensing (Basel)*, *12*(15), 2427. doi:10.3390/rs12152427

Cao, X. (2022). *Pose Estimation of Swimmers from Digital Images Using Deep Learning.* [Master's Thesis, Auckland University of Technology].

Cao, W., Li, L., Gong, S., & Dong, X. (2023, May). Research on Human Behavior Feature Recognition and Intelligent Early Warning Methods in Safety Supervision Scene Video based on Yolov7. []. IOP Publishing.]. *Journal of Physics: Conference Series*, *2496*(1), 012019. doi:10.1088/1742-6596/2496/1/012019

Cao, X., & Yan, W. (2022). *Pose estimation for swimmers in video surveillance. Multimedia Tools and Applications*. Springer.

Cao, Z., Simon, T., Wei, S. E., & Sheikh, Y. (2017), Realtime multi-person 2D pose estimation using part affinity fields. *IEEE Conference on Computer Vision and Pattern Recognition*, (pp. 7291-7299). IEEE. 10.1109/CVPR.2017.143

Cao, Z., Xu, S., Peng, H., Yang, D., & Zidek, R. (2021). Confidence-Aware Reinforcement Learning for Self-Driving Cars. *IEEE Transactions on Intelligent Transportation Systems*, *23*(7), 7419–7430. doi:10.1109/TITS.2021.3069497

Carlini, N., & Wagner, D. (2017). Towards evaluating the robustness of neural networks. *2017 Ieee Symposium on Security and Privacy (Sp).* IEEE. 10.1109/SP.2017.49

Carreira, J., & Zisserman, A. (2017), Quo vadis, action recognition? A new model and the kinetics dataset. *IEEE Conference on Computer Vision and Pattern Recognition*, (pp. 6299-6308). IEEE. 10.1109/CVPR.2017.502

Chandan, R. R., Soni, S., Raj, A., Veeraiah, V., Dhabliya, D., Pramanik, S., & Gupta, A. (2023). Genetic Algorithm and Machine Learning. Advanced Bioinspiration Methods for Healthcare Standards, Policies, and Reform. IGI Global. doi:10.4018/978-1-6684-5656-9

Chaudhari, P. R., Jhaveri, R. V., & Maheta, K. V. (2019). K-Nearest Neighbor Algorithm for Phishing Detection. *Procedia Computer Science*, *165*, 272–279.

Chen, T.-C. T. (2023). Explainable Artificial Intelligence (XAI) in Manufacturing, in Explainable Artificial Intelligence (XAI) in Manufacturing: Methodology, Tools, and Applications. Springer.

Chen, P.-Y., Chang, M.-C., Hsieh, J.-W., & Chen, Y.-S. (2021). Parallel Residual Bi-Fusion Feature Pyramid Network for Accurate Single-Shot Object Detection. *IEEE Transactions on Image Processing*, *30*, 9099–9111. doi:10.1109/TIP.2021.3118953 PMID:34735334

Chen, S. X., Liu, H. Q., & Lin, Y. Q. (2018). Deep Learning for 3D Shape Prediction from a Single Image. In *Proceedings of the IEEE Conference on Computer Vision and Pattern Recognition* (pp. 7847-7856). IEEE.

Chen, X.-Q., Ma, C.-Q., Ren, Y.-S., Lei, Y.-T., Huynh, N. Q. A., & Narayan, S. (2023). Explainable artificial intelligence in finance: A bibliometric review. *Finance Research Letters*, *56*, 104145. doi:10.1016/j.frl.2023.104145

Chen, X., Yao, L., McAuley, J., Zhou, G., & Wang, X. (2023). Deep Reinforcement Learning in Recommender Systems: A Survey and New Perspectives. *Knowledge-Based Systems*, *264*, 110335. doi:10.1016/j.knosys.2023.110335

Chen, Y., Wang, Z., Peng, Y., Zhang, Z., Yu, G., & Sun, J. (2018), Cascaded pyramid network for multi-person pose estimation. *IEEE Conference on Computer Vision and Pattern Recognition*, (pp. 7103-7112). IEEE. 10.1109/CVPR.2018.00742

Chen, Z. (2023). *Real-Time Pose Recognition for Billiard Players Using Deep Learning. Research Report*. Auckland University of Technology.

ChienyaoW.AlexeyB.MarkL. (2022). YOLOv7: Trainable bag-of-freebies sets new state-of-the-art for real-time object detectors. Computer Vision and Pattern Recognition, arXiv:2207.02696

Chirra, V. R. R., Reddy, U. S., & Kolli, V. K. K. (2021). Virtual facial expression recognition using deep CNN with ensemble learning. *Journal of Ambient Intelligence and Humanized Computing*, *12*(12), 10581–10599. doi:10.1007/s12652-020-02866-3

Chiu, T.-Y., & Gurari, D. (2022). PhotoWCT2: Compact Autoencoder for Photorealistic Style Transfer Resulting from Blockwise Training and Skip Connections of High-Frequency Residuals. *In Proceedings of the IEEE/CVF Winter Conference on Applications of Computer Vision,* (pp. 2868-2877). IEEE. 10.1109/WACV51458.2022.00303

Choi, E., Hewlett, D., Uszkoreit, J., Polosukhin, I., Lacoste, A., & Berant, J. (2017). Coarse-to-Fine Question Answering for Long Documents. In *Proceedings of the 55th Annual Meeting of the Association for Computational Linguistics (*Volume 1*: Long Papers)*, (pp. 209–20). IEEE. 10.18653/v1/P17-1020

Choutas, V., Weinzaepfel, P., Revaud, J., & Schmid, C. (2018), Potion: Pose motion representation for action recognition. *IEEE Conference on Computer Vision and Pattern Recognition*, (pp. 7024-7033). IEEE. 10.1109/CVPR.2018.00734

Čík, I. (2021). Explaining deep neural network using layer-wise relevance propagation and integrated gradients. In *2021 IEEE 19th world symposium on applied machine intelligence and informatics (SAMI)*. IEEE. 10.1109/SAMI50585.2021.9378686

Clement, T., Kemmerzell, N., Abdelaal, M., & Amberg, M. (2023). XAIR: A Systematic Metareview of Explainable AI (XAI) Aligned to the Software Development Process. *Machine Learning and Knowledge Extraction*, *5*(1), 78–108. doi:10.3390/make5010006

Connie, T., Al-Shabi, M., Cheah, W. P., & Goh, M. K. O. (2017). Facial expression recognition using a hybrid CNN–SIFT aggregator. In Lecture Notes in Computer Science (pp. 139–149). Springer. doi:10.1007/978-3-319-69456-6_12

Coronato, A., Naeem, M., De Pietro, G., & Paragliola, G. (2020). Reinforcement Learning for Intelligent Healthcare Applications: A Survey. *Artificial Intelligence in Medicine*, *109*(September), 101964. doi:10.1016/j.artmed.2020.101964 PMID:34756216

Cui, W., & Yan, W. (2016). A scheme for face recognition in complex environments. [IJDCF]. *International Journal of Digital Crime and Forensics*, *8*(1), 26–36. doi:10.4018/IJDCF.2016010102

Cunha, B., & Manikonda, L. (2022). *Classification of Misinformation in New Articles using Natural Language Processing and a Recurrent Neural Network*. arXiv preprint arXiv:2210.13534.

Dai, Y., Wang, G., Muhammad, K., & Liu, S. (2020). A Closed-Loop Healthcare Processing Approach Based on Deep Reinforcement Learning. *Multimedia Tools and Applications*, no. 2017.

Das, N., Shanbhogue, M., Chen, S.-T., Hohman, F., Chen, L., Kounavis, M. E., & Chau, D. H. 2017. Keeping the bad guys out: Protecting and vaccinating deep learning with jpeg compression. arXiv Prepr. arXiv1705.02900.

Datta, S., & Li, Y. (2021). Reinforcement Learning in Surgery. *Surgery, 170*(1), 329–32. https://doi.org/10.1016/j.surg.2020.11.040

Delanoy, J., Aubry, M., Isola, P., Efros, A. A., & Bousseau, A. (2018). 3D Sketching using Multi-View Deep Volumetric Prediction. In *Proceedings of the ACM Conference on Computer-Aided Design* (pp. 1-20). ACM. 10.1145/3203197

Demetriou, D., Mavromatidis, P., Robert, P. M., Papadopoulos, H., Petrou, M. F., & Nicolaides, D. (2023). *Real-Time Construction Demolition Waste Detection Using State-of-The-Art Deep Learning Methods; Single – Stage vs Two-Stage Detectors* [Preprint].

Desai, P., Sujatha, S., Chakraborty, S., Saurav, S., Bhandari, S., & Sanika, S. (2022). Next frame prediction using ConvLSTM. *Journal of Physics: Conference Series*, *2161*(1), 012024. doi:10.1088/1742-6596/2161/1/012024

Dhiman, G., Kumar, A. V., Nirmalan, R., Sujitha, S., Srihari, K., Yuvaraj, N., Arulprakash, P., & Raja, R. A. (2023). Multi-Modal Active Learning with Deep Reinforcement Learning for Target Feature Extraction in Multi-Media Image Processing Applications. *Multimedia Tools and Applications*, *82*(4), 5343–5367. doi:10.1007/s11042-022-12178-7

Dikshit, A., & Pradhan, B. (2021). Interpretable and explainable AI (XAI) model for spatial drought prediction. *The Science of the Total Environment*, *801*, 149797. doi:10.1016/j.scitotenv.2021.149797 PMID:34467917

Ding, H., Wu, Y., & Wang, L. (2022). Deep attentive style transfer for images with wavelet decomposition. *Information Sciences*, *587*, 63–81. doi:10.1016/j.ins.2021.11.077

Dosovitskiy, A., Beyer, L., Kolesnikov, A., Weissenborn, D., Zhai, X., Unterthiner, T., & Houlsby, N. (2020). An image is worth 16x16 words: Transformers for image recognition at scale. arXiv preprint arXiv:2010.11929.

Du, W., Chen, H., & Yang, H. (2020). Learning invariant representation for unsupervised image restoration. In *Proceedings of the IEEE/CVF Conference on Computer Vision and Pattern Recognition* (pp. 14483–14492). IEEE. 10.1109/CVPR42600.2020.01449

Du, W., Wang, Y., & Qiao, Y. (2017). Rpan: An end-to-end recurrent poseattention network for action recognition in videos. In *Proceedings of the ieee international conference on computer vision* (pp. 3725–3734). IEEE. 10.1109/ICCV.2017.402

Emami, H., Aliabadi, M. M., Dong, M., & Chinnam, R. (2020). Spa-GAN: Spatial Attention GAN for image-to-image translation. *IEEE Transactions on Multimedia.*

Fan, Y., Lam, J. C., & Li, V. O. K. (2018). Multi-region ensemble convolutional neural network for facial expression recognition. In Lecture Notes in Computer Science (pp. 84–94). Springer. doi:10.1007/978-3-030-01418-6_9

Fan, J., & Li, W. (2021). Adversarial training and provable robustness: A tale of two objectives. *Proceedings of the AAAI Conference on Artificial Intelligence*, (pp. 7367–7376). AAAI. 10.1609/aaai.v35i8.16904

Fayaz, M. (2020). *Ensemble Machine Learning Model for Classification of Spam Product Reviews*. Complexity Volume. doi:10.1155/2020/8857570

Fayek, H. M., Lech, M., & Cavedon, L. (2016). Modeling subjectiveness in emotion recognition with deep neural networks: Ensembles *vs* soft labels. *International Joint Conference on Neural Networks (IJCNN).* IJCNN. 10.1109/IJCNN.2016.7727250

Feichtenhofer, C., Pinz, A., & Zisserman, A. (2016). Convolutional two-stream network fusion for video action recognition. In *Proceedings of the ieee conference on computer vision and pattern recognition* (pp. 1933–1941). IEEE. 10.1109/CVPR.2016.213

Feng, Y., Pang, T., Li, M., & Guan, Y. (2020). Small sample face recognition based on ensemble deep learning. *Chinese Control and Decision Conference (CCDC).* CCDC. 10.1109/CCDC49329.2020.9163968

Freeborough, W., & van Zyl, T. (2022). Investigating explainability methods in recurrent neural network architectures for financial time series data. *Applied Sciences (Basel, Switzerland)*, *12*(3), 1427. doi:10.3390/app12031427

Fuentes-Hurtado, F., Delaire, T., Levet, F., Sibarita, J.-B., & Viasnoff, V. (2022). MID3A: Microscopy Image Denoising meets Differentiable Data Augmentation. *International Joint Conference on Neural Networks (IJCNN),* (pp. 1–9). IEEE. 10.1109/IJCNN55064.2022.9892954

Fukushima, H., & Farzad, D. (2017). Scene Understanding Using Deep Learning. Academic Press.

Furuta, R., Inoue, N., & Yamasaki, T. (2019). Pixelrl: Fully Convolutional Network with Reinforcement Learning for Image Processing. *IEEE Transactions on Multimedia*, *22*(7), 1704–1719. doi:10.1109/TMM.2019.2960636

Gao, X., Nguyen, M., & Yan, W. (2022) A face image inpainting method based on autoencoder and adversarial generative networks. *Pacific-Rim Symposium on Image and Video Technology*.

Gao, X., Nguyen, M., & Yan, W. Q. (2021). Face image inpainting based on generative adversarial network. In 2021 36th international conference on image and vision computing new zealand (ivcnz) (pp. 1–6). 10.1109/IVCNZ54163.2021.9653347

Gao, Z., Tan, C., Wu, L., & Li, S. Z. (2022). Simvp: Simpler yet better video prediction. *In Proceedings of the IEEE/CVF Conference on Computer Vision and Pattern Recognition*, (pp. 3170-3180). IEEE.

García, S., & Herrera, F. (2009). Evolutionary undersampling for classification with imbalanced datasets: Proposals and taxonomy. *Evolutionary Computation*, *17*(3), 275–306. doi:10.1162/evco.2009.17.3.275 PMID:19708770

Geeksforgeeks.org. (2023). *NLP Gensim Tutorial – Complete Guide For Beginners*. Geeksforgeeks. https://www.geeksforgeeks.org/nlp-gensim-tutorial-complete-guide-for-beginners/#article-meta-div

Ghimire, D., Kil, D., & Kim, S. (2022). A survey on efficient convolutional neural networks and hardware acceleration. *Electronics (Basel)*, *11*(6), 945. doi:10.3390/electronics11060945

Gibert, K., Pevný, T., & Bourdaillet, J. (2014).Phishstorm: Detecting phishing with streaming analytics, (2014). In *Proceedings of the 2014 ACM SIGSAC Conference on Computer and Communications Security* (pp. 1115-1126). ACM.

Github.Com. (2023). *Pragmatic machine learning and NLP*. Github.Com. https://github.com/RaRe-Technologies/gensim

Goodfellow, I.J., Shlens, J., & Szegedy, C. (2014). *Explaining and harnessing adversarial examples*. arXiv Prepr. arXiv1412.6572.

Goodfellow, I., Pouget-Abadie, J., Mirza, M., Xu, B., Warde-Farley, D., Ozair, S., Courville, A., & Bengio, Y. (2014). Generative Adversarial Networks. *Advances in Neural Information Processing Systems*, 3.

Gorelick, L., Blank, M., Shechtman, E., Irani, M., & Basri, R. (2007, December). Actions as space-time shapes. *IEEE Transactions on Pattern Analysis and Machine Intelligence*, *29*(12), 2247–2253. doi:10.1109/TPAMI.2007.70711 PMID:17934233

Gramegna, A., & Giudici, P. (2021). SHAP and LIME: An evaluation of discriminative power in credit risk. *Frontiers in Artificial Intelligence*, *4*, 752558. doi:10.3389/frai.2021.752558 PMID:34604738

Grissom, I. I. (2014). Don't until the Final Verb Wait: Reinforcement Learning for Simultaneous Machine Translation. In *Proceedings of the 2014 Conference on Empirical Methods in Natural Language Processing (EMNLP)*, (pp. 1342–52). ACL. 10.3115/v1/D14-1140

Grosse, K., Papernot, N., Manoharan, P., Backes, M., & McDaniel, P. (2017). Adversarial examples for malware detection. *Computer Security–ESORICS 2017: 22nd European Symposium on Research in Computer Security*. Springer.

Güler, R. A., Neverova, N., & Kokkinos, I. (2018). Densepose: Dense human pose estimation in the wild. In *Proceedings of the IEEE conference on computer vision and pattern recognition* (pp. 7297-7306). IEEE.10.1109/CVPR.2018.00762

Guo, C., Rana, M., Cisse, M., & Van Der Maaten, L. 2017. Countering adversarial images using input transformations. arXiv Prepr. arXiv1711.00117.

Guo, J., Wang, J., Wang, H., Xiao, B., He, Z., & Li, L. (2023). Research on road scene understanding of autonomous vehicles based on multi-task learning. *Sensors (Basel)*, *23*(13), 6238. doi:10.3390/s23136238 PMID:37448087

Gupta, R., Dey, D., & Mukherjee, A. (2013). Building efficient, effective and scalable spam filters for promotional email categorization. *Knowledge-Based Systems*, *53*, 45–57.

Gu, S., Holly, E., Lillicrap, T., & Levine, S. (2017). Deep Reinforcement Learning for Robotic Manipulation with Asynchronous Off-Policy Updates. In *2017 IEEE International Conference on Robotics and Automation (ICRA)*, (pp. 3389–96). IEEE. 10.1109/ICRA.2017.7989385

Habib, A. S. B., & Tasnim, T. (2020). An ensemble hard voting model for cardiovascular disease prediction. *International Conference on Sustainable Technologies for Industry 4.0 (STI)*. IEEE. 10.1109/STI50764.2020.9350514

Han, T., Zhao, L., & Wang, C. (2023). Research on Super-resolution Image Based on Deep Learning. *International Journal of Advanced Network. Monitoring and Controls*, *8*(1), 58–65. doi:10.2478/ijanmc-2023-0046

Han, W., Cao, Y., Bertino, E., & Yong, J. (2012). Using automated individual white-list to protect web digital identities. *Expert Systems with Applications*, *2012*(39), 11861–11869. doi:10.1016/j.eswa.2012.02.020

Hare, R., & Tang, Y. (2023). Hierarchical Deep Reinforcement Learning With Experience Sharing for Metaverse in Education. *IEEE Transactions on Systems, Man, and Cybernetics. Systems*, *53*(4), 2047–2055. doi:10.1109/TSMC.2022.3227919

He, K., Zhang, X., Ren, S., & Sun, J. (2015). Spatial pyramid pooling in deep convolutional networks for visual recognition. *IEEE Transactions on Pattern Analysis and Machine Intelligence*, *37*(9), 1904–1916. doi:10.1109/TPAMI.2015.2389824 PMID:26353135

He, K., Zhang, X., Ren, S., & Sun, J. (2016), Deep residual learning for image recognition. *IEEE Conference on Computer Vision and Pattern Recognition*, (pp. 770-778). IEEE.

He, K., Zhang, X., Ren, S., & Sun, J. (2016). Deep Residual Learning for Image Recognition. 2016 *IEEE Conference on Computer Vision and Pattern Recognition (CVPR)*, (pp. 770–778). IEEE. 10.1109/CVPR.2016.90

Herrera, A., Beck, A., Bell, D., Miller, P., Wu, Q., & Yan, W. (2008) Behavior analysis and prediction in image sequences using rough sets. *International Machine Vision and Image Processing Conference* (pp.71-76). IEEE.

He, X., Lou, B., Yang, H., & Lv, C. (2022a). Robust decision making for autonomous vehicles at highway on-ramps: A constrained adversarial reinforcement learning approach. *IEEE Transactions on Intelligent Transportation Systems*, *24*(4), 4103–4113. doi:10.1109/TITS.2022.3229518

He, X., Yang, H., Hu, Z., & Lv, C. (2022b). Robust lane change decision making for autonomous vehicles: An observation adversarial reinforcement learning approach. *IEEE Transactions on Intelligent Vehicles*, *8*(1), 184–193. doi:10.1109/TIV.2022.3165178

He, Z., Yang, Q., Zhao, X., Zhang, S., & Tan, J. (2020). Spatiotemporal visual odometry using ground plane in dynamic indoor environment. *Optik (Stuttgart)*, *220*, 165165. doi:10.1016/j.ijleo.2020.165165

Hochreiter, S., & Schmidhuber, J. (1997). Long short-term memory. *Neural Computation*, *9*(8), 1735–1780. doi:10.1162/neco.1997.9.8.1735 PMID:9377276

Holden, D., Saito, J., & Komura, T. (2016). A deep learning framework for character motion synthesis and editing. *ACM Transactions on Graphics*, *35*(4), 138. doi:10.1145/2897824.2925975

Huang, K. C., Huang, Y. K., & Hsu, W. H. (2021). *Multi-Stream Attention Learning for Monocular Vehicle Velocity and Inter-Vehicle Distance Estimation.* arXiv preprint arXiv:2110.11608.

Huang, S., Papernot, N., Goodfellow, I., Duan, Y., & Abbeel, P. 2017. Adversarial attacks on neural network policies. arXiv Prepr. arXiv1702.02284.

Huang, Y., & Zhu, Q. (2019). Deceptive reinforcement learning under adversarial manipulations on cost signals. *Decision and Game Theory for Security: 10th International Conference, GameSec 2019*. Springer. 10.1007/978-3-030-32430-8_14

Huang, L., Fu, M., Li, F., Qu, H., Liu, Y., & Chen, W. (2021). A Deep Reinforcement Learning Based Long-Term Recommender System. *Knowledge-Based Systems*, *213*(1), 106706. doi:10.1016/j.knosys.2020.106706

Huang, M., Liu, Z., Liu, T., & Wang, J. (2023). CCDS-YOLO: Multi-Category Synthetic Aperture Radar Image Object Detection Model Based on YOLOv5s. *Electronics (Basel)*, *12*(16), 3497. doi:10.3390/electronics12163497

Hui, Z., Wang, X., & Gao, X. (2018). Fast and accurate single image super resolution via information distillation network. In *Proceedings of the IEEE Conference on Computer Vision and Pattern Recognition,* (pp. 723-731). IEEE. 10.1109/CVPR.2018.00082

Hu, J., Tan, C. W., Wang, W., & Li, J. (2018). A novel feature engineering approach to phishing email detection. *Information Sciences*, *450*, 19–31.

Hulsen, T. (2023). Explainable Artificial Intelligence (XAI): Concepts and Challenges in Healthcare. *AI*, *4*(3), 652–666. doi:10.3390/ai4030034

Ibarz, J., Tan, J., Finn, C., Kalakrishnan, M., Pastor, P., & Levine, S. (2021). How to Train Your Robot with Deep Reinforcement Learning: Lessons We Have Learned. *The International Journal of Robotics Research*, *40*(4–5), 698–721. doi:10.1177/0278364920987859

Ignatious, H. A., El-Sayed, H., Khan, M. A., & Mokhtar, B. M. (2023). Analyzing Factors Influencing Situation Awareness in Autonomous Vehicles—A Survey. *Sensors (Basel)*, *23*(8), 4075. doi:10.3390/s23084075 PMID:37112416

Iman, M. R. (2022). EXPANSE: A Continual and Progressive Learning System for Deep Transfer Learning. *2022 International Conference on Computational Science and Computational Intelligence (CSCI)*. IEEE. 10.1109/CSCI58124.2022.00016

Ioffe, S., & Szegedy, C. (2015). *Batch normalization: Accelerating deep network training by reducing internal covariate shift*.arXiv. http://export.arxiv.org/pdf/1502.03167

Isogawa, M., Mikami, D., Iwai, D., Kimata, H., & Sato, K. (2018). Mask optimization for image inpainting. *IEEE Access : Practical Innovations, Open Solutions*, *6*, 69728–69741. doi:10.1109/ACCESS.2018.2877401

Isola, P., Zhu, J.-Y., Zhou, T., & Efros, A. A. (2017). Image-to-Image Translation with Conditional Adversarial Networks. 2017 *IEEE Conference on Computer Vision and Pattern Recognition (CVPR)*, (pp. 5967–5976). IEEE. 10.1109/CVPR.2017.632

Ivanovs, M., Kadikis, R., & Ozols, K. (2021). Perturbation-based methods for explaining deep neural networks: A survey. *Pattern Recognition Letters*, *150*, 228–234. doi:10.1016/j.patrec.2021.06.030

Jain, V., Rastogi, M., Ramesh, J. V. N., Chauhan, A., Agarwal, P., Pramanik, S., & Gupta, A. (2023). FinTech and Artificial Intelligence in Relationship Banking and Computer Technology. In K. Saini, A. Mummoorthy, R. Chandrika, N. S. Gowri Ganesh, & I. G. I. Global (Eds.), *AI, IoT, and Blockchain Breakthroughs in E-Governance*. doi:10.4018/978-1-6684-7697-0.ch011

Jasti, R., Jampani, V., Sun, D., & Yang, M.-H. (2022). Multi-Frame Video Prediction with Learnable Motion Encodings. In 2022 *IEEE International Conference on Image Processing (ICIP)*, (pp. 4198-4202). IEEE. 10.1109/ICIP46576.2022.9897483

Javapoint.com. (2021). K-Nearest Neighbor (KNN) Algorithm for Machine Learning. Javapoint.com. https://www.javatpoint.com/k-nearest-neighbor-algorithm-for-machine-learning

Javed, A. R., Ahmed, W., Pandya, S., Maddikunta, P. K. R., Alazab, M., & Gadekallu, T. R. (2023). A survey of explainable artificial intelligence for smart cities. *Electronics (Basel)*, *12*(4), 1020. doi:10.3390/electronics12041020

Jia, C., Li, C. L., & Zhou, Y. (2020). Facial expression recognition based on the ensemble learning of CNNs. *IEEE International Conference on Signal Processing*. IEEE. 10.1109/ICSPCC50002.2020.9259543

Ji, S., Xu, W., Yang, M., & Yu, K. (2012). 3d convolutional neural networks for human action recognition. *IEEE Transactions on Pattern Analysis and Machine Intelligence*, *35*(1), 221–231. doi:10.1109/TPAMI.2012.59 PMID:22392705

Junayed, M. S., & Islam, M. B. (2022). Automated Physical Distance Estimation and Crowd Monitoring Through Surveillance Video. *SN Computer Science*, *4*(1), 67. doi:10.1007/s42979-022-01480-8 PMID:36467857

Karimanzira, D., Pfützenreuter, T., & Renkewitz, H. (2021). Deep learning for long and short range object detection in underwater environment. *Adv Robot Automn*, *5*(1), 1–10.

Katrakazas, C., Quddus, M., Chen, W.-H., & Deka, L. (2015). Real-Time Motion Planning Methods for Autonomous on-Road Driving: State-of-the-Art and Future Research Directions. *Transportation Research Part C, Emerging Technologies*, *60*, 416–442. https://doi.org/10.1016/j.trc.2015.09.011. doi:10.1016/j.trc.2015.09.011

Kaul, D., Raju, H., & Tripathy, B. (2022). Deep learning in healthcare. *Deep Learning in Data Analytics: Recent Techniques, Practices and Applications*. Research Gate.

Keane, M. T., & Smyth, B. (2020). *Good counterfactuals and where to find them: A case-based technique for generating counterfactuals for explainable AI (XAI)*. Case-Based Reasoning Research and Development: 28th International Conference, ICCBR 2020, Salamanca, Spain.

Khan, M. A., Javed, K., Khan, S. A., Saba, T., Habib, U., Khan, J. A., & Abbasi, A. A. (2020). Human action recognition using fusion of Multiview and deep features: An application to video surveillance. *Multimedia Tools and Applications*, *83*(5), 1–27. doi:10.1007/s11042-020-08806-9

Khan, M. Q., Shahid, A., Uddin, M. I., Roman, M., Alharbi, A., Alosaimi, W., Almalki, J., & Alshahrani, S. M. (2022). Impact analysis of keyword extraction using contextual word embedding. *PeerJ. Computer Science*, *8*, e967. doi:10.7717/peerj-cs.967 PMID:35721401

Khatami, A., Nazari, A., Khosravi, A., Lim, C. P., & Nahavandi, S. (2020). A weight perturbation-based regularisation technique for convolutional neural networks and the application in medical imaging. *Expert Systems with Applications*, *149*, 113196. doi:10.1016/j.eswa.2020.113196

Kim, B. (2018). *Interpretability beyond feature attribution: Quantitative testing with concept activation vectors (tcav). International conference on machine learning*. PMLR.

Kim, B., Dong, S., Roh, J., Kim, G., & Lee, S. Y. (2016). Fusing aligned and non-aligned face information for automatic affect recognition in the wild: A deep learning approach. *IEEE Conference on Computer Vision and Pattern Recognition Workshops (CVPRW)*. IEEE. 10.1109/CVPRW.2016.187

Kim, H., Ha, Y. J., & Kim, J. (2021). Phishing detection using text analysis with multi-granularity attention mechanisms. *Computers & Security*, *106*, 102317.

Kim, S., Baek, J., Park, J., Kim, G., & Kim, S. (2022). InstaFormer: Instance-aware image-to-image translation with transformer. In *Proceedings of the IEEE/CVF Conference on Computer Vision and Pattern Recognition* (pp. 18321-18331). IEEE.

Kober, J., Bagnell, J. A., & Peters, J. (2013). Reinforcement Learning in Robotics: A Survey. *The International Journal of Robotics Research*, *32*(11), 1238–1274. doi:10.1177/0278364913495721

Kollias, D., & Zafeiriou, S. (2021). Exploiting Multi-CNN Features in CNN-RNN Based Dimensional Emotion Recognition on the OMG in-the-Wild Dataset. *IEEE Transactions on Affective Computing*, *12*(3), 595–606. doi:10.1109/TAFFC.2020.3014171

Kontes, G. D., Scherer, D. D., Nisslbeck, T., Fischer, J., & Mutschler, C. 2020. High-speed collision avoidance using deep reinforcement learning and domain randomization for autonomous vehicles. *2020 IEEE 23rd International Conference on Intelligent Transportation Systems (ITSC)*. IEEE. 10.1109/ITSC45102.2020.9294396

Kos, J., & Song, D. (2017). *Delving into adversarial attacks on deep policies*. arXiv Prepr. arXiv1705.06452.

Ku, H., & Lee, M. (2023). TextControlGAN: Text-to-Image Synthesis with Controllable Generative Adversarial Networks. *Applied Sciences (Basel, Switzerland)*, *13*(8), 5098. doi:10.3390/app13085098

Kuppa, A., & Le-Khac, N.-A. (2020). *Black box attacks on explainable artificial intelligence (XAI) methods in cyber security*. in *2020 International Joint Conference on neural networks (IJCNN)*. IEEE. 10.1109/IJCNN48605.2020.9206780

Kyeremateng-Boateng, H., Josyula, D. P., & Conn, M. (2023). Computing confidence score for neural network predictions from latent features. *International Conference on Control, Communication and Computing (ICCC)*. IEEE. 10.1109/ICCC57789.2023.10165294

Lample, G., & Chaplot, D. S. (2017). Playing FPS Games with Deep Reinforcement Learning. In *Proceedings of the AAAI Conference on Artificial Intelligence*. AAAI. 10.1609/aaai.v31i1.10827

Le, H., Nguyen, M., Yan, W. Q., & Lo, S. (2021). Training a convolutional neural network for transportation sign detection using synthetic dataset. *2021 36th International Conference on Image and Vision Computing New Zealand (IVCNZ)*. IEEE. 10.1109/IVCNZ54163.2021.9653398

Lecue, F. (2020). On the role of knowledge graphs in explainable AI. *Semantic Web*, *11*(1), 41–51. doi:10.3233/SW-190374

LeCun, Y., Bengio, Y., & Hinton, G. (2015). Deep learning. *Nature*, *521*(7553), 436–444. doi:10.1038/nature14539 PMID:26017442

Lee, S., Ullah, Z., Zeb, A., Ullah, I., Awan, K. M., Saeed, Y., Uddin, M. I., Al-Khasawneh, M. A., Mahmoud, M., & Zareei, M. (2020). Certificateless Proxy Reencryption Scheme (CPRES) Based on Hyperelliptic Curve for Access Control in Content-Centric Network (CCN). *Mobile Information Systems*, *2020*, 4138516.

Li, B., Qi, X., Lukasiewicz, T., & Torr, P. (2019). Controllable Text-to-Image Generation. In Advances in Neural Information Processing Systems, 32.

Li, F., Zhang, Y., Yan, W., & Klette, R. (2016) Adaptive and compressive target tracking based on feature point matching. *International Conference on Pattern Recognition* (ICPR), (pp.2734-2739). IEEE. 10.1109/ICPR.2016.7900049

Li, J., Monroe, W., Ritter, A., Galley, M., Gao, J., & Jurafsky, D. (2016). Deep Reinforcement Learning for Dialogue Generation. *ArXiv Preprint ArXiv:1606.01541*. doi:10.18653/v1/D16-1127

Liang, C., Lu, J., & Yan, W. (2022). *Human action recognition from digital videos based on deep learning.* ACM.

Lian, G., Wang, Y., Qin, H., & Chen, G. (2022). *Towards unified on-road object detection and depth estimation from a single image.* Machine Learning and Cybernetics. doi:10.1007/s13042-021-01444-z

Liang, C., Lu, J., & Yan, W. (2022). *Human action recognition from digital videos based on deep learning.* ACM ICCCV. doi:10.1145/3561613.3561637

Liao, W., Hu, K., Yang, M. Y., & Rosenhahn, B. (2022). Text to Image Generation with Semantic-Spatial Aware GAN. In *2022 IEEE/CVF Conference on Computer Vision and Pattern Recognition (CVPR)*, (pp. 18166-18175). IEEE. 10.1109/CVPR52688.2022.01765

Li, C., Li, D., Zhao, M., & Li, H. (2022). A light-weight convolutional neural network for facial expression recognition using Mini-Xception neural networks. *IEEE International Conference on Current Development in Engineering and Technology (CCET)* IEEE. 10.1109/QRS-C57518.2022.00104

LiC.LiL.GengY.JiangH.ChengM.ZhangB.KeZ.XuX.ChuX. (2023). YOLOv6 v3.0: A Full-Scale Reloading. https://doi.org/ doi:10.48550/ARXIV.2301.05586

Li, C., Zia, M. Z., Tran, Q.-H., Yu, X., Hager, G. D., & Chandraker, M. (2017). Deep supervision with shape concepts for occlusion-aware 3D object parsing. In *Proceedings of the IEEE Conference on Computer Vision and Pattern Recognition* (pp. 5884-5893). IEEE. 10.1109/CVPR.2017.49

Li, H., Tan, Y., Miao, J., Liang, P., Gong, J., He, H., Jiao, Y., Zhang, F., Xing, Y., & Wu, D. (2023). Attention-based and micro designed EfficientNetB2 for diagnosis of Alzheimer's disease. *Biomedical Signal Processing and Control*, *82*, 104571. doi:10.1016/j.bspc.2023.104571

Li, K., Wang, S., Zhang, X., Xu, Y., Xu, W., & Tu, Z. (2021). Pose recognition with cascade transformers. In *Proceedings of the IEEE/CVF conference on computer vision and pattern recognition* (pp. 1944-1953). IEEE.

Lin, Y.-C., Hong, Z.-W., Liao, Y.-H., Shih, M.-L., Liu, M.-Y., & Sun, M. 2017. Tactics of adversarial attack on deep reinforcement learning agents. arXiv Prepr. arXiv1703.06748. doi:10.24963/ijcai.2017/525

Lin, Y., Lin, F., Zeng, W., Xiahou, J., Li, L., Wu, P., Liu, Y., & Miao, C. (2022). Hierarchical Reinforcement Learning with Dynamic Recurrent Mechanism for Course Recommendation. *Knowledge-Based Systems*, *244*, 108546. doi:10.1016/j.knosys.2022.108546

Lin, Y., Liu, Y., Lin, F., Zou, L., Wu, P., Zeng, W., Chen, H., & Miao, C. (2023). A Survey on Reinforcement Learning for Recommender Systems. *IEEE Transactions on Neural Networks and Learning Systems*, 1–21. doi:10.1109/TNNLS.2023.3280161 PMID:37279123

Li, S., Wang, W., Li, Y., & Tan, C. W. (2019). Phishing URL detection based on visual similarity and machine learning. *IEEE Access : Practical Innovations, Open Solutions*, *7*, 24854–24864.

Liu, G., Reda, F. A., & Shih, K. J. (2018). Image inpainting for irregular holes using partial convolutions. In *Proceedings of the European Conference on Computer Vision (ECCV)* (pp. 85–100). Springer. 10.1007/978-3-030-01252-6_6

Liu, M.-Y., Breuel, T., & Kautz, J. (2017). Unsupervised Image-to-Image Translation Networks. *Proceedings of the 31st International Conference on Neural Information Processing Systems,* (pp. 700–708). Springer.

Liu, X. (2019). *Vehicle-related Scene Understanding Using Deep Learning*. [Master's Thesis, Auckland University of Technology, New Zealand].

Liu, Z. (2021). Swin transformer: Hierarchical vision transformer using shifted windows. Computer vision, 37- 49

Liu, K., Zhang, M., & Pan, Z. (2016). Facial expression recognition with CNN ensemble. *International Conference on Cyberworlds*. IEEE.

Liu, M., Shen, X., & Pan, W. (2022). Deep Reinforcement Learning for Personalized Treatment Recommendation. *Statistics in Medicine*, *1*(23), 1–23. doi:10.1002/sim.9491 PMID:35716038

Liu, M., & Yan, W. (2022). *Masked face recognition in real-time using MobileNetV2*. ACM ICCCV.

Liu, S., Chen, Y., Huang, H., Xiao, L., & Hei, X. (2018). Towards Smart Educational Recommendations with Reinforcement Learning in Classroom. In *2018 IEEE International Conference on Teaching, Assessment, and Learning for Engineering (TALE)*, (pp. 1079–84). IEEE. 10.1109/TALE.2018.8615217

Liu, T., Wang, K., Sha, L., Chang, B., & Sui, Z. (2018, April). Table-to-text generation by structure-aware seq2seq learning. *Proceedings of the AAAI Conference on Artificial Intelligence*, *32*(1). doi:10.1609/aaai.v32i1.11925

Liu, X. (2023). Liean Cao"Old-Photo Restoration with Detail- and Structure-Enhanced Cascaded Learning. *IEEE International Conference on Multimedia and Expo Workshops (ICMEW).*

Liu, X., Nguyen, M., & Yan, W. (2019). Vehicle-related scene understanding using deep learn. *Pattern Recognition*, 61–73.

Liu, X., & Yan, W. (2021). *Traffic-light sign recognition using Capsule network.* Springer Multimedia Tools and Applications. doi:10.1007/s11042-020-10455-x

Liu, X., & Yan, W. (2022). *Depth estimation of traffic scenes from image sequence using deep learning*. PSIVT.

Liu, X., Yan, W., & Kasabov, N. (2020). *Vehicle-related scene segmentation using CapsNets.* IEEE IVCNZ. doi:10.1109/IVCNZ51579.2020.9290664

Liu, Y., Ma, Y., & Wei, Y. (2018). 3D Shape Reconstruction from a Single Image using a Deep Convolutional Neural Network. In *Proceedings of the IEEE Conference on Computer Vision and Pattern Recognition* (pp. 7847-7856). IEEE.

Liu, Y., Zhang, L., & Li, W. (2016). Detecting phishing websites with lexical and sentiment features. *Computers & Security*, *59*, 158–168.

Liu, Z., Lin, Y., Cao, Y., Hu, H., Wei, Y., Zhang, Z., & Guo, B. (2021). Swin transformer: Hierarchical vision transformer using shifted windows. In *Proceedings of the IEEE/CVF International Conference on Computer Vision* (pp. 10012-10022). IEEE. 10.1109/ICCV48922.2021.00986

Li, X., Li, Y., Feng, Z., Wang, Z., & Pan, Q. (2023). ATS-O2A: A state-based adversarial attack strategy on deep reinforcement learning. *Computers & Security*, *129*, 103259. doi:10.1016/j.cose.2023.103259

Li, X., Xiong, H., Li, X., Wu, X., Zhang, X., Liu, J., Bian, J., & Dou, D. (2022). Interpretable deep learning: Interpretation, interpretability, trustworthiness, and beyond. *Knowledge and Information Systems*, *64*(12), 3197–3234. doi:10.1007/s10115-022-01756-8

Li, Y., Tang, S., Zhang, R., Zhang, Y., Li, J., & Yan, S. (2019). Asymmetric GAN for unpaired image-to-image translation. *IEEE Transactions on Image Processing*, *28*(12), 5881–5896. doi:10.1109/TIP.2019.2922854 PMID:31226077

Lu, J. (2016). *Empirical Approaches for Human Behavior Analytics.* [Master's Thesis. Auckland University of Technology, New Zealand].

Lu, J., Nguyen, M., & Yan, W. (2020) Comparative evaluations of human behavior recognition using deep learning. Handbook of Research on Multimedia Cyber Security, (pp. 176-189). Research Gate.

Lu, J., Nguyen, M., & Yan, W. Q. (2020). Deep learning methods for human behaviour recognition. In IEEE international conference on image and vision computing New Zealand (IVCNZ) (pp. 1–6). IEEE.

Lu, J., Yan, W. Q., & Nguyen, M. (2018). Human behaviour recognition usingdeep learning. In IEEE international conference on advanced video and signal based surveillance (AVSS) (pp. 1–6). IEEE.

Luan, F., Chen, T., & Hu, X. (2017). Deep photo style transfer. In *Proceedings of the IEEE Conference on Computer Vision and Pattern Recognition,* (pp. 4990-4998). IEEE.

Lugaresi, C., Tang, J., Nash, H., McClanahan, C., Uboweja, E., Hays, M., & Grund-mann, M. (2019). *Mediapipe: A framework for perceiving and processing reality* (Vol. 2019). IEEE.

Lu, J., Nguyen, M., & Yan, W. (2018). *Pedestrian detection using deep learning*. IEEE AVSS.

Lu, J., Nguyen, M., & Yan, W. (2020) Human behavior recognition using deep learning. *International Conference on Image and Vision Computing New Zealand*. IEEE.

Lu, J., Shen, J., Yan, W., & Boris, B. (2017). An empirical study for human behaviors analysis. *International Journal of Digital Crime and Forensics*, *9*(3), 11–17. doi:10.4018/IJDCF.2017070102

Lun, Z., Gadelha, M., Kalogerakis, E., Maji, S., & Wang, R. (2017). 3D Shape Reconstruction from Sketches via Multi-view Convolutional Networks. In *2017 IEEE International Conference on 3D Vision (3DV)* (pp. 441-450). IEEE.

Lu, W., Cui, J., Chang, Y., & Zhang, L. (2021). A Video Prediction Method Based on Optical Flow Estimation and Pixel Generation. *IEEE Access : Practical Innovations, Open Solutions*, *9*, 100395–100406. doi:10.1109/ACCESS.2021.3096788

Lyu, C., Huang, K., & Liang, H.-N. 2015. A unified gradient regularization family for adversarial examples. *2015 IEEE International Conference on Data Mining*. IEEE. 10.1109/ICDM.2015.84

Ma, R. (2022). Forecasting and XAI for Applications Usage in OS. *Machine Learning and Artificial Intelligence*. IOS Press.

Madry, A., Makelov, A., Schmidt, L., Tsipras, D., & Vladu, A. (2017). *Towards deep learning models resistant to adversarial attacks*. arXiv Prepr. arXiv1706.06083.

Mahalakshmi, V., Kulkarni, N., Pradeep Kumar, K. V., Suresh Kumar, K., Nidhi Sree, D., & Durga, S. (2022). The Role of implementing Artificial Intelligence and Machine Learning Technologies in the financial services Industry for creating Competitive Intelligence. *Materials Today: Proceedings*, *56*, 2252–2255. doi:10.1016/j.matpr.2021.11.577

Mandal, A., Dutta, S., & Pramanik, S. (2021). Machine Intelligence of Pi from Geometrical Figures with Variable Parameters using SCILab. In D. Samanta, R. R. Althar, S. Pramanik, & S. Dutta (Eds.), *Methodologies and Applications of Computational Statistics for Machine Learning* (pp. 38–63). IGI Global. doi:10.4018/978-1-7998-7701-1.ch003

Mao, W., Ge, Y., Shen, C., Tian, Z., Wang, X., & Wang, Z. (2021). *TFPose: Direct human pose estimation with transformers*. arXiv preprint arXiv:2103.15320.

Martínez, J. (2021). *TensorFlow 2.0 Computer Vision Cookbook: Implement machine learning solutions to overcome various computer vision challenges*. Packt Publishing.

Masoumian, A., Rashwan, H. A., Cristiano, J., Asif, M. S., & Puig, D. (2022). Monocular depth estimation using deep learning: A review. *Sensors (Basel)*, *22*(14), 5353. doi:10.3390/s22145353 PMID:35891033

Mehta, S., & Mohammad, R. (2021). *MobileViT: Light-weight, general-purpose, and mobile friendly vision transformer.* arXiv preprint arXiv:2110.02178.

Mehtab, S., & Yan, W. (2021). Flexible neural network for fast and accurate road scene perception. *Multimedia Tools and Applications*, 7169–7181.

Mehtab, S., Yan, W., & Narayanan, A. (2021). *3D vehicle detection using cheap LiDAR and camera sensors*. IEEE IVCNZ. doi:10.1109/IVCNZ54163.2021.9653358

Mehta, S., Kanhangad, V., & Ravi, T. M. (2015). Phishing Detection using Machine Learning Techniques. *International Journal of Computer Applications*, *117*(22), 9–13.

Meng, J., Zhu, F., Ge, Y., & Zhao, P. (2023). Integrating safety constraints into adversarial training for robust deep reinforcement learning. *Information Sciences*, *619*, 310–323. doi:10.1016/j.ins.2022.11.051

Meslie, Y., Enbeyle, W., Pandey, B. K., Pramanik, S., Pandey, D., Dadeech, P., Belay, A., & Saini, A. (2021). Machine Intelligence-based Trend Analysis of COVID-19 for Total Daily Confirmed Cases in Asia and Africa. In D. Samanta, R. R. Althar, S. Pramanik, & S. Dutta (Eds.), *Methodologies and Applications of Computational Statistics for Machine Learning* (pp. 164–185). IGI Global. doi:10.4018/978-1-7998-7701-1.ch009

Ming, Y., Meng, X., Fan, C., & Yu, H. (2021). Deep learning for monocular depth estimation: A review. *Neurocomputing*, *438*, 14–33. doi:10.1016/j.neucom.2020.12.089

Mir, I., Gul, F., Mir, S., Mansoor A Khan, N. S., Abualigah, L., Abuhaija, B., & Amir, H. (2022, September 06). A Survey of Trajectory Planning Techniques for Autonomous Systems. *Electronics (Basel)*, *11*(18), 2801. doi:10.3390/electronics11182801

Moghimi, M., & Varjani, A. Y. (2016). New rule-based phishing detection method. *Expert Systems with Applications*, *2016*(53), 231–242. doi:10.1016/j.eswa.2016.01.028

Mon, F., Bisni, A. W., Hayajneh, M., Slim, A., & Abu Ali, N. (2023). Reinforcement Learning in Education: A Literature Review. [MDPI.]. *Informatics (MDPI)*, *10*(3), 74. doi:10.3390/informatics10030074

Montavon, G. (2019). *Layer-wise relevance propagation: an overview.* Explainable AI: interpreting, explaining and visualizing deep learning, 193-209.

Moosavi-Dezfooli, S.-M., Fawzi, A., & Frossard, P. 2016. Deepfool: a simple and accurate method to fool deep neural networks. *Proceedings of the IEEE Conference on Computer Vision and Pattern Recognition,* (pp. 2574–2582). IEEE. 10.1109/CVPR.2016.282

Muddala, S. M., Olsson, R., & Sjöström, M. (2016). Spatio-temporal consistent depth-image-based rendering using layered depth image and inpainting. *EURASIP Journal on Image and Video Processing*, *2016*(1), 1–19. doi:10.1186/s13640-016-0109-6

Mundhenk, T. N., Chen, B. Y., & Friedland, G. (2019). *Efficient saliency maps for explainable AI.* arXiv preprint arXiv:1911.11293.

Munemasa, I., Tomomatsu, Y., Hayashi, K., & Takagi, T. (2018). Deep Reinforcement Learning for Recommender Systems. In *2018 International Conference on Information and Communications Technology (ICOIACT)*, (pp. 226–33). IEEE. 10.1109/ICOIACT.2018.8350761

Murindanyi, S. (2023). *Interpretable Machine Learning for Predicting Customer Churn in Retail Banking. 2023 7th International Conference on Trends in Electronics and Informatics (ICOEI).* IEEE. 10.1109/ICOEI56765.2023.10125859

Nallamothu, L. H., Ramisetti, T. P., Mekala, V. K., Aramandla, K., & Duvvada, R. R. (2023). Interactive Image Generation Using Cycle GAN Over AWS Cloud. In S. Shakya, V. E. Balas, & W. Haoxiang (Eds.), *Proceedings of Third International Conference on Sustainable Expert Systems* (pp. 587). Springer, Singapore. 10.1007/978-981-19-7874-6_30

Naseem, R. (2020). Performance Assessment of Classification Algorithms on Early Detection of Liver Syndrome. *Journal of Healthcare and Engineering.*

Naveen, S. S., Kiran, M., Indupriya, M., Manikanta, T. S., & Sudeep, P. V. (2021). Transformer models for enhancing AttnGAN based text to image generation. *Image and Vision Computing*, *115*, 104284. doi:10.1016/j.imavis.2021.104284

Nazir, S., Naseem, R., Khan, B., Shah, M. A., Wakil, K., Khan, A., Alosaimi, W., Uddin, M. I., & Alouffi, B. (2020). Performance Assessment of Classification Algorithms on Early Detection of Liver Syndrome. *Journal of Healthcare Engineering*, *2020*, 6680002. PMID:33489060

Nguyen, A. T., & Bui, H. A. (2023, March). Multiple Target Activity Recognition by Combining YOLOv5 with LSTM Network. In *The International Conference on Intelligent Systems & Networks* (pp. 400-408). Singapore: Springer Nature Singapore. 10.1007/978-981-99-4725-6_49

Nguyen, A., Yosinski, J., & Clune, J. (2019). Understanding neural networks via feature visualization: A survey. *Explainable AI: interpreting, explaining and visualizing deep learning* (p. 55-76). Research Gate.

Nguyen, M., Yan, W. (2022) Temporal color-coded facial-expression recognition using convolutional neural network. *International Summit Smart City 360°: Science and Technologies for Smart Cities*. IEEE.

Nguyen, M., & Yan, W. (2023) From faces to traffic lights: A multi-scale approach for emotional state representation. *IEEE International Conference on Smart City*. IEEE.

Nielsen, I. E., Dera, D., Rasool, G., Ramachandran, R. P., & Bouaynaya, N. C. (2022). Robust explainability: A tutorial on gradient-based attribution methods for deep neural networks. *IEEE Signal Processing Magazine*, *39*(4), 73–84. doi:10.1109/MSP.2022.3142719

Niu, C., Li, J., & Xu, K. (2018). Im2Struct: Recovering 3D Shape Structure from a Single RGB Image. In *Proceedings of the IEEE Conference on Computer Vision and Pattern Recognition* (pp. 80-89). IEEE. 10.1109/CVPR.2018.00475

Oppenlaender, J. (2022). The Creativity of Text-to-Image Generation. In *25th International Academic Mindtrek Conference (Academic Mindtrek 2022)*. ACM. 10.1145/3569219.3569352

Özcan, M., Aliew, F., & Görgün, H. (2020). Accurate and precise distance estimation for noisy IR sensor readings contaminated by outliers. *Measurement*, *156*, 107633. doi:10.1016/j.measurement.2020.107633

Palatnik de Sousa, I., Maria Bernardes Rebuzzi Vellasco, M., & Costa da Silva, E. (2019). Local interpretable model-agnostic explanations for classification of lymph node metastases. *Sensors (Basel)*, *19*(13), 2969. doi:10.3390/s19132969 PMID:31284419

Pang, Y., Lin, J., Qin, T., & Chen, Z. (2021). Image-to-image translation: Methods and applications. *IEEE Transactions on Multimedia*, *24*, 3859–3881. doi:10.1109/TMM.2021.3109419

Papernot, N., McDaniel, P., Sinha, A., & Wellman, M. (2016). *Towards the science of security and privacy in machine learning*. arXiv Prepr. arXiv1611.03814.

Parihar, S. S., Gupta, J. P., & Kumar, V. (2019). Phishing Detection based on the Features of Phishing Webpages Using K-Nearest Neighbor Algorithm. *International Journal of Computer Applications*, *182*(2), 38–43.

Parker, P. R., Abe, E. T., Beatie, N. T., Leonard, E. S., Martins, D. M., Sharp, S. L., Wyrick, D. G., Mazzucato, L., & Niell, C. M. (2022). Distance estimation from monocular cues in an ethological visuomotor task. *eLife*, *11*, 74708. doi:10.7554/eLife.74708 PMID:36125119

Parmar, A., Katariya, R., & Patel, V. (2018). A review on random forest: An ensemble classifier. *International conference on intelligent data communication technologies and internet of things (ICICI)*. Springer.

Pattanaik, A., Tang, Z., Liu, S., Bommannan, G., & Chowdhary, G. (2017). *Robust deep reinforcement learning with adversarial attacks*. arXiv Prepr. arXiv1712.03632.

Paulus, R., Xiong, C., & Socher, R. (2017). A Deep Reinforced Model for Abstractive Summarization. *ArXiv Preprint ArXiv:1705.04304*.

Pauzi, A. S. B., Mohd Nazri, F. B., Sani, S., Bataineh, A. M., Hisyam, M. N., Jaafar, M. H., & Mohamed, A. (2021). *Movement estimation using MediaPipe blazepose*. IVIC. doi:10.1007/978-3-030-90235-3_49

Pham, T. N., Van Tran, L., & Dao, S. V. T. (2020). Early disease classification of mango leaves using feed-forward neural network and hybrid metaheuristic feature selection. *IEEE Access : Practical Innovations, Open Solutions*, *8*, 189960–189973. doi:10.1109/ACCESS.2020.3031914

Pinto, L., Davidson, J., Sukthankar, R., & Gupta, A. (2017). Robust adversarial reinforcement learning. *International Conference on Machine Learning*. IEEE.

Pothen, A.S. (2022). Artificial intelligence and its increasing importance. Success is no accident. It is hard work, perseverance, learning, studying, sacrifice and most of all, love of what you are doing or learning to do.

Powers, D. (2020). *Evaluation: from precision, recall and F-measure to ROC, informedness, markedness and correlation.* Cornell University. https://doi.org//arxiv.2010.16061 doi:10.48550

Pramanik, S. (2023). A Novel Data Hiding Locating Approach in Image Steganography. *Multimedia Tools and Applications, 2023*. doi:10.1007/s11042-023-16762-3

Pramanik, S. (2023). An Adaptive Image Steganography Approach depending on Integer Wavelet Transform and Genetic Algorithm. *Multimedia Tools and Applications*, *82*(22), 34287–34319. Advance online publication. doi:10.1007/s11042-023-14505-y

Prasad. (2016). *Top 20 Python Machine Learning Open Source Projects*. KD nuggets. https://www.kdnuggets.com/2016/11/top-20-python-machine-learning-opensource-updated.html

Praveenkumar, S., Veeraiah, V., Pramanik, S., Basha, S. M., Lira Neto, A. V., De Albuquerque, V. H. C., & Gupta, A. (2023). *Prediction of Patients' Incurable Diseases Utilizing Deep Learning Approaches, ICICC 2023*. Springer. doi:10.1007/978-981-99-3315-0_4

Qiao, Y., Wu, Y., & Wang, L. (2021). Efficient style-corpus constrained learning for photorealistic style transfer. *IEEE Transactions on Image Processing*, *30*(01), 1–1. doi:10.1109/TIP.2021.3058566 PMID:33617453

Qu, Y., Shao, Z., & Qi, H. (2021). Non-local representation based mutual affine-transfer network for photorealistic stylization. *IEEE Transactions on Pattern Analysis and Machine Intelligence*, *01*(01), 1–1. PMID:34260345

Radford, A., Metz, L., & Chintala, S. (2015). Unsupervised Representation Learning with Deep Convolutional Generative Adversarial Networks. *CoRR,* abs/1511.06434.

Rafailov, R., Yu, T., Rajeswaran, A., & Finn, C. (2021). Offline reinforcement learning from images with latent space models. In *Learning for Dynamics and Control* (pp. 1154–1168). PMLR.

Raghu, M. (2017). *Singular vector canonical correlation analysis for deep learning dynamics and interpretability. 2017*. 31st Conference on Neural Information Processing Systems (NIPS 2017), Long Beach: Neural Info Process Sys F, La Jolla.

Ramakrishna, M. Z., Efros, A. A., & Shechtman, Y. (2018). Photorealistic 3D Modeling from a Single Image using a Deep Convolutional Neural Network. In *Proceedings of the IEEE Conference on Computer Vision and Pattern Recognition* (pp. 7847-7856). IEEE.

Ramzan, S., Iqbal, M. M., & Kalsum, T. (2022). Text-to-Image Generation Using Deep Learning. *Engineering Proceedings*, *20*(1), 16.

Rao, R. S., Vaishnavi, T., & Pais, A. R. (2019). CatchPhish: Detection of phishing websites by inspecting URLs. *Journal of Ambient Intelligence and Humanized Computing*, *11*(2), 813–825. doi:10.1007/s12652-019-01311-4

Redmon, J., Divvala, S., Girshick, R., & Farhadi, A. (2016). You only look once: Unified, real-time object detection. In *Proceedings of the ieee conference on computer vision and pattern recognition* (pp. 779–788). IEEE. 10.1109/CVPR.2016.91

Reed, S., Akata, Z., Yan, X., Logeswaran, L., Schiele, B., & Lee, H. (2016, June). Generative Adversarial Text to Image Synthesis. In *International Conference on Machine Learning* (pp. 1060-1069). PMLR.

Reepu, K. S., Chaudhary, M. G., Gupta, K. G., Pramanik, S. and Gupta, A. (2023). Information Security and Privacy in IoT. J. Zhao, V. V. Kumar, R. Natarajan and T. R. Mahesh, (eds.) Handbook of Research in Advancements in AI and IoT Convergence Technologies. IGI Global.

Renda, A., Barsacchi, M., Bechini, A., & Marcelloni, F. (2019). Comparing ensemble strategies for deep learning: An application to facial expression recognition. *Expert Systems with Applications*, *136*, 1–11. doi:10.1016/j.eswa.2019.06.025

Riek, L. D. (2013). Embodied Computation: An Active-Learning Approach to Mobile Robotics Education. *IEEE Transactions on Education*, *56*(1), 67–72. doi:10.1109/TE.2012.2221716

Rojat, T. (2021). *Explainable artificial intelligence (xai) on timeseries data: A survey.* arXiv preprint arXiv:2104.00950.

Rosenfeld, A. (2021). *Better metrics for evaluating explainable artificial intelligence.* in *Proceedings of the 20th international conference on autonomous agents and multiagent systems*. IEEE.

Sahingoz, O. K., Buber, E., Demir, O., & Diri, B. (2019). Machine learning based phishing detection from URLs. *Expert Systems with Applications*, *2019*(117), 345–357. doi:10.1016/j.eswa.2018.09.029

Sanjaya, S. A., & Adi Rakhmawan, S. (2020). Face mask detection using mobilenetv2 in the era of COVID-19 pandemic. *2020 International Conference on Data Analytics for Business and Industry: Way Towards a Sustainable Economy (ICDABI)*. IEEE. 10.1109/ICDABI51230.2020.9325631

Sankaranarayanan, S., Jain, A., Chellappa, R., & Lim, S. N. 2018. Regularizing deep networks using efficient layerwise adversarial training. *Proceedings of the AAAI Conference on Artificial Intelligence.* AAAI. 10.1609/aaai.v32i1.11688

Sarkar, A. (2022). A framework for learning ante-hoc explainable models via concepts. *Proceedings of the IEEE/CVF Conference on Computer Vision and Pattern Recognition.* IEEE. 10.1109/CVPR52688.2022.01004

Sawant, R., Shaikh, A., Sabat, S., & Bhole, V. (2021). Text to Image Generation using GAN. *Proceedings of the International Conference on IoT Based Control Networks & Intelligent Systems - ICICNIS 2021*. SSRN. 10.2139/ssrn.3882570

Schuldt, C., Laptev, I., & Caputo, B. (2004). Recognizing human actions: A local svm approach. In IEEE international conference on pattern recognition (Vol. 3, pp. 32–36). IEEE. doi:10.1109/ICPR.2004.1334462

Sewak, M. (2019). In M. Sewak (Ed.), *Deep Q Network (DQN), Double DQN, and Dueling DQN BT - Deep Reinforcement Learning: Frontiers of Artificial Intelligence* (pp. 95–108). Springer Singapore. doi:10.1007/978-981-13-8285-7_8

Shaham, U., Yamada, Y., & Negahban, S. (2018). Understanding adversarial training: Increasing local stability of supervised models through robust optimization. *Neurocomputing*, *307*, 195–204. doi:10.1016/j.neucom.2018.04.027

Shao, L., Zhu, F., & Li, X. (2015). Transfer Learning for Visual Categorization: A Survey. *IEEE Transactions on Neural Networks and Learning Systems*. PMID:25014970

Sharma, D., & Gomase, V. (2017). An Approach for Detecting Phishing Websites Based on K-Nearest Neighbors Algorithm. *International Journal of Computer Applications*, *176*(3), 22–26.

Shawky, D., & Badawi, A. (2019). In A. E. Hassanien (Ed.), *Towards a Personalized Learning Experience Using Reinforcement Learning BT - Machine Learning Paradigms: Theory and Application* (pp. 169–187). Springer International Publishing. doi:10.1007/978-3-030-02357-7_8

Shen, D., Chen, X., Nguyen, M., & Yan, W. Q. (2018). Flame detection using Deep Learning. *2018 4th International Conference on Control, Automation and Robotics (ICCAR)*. IEEE. doi:10.1109/ICCAR.2018.8384711

Sheng, S., Holbrook, M., Kumaraguru, P., Cranor, L. F., & Downs, J. (2010). Who falls for phishing scams? A demographic analysis of phishing susceptibility and effectiveness of interventions.In *Proceedings of the SIGCHI Conference on Human Factors in Computing Systems (CHI)* (pp. 373-382). ACM. 10.1145/1753326.1753383

Sigut, J., Castro, M., Arnay, R., & Sigut, M. (2020). OpenCV Basics: A Mobile Application to Support the Teaching of Computer Vision Concepts". *IEEE Transactions on Education*, *63*(4), 328–335. doi:10.1109/TE.2020.2993013

Silver, D., Hubert, T., Schrittwieser, J., Antonoglou, I., Lai, M., Guez, A., Lanctot, M., Sifre, L., Kumaran, D., Graepel, T., Lillicrap, T., Simonyan, K., & Hassabis, D. (2018). A General Reinforcement Learning Algorithm That Masters Chess, Shogi, and Go through Self-Play. *Science*, *362*(6419), 1140–1144. doi:10.1126/science.aar6404 PMID:30523106

Simonyan, K., & Zisserman, A. (2014). Two-stream convolutional networks for action recognition in videos. *Advances in Neural Information Processing Systems*, 27.

Singh, A. K., Kumbhare, V. A., & Arthi, K. (2021). Real-time human pose detection and recognition using MediaPipe. *International Conference on Soft Computing and Signal Processing*, (pp. 145-154). IEEE.

Singh, B., Kumar, R., & Singh, V. P. (2022). Reinforcement Learning in Robotic Applications: A Comprehensive Survey. *Artificial Intelligence Review*, *55*(2), 1–46. doi:10.1007/s10462-021-09997-9

Singh, S., Ahuja, U., Kumar, M., Kumar, K., & Sachdeva, M. (2021). Face mask detection using yolov3 and faster R-CNN models: COVID-19 environment. *Multimedia Tools and Applications*, *80*(13), 19753–19768. doi:10.1007/s11042-021-10711-8 PMID:33679209

Smith, M., Banerjee, I., & Laskowski, S. (2017). A novel machine learning approach to detect phishing URLs using natural language processing. *Journal of Computer and System Sciences*, *86*, 13–26.

Sofianidis, G. (2021). *A review of explainable artificial intelligence in manufacturing*. Trusted Artificial Intelligence in Manufacturing.

Song, C., He, L., Yan, W., & Nand, P. (2019) An improved selective facial extraction model for age estimation. *International Conference on Image and Vision Computing New Zealand.* IEEE. 10.1109/IVCNZ48456.2019.8960965

Song, X., Gao, H., Ding, T., Gu, Y., Liu, J., & Tian, K. (2023). A Review of the Motion Planning and Control Methods for Automated Vehicles. *Sensors (Basel)*, *23*(13), 6140. doi:10.3390/s23136140 PMID:37447989

Soomro, K., & Zamir, A. R. (2014). Action recognition in realistic sports videos. In *Computer vision in sports* (pp. 181–208). Springer. doi:10.1007/978-3-319-09396-3_9

Sridhar, K., Lin, W., & Busso, C. (2021). Generative approach using soft-labels to learn uncertainty in predicting emotional attributes. *International Conference on Affective Computing and Intelligent Interaction (ACII).* IEEE. 10.1109/ACII52823.2021.9597461

Sujatha, K., Amrutha, K., & Veeranjaneyulu, N. (2023). Enhancing Object Detection with Mask R-CNN: A Deep Learning Perspective. *International Conference on Network, Multimedia and Information Technology (NMITCON)*, (pp. 1–6). IEEE. 10.1109/NMITCON58196.2023.10276033

Sun, J., Zhang, T., Xie, X., Ma, L., Zheng, Y., Chen, K., & Liu, Y. (2020). Stealthy and efficient adversarial attacks against deep reinforcement learning. *Proceedings of the AAAI Conference on Artificial Intelligence*, (pp. 5883–5891). AAAI. 10.1609/aaai.v34i04.6047

Sun, K., Xiao, B., Liu, D., & Wang, J. (2019), Deep high-resolution representation learning for human pose estimation. *IEEE Conference on Computer Vision and Pattern Recognition*, (pp. 5693-5703). IEEE. 10.1109/CVPR.2019.00584

Sun, L., Ge, C., & Zhong, Y. (2021). Design and implementation of face emotion recognition system based on CNN Mini-Xception Frameworks. *Journal of Physics: Conference Series*, *2010*(1), 012123. doi:10.1088/1742-6596/2010/1/012123

Sun, X., Wu, P., & Hoi, S. C. (2018). Face detection using deep learning: An improved Faster R-CNN approach. *Neurocomputing*, *299*, 42–50. doi:10.1016/j.neucom.2018.03.030

Susheelkumar, K., Semwal, V., Prasad, S., & Tripathi, R. (2011). Generating 3D Model Using 2D Images of an Object. In *2011 International Conference on Computing Communication and Automation (ICCCA)* (pp. 1-6). IEEE.

Sutton, R. (2018). *Reinforcement Learning : An Introduction*. The MIT Press.

Szegedy, C., Zaremba, W., Sutskever, I., Bruna, J., Erhan, D., Goodfellow, I., & Fergus, R. (2013). *Intriguing properties of neural networks*. arXiv Prepr. arXiv1312.6199.

Talaat, F. M., Aljadani, A., Alharthi, B., Farsi, M. A., Badawy, M., & Elhosseini, M. (2023). A Mathematical Model for Customer Segmentation Leveraging Deep Learning, Explainable AI, and RFM Analysis in Targeted Marketing. *Mathematics*, *11*(18), 3930. doi:10.3390/math11183930

Tang, J., Su, Q., Su, B., Fong, S., Cao, W., & Gong, X. (2020). Parallel ensemble learning of convolutional neural networks and local binary patterns for face recognition. *Computer Methods and Programs in Biomedicine*, *197*, 105622. doi:10.1016/j.cmpb.2020.105622 PMID:32629293

Tang, Y. (2013). *Deep learning using linear support vector machines*. Cornell University.

Tessler, C., Efroni, Y., & Mannor, S. (2019). Action robust reinforcement learning and applications in continuous control. *International Conference on Machine Learning*. PMLR.

Tirer, T., & Giryes, R. (2019). Image restoration by iterative denoising and backward projections. *IEEE Transactions on Image Processing*, *28*(3), 1220–1234. doi:10.1109/TIP.2018.2875569 PMID:30307870

Tirer, T., & Giryes, R. (2019). Super-resolution based on image-adapted CNN denoisers: Incorporating generalization of training data and internal learning in test time. [IEEE]. *Institute of Electrical and Electronics Engineers*, *26*(7), 1080–1084.

Tran, D., Bourdev, L., Fergus, R., Torresani, L., & Paluri, M. (2015). Learning spatiotemporal features with 3d convolutional networks. In *Proceedings of the ieee international conference on computer vision* (pp. 4489–4497). IEEE. 10.1109/ICCV.2015.510

Turing.Com. (2023). *A Guide on Word Embeddings in NLP*. Turing.com. https://www.turing.com/kb/guide-on-word-embeddings-in-nlp

Tzeng, J.-W., Huang, N.-F., Chuang, A.-C., Huang, T.-W., & Chang, H.-Y. (2023). Massive Open Online Course Recommendation System Based on a Reinforcement Learning Algorithm. *Neural Computing & Applications*. Advance online publication. doi:10.1007/s00521-023-08686-8

Ullah, I., Amin, N. U., Almogren, A., Khan, M. A., Uddin, M. I., & Hua, Q. (2020). A Lightweight and Secured Certificate-Based Proxy Signcryption (CB-PS) Scheme for E-Prescription Systems. *IEEE Access : Practical Innovations, Open Solutions*, *8*, 199197–199212. doi:10.1109/ACCESS.2020.3033758

Vakili, E., Shoaran, M., & Sarmadi, M. R. (2020). Single-camera vehicle speed measurement using the geometry of the imaging system. *Multimedia Tools and Applications*, *79*(27-28), 19307–19327. doi:10.1007/s11042-020-08761-5

Valente, J., António, J., Mora, C., & Jardim, S. (2023). Developments in Image Processing Using Deep Learning and Reinforcement Learning. *Journal of Imaging*, *9*(10), 207. doi:10.3390/jimaging9100207 PMID:37888314

Vasanthi, P., & Mohan, L. (2023). Multi-Head-Self-Attention based YOLOv5X-transformer for multi-scale object detection. *Multimedia Tools and Applications*.

Vaswani, A., Shazeer, N., Parmar, N., Uszkoreit, J., Jones, L., Gomez, A. N., Kaiser, Ł., & Polosukhin, I. (2017). Attention is All you Need. In I. Guyon, U. V. Luxburg, S. Bengio, H. Wallach, R. Fergus, S. Vishwanathan, & R. Garnett (Eds.), Advances in Neural Information Processing Systems: Vol. 30. *Curran Associates, Inc.*

Vaswani, A., Shazeer, N., Parmar, N., Uszkoreit, J., Jones, L., Gomez, A. N., & Polosukhin, I. (2017). Attention is all you need. *Advances in Neural Information Processing Systems*, 30.

Veeraiah, V., Talukdar, V., Manikandan, K., Talukdar, S. B., Solavande, V. D., Pramanik, S., & Gupta, A. (2023). Machine Learning Frameworks in Carpooling. In R. Hossain, C. Ho, & G. Trajkovski, Handbook of Research on AI and Machine Learning Applications in Customer Support and Analytics. IGI Global. doi:10.4018/978-1-6684-7105-0.ch009

Velthoen, J. (2023). Gradient boosting for extreme quantile regression. *Extremes*, 1–29.

Venkateswarlu, I. B., Kakarla, J., & Prakash, S. (2020). Face mask detection using mobilenet and global pooling block. 2020 IEEE 4th Conference on Information & Communication Technology (CICT). doi:10.1109/CICT51604.2020.9312083

Vidya, C. V., Veeraiah, V., Khanna, A., Sheikh, T. H., Pramanik, S., & Dhabliya, D. (2023). A Machine Vision-based Approach for Tuberculosis Identification in Chest X-Rays Images of Patients. *ICICC 2023*. Springer. doi:10.1007/978-981-99-3315-0_3

Vijayanarasimhan, S. (2017). Sfm-net: Learning of structure and motion from video. arXiv preprint arXiv:1704.07804.

Vilone, G., & Longo, L. (2020). *Explainable artificial intelligence: a systematic review.* arXiv preprint arXiv:2006.00093.

Vilone, G., & Longo, L. (2021). Notions of explainability and evaluation approaches for explainable artificial intelligence. *Information Fusion*, *76*, 89–106. doi:10.1016/j.inffus.2021.05.009

Vinitsky, E., Du, Y., Parvate, K., Jang, K., Abbeel, P., & Bayen, A. 2020. Robust reinforcement learning using adversarial populations. arXiv Prepr. arXiv2008.01825.

Vinogradova, K., Dibrov, A., & Myers, G. (2020). Towards interpretable semantic segmentation via gradient-weighted class activation mapping (student abstract). *Proceedings of the AAAI conference on artificial intelligence*. AAAI. 10.1609/aaai.v34i10.7244

Vitelli, M. (2022). *Safetynet: Safe planning for real-world self-driving vehicles using machine-learned policies. 2022 International Conference on Robotics and Automation (ICRA).* IEEE. 10.1109/ICRA46639.2022.9811576

Volchenkov, D., Mast, N., Khan, M. A., Uddin, M. I., Ali Shah, S. A., Khan, A., Al-Khasawneh, M. A., & Mahmoud, M. (2021). Channel Contention-Based Routing Protocol for Wireless Ad Hoc Networks. *Complexity*, *2021*, 2051796.

Wang, C. (2020). Generalization and Visual Comprehension of CNN Models on Chromosome Images. Journal of Physics: Conference Series. IOP Publishing. doi:10.1088/1742-6596/1487/1/012027

Wang, C., He, W., Nie, Y., Guo, J., Liu, C., Han, K., & Wang, Y. (2023). *Gold-YOLO: Efficient Object Detector via Gather-and-Distribute Mechanism.*

Wang, C.-Y., & Bochkovskiy, A., & Liao, H.-Y. M. (2023). YOLOv7: Trainable Bag-of-Freebies Sets New State-of-the-Art for Real-Time Object Detectors. *2023 IEEE Conference on Computer Vision and Pattern Recognition (CVPR)*, (pp. 7464–7475). IEEE. 10.1109/CVPR52729.2023.00721

Wang, C.-Y., Bochkovskiy, A., & Liao, H.-Y. M. (2022). *YOLOv7: Trainable bag-of-freebies sets new state-of-the-art for real-time object detectors*. arXiv preprint arXiv:2207.02696.

Wang, D. & Hu, M. (2021). Deep Deterministic Policy Gradient With Compatible Critic Network. *IEEE Trans. Neural Networks Learn. Syst*. IEEE.

Wang, D. (2022). Meta Reinforcement Learning with Hebbian Learning. 2022 IEEE 13th Annual Ubiquitous Computing, Electronics & Mobile Communication Conference (UEMCON). IEEE. doi:10.1109/UEMCON54665.2022.9965711

Wang, D. (2023a). Obstacle-aware Simultaneous Task and Energy Planning with Ordering Constraints. *2023 11th International Conference on Information and Communication Technology (ICoICT)*. IEEE. 10.1109/ICoICT58202.2023.10262644

Wang, D., Hu, M., & Gao, Y. (2018). Multi-criteria mission planning for a solar-powered multi-robot system. *International Design Engineering Technical Conferences and Computers and Information in Engineering Conference*. IEEE. 10.1115/DETC2018-85683

Wang, D., Hu, M., & Weir, J.D. (2022). *Simultaneous Task and Energy Planning using Deep Reinforcement Learning. Inf. Sci.* (Ny).

Wang, L., Xiong, Y., Wang, Z., Qiao, Y., Lin, D., Tang, X., & Gool, L. V. (2016). Temporal segment networks: Towards good practices for deep action recognition. In *European conference on computer vision* (pp. 20–36).

Wang, X., & Hu, H.-M., & Zhang, Y. (2019). Pedestrian detection based on spatial attention module for outdoor video surveillance. *2019 IEEE Fifth International Conference on Multimedia Big Data (BigMM)*. IEEE. 10.1109/BigMM.2019.00-17

Wang, B., Wu, T., Zhu, M., & Du, P. (2022). Interactive image synthesis with panoptic layout generation. In *Proceedings of the IEEE/CVF Conference on Computer Vision and Pattern Recognition* (pp. 7783-7792). IEEE. 10.1109/CVPR52688.2022.00763

Wang, D. (2023b). Explainable Deep Reinforcement Learning for Knowledge Graph Reasoning. In *Recent Developments in Machine and Human Intelligence* (pp. 168–183). IGI Global. doi:10.4018/978-1-6684-9189-8.ch012

Wang, D. (2023c). Out-of-Distribution Detection with Confidence Deep Reinforcement Learning. *2023 International Conference on Communications, Computing, Cybersecurity, and Informatics (CCCI)*. IEEE. 10.1109/CCCI58712.2023.10290768

Wang, D. (2023d). Reinforcement Learning for Combinatorial Optimization. In *Encyclopedia of Data Science and Machine Learning* (pp. 2857–2871). IGI Global.

Wang, D., & Hu, M. (2023). Contrastive Learning Methods for Deep Reinforcement Learning. *IEEE Access : Practical Innovations, Open Solutions*, *11*, 97107–97117. doi:10.1109/ACCESS.2023.3312383

WangD.ZhaoJ.HanM.LiL. (n.d). 4d Printing-Enabled Circular Economy: Disassembly Sequence Planning Using Reinforcement Learning. SSRN 4429186. doi:10.2139/ssrn.4429186

Wang, H., & Yan, W. (2022). *Face detection and recognition from distance based on deep learning. Aiding Forensic Investigation Through Deep Learning and Machine Learning Framework*. IGI Global.

Wang, H., & Yan, W. Q. (2022). Face detection and recognition from distance based on Deep Learning. *Advances in Digital Crime, Forensics, and Cyber Terrorism*, 144–160. doi:10.4018/978-1-6684-4558-7.ch006

Wang, J., Qiu, K., Peng, H., Fu, J., & Zhu, J. (2019, October). Ai coach: Deep human pose estimation and analysis for personalized athletic training assistance. In *Proceedings of the 27th ACM international conference on multimedia* (pp. 374-382). ACM. 10.1145/3343031.3350910

Wang, N., Li, J., & Zhang, L. (2019). Musical: Multi-scale image contextual attention learning for inpainting. In *Proceedings of the Twenty-Eighth International Joint Conference on Artificial Intelligence (IJCAI-19)* (pp. 3748–3754). IEEE.10.24963/ijcai.2019/520

Wang, P., Liu, D., Chen, J., Li, H., & Chan, C.-Y. (2021). Decision making for autonomous driving via augmented adversarial inverse reinforcement learning. *2021 IEEE International Conference on Robotics and Automation (ICRA)*. IEEE. 10.1109/ICRA48506.2021.9560907

Wang, X., & Yan, W. Q. (2020). Human gait recognition based on frameby-frame gait energy images and convolutional long short-term memory. *International Journal of Neural Systems*, *30*(01), 1950027. doi:10.1142/S0129065719500278 PMID:31747820

Wang, X., Zhang, J., & Yan, W. Q. (2020). Gait recognition using multichannel convolution neural networks. *Neural Computing & Applications*, *32*(18), 14275–14285. doi:10.1007/s00521-019-04524-y

Wang, Y., Liu, W., & Liu, X. (2022). Explainable AI techniques with application to NBA gameplay prediction. *Neurocomputing*, *483*, 59–71. doi:10.1016/j.neucom.2022.01.098

Wang, Y., & Lu, F. (2021). An adaptive boosting algorithm based on weighted feature selection and category classification confidence. *Applied Intelligence*, *51*(10), 6837–6858. doi:10.1007/s10489-020-02184-3

Wang, Y., & Wang, X. (2022). "Why Not Other Classes?": Towards Class-Contrastive Back-Propagation Explanations. *Advances in Neural Information Processing Systems, 35*, 9085–9097.

Wang, Y., Zhang, L., Zhang, D., & Li, W. (2018). Detecting phishing emails using a hierarchical classification framework. *IEEE Transactions on Information Forensics and Security, 13*(8), 1906–1919.

Wang, Z. J., Turko, R., Shaikh, O., Park, H., Das, N., Hohman, F., Kahng, M., & Polo Chau, D. H. (2020). CNN explainer: Learning convolutional neural networks with interactive visualization. *IEEE Transactions on Visualization and Computer Graphics, 27*(2), 1396–1406. doi:10.1109/TVCG.2020.3030418 PMID:33048723

Webb, G. I., & Zheng, Z. (2004). Multistrategy ensemble learning: Reducing error by combining ensemble learning methods. *IEEE Transactions on Knowledge and Data Engineering, 16*(8), 980–991. doi:10.1109/TKDE.2004.29

Wen, Y., Zhang, K., Li, Z., & Qiao, Y. (2016), A discriminative feature learning approach for deep face recognition. In ECCV (pp. 499-515). Springer. doi:10.1007/978-3-319-46478-7_31

Wildi, M., & Misheva, B. H. (2022). *A Time Series Approach to Explainability for Neural Nets with Applications to Risk-Management and Fraud Detection.* arXiv preprint arXiv:2212.02906.

Wiriyathammabhum, P., Summers-Stay, D., Ferm¨uller, C., & Aloimonos, Y. (2016). Computer vision and natural language processing: Recent approaches in multimedia and robotics. *ACM Computing Surveys, 49*(4), 1–44. doi:10.1145/3009906

Woo, S., Park, J., Lee, J.-Y., & Kweon, I. S. (2018). CBAM: Convolutional Block Attention Module. *Computer Vision – ECCV 2018.* Springer. doi:10.1007/978-3-030-01234-2_1

Woo, S., Park, J., Lee, J.-Y., & Kweon, I. S. (2018). Cbam: Convolutional block attention module. In *Proceedings of the european conference on computer vision (eccv)* (pp. 3–19). IEEE.

Woo, S., Park, J., Lee, J. Y., & Kweon, I. S. (2019). *CBAM: Convolutional block attention module.* Computer Vision.

Woschank, M., Rauch, E., & Zsifkovits, H. (2020). A review of further directions for artificial intelligence, machine learning, and deep learning in smart logistics. *Sustainability (Basel), 12*(9), 3760. doi:10.3390/su12093760

Wu, Q., Wang, W., Chen, X., & Li, W. (2019). Video Prediction with Temporal-Spatial Attention Mechanism and Deep Perceptual Similarity Branch. In 2019 *IEEE International Conference on Multimedia and Expo (ICME),* (pp. 1594-1599). IEEE. 10.1109/ICME.2019.00275

Wu, P., Li, H., Zeng, N., & Li, F. (2022). FMD-Yolo: An efficient face mask detection method for covid-19 prevention and control in public. *Image and Vision Computing, 117*, 104341. doi:10.1016/j.imavis.2021.104341 PMID:34848910

Xiaolin, L., & Yuwei, G. (2020). *Research on Text to Image Based on Generative Adversarial Network.* In 2020 2nd International Conference on Information Technology and Computer Application (ITCA), Guangzhou, China (pp. 330-334). 10.1109/ITCA52113.2020.00077

Xia, X., Wu, Y., & Wang, L. (2021). Real-time localized photorealistic video style transfer. *In Proceedings of the IEEE/CVF Winter Conference on Applications of Computer Vision*, (pp. 1089-1098). IEEE.

Xin, X., Karatzoglou, A., & Arapakis, I., & Joemon, M. (2020). Self-Supervised Reinforcement Learning for Recommender Systems. In *Proceedings of the 43rd International ACM SIGIR Conference on Research and Development in Information Retrieval.* ACM.

Xu, Y. & Singh, G. (2023). *Black-Box Targeted Reward Poisoning Attack Against Online Deep Reinforcement Learning*. arXiv Prepr. arXiv2305.10681.

Xu, Y., Zeng, Q., & Singh, G. (2022). *Efficient reward poisoning attacks on online deep reinforcement learning*. arXiv Prepr. arXiv2205.14842.

Xu, D. (2020). Adversarial counterfactual learning and evaluation for recommender system. *Advances in Neural Information Processing Systems*, *33*, 13515–13526.

Yang, G., Feng, W., Jin, J., Lei, Q., Li, X., Gui, G., & Wang, W. (2020). Face mask recognition system with Yolov5 based on image recognition. *2020 IEEE 6th International Conference on Computer and Communications (ICCC).* IEEE. doi:10.1109/ICCC51575.2020.9345042

Yang, Z., Zhang, K., Liang, Y., & Wang, J. (2017), Single image super-resolution with a parameter economic residual-like convolutional neural network. In MultiMedia Modeling, (pp. 353-364). Springer. doi:10.1007/978-3-319-51811-4_29

Yang, C. C. (2022). Explainable artificial intelligence for predictive modeling in healthcare. *Journal of Healthcare Informatics Research*, *6*(2), 228–239. doi:10.1007/s41666-022-00114-1 PMID:35194568

Yang, L., Zhang, R.-Y., Li, L., & Xie, X. (2021). Simam: A simple, parameterfree attention module for convolutional neural networks. In *International conference on machine learning* (pp. 11863–11874). IEEE.

Yan, S., Wang, C., Chen, W., & Lyu, J. (2022). Swin transformer-based GAN for multi-modal medical image translation. *Frontiers in Oncology*, *12*, 942511. doi:10.3389/fonc.2022.942511 PMID:36003791

Yan, W. (2023). *Computational Methods for Deep Learning: Theory, Algorithms, and Implementations*. Springer Nature. doi:10.1007/978-981-99-4823-9

Yan, W. Q. (2019). *Introduction to intelligent surveillance*. Springer. doi:10.1007/978-3-030-10713-0

Yan, W. Q. (2021). *Computational methods for deep learning: Theoretic, practice and applications*. Springer. doi:10.1007/978-3-030-61081-4

Yi, Z., Tang, Q., & Azizi, S. (2020). Contextual residual aggregation for ultra high-resolution image inpainting. In *Proceedings of the IEEE/CVF Conference on Computer Vision and Pattern Recognition* (pp. 7508–7517). IEEE. 10.1109/CVPR42600.2020.00753

Yi, Z., Zhang, H., Tan, P., & Gong, M. (2017). Dualgan: Unsupervised dual learning for image-to-image translation. In *Proceedings of the IEEE International Conference on Computer Vision* (pp. 2849-2857). IEEE. 10.1109/ICCV.2017.310

Yu, Z., & Yan, W. Q. (2020). Human action recognition using deep learning methods. In Ieee international conference on image and vision computing new zealand (ivcnz) (pp. 1–6). IEEE. doi:10.1109/IVCNZ51579.2020.9290594

Yuan, J., Liu, Z., & Wu, Y. (2011). Discriminative video pattern search for efficient action detection. *IEEE Transactions on Pattern Analysis and Machine Intelligence*, *33*(9), 1728–1743. doi:10.1109/TPAMI.2011.38 PMID:21339530

Yuan, Y., Liu, S., Zhang, J., Zhang, Y., Dong, C., & Lin, L. (2018). Unsupervised image super-resolution using cycle-in-cycle generative adversarial networks. In *2018 IEEE Conference on Computer Vision and Pattern Recognition Workshops*, (pp. 814-823). IEEE. 10.1109/CVPRW.2018.00113

Yu, J., & Zhang, W. (2021). Face mask wearing detection algorithm based on improved Yolo-V4. *Sensors (Basel)*, *21*(9), 3263. doi:10.3390/s21093263 PMID:34066802

Yun, L., Wang, D., & Li, L. (2023). Explainable multi-agent deep reinforcement learning for real-time demand response towards sustainable manufacturing. *Applied Energy*, *347*, 121324. doi:10.1016/j.apenergy.2023.121324

Zalevsky, Z., Buller, G. S., Chen, T., Cohen, M., & Barton-Grimley, R. (2021). Light detection and ranging (lidar): Introduction. *Journal of the Optical Society of America. A, Optics, Image Science, and Vision*, *38*(11), LID1–LID2. doi:10.1364/JOSAA.445792 PMID:34807027

Zehra, N., Azeem, S. H., & Farhan, M. (2021). Human activity recognition through ensemble learning of multiple convolutional neural networks. *Annual Conference on Information Sciences and Systems (CISS)*. IEEE. 10.1109/CISS50987.2021.9400290

Zeiler, M. D., & Fergus, R. (2014). Visualizing and understanding convolutional networks. In ECCV (pp. 818-833). doi:10.1007/978-3-319-10590-1_53

Zhai, P., Luo, J., Dong, Z., Zhang, L., Wang, S., & Yang, D. (2022). Robust adversarial reinforcement learning with dissipation inequation constraint. *Proceedings of the AAAI Conference on Artificial Intelligence*, (pp. 5431–5439). AAAI. 10.1609/aaai.v36i5.20481

Zhang, H., Chen, H., Boning, D., & Hsieh, C.-J. (2021). *Robust reinforcement learning on state observations with learned optimal adversary.* arXiv Prepr. arXiv2101.08452.

Zhang, X., Chen, Y., Zhu, X., & Sun, W. (2021). Robust policy gradient against strong data corruption. International Conference on Machine Learning. PMLR, (pp. 12391–12401). IEEE.

Zhang, X., Ma, Y., Singla, A., & Zhu, X. (2020). Adaptive reward-poisoning attacks against reinforcement learning. *International Conference on Machine Learning*. PMLR.

Zhang, D. (2023). STA-YOLOv7: Swin-Transformer-Enabled YOLOv7 for Road Damage Detection. *Computer Science and Application.*, *13*(5), 1157–1165. doi:10.12677/CSA.2023.135113

Zhang, H., Chen, H., Xiao, C., Li, B., Liu, M., Boning, D., & Hsieh, C.-J. (2020). Robust deep reinforcement learning against adversarial perturbations on state observations. *Advances in Neural Information Processing Systems*, *33*, 21024–21037.

Zhang, H., Xu, T., Li, H., Zhang, S., Wang, X., Huang, X., & Metaxas, D. (2017). StackGAN: Text to Photo-Realistic Image Synthesis with Stacked Generative Adversarial Networks. 2017 *IEEE International Conference on Computer Vision (ICCV),* (pp. 5908–5916). IEEE. 10.1109/ICCV.2017.629

Zhang, K., Zuo, W., Gu, S., & Zhang, L. (2017). Learning deep CNN denoiser prior for image restoration. In *Proceedings of the IEEE Conference on Computer Vision and Pattern Recognition*, (pp. 3929-3938). IEEE. 10.1109/CVPR.2017.300

Zhang, T. (2019). ANODEV2: A coupled neural ODE framework. *Advances in Neural Information Processing Systems*, 32.

Zhang, W., Ding, Y. X., Tang, Y., & Zhao, B. (2011). *Malicious web page detection based on on-line learning algorithm.* In *Proceedings of the 2011 International Conference on Machine Learning and Cybernetics*, Guilin, China. 10.1109/ICMLC.2011.6016954

Zhang, Y. (2021). XAI Evaluation: Evaluating Black-Box Model Explanations for Prediction. In *2021 II International Conference on Neural Networks and Neurotechnologies (NeuroNT)*. IEEE. 10.1109/NeuroNT53022.2021.9472817

Zhang, Y., Wu, S., Li, Q., & Hu, J. (2020). Detecting phishing emails with lexical and syntactic features. *Information Sciences*, *509*, 48–60.

Zhang, Z., Luo, P., Loy, C. C., & Tang, X. (2015). Learning social relation traits from face images. *IEEE International Conference on Computer Vision (ICCV).* IEEE. 10.1109/ICCV.2015.414

Zhang, Z., Lu, X., Cao, G., Yang, Y., Jiao, L., & Liu, F. (2021). ViT-YOLO: Transformer-Based YOLO for Object Detection. *IEEE/CVF International Conference on Computer Vision Workshops (ICCVW),* (pp. 2799–2808). IEEE. 10.1109/ICCVW54120.2021.00314

Zhao, L., Mo, Q., & Lin, S. (2020). Uctgan: Diverse image inpainting based on unsupervised cross-space translation. In *Proceedings of the IEEE/CVF Conference on Computer Vision and Pattern Recognition* (pp. 5741–5750). IEEE. 10.1109/CVPR42600.2020.00578

Zhao, Y. (2022). Deep Learning of 3D High-Precision Model Digital Engraving of Next-Generation Games Based on Artificial Intelligence. *IEEE Access : Practical Innovations, Open Solutions*, *10*, 10976–10984.

Zhou, D., Fang, J., Song, X., Guan, C., Yin, J., Dai, Y., & Yang, R. (2019). IOU loss for 2D/3D object detection. *2019 International Conference on 3D Vision (3DV)*. IEEE. doi:10.1109/3DV.2019.00019

Zhou, H., Nguyen, M., Yan, W. (2023) Computational analysis of table tennis matches from real-time videos using deep learning. *PSIVT 2023*. IEEE.

Zhou, L., Wei, S., Cui, Z., & Ding, W. (2019). YOLO-RD: A lightweight object detection network for range doppler radar images. *IOP Conference Series. Materials Science and Engineering*, *563*(4), 042027. doi:10.1088/1757-899X/563/4/042027

Zhou, Y.-F., Jiang, R.-H., Wu, X., He, J.-Y., Weng, S., & Peng, Q. (2019). BranchGAN: Unsupervised mutual image-to-image transfer with a single encoder and dual decoders. *IEEE Transactions on Multimedia*, *21*(12), 3136–3149. doi:10.1109/TMM.2019.2920613

Zhou, Y., Zhang, R., Gu, J., Tensmeyer, C., Yu, T., Chen, C., Xu, J., & Sun, T. (2022). TiGAN: Text-Based Interactive Image Generation and Manipulation. *Proceedings of the AAAI Conference on Artificial Intelligence*, *36*(3), 3580–3588. doi:10.1609/aaai.v36i3.20270

Zhu, J. Y., Krähenbühl, P., Shechtman, E., & Efros, A. A. (2016). Generative visual manipulation on the natural image manifold. In *Proceedings of the 14th European Conference on Computer Vision (ECCV 2016)* (pp. 597-613). Amsterdam, The Netherlands: Springer International Publishing. 10.1007/978-3-319-46454-1_36

Zhu, J.-Y., Park, T., Isola, P., & Efros, A. A. (2017). Unpaired Image-to-Image Translation Using Cycle-Consistent Adversarial Networks. *2017 IEEE International Conference on Computer Vision (ICCV)*, (pp. 2242–2251). IEEE. 10.1109/ICCV.2017.244

Zhu, Y., & Yan, W. (2022). *Ski fall detection from digital images using deep learning*. ACM ICCCV. doi:10.1145/3561613.3561625

Zou, Z., Chen, K., Shi, Z., & Guo, Y., & Ye, J. (2023). Object detection in 20 years: A survey. *Proceedings of the IEEE, 111*(3), 257–276. 10.1109/JPROC.2023.3238524

Zou, L., Xia, L., Ding, Z., Song, J., Liu, W., & Yin, D. (2019). Reinforcement Learning to Optimize Long-Term User Engagement in Recommender Systems. In *Proceedings of the 25th ACM SIGKDD International Conference on Knowledge Discovery & Data Mining*. ACM. 10.1145/3292500.3330668

Related References

To continue our tradition of advancing information science and technology research, we have compiled a list of recommended IGI Global readings. These references will provide additional information and guidance to further enrich your knowledge and assist you with your own research and future publications.

Aasi, P., Rusu, L., & Vieru, D. (2017). The Role of Culture in IT Governance Five Focus Areas: A Literature Review. *International Journal of IT/Business Alignment and Governance, 8*(2), 42-61. https://doi.org/ doi:10.4018/IJITBAG.2017070103

Abdrabo, A. A. (2018). Egypt's Knowledge-Based Development: Opportunities, Challenges, and Future Possibilities. In A. Alraouf (Ed.), *Knowledge-Based Urban Development in the Middle East* (pp. 80–101). Hershey, PA: IGI Global. doi:10.4018/978-1-5225-3734-2.ch005

Abu Doush, I., & Alhami, I. (2018). Evaluating the Accessibility of Computer Laboratories, Libraries, and Websites in Jordanian Universities and Colleges. *International Journal of Information Systems and Social Change*, *9*(2), 44–60. doi:10.4018/IJISSC.2018040104

Adegbore, A. M., Quadri, M. O., & Oyewo, O. R. (2018). A Theoretical Approach to the Adoption of Electronic Resource Management Systems (ERMS) in Nigerian University Libraries. In A. Tella & T. Kwanya (Eds.), *Handbook of Research on Managing Intellectual Property in Digital Libraries* (pp. 292–311). Hershey, PA: IGI Global. doi:10.4018/978-1-5225-3093-0.ch015

Afolabi, O. A. (2018). Myths and Challenges of Building an Effective Digital Library in Developing Nations: An African Perspective. In A. Tella & T. Kwanya (Eds.), *Handbook of Research on Managing Intellectual Property in Digital Libraries* (pp. 51–79). Hershey, PA: IGI Global. doi:10.4018/978-1-5225-3093-0.ch004

Agarwal, P., Kurian, R., & Gupta, R. K. (2022). Additive Manufacturing Feature Taxonomy and Placement of Parts in AM Enclosure. In S. Salunkhe, H. Hussein, & J. Davim (Eds.), *Applications of Artificial Intelligence in Additive Manufacturing* (pp. 138–176). IGI Global. https://doi.org/10.4018/978-1-7998-8516-0.ch007

Al-Alawi, A. I., Al-Hammam, A. H., Al-Alawi, S. S., & AlAlawi, E. I. (2021). The Adoption of E-Wallets: Current Trends and Future Outlook. In Y. Albastaki, A. Razzaque, & A. Sarea (Eds.), *Innovative Strategies for Implementing FinTech in Banking* (pp. 242–262). IGI Global. https://doi.org/10.4018/978-1-7998-3257-7.ch015

Alsharo, M. (2017). Attitudes Towards Cloud Computing Adoption in Emerging Economies. *International Journal of Cloud Applications and Computing*, *7*(3), 44–58. doi:10.4018/IJCAC.2017070102

Amer, T. S., & Johnson, T. L. (2017). Information Technology Progress Indicators: Research Employing Psychological Frameworks. In A. Mesquita (Ed.), *Research Paradigms and Contemporary Perspectives on Human-Technology Interaction* (pp. 168–186). Hershey, PA: IGI Global. doi:10.4018/978-1-5225-1868-6.ch008

Andreeva, A., & Yolova, G. (2021). Liability in Labor Legislation: New Challenges Related to the Use of Artificial Intelligence. In B. Vassileva & M. Zwilling (Eds.), *Responsible AI and Ethical Issues for Businesses and Governments* (pp. 214–232). IGI Global. https://doi.org/10.4018/978-1-7998-4285-9.ch012

Anohah, E. (2017). Paradigm and Architecture of Computing Augmented Learning Management System for Computer Science Education. *International Journal of Online Pedagogy and Course Design*, *7*(2), 60–70. doi:10.4018/IJOPCD.2017040105

Anohah, E., & Suhonen, J. (2017). Trends of Mobile Learning in Computing Education from 2006 to 2014: A Systematic Review of Research Publications. *International Journal of Mobile and Blended Learning*, *9*(1), 16–33. doi:10.4018/IJMBL.2017010102

Arbaiza, C. S., Huerta, H. V., & Rodriguez, C. R. (2021). Contributions to the Technological Adoption Model for the Peruvian Agro-Export Sector. *International Journal of E-Adoption*, *13*(1), 1–17. https://doi.org/10.4018/IJEA.2021010101

Bailey, E. K. (2017). Applying Learning Theories to Computer Technology Supported Instruction. In M. Grassetti & S. Brookby (Eds.), *Advancing Next-Generation Teacher Education through Digital Tools and Applications* (pp. 61–81). Hershey, PA: IGI Global. doi:10.4018/978-1-5225-0965-3.ch004

Baker, J. D. (2021). Introduction to Machine Learning as a New Methodological Framework for Performance Assessment. In M. Bocarnea, B. Winston, & D. Dean (Eds.), *Handbook of Research on Advancements in Organizational Data Collection and Measurements: Strategies for Addressing Attitudes, Beliefs, and Behaviors* (pp. 326–342). IGI Global. https://doi.org/10.4018/978-1-7998-7665-6.ch021

Banerjee, S., Sing, T. Y., Chowdhury, A. R., & Anwar, H. (2018). Let's Go Green: Towards a Taxonomy of Green Computing Enablers for Business Sustainability. In M. Khosrow-Pour (Ed.), *Green Computing Strategies for Competitive Advantage and Business Sustainability* (pp. 89–109). Hershey, PA: IGI Global. doi:10.4018/978-1-5225-5017-4.ch005

Basham, R. (2018). Information Science and Technology in Crisis Response and Management. In M. Khosrow-Pour, D.B.A. (Ed.), Encyclopedia of Information Science and Technology, Fourth Edition (pp. 1407-1418). Hershey, PA: IGI Global. doi:10.4018/978-1-5225-2255-3.ch121

Batyashe, T., & Iyamu, T. (2018). Architectural Framework for the Implementation of Information Technology Governance in Organisations. In M. Khosrow-Pour, D.B.A. (Ed.), Encyclopedia of Information Science and Technology, Fourth Edition (pp. 810-819). Hershey, PA: IGI Global. doi:10.4018/978-1-5225-2255-3.ch070

Bekleyen, N., & Çelik, S. (2017). Attitudes of Adult EFL Learners towards Preparing for a Language Test via CALL. In D. Tafazoli & M. Romero (Eds.), *Multiculturalism and Technology-Enhanced Language Learning* (pp. 214–229). Hershey, PA: IGI Global. doi:10.4018/978-1-5225-1882-2.ch013

Bergeron, F., Croteau, A., Uwizeyemungu, S., & Raymond, L. (2017). A Framework for Research on Information Technology Governance in SMEs. In S. De Haes & W. Van Grembergen (Eds.), *Strategic IT Governance and Alignment in Business Settings* (pp. 53–81). Hershey, PA: IGI Global. doi:10.4018/978-1-5225-0861-8.ch003

Bhardwaj, M., Shukla, N., & Sharma, A. (2021). Improvement and Reduction of Clustering Overhead in Mobile Ad Hoc Network With Optimum Stable Bunching Algorithm. In S. Kumar, M. Trivedi, P. Ranjan, & A. Punhani (Eds.), *Evolution of Software-Defined Networking Foundations for IoT and 5G Mobile Networks* (pp. 139–158). IGI Global. https://doi.org/10.4018/978-1-7998-4685-7.ch008

Bhatt, G. D., Wang, Z., & Rodger, J. A. (2017). Information Systems Capabilities and Their Effects on Competitive Advantages: A Study of Chinese Companies. *Information Resources Management Journal*, *30*(3), 41–57. doi:10.4018/IRMJ.2017070103

Bhattacharya, A. (2021). Blockchain, Cybersecurity, and Industry 4.0. In A. Tyagi, G. Rekha, & N. Sreenath (Eds.), *Opportunities and Challenges for Blockchain Technology in Autonomous Vehicles* (pp. 210–244). IGI Global. https://doi.org/10.4018/978-1-7998-3295-9.ch013

Bhyan, P., Shrivastava, B., & Kumar, N. (2022). Requisite Sustainable Development Contemplating Buildings: Economic and Environmental Sustainability. In A. Hussain, K. Tiwari, & A. Gupta (Eds.), *Addressing Environmental Challenges Through Spatial Planning* (pp. 269–288). IGI Global. https://doi.org/10.4018/978-1-7998-8331-9.ch014

Boido, C., Davico, P., & Spallone, R. (2021). Digital Tools Aimed to Represent Urban Survey. In M. Khosrow-Pour D.B.A. (Ed.), *Encyclopedia of Information Science and Technology, Fifth Edition* (pp. 1181-1195). IGI Global. https://doi.org/10.4018/978-1-7998-3479-3.ch082

Borkar, P. S., Chanana, P. U., Atwal, S. K., Londe, T. G., & Dalal, Y. D. (2021). The Replacement of HMI (Human-Machine Interface) in Industry Using Single Interface Through IoT. In R. Raut & A. Mihovska (Eds.), *Examining the Impact of Deep Learning and IoT on Multi-Industry Applications* (pp. 195–208). IGI Global. https://doi.org/10.4018/978-1-7998-7511-6.ch011

Brahmane, A. V., & Krishna, C. B. (2021). Rider Chaotic Biography Optimization-driven Deep Stacked Auto-encoder for Big Data Classification Using Spark Architecture: Rider Chaotic Biography Optimization. *International Journal of Web Services Research, 18*(3), 42–62. https://doi.org/10.4018/ijwsr.2021070103

Burcoff, A., & Shamir, L. (2017). Computer Analysis of Pablo Picasso's Artistic Style. *International Journal of Art, Culture and Design Technologies, 6*(1), 1–18. doi:10.4018/IJACDT.2017010101

Byker, E. J. (2017). I Play I Learn: Introducing Technological Play Theory. In C. Martin & D. Polly (Eds.), *Handbook of Research on Teacher Education and Professional Development* (pp. 297–306). Hershey, PA: IGI Global. doi:10.4018/978-1-5225-1067-3.ch016

Calongne, C. M., Stricker, A. G., Truman, B., & Arenas, F. J. (2017). Cognitive Apprenticeship and Computer Science Education in Cyberspace: Reimagining the Past. In A. Stricker, C. Calongne, B. Truman, & F. Arenas (Eds.), *Integrating an Awareness of Selfhood and Society into Virtual Learning* (pp. 180–197). Hershey, PA: IGI Global. doi:10.4018/978-1-5225-2182-2.ch013

Carneiro, A. D. (2017). Defending Information Networks in Cyberspace: Some Notes on Security Needs. In M. Dawson, D. Kisku, P. Gupta, J. Sing, & W. Li (Eds.), Developing Next-Generation Countermeasures for Homeland Security Threat Prevention (pp. 354-375). Hershey, PA: IGI Global. https://doi.org/ doi:10.4018/978-1-5225-0703-1.ch016

Carvalho, W. F., & Zarate, L. (2021). Causal Feature Selection. In A. Azevedo & M. Santos (Eds.), *Integration Challenges for Analytics, Business Intelligence, and Data Mining* (pp. 145-160). IGI Global. https://doi.org/10.4018/978-1-7998-5781-5.ch007

Chase, J. P., & Yan, Z. (2017). Affect in Statistics Cognition. In *Assessing and Measuring Statistics Cognition in Higher Education Online Environments: Emerging Research and Opportunities* (pp. 144–187). Hershey, PA: IGI Global. doi:10.4018/978-1-5225-2420-5.ch005

Chatterjee, A., Roy, S., & Shrivastava, R. (2021). A Machine Learning Approach to Prevent Cancer. In G. Rani & P. Tiwari (Eds.), *Handbook of Research on Disease Prediction Through Data Analytics and Machine Learning* (pp. 112–141). IGI Global. https://doi.org/10.4018/978-1-7998-2742-9.ch007

Cifci, M. A. (2021). Optimizing WSNs for CPS Using Machine Learning Techniques. In A. Luhach & A. Elçi (Eds.), *Artificial Intelligence Paradigms for Smart Cyber-Physical Systems* (pp. 204–228). IGI Global. https://doi.org/10.4018/978-1-7998-5101-1.ch010

Cimermanova, I. (2017). Computer-Assisted Learning in Slovakia. In D. Tafazoli & M. Romero (Eds.), *Multiculturalism and Technology-Enhanced Language Learning* (pp. 252–270). Hershey, PA: IGI Global. doi:10.4018/978-1-5225-1882-2.ch015

Cipolla-Ficarra, F. V., & Cipolla-Ficarra, M. (2018). Computer Animation for Ingenious Revival. In F. Cipolla-Ficarra, M. Ficarra, M. Cipolla-Ficarra, A. Quiroga, J. Alma, & J. Carré (Eds.), *Technology-Enhanced Human Interaction in Modern Society* (pp. 159–181). Hershey, PA: IGI Global. doi:10.4018/978-1-5225-3437-2.ch008

Cockrell, S., Damron, T. S., Melton, A. M., & Smith, A. D. (2018). Offshoring IT. In M. Khosrow-Pour, D.B.A. (Ed.), Encyclopedia of Information Science and Technology, Fourth Edition (pp. 5476-5489). Hershey, PA: IGI Global. https://doi.org/ doi:10.4018/978-1-5225-2255-3.ch476

Coffey, J. W. (2018). Logic and Proof in Computer Science: Categories and Limits of Proof Techniques. In J. Horne (Ed.), *Philosophical Perceptions on Logic and Order* (pp. 218–240). Hershey, PA: IGI Global. doi:10.4018/978-1-5225-2443-4.ch007

Dale, M. (2017). Re-Thinking the Challenges of Enterprise Architecture Implementation. In M. Tavana (Ed.), *Enterprise Information Systems and the Digitalization of Business Functions* (pp. 205–221). Hershey, PA: IGI Global. doi:10.4018/978-1-5225-2382-6.ch009

Das, A., & Mohanty, M. N. (2021). An Useful Review on Optical Character Recognition for Smart Era Generation. In A. Tyagi (Ed.), *Multimedia and Sensory Input for Augmented, Mixed, and Virtual Reality* (pp. 1–41). IGI Global. https://doi.org/10.4018/978-1-7998-4703-8.ch001

Dash, A. K., & Mohapatra, P. (2021). A Survey on Prematurity Detection of Diabetic Retinopathy Based on Fundus Images Using Deep Learning Techniques. In S. Saxena & S. Paul (Eds.), *Deep Learning Applications in Medical Imaging* (pp. 140–155). IGI Global. https://doi.org/10.4018/978-1-7998-5071-7.ch006

De Maere, K., De Haes, S., & von Kutzschenbach, M. (2017). CIO Perspectives on Organizational Learning within the Context of IT Governance. *International Journal of IT/Business Alignment and Governance, 8*(1), 32-47. https://doi.org/doi:10.4018/IJITBAG.2017010103

Demir, K., Çaka, C., Yaman, N. D., İslamoğlu, H., & Kuzu, A. (2018). Examining the Current Definitions of Computational Thinking. In H. Ozcinar, G. Wong, & H. Ozturk (Eds.), *Teaching Computational Thinking in Primary Education* (pp. 36–64). Hershey, PA: IGI Global. doi:10.4018/978-1-5225-3200-2.ch003

Deng, X., Hung, Y., & Lin, C. D. (2017). Design and Analysis of Computer Experiments. In S. Saha, A. Mandal, A. Narasimhamurthy, S. V, & S. Sangam (Eds.), Handbook of Research on Applied Cybernetics and Systems Science (pp. 264-279). Hershey, PA: IGI Global. doi:10.4018/978-1-5225-2498-4.ch013

Denner, J., Martinez, J., & Thiry, H. (2017). Strategies for Engaging Hispanic/Latino Youth in the US in Computer Science. In Y. Rankin & J. Thomas (Eds.), *Moving Students of Color from Consumers to Producers of Technology* (pp. 24–48). Hershey, PA: IGI Global. doi:10.4018/978-1-5225-2005-4.ch002

Devi, A. (2017). Cyber Crime and Cyber Security: A Quick Glance. In R. Kumar, P. Pattnaik, & P. Pandey (Eds.), *Detecting and Mitigating Robotic Cyber Security Risks* (pp. 160–171). Hershey, PA: IGI Global. doi:10.4018/978-1-5225-2154-9.ch011

Dhaya, R., & Kanthavel, R. (2022). Futuristic Research Perspectives of IoT Platforms. In D. Jeya Mala (Ed.), *Integrating AI in IoT Analytics on the Cloud for Healthcare Applications* (pp. 258–275). IGI Global. doi:10.4018/978-1-7998-9132-1.ch015

Doyle, D. J., & Fahy, P. J. (2018). Interactivity in Distance Education and Computer-Aided Learning, With Medical Education Examples. In M. Khosrow-Pour, D.B.A. (Ed.), Encyclopedia of Information Science and Technology, Fourth Edition (pp. 5829-5840). Hershey, PA: IGI Global. https://doi.org/ doi:10.4018/978-1-5225-2255-3.ch507

Eklund, P. (2021). Reinforcement Learning in Social Media Marketing. In B. Christiansen & T. Škrinjarić (Eds.), *Handbook of Research on Applied AI for International Business and Marketing Applications* (pp. 30–48). IGI Global. https://doi.org/10.4018/978-1-7998-5077-9.ch003

El Ghandour, N., Benaissa, M., & Lebbah, Y. (2021). An Integer Linear Programming-Based Method for the Extraction of Ontology Alignment. *International Journal of Information Technology and Web Engineering*, *16*(2), 25–44. https://doi.org/10.4018/IJITWE.2021040102

Elias, N. I., & Walker, T. W. (2017). Factors that Contribute to Continued Use of E-Training among Healthcare Professionals. In F. Topor (Ed.), *Handbook of Research on Individualism and Identity in the Globalized Digital Age* (pp. 403–429). Hershey, PA: IGI Global. doi:10.4018/978-1-5225-0522-8.ch018

Fisher, R. L. (2018). Computer-Assisted Indian Matrimonial Services. In M. Khosrow-Pour, D.B.A. (Ed.), Encyclopedia of Information Science and Technology, Fourth Edition (pp. 4136-4145). Hershey, PA: IGI Global. doi:10.4018/978-1-5225-2255-3.ch358

Galiautdinov, R. (2021). Nonlinear Filtering in Artificial Neural Network Applications in Business and Engineering. In Q. Do (Ed.), *Artificial Neural Network Applications in Business and Engineering* (pp. 1–23). IGI Global. https://doi.org/10.4018/978-1-7998-3238-6.ch001

Gardner-McCune, C., & Jimenez, Y. (2017). Historical App Developers: Integrating CS into K-12 through Cross-Disciplinary Projects. In Y. Rankin & J. Thomas (Eds.), *Moving Students of Color from Consumers to Producers of Technology* (pp. 85–112). Hershey, PA: IGI Global. doi:10.4018/978-1-5225-2005-4.ch005

Garg, P. K. (2021). The Internet of Things-Based Technologies. In S. Kumar, M. Trivedi, P. Ranjan, & A. Punhani (Eds.), *Evolution of Software-Defined Networking Foundations for IoT and 5G Mobile Networks* (pp. 37–65). IGI Global. https://doi.org/10.4018/978-1-7998-4685-7.ch003

Garg, T., & Bharti, M. (2021). Congestion Control Protocols for UWSNs. In N. Goyal, L. Sapra, & J. Sandhu (Eds.), *Energy-Efficient Underwater Wireless Communications and Networking* (pp. 85–100). IGI Global. https://doi.org/10.4018/978-1-7998-3640-7.ch006

Gauttier, S. (2021). A Primer on Q-Method and the Study of Technology. In M. Khosrow-Pour D.B.A. (Eds.), *Encyclopedia of Information Science and Technology, Fifth Edition* (pp. 1746-1756). IGI Global. https://doi.org/10.4018/978-1-7998-3479-3.ch120

Ghafele, R., & Gibert, B. (2018). Open Growth: The Economic Impact of Open Source Software in the USA. In M. Khosrow-Pour (Ed.), *Optimizing Contemporary Application and Processes in Open Source Software* (pp. 164–197). Hershey, PA: IGI Global. doi:10.4018/978-1-5225-5314-4.ch007

Ghobakhloo, M., & Azar, A. (2018). Information Technology Resources, the Organizational Capability of Lean-Agile Manufacturing, and Business Performance. *Information Resources Management Journal, 31*(2), 47–74. doi:10.4018/IRMJ.2018040103

Gikandi, J. W. (2017). Computer-Supported Collaborative Learning and Assessment: A Strategy for Developing Online Learning Communities in Continuing Education. In J. Keengwe & G. Onchwari (Eds.), *Handbook of Research on Learner-Centered Pedagogy in Teacher Education and Professional Development* (pp. 309–333). Hershey, PA: IGI Global. doi:10.4018/978-1-5225-0892-2.ch017

Gokhale, A. A., & Machina, K. F. (2017). Development of a Scale to Measure Attitudes toward Information Technology. In L. Tomei (Ed.), *Exploring the New Era of Technology-Infused Education* (pp. 49–64). Hershey, PA: IGI Global. doi:10.4018/978-1-5225-1709-2.ch004

Goswami, J. K., Jalal, S., Negi, C. S., & Jalal, A. S. (2022). A Texture Features-Based Robust Facial Expression Recognition. *International Journal of Computer Vision and Image Processing, 12*(1), 1–15. https://doi.org/10.4018/IJCVIP.2022010103

Hafeez-Baig, A., Gururajan, R., & Wickramasinghe, N. (2017). Readiness as a Novel Construct of Readiness Acceptance Model (RAM) for the Wireless Handheld Technology. In N. Wickramasinghe (Ed.), *Handbook of Research on Healthcare Administration and Management* (pp. 578–595). Hershey, PA: IGI Global. doi:10.4018/978-1-5225-0920-2.ch035

Hanafizadeh, P., Ghandchi, S., & Asgarimehr, M. (2017). Impact of Information Technology on Lifestyle: A Literature Review and Classification. *International Journal of Virtual Communities and Social Networking*, *9*(2), 1–23. doi:10.4018/IJVCSN.2017040101

Haseski, H. İ., Ilic, U., & Tuğtekin, U. (2018). Computational Thinking in Educational Digital Games: An Assessment Tool Proposal. In H. Ozcinar, G. Wong, & H. Ozturk (Eds.), *Teaching Computational Thinking in Primary Education* (pp. 256–287). Hershey, PA: IGI Global. doi:10.4018/978-1-5225-3200-2.ch013

Hee, W. J., Jalleh, G., Lai, H., & Lin, C. (2017). E-Commerce and IT Projects: Evaluation and Management Issues in Australian and Taiwanese Hospitals. *International Journal of Public Health Management and Ethics*, *2*(1), 69–90. doi:10.4018/IJPHME.2017010104

Hernandez, A. A. (2017). Green Information Technology Usage: Awareness and Practices of Philippine IT Professionals. *International Journal of Enterprise Information Systems*, *13*(4), 90–103. doi:10.4018/IJEIS.2017100106

Hernandez, M. A., Marin, E. C., Garcia-Rodriguez, J., Azorin-Lopez, J., & Cazorla, M. (2017). Automatic Learning Improves Human-Robot Interaction in Productive Environments: A Review. *International Journal of Computer Vision and Image Processing*, *7*(3), 65–75. doi:10.4018/IJCVIP.2017070106

Hirota, A. (2021). Design of Narrative Creation in Innovation: "Signature Story" and Two Types of Pivots. In T. Ogata & J. Ono (Eds.), *Bridging the Gap Between AI, Cognitive Science, and Narratology With Narrative Generation* (pp. 363–376). IGI Global. https://doi.org/10.4018/978-1-7998-4864-6.ch012

Hond, D., Asgari, H., Jeffery, D., & Newman, M. (2021). An Integrated Process for Verifying Deep Learning Classifiers Using Dataset Dissimilarity Measures. *International Journal of Artificial Intelligence and Machine Learning*, *11*(2), 1–21. https://doi.org/10.4018/IJAIML.289536

Horne-Popp, L. M., Tessone, E. B., & Welker, J. (2018). If You Build It, They Will Come: Creating a Library Statistics Dashboard for Decision-Making. In L. Costello & M. Powers (Eds.), *Developing In-House Digital Tools in Library Spaces* (pp. 177–203). Hershey, PA: IGI Global. doi:10.4018/978-1-5225-2676-6.ch009

Hu, H., Hu, P. J., & Al-Gahtani, S. S. (2017). User Acceptance of Computer Technology at Work in Arabian Culture: A Model Comparison Approach. In M. Khosrow-Pour (Ed.), *Handbook of Research on Technology Adoption, Social Policy, and Global Integration* (pp. 205–228). Hershey, PA: IGI Global. doi:10.4018/978-1-5225-2668-1.ch011

Huang, C., Sun, Y., & Fuh, C. (2022). Vehicle License Plate Recognition With Deep Learning. In C. Chen, W. Yang, & L. Chen (Eds.), *Technologies to Advance Automation in Forensic Science and Criminal Investigation* (pp. 161-219). IGI Global. https://doi.org/10.4018/978-1-7998-8386-9.ch009

Ifinedo, P. (2017). Using an Extended Theory of Planned Behavior to Study Nurses' Adoption of Healthcare Information Systems in Nova Scotia. *International Journal of Technology Diffusion*, *8*(1), 1–17. doi:10.4018/IJTD.2017010101

Ilie, V., & Sneha, S. (2018). A Three Country Study for Understanding Physicians' Engagement With Electronic Information Resources Pre and Post System Implementation. *Journal of Global Information Management*, *26*(2), 48–73. doi:10.4018/JGIM.2018040103

Ilo, P. I., Nkiko, C., Ugwu, C. I., Ekere, J. N., Izuagbe, R., & Fagbohun, M. O. (2021). Prospects and Challenges of Web 3.0 Technologies Application in the Provision of Library Services. In M. Khosrow-Pour D.B.A. (Ed.), *Encyclopedia of Information Science and Technology, Fifth Edition* (pp. 1767-1781). IGI Global. https://doi.org/10.4018/978-1-7998-3479-3.ch122

Inoue-Smith, Y. (2017). Perceived Ease in Using Technology Predicts Teacher Candidates' Preferences for Online Resources. *International Journal of Online Pedagogy and Course Design*, *7*(3), 17–28. doi:10.4018/IJOPCD.2017070102

Islam, A. Y. (2017). Technology Satisfaction in an Academic Context: Moderating Effect of Gender. In A. Mesquita (Ed.), *Research Paradigms and Contemporary Perspectives on Human-Technology Interaction* (pp. 187–211). Hershey, PA: IGI Global. doi:10.4018/978-1-5225-1868-6.ch009

Jagdale, S. C., Hable, A. A., & Chabukswar, A. R. (2021). Protocol Development in Clinical Trials for Healthcare Management. In M. Khosrow-Pour D.B.A. (Ed.), *Encyclopedia of Information Science and Technology, Fifth Edition* (pp. 1797-1814). IGI Global. https://doi.org/10.4018/978-1-7998-3479-3.ch124

Jamil, G. L., & Jamil, C. C. (2017). Information and Knowledge Management Perspective Contributions for Fashion Studies: Observing Logistics and Supply Chain Management Processes. In G. Jamil, A. Soares, & C. Pessoa (Eds.), *Handbook of Research on Information Management for Effective Logistics and Supply Chains* (pp. 199–221). Hershey, PA: IGI Global. doi:10.4018/978-1-5225-0973-8.ch011

Jamil, M. I., & Almunawar, M. N. (2021). Importance of Digital Literacy and Hindrance Brought About by Digital Divide. In M. Khosrow-Pour D.B.A. (Ed.), *Encyclopedia of Information Science and Technology, Fifth Edition* (pp. 1683-1698). IGI Global. https://doi.org/10.4018/978-1-7998-3479-3.ch116

Janakova, M. (2018). Big Data and Simulations for the Solution of Controversies in Small Businesses. In M. Khosrow-Pour, D.B.A. (Ed.), Encyclopedia of Information Science and Technology, Fourth Edition (pp. 6907-6915). Hershey, PA: IGI Global. doi:10.4018/978-1-5225-2255-3.ch598

Jhawar, A., & Garg, S. K. (2018). Logistics Improvement by Investment in Information Technology Using System Dynamics. In A. Azar & S. Vaidyanathan (Eds.), *Advances in System Dynamics and Control* (pp. 528–567). Hershey, PA: IGI Global. doi:10.4018/978-1-5225-4077-9.ch017

Kalelioğlu, F., Gülbahar, Y., & Doğan, D. (2018). Teaching How to Think Like a Programmer: Emerging Insights. In H. Ozcinar, G. Wong, & H. Ozturk (Eds.), *Teaching Computational Thinking in Primary Education* (pp. 18–35). Hershey, PA: IGI Global. doi:10.4018/978-1-5225-3200-2.ch002

Kamberi, S. (2017). A Girls-Only Online Virtual World Environment and its Implications for Game-Based Learning. In A. Stricker, C. Calongne, B. Truman, & F. Arenas (Eds.), *Integrating an Awareness of Selfhood and Society into Virtual Learning* (pp. 74–95). Hershey, PA: IGI Global. doi:10.4018/978-1-5225-2182-2.ch006

Kamel, S., & Rizk, N. (2017). ICT Strategy Development: From Design to Implementation – Case of Egypt. In C. Howard & K. Hargiss (Eds.), *Strategic Information Systems and Technologies in Modern Organizations* (pp. 239–257). Hershey, PA: IGI Global. doi:10.4018/978-1-5225-1680-4.ch010

Kamel, S. H. (2018). The Potential Role of the Software Industry in Supporting Economic Development. In M. Khosrow-Pour, D.B.A. (Ed.), Encyclopedia of Information Science and Technology, Fourth Edition (pp. 7259-7269). Hershey, PA: IGI Global. doi:10.4018/978-1-5225-2255-3.ch631

Kang, H., Kang, Y., & Kim, J. (2022). Improved Fall Detection Model on GRU Using PoseNet. *International Journal of Software Innovation, 10*(2), 1–11. https://doi.org/10.4018/IJSI.289600

Kankam, P. K. (2021). Employing Case Study and Survey Designs in Information Research. *Journal of Information Technology Research, 14*(1), 167–177. https://doi.org/10.4018/JITR.2021010110

Karas, V., & Schuller, B. W. (2021). Deep Learning for Sentiment Analysis: An Overview and Perspectives. In F. Pinarbasi & M. Taskiran (Eds.), *Natural Language Processing for Global and Local Business* (pp. 97–132). IGI Global. https://doi.org/10.4018/978-1-7998-4240-8.ch005

Kaufman, L. M. (2022). Reimagining the Magic of the Workshop Model. In T. Driscoll III, (Ed.), *Designing Effective Distance and Blended Learning Environments in K-12* (pp. 89–109). IGI Global. https://doi.org/10.4018/978-1-7998-6829-3.ch007

Kawata, S. (2018). Computer-Assisted Parallel Program Generation. In M. Khosrow-Pour, D.B.A. (Ed.), Encyclopedia of Information Science and Technology, Fourth Edition (pp. 4583-4593). Hershey, PA: IGI Global. doi:10.4018/978-1-5225-2255-3.ch398

Kharb, L., & Singh, P. (2021). Role of Machine Learning in Modern Education and Teaching. In S. Verma & P. Tomar (Ed.), *Impact of AI Technologies on Teaching, Learning, and Research in Higher Education* (pp. 99-123). IGI Global. https://doi.org/10.4018/978-1-7998-4763-2.ch006

Khari, M., Shrivastava, G., Gupta, S., & Gupta, R. (2017). Role of Cyber Security in Today's Scenario. In R. Kumar, P. Pattnaik, & P. Pandey (Eds.), *Detecting and Mitigating Robotic Cyber Security Risks* (pp. 177–191). Hershey, PA: IGI Global. doi:10.4018/978-1-5225-2154-9.ch013

Khekare, G., & Sheikh, S. (2021). Autonomous Navigation Using Deep Reinforcement Learning in ROS. *International Journal of Artificial Intelligence and Machine Learning, 11*(2), 63–70. https://doi.org/10.4018/IJAIML.20210701.oa4

Khouja, M., Rodriguez, I. B., Ben Halima, Y., & Moalla, S. (2018). IT Governance in Higher Education Institutions: A Systematic Literature Review. *International Journal of Human Capital and Information Technology Professionals, 9*(2), 52–67. doi:10.4018/IJHCITP.2018040104

Kiourt, C., Pavlidis, G., Koutsoudis, A., & Kalles, D. (2017). Realistic Simulation of Cultural Heritage. *International Journal of Computational Methods in Heritage Science, 1*(1), 10–40. doi:10.4018/IJCMHS.2017010102

Köse, U. (2017). An Augmented-Reality-Based Intelligent Mobile Application for Open Computer Education. In G. Kurubacak & H. Altinpulluk (Eds.), *Mobile Technologies and Augmented Reality in Open Education* (pp. 154–174). Hershey, PA: IGI Global. doi:10.4018/978-1-5225-2110-5.ch008

Lahmiri, S. (2018). Information Technology Outsourcing Risk Factors and Provider Selection. In M. Gupta, R. Sharman, J. Walp, & P. Mulgund (Eds.), *Information Technology Risk Management and Compliance in Modern Organizations* (pp. 214–228). Hershey, PA: IGI Global. doi:10.4018/978-1-5225-2604-9.ch008

Lakkad, A. K., Bhadaniya, R. D., Shah, V. N., & Lavanya, K. (2021). Complex Events Processing on Live News Events Using Apache Kafka and Clustering Techniques. *International Journal of Intelligent Information Technologies, 17*(1), 39–52. https://doi.org/10.4018/IJIIT.2021010103

Landriscina, F. (2017). Computer-Supported Imagination: The Interplay Between Computer and Mental Simulation in Understanding Scientific Concepts. In I. Levin & D. Tsybulsky (Eds.), *Digital Tools and Solutions for Inquiry-Based STEM Learning* (pp. 33–60). Hershey, PA: IGI Global. doi:10.4018/978-1-5225-2525-7.ch002

Lara López, G. (2021). Virtual Reality in Object Location. In A. Negrón & M. Muñoz (Eds.), *Latin American Women and Research Contributions to the IT Field* (pp. 307–324). IGI Global. https://doi.org/10.4018/978-1-7998-7552-9.ch014

Lee, W. W. (2018). Ethical Computing Continues From Problem to Solution. In M. Khosrow-Pour, D.B.A. (Ed.), Encyclopedia of Information Science and Technology, Fourth Edition (pp. 4884-4897). Hershey, PA: IGI Global. doi:10.4018/978-1-5225-2255-3.ch423

Lin, S., Chen, S., & Chuang, S. (2017). Perceived Innovation and Quick Response Codes in an Online-to-Offline E-Commerce Service Model. *International Journal of E-Adoption, 9*(2), 1–16. doi:10.4018/IJEA.2017070101

Liu, M., Wang, Y., Xu, W., & Liu, L. (2017). Automated Scoring of Chinese Engineering Students' English Essays. *International Journal of Distance Education Technologies, 15*(1), 52–68. doi:10.4018/IJDET.2017010104

Ma, X., Li, X., Zhong, B., Huang, Y., Gu, Y., Wu, M., Liu, Y., & Zhang, M. (2021). A Detector and Evaluation Framework of Abnormal Bidding Behavior Based on Supplier Portrait. *International Journal of Information Technology and Web Engineering, 16*(2), 58–74. https://doi.org/10.4018/IJITWE.2021040104

Mabe, L. K., & Oladele, O. I. (2017). Application of Information Communication Technologies for Agricultural Development through Extension Services: A Review. In T. Tossy (Ed.), *Information Technology Integration for Socio-Economic Development* (pp. 52–101). Hershey, PA: IGI Global. doi:10.4018/978-1-5225-0539-6.ch003

Mahboub, S. A., Sayed Ali Ahmed, E., & Saeed, R. A. (2021). Smart IDS and IPS for Cyber-Physical Systems. In A. Luhach & A. Elçi (Eds.), *Artificial Intelligence Paradigms for Smart Cyber-Physical Systems* (pp. 109–136). IGI Global. https://doi.org/10.4018/978-1-7998-5101-1.ch006

Manogaran, G., Thota, C., & Lopez, D. (2018). Human-Computer Interaction With Big Data Analytics. In D. Lopez & M. Durai (Eds.), *HCI Challenges and Privacy Preservation in Big Data Security* (pp. 1–22). Hershey, PA: IGI Global. doi:10.4018/978-1-5225-2863-0.ch001

Margolis, J., Goode, J., & Flapan, J. (2017). A Critical Crossroads for Computer Science for All: "Identifying Talent" or "Building Talent," and What Difference Does It Make? In Y. Rankin & J. Thomas (Eds.), *Moving Students of Color from Consumers to Producers of Technology* (pp. 1–23). Hershey, PA: IGI Global. doi:10.4018/978-1-5225-2005-4.ch001

Mazzù, M. F., Benetton, A., Baccelloni, A., & Lavini, L. (2022). A Milk Blockchain-Enabled Supply Chain: Evidence From Leading Italian Farms. In P. De Giovanni (Ed.), *Blockchain Technology Applications in Businesses and Organizations* (pp. 73–98). IGI Global. https://doi.org/10.4018/978-1-7998-8014-1.ch004

Mbale, J. (2018). Computer Centres Resource Cloud Elasticity-Scalability (CRECES): Copperbelt University Case Study. In S. Aljawarneh & M. Malhotra (Eds.), *Critical Research on Scalability and Security Issues in Virtual Cloud Environments* (pp. 48–70). Hershey, PA: IGI Global. doi:10.4018/978-1-5225-3029-9.ch003

McKee, J. (2018). The Right Information: The Key to Effective Business Planning. In *Business Architectures for Risk Assessment and Strategic Planning: Emerging Research and Opportunities* (pp. 38–52). Hershey, PA: IGI Global. doi:10.4018/978-1-5225-3392-4.ch003

Meddah, I. H., Remil, N. E., & Meddah, H. N. (2021). Novel Approach for Mining Patterns. *International Journal of Applied Evolutionary Computation, 12*(1), 27–42. https://doi.org/10.4018/IJAEC.2021010103

Mensah, I. K., & Mi, J. (2018). Determinants of Intention to Use Local E-Government Services in Ghana: The Perspective of Local Government Workers. *International Journal of Technology Diffusion, 9*(2), 41–60. doi:10.4018/IJTD.2018040103

Mohamed, J. H. (2018). Scientograph-Based Visualization of Computer Forensics Research Literature. In J. Jeyasekar & P. Saravanan (Eds.), *Innovations in Measuring and Evaluating Scientific Information* (pp. 148–162). Hershey, PA: IGI Global. doi:10.4018/978-1-5225-3457-0.ch010

Montañés-Del Río, M. Á., Cornejo, V. R., Rodríguez, M. R., & Ortiz, J. S. (2021). Gamification of University Subjects: A Case Study for Operations Management. *Journal of Information Technology Research, 14*(2), 1–29. https://doi.org/10.4018/JITR.2021040101

Moore, R. L., & Johnson, N. (2017). Earning a Seat at the Table: How IT Departments Can Partner in Organizational Change and Innovation. *International Journal of Knowledge-Based Organizations, 7*(2), 1–12. doi:10.4018/IJKBO.2017040101

Mukul, M. K., & Bhattaharyya, S. (2017). Brain-Machine Interface: Human-Computer Interaction. In E. Noughabi, B. Raahemi, A. Albadvi, & B. Far (Eds.), *Handbook of Research on Data Science for Effective Healthcare Practice and Administration* (pp. 417–443). Hershey, PA: IGI Global. doi:10.4018/978-1-5225-2515-8.ch018

Na, L. (2017). Library and Information Science Education and Graduate Programs in Academic Libraries. In L. Ruan, Q. Zhu, & Y. Ye (Eds.), *Academic Library Development and Administration in China* (pp. 218–229). Hershey, PA: IGI Global. doi:10.4018/978-1-5225-0550-1.ch013

Nagpal, G., Bishnoi, G. K., Dhami, H. S., & Vijayvargia, A. (2021). Use of Data Analytics to Increase the Efficiency of Last Mile Logistics for Ecommerce Deliveries. In B. Patil & M. Vohra (Eds.), *Handbook of Research on Engineering, Business, and Healthcare Applications of Data Science and Analytics* (pp. 167–180). IGI Global. https://doi.org/10.4018/978-1-7998-3053-5.ch009

Nair, S. M., Ramesh, V., & Tyagi, A. K. (2021). Issues and Challenges (Privacy, Security, and Trust) in Blockchain-Based Applications. In A. Tyagi, G. Rekha, & N. Sreenath (Eds.), *Opportunities and Challenges for Blockchain Technology in Autonomous Vehicles* (pp. 196–209). IGI Global. https://doi.org/10.4018/978-1-7998-3295-9.ch012

Naomi, J. F. M., K., & V., S. (2021). Machine and Deep Learning Techniques in IoT and Cloud. In S. Velayutham (Ed.), *Challenges and Opportunities for the Convergence of IoT, Big Data, and Cloud Computing* (pp. 225-247). IGI Global. https://doi.org/10.4018/978-1-7998-3111-2.ch013

Nath, R., & Murthy, V. N. (2018). What Accounts for the Differences in Internet Diffusion Rates Around the World? In M. Khosrow-Pour, D.B.A. (Ed.), Encyclopedia of Information Science and Technology, Fourth Edition (pp. 8095-8104). Hershey, PA: IGI Global. https://doi.org/ doi:10.4018/978-1-5225-2255-3.ch705

Nedelko, Z., & Potocan, V. (2018). The Role of Emerging Information Technologies for Supporting Supply Chain Management. In M. Khosrow-Pour, D.B.A. (Ed.), Encyclopedia of Information Science and Technology, Fourth Edition (pp. 5559-5569). Hershey, PA: IGI Global. doi:10.4018/978-1-5225-2255-3.ch483

Negrini, L., Giang, C., & Bonnet, E. (2022). Designing Tools and Activities for Educational Robotics in Online Learning. In N. Eteokleous & E. Nisiforou (Eds.), *Designing, Constructing, and Programming Robots for Learning* (pp. 202–222). IGI Global. https://doi.org/10.4018/978-1-7998-7443-0.ch010

Ngafeeson, M. N. (2018). User Resistance to Health Information Technology. In M. Khosrow-Pour, D.B.A. (Ed.), Encyclopedia of Information Science and Technology, Fourth Edition (pp. 3816-3825). Hershey, PA: IGI Global. doi:10.4018/978-1-5225-2255-3.ch331

Nguyen, T. T., Giang, N. L., Tran, D. T., Nguyen, T. T., Nguyen, H. Q., Pham, A. V., & Vu, T. D. (2021). A Novel Filter-Wrapper Algorithm on Intuitionistic Fuzzy Set for Attribute Reduction From Decision Tables. *International Journal of Data Warehousing and Mining*, *17*(4), 67–100. https://doi.org/10.4018/IJDWM.2021100104

Nigam, A., & Dewani, P. P. (2022). Consumer Engagement Through Conditional Promotions: An Exploratory Study. *Journal of Global Information Management*, *30*(5), 1–19. https://doi.org/10.4018/JGIM.290364

Odagiri, K. (2017). Introduction of Individual Technology to Constitute the Current Internet. In *Strategic Policy-Based Network Management in Contemporary Organizations* (pp. 20–96). Hershey, PA: IGI Global. doi:10.4018/978-1-68318-003-6.ch003

Odia, J. O., & Akpata, O. T. (2021). Role of Data Science and Data Analytics in Forensic Accounting and Fraud Detection. In B. Patil & M. Vohra (Eds.), *Handbook of Research on Engineering, Business, and Healthcare Applications of Data Science and Analytics* (pp. 203–227). IGI Global. https://doi.org/10.4018/978-1-7998-3053-5.ch011

Okike, E. U. (2018). Computer Science and Prison Education. In I. Biao (Ed.), *Strategic Learning Ideologies in Prison Education Programs* (pp. 246–264). Hershey, PA: IGI Global. doi:10.4018/978-1-5225-2909-5.ch012

Olelewe, C. J., & Nwafor, I. P. (2017). Level of Computer Appreciation Skills Acquired for Sustainable Development by Secondary School Students in Nsukka LGA of Enugu State, Nigeria. In C. Ayo & V. Mbarika (Eds.), *Sustainable ICT Adoption and Integration for Socio-Economic Development* (pp. 214–233). Hershey, PA: IGI Global. doi:10.4018/978-1-5225-2565-3.ch010

Oliveira, M., Maçada, A. C., Curado, C., & Nodari, F. (2017). Infrastructure Profiles and Knowledge Sharing. *International Journal of Technology and Human Interaction*, *13*(3), 1–12. doi:10.4018/IJTHI.2017070101

Otarkhani, A., Shokouhyar, S., & Pour, S. S. (2017). Analyzing the Impact of Governance of Enterprise IT on Hospital Performance: Tehran's (Iran) Hospitals – A Case Study. *International Journal of Healthcare Information Systems and Informatics*, *12*(3), 1–20. doi:10.4018/IJHISI.2017070101

Otunla, A. O., & Amuda, C. O. (2018). Nigerian Undergraduate Students' Computer Competencies and Use of Information Technology Tools and Resources for Study Skills and Habits' Enhancement. In M. Khosrow-Pour, D.B.A. (Ed.), Encyclopedia of Information Science and Technology, Fourth Edition (pp. 2303-2313). Hershey, PA: IGI Global. https://doi.org/ doi:10.4018/978-1-5225-2255-3.ch200

Özçınar, H. (2018). A Brief Discussion on Incentives and Barriers to Computational Thinking Education. In H. Ozcinar, G. Wong, & H. Ozturk (Eds.), *Teaching Computational Thinking in Primary Education* (pp. 1–17). Hershey, PA: IGI Global. doi:10.4018/978-1-5225-3200-2.ch001

Pandey, J. M., Garg, S., Mishra, P., & Mishra, B. P. (2017). Computer Based Psychological Interventions: Subject to the Efficacy of Psychological Services. *International Journal of Computers in Clinical Practice*, *2*(1), 25–33. doi:10.4018/IJCCP.2017010102

Pandkar, S. D., & Paatil, S. D. (2021). Big Data and Knowledge Resource Centre. In S. Dhamdhere (Ed.), *Big Data Applications for Improving Library Services* (pp. 90–106). IGI Global. https://doi.org/10.4018/978-1-7998-3049-8.ch007

Patro, C. (2017). Impulsion of Information Technology on Human Resource Practices. In P. Ordóñez de Pablos (Ed.), *Managerial Strategies and Solutions for Business Success in Asia* (pp. 231–254). Hershey, PA: IGI Global. doi:10.4018/978-1-5225-1886-0.ch013

Patro, C. S., & Raghunath, K. M. (2017). Information Technology Paraphernalia for Supply Chain Management Decisions. In M. Tavana (Ed.), *Enterprise Information Systems and the Digitalization of Business Functions* (pp. 294–320). Hershey, PA: IGI Global. doi:10.4018/978-1-5225-2382-6.ch014

Paul, P. K. (2018). The Context of IST for Solid Information Retrieval and Infrastructure Building: Study of Developing Country. *International Journal of Information Retrieval Research*, *8*(1), 86–100. doi:10.4018/IJIRR.2018010106

Paul, P. K., & Chatterjee, D. (2018). iSchools Promoting "Information Science and Technology" (IST) Domain Towards Community, Business, and Society With Contemporary Worldwide Trend and Emerging Potentialities in India. In M. Khosrow-Pour, D.B.A. (Ed.), Encyclopedia of Information Science and Technology, Fourth Edition (pp. 4723-4735). Hershey, PA: IGI Global. https://doi.org/ doi:10.4018/978-1-5225-2255-3.ch410

Pessoa, C. R., & Marques, M. E. (2017). Information Technology and Communication Management in Supply Chain Management. In G. Jamil, A. Soares, & C. Pessoa (Eds.), *Handbook of Research on Information Management for Effective Logistics and Supply Chains* (pp. 23–33). Hershey, PA: IGI Global. doi:10.4018/978-1-5225-0973-8.ch002

Pineda, R. G. (2018). Remediating Interaction: Towards a Philosophy of Human-Computer Relationship. In M. Khosrow-Pour (Ed.), *Enhancing Art, Culture, and Design With Technological Integration* (pp. 75–98). Hershey, PA: IGI Global. doi:10.4018/978-1-5225-5023-5.ch004

Prabha, V. D., & R., R. (2021). Clinical Decision Support Systems: Decision-Making System for Clinical Data. In G. Rani & P. Tiwari (Eds.), *Handbook of Research on Disease Prediction Through Data Analytics and Machine Learning* (pp. 268-280). IGI Global. https://doi.org/10.4018/978-1-7998-2742-9.ch014

Pushpa, R., & Siddappa, M. (2021). An Optimal Way of VM Placement Strategy in Cloud Computing Platform Using ABCS Algorithm. *International Journal of Ambient Computing and Intelligence*, *12*(3), 16–38. https://doi.org/10.4018/IJACI.2021070102

Qian, Y. (2017). Computer Simulation in Higher Education: Affordances, Opportunities, and Outcomes. In P. Vu, S. Fredrickson, & C. Moore (Eds.), *Handbook of Research on Innovative Pedagogies and Technologies for Online Learning in Higher Education* (pp. 236–262). Hershey, PA: IGI Global. doi:10.4018/978-1-5225-1851-8.ch011

Rahman, N. (2017). Lessons from a Successful Data Warehousing Project Management. *International Journal of Information Technology Project Management*, *8*(4), 30–45. doi:10.4018/IJITPM.2017100103

Rahman, N. (2018). Environmental Sustainability in the Computer Industry for Competitive Advantage. In M. Khosrow-Pour (Ed.), *Green Computing Strategies for Competitive Advantage and Business Sustainability* (pp. 110–130). Hershey, PA: IGI Global. doi:10.4018/978-1-5225-5017-4.ch006

Rajh, A., & Pavetic, T. (2017). Computer Generated Description as the Required Digital Competence in Archival Profession. *International Journal of Digital Literacy and Digital Competence*, *8*(1), 36–49. doi:10.4018/IJDLDC.2017010103

Raman, A., & Goyal, D. P. (2017). Extending IMPLEMENT Framework for Enterprise Information Systems Implementation to Information System Innovation. In M. Tavana (Ed.), *Enterprise Information Systems and the Digitalization of Business Functions* (pp. 137–177). Hershey, PA: IGI Global. doi:10.4018/978-1-5225-2382-6.ch007

Rao, A. P., & Reddy, K. S. (2021). Automated Soil Residue Levels Detecting Device With IoT Interface. In V. Sathiyamoorthi & A. Elci (Eds.), *Challenges and Applications of Data Analytics in Social Perspectives* (Vol. S, pp. 123–135). IGI Global. https://doi.org/10.4018/978-1-7998-2566-1.ch007

Rao, Y. S., Rauta, A. K., Saini, H., & Panda, T. C. (2017). Mathematical Model for Cyber Attack in Computer Network. *International Journal of Business Data Communications and Networking*, *13*(1), 58–65. doi:10.4018/IJBDCN.2017010105

Rapaport, W. J. (2018). Syntactic Semantics and the Proper Treatment of Computationalism. In M. Danesi (Ed.), *Empirical Research on Semiotics and Visual Rhetoric* (pp. 128–176). Hershey, PA: IGI Global. doi:10.4018/978-1-5225-5622-0.ch007

Raut, R., Priyadarshinee, P., & Jha, M. (2017). Understanding the Mediation Effect of Cloud Computing Adoption in Indian Organization: Integrating TAM-TOE- Risk Model. *International Journal of Service Science, Management, Engineering, and Technology*, *8*(3), 40–59. doi:10.4018/IJSSMET.2017070103

Rezaie, S., Mirabedini, S. J., & Abtahi, A. (2018). Designing a Model for Implementation of Business Intelligence in the Banking Industry. *International Journal of Enterprise Information Systems*, *14*(1), 77–103. doi:10.4018/IJEIS.2018010105

Rezende, D. A. (2018). Strategic Digital City Projects: Innovative Information and Public Services Offered by Chicago (USA) and Curitiba (Brazil). In M. Lytras, L. Daniela, & A. Visvizi (Eds.), *Enhancing Knowledge Discovery and Innovation in the Digital Era* (pp. 204–223). Hershey, PA: IGI Global. doi:10.4018/978-1-5225-4191-2.ch012

Rodriguez, A., Rico-Diaz, A. J., Rabuñal, J. R., & Gestal, M. (2017). Fish Tracking with Computer Vision Techniques: An Application to Vertical Slot Fishways. In M. S., & V. V. (Eds.), Multi-Core Computer Vision and Image Processing for Intelligent Applications (pp. 74-104). Hershey, PA: IGI Global. https://doi.org/doi:10.4018/978-1-5225-0889-2.ch003

Romero, J. A. (2018). Sustainable Advantages of Business Value of Information Technology. In M. Khosrow-Pour, D.B.A. (Ed.), Encyclopedia of Information Science and Technology, Fourth Edition (pp. 923-929). Hershey, PA: IGI Global. doi:10.4018/978-1-5225-2255-3.ch079

Romero, J. A. (2018). The Always-On Business Model and Competitive Advantage. In N. Bajgoric (Ed.), *Always-On Enterprise Information Systems for Modern Organizations* (pp. 23–40). Hershey, PA: IGI Global. doi:10.4018/978-1-5225-3704-5.ch002

Rosen, Y. (2018). Computer Agent Technologies in Collaborative Learning and Assessment. In M. Khosrow-Pour, D.B.A. (Ed.), Encyclopedia of Information Science and Technology, Fourth Edition (pp. 2402-2410). Hershey, PA: IGI Global. doi:10.4018/978-1-5225-2255-3.ch209

Roy, D. (2018). Success Factors of Adoption of Mobile Applications in Rural India: Effect of Service Characteristics on Conceptual Model. In M. Khosrow-Pour (Ed.), *Green Computing Strategies for Competitive Advantage and Business Sustainability* (pp. 211–238). Hershey, PA: IGI Global. doi:10.4018/978-1-5225-5017-4.ch010

Ruffin, T. R., & Hawkins, D. P. (2018). Trends in Health Care Information Technology and Informatics. In M. Khosrow-Pour, D.B.A. (Ed.), Encyclopedia of Information Science and Technology, Fourth Edition (pp. 3805-3815). Hershey, PA: IGI Global. doi:10.4018/978-1-5225-2255-3.ch330

Sadasivam, U. M., & Ganesan, N. (2021). Detecting Fake News Using Deep Learning and NLP. In S. Misra, C. Arumugam, S. Jaganathan, & S. S. (Eds.), *Confluence of AI, Machine, and Deep Learning in Cyber Forensics* (pp. 117-133). IGI Global. https://doi.org/10.4018/978-1-7998-4900-1.ch007

Safari, M. R., & Jiang, Q. (2018). The Theory and Practice of IT Governance Maturity and Strategies Alignment: Evidence From Banking Industry. *Journal of Global Information Management*, *26*(2), 127–146. doi:10.4018/JGIM.2018040106

Sahin, H. B., & Anagun, S. S. (2018). Educational Computer Games in Math Teaching: A Learning Culture. In E. Toprak & E. Kumtepe (Eds.), *Supporting Multiculturalism in Open and Distance Learning Spaces* (pp. 249–280). Hershey, PA: IGI Global. doi:10.4018/978-1-5225-3076-3.ch013

Sakalle, A., Tomar, P., Bhardwaj, H., & Sharma, U. (2021). Impact and Latest Trends of Intelligent Learning With Artificial Intelligence. In S. Verma & P. Tomar (Eds.), *Impact of AI Technologies on Teaching, Learning, and Research in Higher Education* (pp. 172-189). IGI Global. https://doi.org/10.4018/978-1-7998-4763-2.ch011

Sala, N. (2021). Virtual Reality, Augmented Reality, and Mixed Reality in Education: A Brief Overview. In D. Choi, A. Dailey-Hebert, & J. Estes (Eds.), *Current and Prospective Applications of Virtual Reality in Higher Education* (pp. 48–73). IGI Global. https://doi.org/10.4018/978-1-7998-4960-5.ch003

Salunkhe, S., Kanagachidambaresan, G., Rajkumar, C., & Jayanthi, K. (2022). Online Detection and Prediction of Fused Deposition Modelled Parts Using Artificial Intelligence. In S. Salunkhe, H. Hussein, & J. Davim (Eds.), *Applications of Artificial Intelligence in Additive Manufacturing* (pp. 194–209). IGI Global. https://doi.org/10.4018/978-1-7998-8516-0.ch009

Samy, V. S., Pramanick, K., Thenkanidiyoor, V., & Victor, J. (2021). Data Analysis and Visualization in Python for Polar Meteorological Data. *International Journal of Data Analytics*, *2*(1), 32–60. https://doi.org/10.4018/IJDA.2021010102

Sanna, A., & Valpreda, F. (2017). An Assessment of the Impact of a Collaborative Didactic Approach and Students' Background in Teaching Computer Animation. *International Journal of Information and Communication Technology Education*, *13*(4), 1–16. doi:10.4018/IJICTE.2017100101

Sarivougioukas, J., & Vagelatos, A. (2022). Fused Contextual Data With Threading Technology to Accelerate Processing in Home UbiHealth. *International Journal of Software Science and Computational Intelligence*, *14*(1), 1–14. https://doi.org/10.4018/IJSSCI.285590

Scott, A., Martin, A., & McAlear, F. (2017). Enhancing Participation in Computer Science among Girls of Color: An Examination of a Preparatory AP Computer Science Intervention. In Y. Rankin & J. Thomas (Eds.), *Moving Students of Color from Consumers to Producers of Technology* (pp. 62–84). Hershey, PA: IGI Global. doi:10.4018/978-1-5225-2005-4.ch004

Shanmugam, M., Ibrahim, N., Gorment, N. Z., Sugu, R., Dandarawi, T. N., & Ahmad, N. A. (2022). Towards an Integrated Omni-Channel Strategy Framework for Improved Customer Interaction. In P. Lai (Ed.), *Handbook of Research on Social Impacts of E-Payment and Blockchain Technology* (pp. 409–427). IGI Global. https://doi.org/10.4018/978-1-7998-9035-5.ch022

Sharma, A., & Kumar, S. (2021). Network Slicing and the Role of 5G in IoT Applications. In S. Kumar, M. Trivedi, P. Ranjan, & A. Punhani (Eds.), *Evolution of Software-Defined Networking Foundations for IoT and 5G Mobile Networks* (pp. 172–190). IGI Global. https://doi.org/10.4018/978-1-7998-4685-7.ch010

Siddoo, V., & Wongsai, N. (2017). Factors Influencing the Adoption of ISO/IEC 29110 in Thai Government Projects: A Case Study. *International Journal of Information Technologies and Systems Approach*, *10*(1), 22–44. doi:10.4018/IJITSA.2017010102

Silveira, C., Hir, M. E., & Chaves, H. K. (2022). An Approach to Information Management as a Subsidy of Global Health Actions: A Case Study of Big Data in Health for Dengue, Zika, and Chikungunya. In J. Lima de Magalhães, Z. Hartz, G. Jamil, H. Silveira, & L. Jamil (Eds.), *Handbook of Research on Essential Information Approaches to Aiding Global Health in the One Health Context* (pp. 219–234). IGI Global. https://doi.org/10.4018/978-1-7998-8011-0.ch012

Simões, A. (2017). Using Game Frameworks to Teach Computer Programming. In R. Alexandre Peixoto de Queirós & M. Pinto (Eds.), *Gamification-Based E-Learning Strategies for Computer Programming Education* (pp. 221–236). Hershey, PA: IGI Global. doi:10.4018/978-1-5225-1034-5.ch010

Simões de Almeida, R., & da Silva, T. (2022). AI Chatbots in Mental Health: Are We There Yet? In A. Marques & R. Queirós (Eds.), *Digital Therapies in Psychosocial Rehabilitation and Mental Health* (pp. 226–243). IGI Global. https://doi.org/10.4018/978-1-7998-8634-1.ch011

Singh, L. K., Khanna, M., Thawkar, S., & Gopal, J. (2021). Robustness for Authentication of the Human Using Face, Ear, and Gait Multimodal Biometric System. *International Journal of Information System Modeling and Design*, *12*(1), 39–72. https://doi.org/10.4018/IJISMD.2021010103

Sllame, A. M. (2017). Integrating LAB Work With Classes in Computer Network Courses. In H. Alphin Jr, R. Chan, & J. Lavine (Eds.), *The Future of Accessibility in International Higher Education* (pp. 253–275). Hershey, PA: IGI Global. doi:10.4018/978-1-5225-2560-8.ch015

Smirnov, A., Ponomarev, A., Shilov, N., Kashevnik, A., & Teslya, N. (2018). Ontology-Based Human-Computer Cloud for Decision Support: Architecture and Applications in Tourism. *International Journal of Embedded and Real-Time Communication Systems*, *9*(1), 1–19. doi:10.4018/IJERTCS.2018010101

Smith-Ditizio, A. A., & Smith, A. D. (2018). Computer Fraud Challenges and Its Legal Implications. In M. Khosrow-Pour, D.B.A. (Ed.), Encyclopedia of Information Science and Technology, Fourth Edition (pp. 4837-4848). Hershey, PA: IGI Global. doi:10.4018/978-1-5225-2255-3.ch419

Sosnin, P. (2018). Figuratively Semantic Support of Human-Computer Interactions. In *Experience-Based Human-Computer Interactions: Emerging Research and Opportunities* (pp. 244–272). Hershey, PA: IGI Global. doi:10.4018/978-1-5225-2987-3.ch008

Srilakshmi, R., & Jaya Bhaskar, M. (2021). An Adaptable Secure Scheme in Mobile Ad hoc Network to Protect the Communication Channel From Malicious Behaviours. *International Journal of Information Technology and Web Engineering, 16*(3), 54–73. https://doi.org/10.4018/IJITWE.2021070104

Sukhwani, N., Kagita, V. R., Kumar, V., & Panda, S. K. (2021). Efficient Computation of Top-K Skyline Objects in Data Set With Uncertain Preferences. *International Journal of Data Warehousing and Mining, 17*(3), 68–80. https://doi.org/10.4018/IJDWM.2021070104

Susanto, H., Yie, L. F., Setiana, D., Asih, Y., Yoganingrum, A., Riyanto, S., & Saputra, F. A. (2021). Digital Ecosystem Security Issues for Organizations and Governments: Digital Ethics and Privacy. In Z. Mahmood (Ed.), *Web 2.0 and Cloud Technologies for Implementing Connected Government* (pp. 204–228). IGI Global. https://doi.org/10.4018/978-1-7998-4570-6.ch010

Syväjärvi, A., Leinonen, J., Kivivirta, V., & Kesti, M. (2017). The Latitude of Information Management in Local Government: Views of Local Government Managers. *International Journal of Electronic Government Research, 13*(1), 69–85. doi:10.4018/IJEGR.2017010105

Tanque, M., & Foxwell, H. J. (2018). Big Data and Cloud Computing: A Review of Supply Chain Capabilities and Challenges. In A. Prasad (Ed.), *Exploring the Convergence of Big Data and the Internet of Things* (pp. 1–28). Hershey, PA: IGI Global. doi:10.4018/978-1-5225-2947-7.ch001

Teixeira, A., Gomes, A., & Orvalho, J. G. (2017). Auditory Feedback in a Computer Game for Blind People. In T. Issa, P. Kommers, T. Issa, P. Isaías, & T. Issa (Eds.), *Smart Technology Applications in Business Environments* (pp. 134–158). Hershey, PA: IGI Global. doi:10.4018/978-1-5225-2492-2.ch007

Tewari, P., Tiwari, P., & Goel, R. (2022). Information Technology in Supply Chain Management. In V. Garg & R. Goel (Eds.), *Handbook of Research on Innovative Management Using AI in Industry 5.0* (pp. 165–178). IGI Global. https://doi.org/10.4018/978-1-7998-8497-2.ch011

Thompson, N., McGill, T., & Murray, D. (2018). Affect-Sensitive Computer Systems. In M. Khosrow-Pour, D.B.A. (Ed.), Encyclopedia of Information Science and Technology, Fourth Edition (pp. 4124-4135). Hershey, PA: IGI Global. doi:10.4018/978-1-5225-2255-3.ch357

Triberti, S., Brivio, E., & Galimberti, C. (2018). On Social Presence: Theories, Methodologies, and Guidelines for the Innovative Contexts of Computer-Mediated Learning. In M. Marmon (Ed.), *Enhancing Social Presence in Online Learning Environments* (pp. 20–41). Hershey, PA: IGI Global. doi:10.4018/978-1-5225-3229-3.ch002

Tripathy, B. K. T. R., S., & Mohanty, R. K. (2018). Memetic Algorithms and Their Applications in Computer Science. In S. Dash, B. Tripathy, & A. Rahman (Eds.), Handbook of Research on Modeling, Analysis, and Application of Nature-Inspired Metaheuristic Algorithms (pp. 73-93). Hershey, PA: IGI Global. https://doi.org/ doi:10.4018/978-1-5225-2857-9.ch004

Turulja, L., & Bajgoric, N. (2017). Human Resource Management IT and Global Economy Perspective: Global Human Resource Information Systems. In M. Khosrow-Pour (Ed.), *Handbook of Research on Technology Adoption, Social Policy, and Global Integration* (pp. 377–394). Hershey, PA: IGI Global. doi:10.4018/978-1-5225-2668-1.ch018

Unwin, D. W., Sanzogni, L., & Sandhu, K. (2017). Developing and Measuring the Business Case for Health Information Technology. In K. Moahi, K. Bwalya, & P. Sebina (Eds.), *Health Information Systems and the Advancement of Medical Practice in Developing Countries* (pp. 262–290). Hershey, PA: IGI Global. doi:10.4018/978-1-5225-2262-1.ch015

Usharani, B. (2022). House Plant Leaf Disease Detection and Classification Using Machine Learning. In M. Mundada, S. Seema, S. K.G., & M. Shilpa (Eds.), *Deep Learning Applications for Cyber-Physical Systems* (pp. 17-26). IGI Global. https://doi.org/10.4018/978-1-7998-8161-2.ch002

Vadhanam, B. R. S., M., Sugumaran, V., V., V., & Ramalingam, V. V. (2017). Computer Vision Based Classification on Commercial Videos. In M. S., & V. V. (Eds.), Multi-Core Computer Vision and Image Processing for Intelligent Applications (pp. 105-135). Hershey, PA: IGI Global. https://doi.org/ doi:10.4018/978-1-5225-0889-2.ch004

Vairinho, S. (2022). Innovation Dynamics Through the Encouragement of Knowledge Spin-Off From Touristic Destinations. In C. Ramos, S. Quinteiro, & A. Gonçalves (Eds.), *ICT as Innovator Between Tourism and Culture* (pp. 170–190). IGI Global. https://doi.org/10.4018/978-1-7998-8165-0.ch011

Valverde, R., Torres, B., & Motaghi, H. (2018). A Quantum NeuroIS Data Analytics Architecture for the Usability Evaluation of Learning Management Systems. In S. Bhattacharyya (Ed.), *Quantum-Inspired Intelligent Systems for Multimedia Data Analysis* (pp. 277–299). Hershey, PA: IGI Global. doi:10.4018/978-1-5225-5219-2.ch009

Vassilis, E. (2018). Learning and Teaching Methodology: "1:1 Educational Computing. In K. Koutsopoulos, K. Doukas, & Y. Kotsanis (Eds.), *Handbook of Research on Educational Design and Cloud Computing in Modern Classroom Settings* (pp. 122–155). Hershey, PA: IGI Global. doi:10.4018/978-1-5225-3053-4.ch007

Verma, S., & Jain, A. K. (2022). A Survey on Sentiment Analysis Techniques for Twitter. In B. Gupta, D. Peraković, A. Abd El-Latif, & D. Gupta (Eds.), *Data Mining Approaches for Big Data and Sentiment Analysis in Social Media* (pp. 57–90). IGI Global. https://doi.org/10.4018/978-1-7998-8413-2.ch003

Wang, H., Huang, P., & Chen, X. (2021). Research and Application of a Multidimensional Association Rules Mining Method Based on OLAP. *International Journal of Information Technology and Web Engineering*, *16*(1), 75–94. https://doi.org/10.4018/IJITWE.2021010104

Wexler, B. E. (2017). Computer-Presented and Physical Brain-Training Exercises for School Children: Improving Executive Functions and Learning. In B. Dubbels (Ed.), *Transforming Gaming and Computer Simulation Technologies across Industries* (pp. 206–224). Hershey, PA: IGI Global. doi:10.4018/978-1-5225-1817-4.ch012

Wimble, M., Singh, H., & Phillips, B. (2018). Understanding Cross-Level Interactions of Firm-Level Information Technology and Industry Environment: A Multilevel Model of Business Value. *Information Resources Management Journal*, *31*(1), 1–20. doi:10.4018/IRMJ.2018010101

Wimmer, H., Powell, L., Kilgus, L., & Force, C. (2017). Improving Course Assessment via Web-based Homework. *International Journal of Online Pedagogy and Course Design*, *7*(2), 1–19. doi:10.4018/IJOPCD.2017040101

Wong, S. (2021). Gendering Information and Communication Technologies in Climate Change. In M. Khosrow-Pour D.B.A. (Eds.), *Encyclopedia of Information Science and Technology, Fifth Edition* (pp. 1408-1422). IGI Global. https://doi.org/10.4018/978-1-7998-3479-3.ch096

Wong, Y. L., & Siu, K. W. (2018). Assessing Computer-Aided Design Skills. In M. Khosrow-Pour, D.B.A. (Ed.), Encyclopedia of Information Science and Technology, Fourth Edition (pp. 7382-7391). Hershey, PA: IGI Global. doi:10.4018/978-1-5225-2255-3.ch642

Wongsurawat, W., & Shrestha, V. (2018). Information Technology, Globalization, and Local Conditions: Implications for Entrepreneurs in Southeast Asia. In P. Ordóñez de Pablos (Ed.), *Management Strategies and Technology Fluidity in the Asian Business Sector* (pp. 163–176). Hershey, PA: IGI Global. doi:10.4018/978-1-5225-4056-4.ch010

Yamada, H. (2021). Homogenization of Japanese Industrial Technology From the Perspective of R&D Expenses. *International Journal of Systems and Service-Oriented Engineering*, *11*(2), 24–51. doi:10.4018/IJSSOE.2021070102

Yang, Y., Zhu, X., Jin, C., & Li, J. J. (2018). Reforming Classroom Education Through a QQ Group: A Pilot Experiment at a Primary School in Shanghai. In H. Spires (Ed.), *Digital Transformation and Innovation in Chinese Education* (pp. 211–231). Hershey, PA: IGI Global. doi:10.4018/978-1-5225-2924-8.ch012

Yilmaz, R., Sezgin, A., Kurnaz, S., & Arslan, Y. Z. (2018). Object-Oriented Programming in Computer Science. In M. Khosrow-Pour, D.B.A. (Ed.), Encyclopedia of Information Science and Technology, Fourth Edition (pp. 7470-7480). Hershey, PA: IGI Global. doi:10.4018/978-1-5225-2255-3.ch650

Yu, L. (2018). From Teaching Software Engineering Locally and Globally to Devising an Internationalized Computer Science Curriculum. In S. Dikli, B. Etheridge, & R. Rawls (Eds.), *Curriculum Internationalization and the Future of Education* (pp. 293–320). Hershey, PA: IGI Global. doi:10.4018/978-1-5225-2791-6.ch016

Yuhua, F. (2018). Computer Information Library Clusters. In M. Khosrow-Pour, D.B.A. (Ed.), Encyclopedia of Information Science and Technology, Fourth Edition (pp. 4399-4403). Hershey, PA: IGI Global. doi:10.4018/978-1-5225-2255-3.ch382

Zakaria, R. B., Zainuddin, M. N., & Mohamad, A. H. (2022). Distilling Blockchain: Complexity, Barriers, and Opportunities. In P. Lai (Ed.), *Handbook of Research on Social Impacts of E-Payment and Blockchain Technology* (pp. 89–114). IGI Global. https://doi.org/10.4018/978-1-7998-9035-5.ch007

Zhang, Z., Ma, J., & Cui, X. (2021). Genetic Algorithm With Three-Dimensional Population Dominance Strategy for University Course Timetabling Problem. *International Journal of Grid and High Performance Computing*, *13*(2), 56–69. https://doi.org/10.4018/IJGHPC.2021040104

About the Contributors

Irfan Uddin is currently working as a faculty member at the Institute of Computing, Kohat University of Science and Technology, Kohat, Pakistan. He has received his academic qualifications in computer science and has worked as a researcher on funded projects. He is involved in teaching and research activities related to different diverse computer science topics and has more than eighteen years of teaching plus research experience. He is a member of IEEE, ACM, and HiPEAC. He has actively organized national and international seminars, workshops, and conferences. He has published over a hundred research papers in international journals and conferences. His research interests include machine learning, data science, artificial neural networks, deep learning, convolutional neural networks, recurrent neural networks, attention models, reinforcement learning, generative adversarial networks, computer vision, image processing, machine translation, natural language processing, speech recognition, big data analytics, parallel programming, Multi-core, Many-core and GPUs.

Wali Khan Mashwani received an M.Sc. degree in mathematics from the University of Peshawar, Khyber Pakhtunkhwa, Pakistan, in 1996, and a Ph.D. degree in mathematics from the University of Essex, U.K., in 2012. He is currently a Full Professor of mathematics and the Director of the Institute of Numerical Sciences, Kohat University of Science and Technology (KUST), Khyber Pakhtunkhwa. He is also the Dean of the Physical and Numerical Sciences faculty at KUST. He has published more than 100 academic papers in peer-reviewed international journals and conference proceedings. His research interests include evolutionary computation, hybrid evolutionary multi-objective algorithms, decomposition-based evolutionary methods for multi-objective optimization, mathematical programming, numerical analysis, and artificial neural networks.

***

Muhammad Adnan is currently serving as a senior lecturer at the Institute of Computing, KUST, Kohat. His area of interest includes machine learning, explainable AI, and deep learning.

Samina Amin received the M.S. degree in computer science from the Institute of Computing, Kohat University of Science and Technology, Kohat, Pakistan, in 2020, where she is currently pursuing the Ph.D. degree. Her research interests include machine learning, deep learning, data science, data mining, natural language processing, social media analysis, neural networks, recurrent neural networks, convolutional neural networks, image processing, health informatics, recommender systems, ensemble learning, and reinforcement learning. She has received the Gold Medal from the Kohat University of Science and Technology. She has published several articles in reputable journals. She serves as a reviewer for different journals.

Zhikang Chen has a Master's student in computer science, his research interest is computer vision and deep learning.

Ankur Gupta has received the B.Tech and M.Tech in Computer Science and Engineering from Ganga Institute of Technology and Management, Kablana affiliated with Maharshi Dayanand University, Rohtak in 2015 and 2017. He is an Assistant Professor in the Department of Computer Science and Engineering at Vaish College of Engineering, Rohtak, and has been working there since January 2019. He has many publications in various reputed national/ international conferences, journals, and online book chapter contributions (Indexed by SCIE, Scopus, ESCI, ACM, DBLP, etc). He is doing research in the field of cloud computing, data security & machine learning. His research work in M.Tech was based on biometric security in cloud computing.

Chenwei Liang is a Master's student, his research interest is human action recognition via computer vision and deep learning.

Xiaoxu Liu is a PhD student with Auckland University of Technology, New Zealand.

Varun V. L. is an experienced problem solver with a range of technical and practical experience gained within academic and business environments. Detail focused, flexible and resourceful with the ability to effectively manage the undertaken works within required performance requirements.

Asim Wadood, hailing from Kohat, Khyber Pakhtunkhwa, Pakistan, was born in 1992. His academic journey began at the Kohat University of Science & Technology, where he earned a B.S. in computer science in 2015. Building upon this foundation, Asim pursued a Master's degree in computer science at Bahria University, Islamabad, Pakistan, graduating in 2019. Currently enrolled in a Ph.D. program at Kohat University of Science & Technology, he exhibits an unwavering commitment to advancing his expertise in computer science. As a researcher, Asim's focus converges on the realms of deep learning and image processing, specifically delving into generative models, classification, detection, and segmentation. These research interests underscore his dedication to exploring cutting-edge solutions within the field of computer science. Asim Wadood actively contributes to the global scholarly community, positioning himself as a promising figure poised to make significant strides in both academia and technological innovation.

GuanQun Xu is a master student in computer science, his research interests include deep learning and computer vision.

Wei Qi Yan is the Director of Centre for Robotics & Vision (CeRV), Auckland University of Technology (AUT), his expertise is in deep learning, intelligent surveillance, computer vision, multimedia, etc. Dr. Yan has published over 250 research papers, his research distinctions include the published Springer monographs: Computational Methods for Deep Learning (2021), Introduction to Intelligent Surveillance (2019), etc. Dr. Yan is the Chair of the ACM Multimedia Chapter of New Zealand, a Member of the ACM, a Senior Member of the IEEE, TC members of the IEEE. Dr. Yan was a visiting professor with the National University of Singapore (NUS, QS Ranking #11), Singapore.

Boning Yang is a Master student, his research interests are deep learning and computer vision.

Index

A

C

D

E

F

G

H

I

K

M

O

P

Q

R

S

T

U

V

Y

www.ingramcontent.com/pod-product-compliance
Lightning Source LLC
LaVergne TN
LVHW080645011026
849160LV00014B/1325
* 9 7 9 8 3 6 9 3 4 5 6 8 9 *